POPULATION PROBLEMS

in

THE VICTORIAN AGE

VICTORIAN SOCIAL CONSCIENCE

A Series of facsimile reprints of selected articles from The Edinburgh Review, The Westminster Review, The Quarterly Review, Blackwood's Magazine and Fraser's Magazine

1802—1870

Volumes in this series

POPULATION PROBLEMS in the VICTORIAN AGE
VOLUME I

THEORY

DEBATES ON THE ISSUE

From

19ᵀᴴ CENTURY CRITICAL JOURNALS

with an introduction

by

JOSEPH J. SPENGLER

1973

GREGG INTERNATIONAL PUBLISHERS LIMITED

100725

301.32
POP

011 0574

COMPLETE SET ISBN 0 576 53252 5
THIS VOLUME ISBN 0 576 53253 3✓

Republished in 1973 by Gregg International Publishers Limited
Westmead, Farnborough, Hants England

Printed in Germany

CONTENTS

INTRODUCTION

The essays on population, herein reprinted from early nineteenth-century English periodicals, reflect the tremendous impact of T. R. Malthus's *Essay on the Principle of Population*, a work that went through six editions between 1798 and 1826. Population questions had, of course, received considerable attention before Malthus wrote. David Hume had undermined the thesis that numbers had been greater in ancient times than in his day and Adam Smith (as had James Steuart) had discussed the determinants of fertility and mortality, though without incorporating in this discussion his belief that "the course of human prosperity" seldom endured "more than two hundred years." There had also been considerable controversy in the second half of the eighteenth century respecting English population growth, whether it had been negligible, significant, or increasing. Yet, not until after Malthus's *Essay* appeared in 1798, had interest in population questions transcended in importance almost all other politico-economic questions.

Malthus's *Essay* incorporated what amounted to a number of distinct propositions. First, populations occupied finite environments. Second, the amount of subsistence derivable from a finite environment was limited as was the access of its inhabitants to supplies from beyond their borders. Third, while the potential procreative capacity of a human population was very high, its capacity to support population growth was conditioned by its finite and hence diminishing-marginal capacity to produce subsistence. Fourth, because of these constraints upon a population's capacity to increase its flow of subsistence, it needed to adjust its natality and rate of natural increase to this flow. Fifth, the proper means to the control of natural increase consisted in the development and/or maintenance of institutions which conduced to "moral restraint," to sufficient deferment of marriage on the part of women, until the age of 27 or 28. Sixth, given good institutions, the availability of want-generating products (e.g., manufactures for which there was mass demand) tends to motivate moral restraint. Seventh, should a community not voluntarily confine its fertility and hence its natural increase within its capacity to support this increase, its growth would be held down by so-called positive checks, generally in the form of heightened mortality. Eighth, it was risky for a country to become dependent upon foreign sources for a significant portion of its food supply, since these sources might be cut off. Ninth,

"population pressure" was not harmful on balance if sufficiently con-
strained, for it compelled men to overcome the inertia common to
most persons.

Since England was the most developed country in the world at the
time Malthus was writing, his estimation of England's past and prospective demographic and economic states, though based upon admittedly
inadequate information, is illuminating.[1] He noted that "the most
cursory view of society in this country must convince us, that throughout
all ranks the preventive check to population prevails in a considerable
degree." But this degree was insufficient, even though "the prolific power
of nature is very far indeed from being called fully into action in this
country." Indeed, were fertility greater, "premature mortality" would
be greater and "happiness" would be less, since it was desirable that a
"well-peopled" country supply its "demand for population" with a
combination of low natality and low mortality. Only in countries "circumstanced like America or Russia," or recovering after a "great mortality" was "a large proportion of births ... a favourable sympton."
In a food-short, backward land, by contrast, a very high natality entailed
a very high mortality. Having inferred, on the basis of information
available before the census of 1811, that Englands' population might be
doubling in something like a century, he said that "we cannot reasonably
suppose that the resources of this country should increase for any long
continuance with such rapidity." When the census of 1811 revealed
"a greatly improved healthfulness of the people" and a rate of population
growth that had risen instead of falling, as one might expect, and that
would if continued double numbers in 55 or less years, he described it
as "a striking illustration of the principle of population." This rate of
increase had been occasioned by a "greatly-increased demand for labour,
combined with a greatly-increased power of production, both in agriculture and manufactures"; it could not "in the nature of things ... be
permanent." Writing in 1825 after the census of 1821 Malthus found
the evidence still in keeping with his earlier inference that the population
was doubling in around 50 years. "This is no doubt a most extraordinary
rate of increase, considering the actual population of this country compared
with its territory, and the number of its great towns and manufactures"; it
reflected "the increasing healthfulness" of the country and a resulting
decrease in mortality and increase in the marriage rate and natality.
But this state of affairs could not continue for, as he observed elsewhere,[2]
a country such as England "could not without extraordinary exertions
be made to support two or three times as many" people as it did in 1817.

England's economy rested on landed products during most of Malthus's lifetime, with over one-third of the labour force still engaged in agriculture in the late eighteenth century. The food supply began to lag behind requirements, with the upsurge of population after 1750, and by 1820 net corn imports approximated 8 per cent of the output of corn. While English wheat yields rose from about 20 to 22 or more bushels per acre in the eighteenth century, they fell during the Napoleonic wars when extension of acreage drove the marginal yield down. Subsequently, with a gradual decline in wheat acreage—about 30 per cent by 1885–94 —and the concentration of wheat production on land suited to it, the yield rose, reaching about 29 bushels by the late 1880's.[3] Yet already by " the late 1870's about 37 per cent of British consumption of cereals, about half of the cheese and butter and about 20 per cent of the meat were imported."[4] Regarding natural increase David Glass writes: "First, mortality in the eighteenth century may have been higher, in the main, than in the first half of the nineteenth century, and the crude death rate was probably higher. Secondly, there is reason to believe that the crude birth rate was high at the end of the eighteenth century ... and that a high rate was maintained during the first three quarters of the nineteenth century."[5] The birth rate did not begin to decline until the late 1870's, falling over one-fourth between 1878–82 and 1908–12. The population of England and Wales grew nearly $1\frac{3}{8}$ per cent per year between 1801 and 1881—at a rate higher than Malthus believed sustainable, but supported in part by imported foodstuffs, at falling prices after 1870.

Malthus's main thesis was subjected to a variety of criticism, many examples of which are included in the articles constituting this volume. Most of these criticisms fell within one or more of four categories. (1) His main argument, with its emphasis upon the finiteness of each nation's territory, was said to impugn the intent of Divine Providence. (2) It underestimated man's capacity to regulate his reproductive behaviour. (3) It was designed to perpetuate undesirable institutions (e.g., property, the church) on the ground that they were essential to the regulation of man's numbers. (4) It undermined man's utopian aspirations by implying that growth of population, being unrestricted in utopian societies, would swamp the programs of these societies. Variously associated with these arguments was a climate of opinion hostile to implications of Malthus's line of argument. It made workers largely responsible for their condition by indicating that they must hold the rate of growth of their numbers below that of the "funds" destined for their employment. It ran counter to the aims of those who looked with favour upon population growth, namely, politicians in search of power, military men in search of cannon fodder, employers in search of cheap and docile labour, and churchmen in search of souls. It ran counter also to the expectations of those who sought in institutional transformation the key to improvement in the condition of the common man.

Although Malthus, in the second and later editions of his essay, touched upon the adjustment of the growth of numbers to the growth of subsistence in all parts of the world, controversy respecting his thesis related mainly to those parts to which European civilisation had spread. If one abstracts from casuistical arguments relating to the intent of Divine Providence or to "natural law" emanating from this source, one might group possible criticisms of Malthus's thesis under three heads. First, one might contend that the means of subsistence would long be subject to increase, with the result that ultimate limits to man's capacity to support himself would not be reached until in the distant future; meanwhile chemical and agricultural revolutions might materialise. Second, one might argue that man's fertility and hence his rate of natural increase would be brought as low as required, to the replacement level if necessary. This argument could assume one or both of two forms. It could be argued that as man's economic and social condition improved, his natural fecundity would decline; or it could be argued that, as those conditions improved, man would become more future-oriented, more prudent, and more inclined to subject his fertility to increasing control, albeit by contraceptive means in addition to the control sanctioned by Malthus, namely, "moral restraint" (i.e., deferment of marriage). Third, it might be argued by utopians and other reformers that a new set of institutions would be much more conducive to both the augmentation of produce and the rational control of numbers than were the contemporary institutions which Malthus defended. This and the preceding argument embodied the belief that as civilisation progressed, fertility would decline sufficiently to offset decline in mortality, with the result that overpopulation would be avoided.

A solution largely in keeping with the classical tradition to which Malthus subscribed in good part was put forward in 1848. That was J. S. Mill's "stationary state." It would not have been acceptable to Malthus insofar as it implied use of contraceptives and a collectivistic approach, or made for inertia which, in Malthus's system, was prevented by population pressure. For Mill held that, since increase in returns to growth of division of labour, theretofore associated with increase in population, was approaching zero, no advantage was to be had from further increase in the size of England's population: the current population would remain large enough to exploit future income-increasing improvements.

The essays comprising this volume, but a few of a large number appearing in pre-1860 English periodicals, both support and criticise Malthus. The three selections from the *Edinburgh Review*, a journal hospitable (as was the *Quarterly Review* after early 1816) to Malthus and his supporters, are directed against critics of Malthus. That in the 1810 number dismisses Ingram's recourse to theological, cannon-fodder, and cheap-labour arguments and dismisses the supposition that control of numbers could result in their diminution. T. B. Macaulay rejected Sadler's arguments, resting upon faith in a " Nature " that " has calculated with utmost precision, and unalterably settled, the different degrees, as well as periods, of prolificness in all things living." One manifestation of this beneficent nature was the alleged tendency of fecundity and fertility to diminish as population density or congestion increased. Unlike those who found Sadler's anti-Malthusian positions tenable, T. B. Macaulay pointed out that Sadler's statistical evidence did not support his conclusions; and he expressed the hope that Sadler would publish no more until he had suitably informed himself. This hope was not realised and Macaulay found it necessary, in the January, 1831, *Edinburgh Review*, to refute Sadler's " refutation " of Macaulay's critique. A belief similar to Sadler's in a beneficent Nature and Providence underlay the arguments of a number of Malthus's critics, among them several represented here.

H. Merivale (1806–74), economist later known for his work in colonisation, supported Malthus in the 1837 *Edinburgh Review*. Merivale deals with the main aspects of Senior's views of political economy, among them his exceptions to Malthus's thesis. Merivale finds confirmation for Malthus's thesis in the failure of real wages to rise and in the deterioration of the economic condition of the people of Ireland and Prussia. Merivale described "the doctrine of population" as "offensive to philosophical pride, and irksome to sanguine temperaments" and hence subject to " endless attempts " "to contradict or to evade it."

Somewhat illustrative of this description is the selection from *Fraser's Magazine* directed against Harriet Martineau (1802–1876), along with Mrs. Jane Marcet (1769–1858) perhaps the leading early populariser of political economy. Her defence of the abolition of the poor laws on the ground that they encouraged population growth was attacked on several grounds. The author found no correlation between the character of the poor laws and the rate of population growth. He declares that their abolition could not be enforced by the state since it would violate the "natural right" of starving men to support—support denied them through past seizure of the commons by dukes, earls, and gentry. Martineau is charged with adopting the "Malthusian fancy that people always breed up to food," a fancy given exaggerated expression in doggerel circa 1830's

> "The daily march of population
> So much outstrips all moderation
> That ev'n prolific herring-shoals
> Keep pace not with our erring souls."

Almost as hostile to Malthus as Miss Martineau's critic was P. G. Scrope (1797–1876), economist and geologist, in his critique of Thomas Chalmers's *On Political Economy* (*Quarterly Review*, XLVIII, 1832) and the latter's "allusion to the Malthusian theory of population, and the Malthusian remedy for its apparent excess, 'the prudential check'." "The idea of an ultimate limit to the globe's possible productiveness tyranises over [Malthusian] imaginations, and gives rise to the strongest opinions and rules of conduct." After all, Britain's empire could support at least 4.2 billion persons, 170 times its then numbers and requiring four centuries to fill, during which time agriculture still would be greatly improved. Not only were the Malthusian assumptions invalid; they had pernicious social and political effects. "The welfare of existing millions—the existence of future myriads, depends on the destruction of the miserable sophism, which lies at the bottom of [Chalmers's] whole economical system." Much more to Scrope's taste were the arguments of Sadler, though not the latter's verbose style, or the failure of his tabular data to demonstrate an inverse relation between fertility and density population, or the questionable character of some of his assertions.

Quite opposed to views such as those expressed by Scrope and Miss Martineau's critic are Russell's arguments in the selection from *Blackwood's Magazine* (Vol. 4, 1818). He condemns the poor laws and other encouragements to population growth, finding in Malthus's doctrine a check upon utopians and "a powerful instrument, not of despotism, but of liberty." He also shared Malthus's concern lest the corn laws be abolished and England become dependent "for subsistence on the precarious fertility, or still more precarious policy, of neighbouring states, to whom she stands jealously opposed by the very tenure of her greatness."

J. B. Sumner's defence of Malthus in the *Quarterly Review* (1817) was in keeping with his earlier *Treatise on the Records of Creation* (1825) wherein the origins and the function of inequality of rank and property, a result of a population growth, are expounded. The cause of man's distress was "moral and political vice" and not "the tendency of population"; it was therefore readily avoided since there were many substitutes for imprudent marriage. G. Taylor (*Quarterly Review*, 1821, pp. 146–68), in his review of Godwin's reply to Malthus, concludes that "the important truth of [Malthus's] principles must not be suppressed, because the unfeeling and the vicious may occasionally pervert them to disguise from others, and perhaps from themselves, the selfishness of their hearts." It needed to be recognised that these principles are compatible with discriminating charity and compassionate beneficence even though they tend to diminish "our sympathy with the poor as a class."

Not many writers stressed the continuing augmentability of the food supply. Scrope's view has already been mentioned. Somewhat similar views occasionally received expression (e.g., by Chambers in the *Edinburgh Review* of 1832, and by T. R. Edmonds, *An Inquiry into the Principles of Population*, 1832). In a review of Comber's study of Britain's food supply George Ellis estimated per capita food consumption of all kinds at 693 English pounds, including ¾ of a quarter of wheat (convertible into 360 lbs of bread). He then concluded "that there can be no doubt that our fisheries might, for centuries to come, effectually supply the deficiencies of our agriculture" (*Quarterly Review*, X, 1813, pp. 173–75).

Malthus's critics placed major emphasis on social and physiological mechanisms that would reduce the rate of natural increase to desirable or tolerable levels. Some writers associated diminution in fecundity and hence in fertility with luxurious living. So runs Hickson's argument in the 1849 *Westminster Review*. Age at marriage, diet, climate, physical habits, pursuit of mental occupations, endogamy—all affect mortality of natality. "The tendency to increase can exist only with the power to spread; when the power to spread ceases there begins a tendency to decay." Sadler's views, it will be recalled, are somewhat similar to Hickson's. Perhaps most notorious was the argument of Thomas Doubleday (1790–1870), a Cobbett type radical. He asserted that fecundity and fertility tended to vary inversely with the harshness of the environment and the scarcity of the means of subsistence for the masses (see selection from 1837 *Blackwood's Magazine*, also Doubleday's *The True Law of Population*, 1853). A century after Doubleday's book appeared, Josue de Castro, in his anti-Malthusian *The Geography of Hunger* (Boston, Little, Brown, 1952), argued that hunger is the cause of overpopulation.

Of all the models describing the probable transit, on physiological grounds, of fecundity and fertility from levels producing a high rate of natural increase to levels in which natality and mortality are in balance, the most rounded was that first developed by Herbert Spencer in the *Westminster Review*, April, 1852. Doubleday as well as other proponents of a physiological theory had failed to derive a self-adjusting principle from their initial premises. Spencer induced that "the degree of fertility varies inversely as the development of the nervous system," since the power to maintain life was antagonistic to the power to propagate the species. With development and individuation, lower fertility was needed to maintain a population; antagonism between the generation and the nervous system increased as man developed mentally. Accordingly, pressure of population, a proximate cause of progress, conduced to man's development and hence to decline in man's fecundity and fertility until natality and mortality were in balance. The analysis did not run in genetic terms as did some twentieth-century explanations of decline in fertility.

Physiological and related explanations of decline in fecundity did not indicate how much it needed to decline to reduce the probability of conception significantly, in part perhaps by reducing the frequency of sexual relations. For if the margin above need were great, reduction in this margin needed to be adequate.

A number of writers reasoned, as did Malthus (*Essay*, Bk. IV, Chap. 13), that there was need for the development of manufactures priced to appeal to the masses, modify their habitual pattern of consumption, and increase the number of products that workers wanted. Workers would then be disposed to defer marriage and regulate family size, to prefer more products and fewer children. For, as David Wakefield put it in his *Essay upon Political Economy* (1804), whereas food stimulated procreation and population growth, activities productive of comforts and enjoyments of life did not and hence were more productive of happiness. A number of writers, among them A. Alison (see selection from 1840 *Blackwood's Magazine*) expressed somewhat similar opinions. Alison assigned a critical role to man's acquired propensities and his development of artificial wants and hence of habits of foresight conducive to planning and the realisation of these wants. Out of these and related changes, together with awareness of the economic burdens of family, issued voluntary constraints upon population growth. The approach of authors along the lines just described, especially when they (as did Wakefield) emphasised not food or (as had Paley) the sum total of happiness but *individual* happiness, contributed to the development of the concept of optimum population.

There is need for a sociological theory to account for the intensity of the attack on Malthus's *Essay*—a spirit manifest in many commentaries, according to accounts of the Malthusian controversy in nineteenth-century England.[6] Presumably it was the supposed incidence of Malthus's interpretations upon so many widely held values, opinions, and special interests that aroused concern. Although the course of events in the century and a half succeeding the appearance of the sixth edition of the *Essay* has altered the dimensions of the population problem, it has not altered its essential character. For, with the replacement of an economy resting upon an organic base by one resting largely upon a base both inorganic and organic, it is the finiteness of a now more broadly defined biosphere that sets limits to how large a population may become and yet remain compatible with man's long-run welfare. Of equal concern are man's social institutions and the degree to which they focus costs and benefits upon responsible decision-makers and thereby prevent imprudent and socially harmful procreation.

Joseph J. Spengler.
September 1972.

1 He deals with England in Chap. 8 of BK ii of *An Essay on the Principle of Population*, with introduction by G. T. Bettany (London, Ward, Lock & Co., 1890); see also D. V. Glass, ed., *Introduction to Malthus* (London, Watts & Co., 1953).

2 *An Essay*, p. 360.

3 Colin Clark, *The Conditions of Economic Progress* (London, Macmillan, 1951), pp. 224–227.

4 Phyllis Deane and W. A. Cole, *British Economic Growth 1688-1959* (Cambridge, University Press, 1962), pp. 32–33, 62–67.

5 D. V. Glass & D. E. C. Eversley, *Population in History* (Chicago, Aldine, 1965), p. 239.

6 E.g., see W. P. Albrecht, *William Hazlitt and the Malthusian Controversy* (Albuquerque, University of New Mexico Press, 1950); Kenneth Smith, *The Malthusian Controversy* (London, Routledge & Kegan Paul, 1951); H. A. Boner, *Hungry Generations* (New York, Columbia University Press, 1955); Glass, *op. cit.*

Art. XI. *Disquisitions on Population.* By Robert Acklom Ingram, B. D. 1809.

Reply to the Essay on Population by the Rev. T. R. Malthus: In a Series of Letters. 8vo. London, 1808.

W E should scarcely have thought it worth while to take any notice of these disquisitions, which consist, in a great degree,

gree, of strange misapprehensions and misrepresentations of the doctrines they profess to discuss, if we had not observed, among many persons, besides Mr Ingram and his anonymous coadjutor, an ignorance of the principles of population, which seems to us nearly unaccountable, considering the careful and detailed manner in which the subject has been lately explained. The excellent work of Mr Malthus, though it has certainly produced a great and salutary impression on the public mind, appears to us to have been much more generally talked of than read, and more generally read than understood. To those who have gone over it with attention, without being able to understand it, we cannot flatter ourselves, that the few observations which we are about to make will be of much use ; but there is a class of readers for whom we cannot help feeling considerable affection, who are tempted, we believe, occasionally to turn over our transitory pages, when they would shrink from the perusal of a bound quarto, or two massive octavos. That these judicious persons are in nowise deterred from discussing the merits of the said quartos and octavos merely because they have not read them, every day's experience sufficiently proves ; and, indeed, it would be a cruel preventive check on conversation, to insist upon such previous drudgery ; but still, if we may judge of the feelings of others from our own under similar circumstances, it is, upon the whole, an advantage to a man to understand something about the subject on which he is going to deliver his opinion. It is a great gratification to us to think, that we have afforded this advantage to our friends, on many important subjects, in morals, politics, and the various branches of science ; and we would fain hope, that we may now render them a small service of the same kind, on the no less important subject of population. At all events, we can promise them, that what we are going to say will, in one respect at least, have a much stronger claim on their attention than the work of Mr Malthus,—that of brevity.

This celebrated work may be said to consist of two separate parts. In the first place, of some very important statements in point of *fact*, the truth of which neither is nor can be denied, though the different parts of the statement had never before been brought together, nor the nature of their connexion pointed out : and, in the second place, of certain *reasonings* and practical inferences deduced from these facts. Now, the first part, or the mere statement of indisputable facts, forms by far the largest and the most important part of the work ; and, strange as it must appear to every one who is capable of forming an opinion on the subject, it is to this part that the most violent objections have been made. It is for having stated, with inimitable caution

and

and accuracy, facts which cannot possibly be called in question, that Mr Malthus has been assailed with such clamorous reproaches, —that he has been accused of sophistry, of presumption, of blasphemy, inhumanity, and love of vice and corruption. Against such charges, we know that he would disdain to be defended; nor would our compassion for those who have advanced them have been quite strong enough to make us undertake the hopeful task of undeceiving them, if their errors did not appear to originate in a few fundamental mistakes, which may probably obstruct the reception of important truths in more dispassionate minds.

The radical proposition, then, which we wish to impress upon our readers is, that throughout the greater part of his invaluable work, Mr Malthus is occupied merely with the statement, detail and illustration, of a few very important and radical *facts*, the truth and certainty of which, none of his detractors have been bold enough to call in question; and that, disclaiming all pretensions to discovery, he has aimed only at fixing the attention of mankind on the true character of certain phenomena that have always been before their eyes. To satisfy the most suspicious of our readers, how very innocent, and, at the same time, how very important this task was, we shall now endeavour to give such a short abstract of the fundamental principles of the work, as, we flatter ourselves, will occasion no perplexity to persons of the most slender capacity.

In the first book of the *Wealth of Nations*, Dr Smith, when explaining the causes which proportion the reward of labour to the extent of the funds for its support, justly observes, ' It is in ' this manner that the demand for *men*, like that for any other com- ' modity, necessarily regulates the production of men ;—quickens ' it, when it goes on too slowly ; and stops it, when it advances too ' fast. It is this demand which regulates and determines the state ' of population in all the different countries of the world—in North ' America, in Europe and in China ; which renders it rapidly pro- ' gressive in the first, slow and gradual in the second, and altoge- ' ther stationary in the last. ' This passage of Dr Smith, which we think we have heard first suggested to Mr Malthus the idea of his essay, is illustrated and confirmed by a crowd of indisputable facts, to whatever country on the globe our view may be directed.

In taking a survey of this kind, it will speedily be discovered to be a fact that admits of no dispute, that the rate of population is by no means the same in all the countries of the world,—and that there is a notable difference in its progress, not only in North America, for instance, compared with Europe or Asia in general, but a similar difference in the different states of Europe, at the same period

riod of time, and in the same state at different periods. As men cannot live without food, it will also be readily admitted to be a fact, that those variations in the rate of population must have been universally preceded and accompanied by variations in the means of maintaining labourers; on which, indeed, the demand before mentioned must necessarily depend. Where these funds are rapidly increasing as in North America, the demand for an increasing number of labourers, makes it easy to provide an ample subsistence for each; and the population of the country is observed to make rapid advances. Where these funds increase only at a moderate rate, as in most of the countries of Europe, there the demand for labourers is moderate; the command of the labourer over the means of subsistence is consequently much diminished; and the population is observed to proceed with a moderate pace, varying in each country, as nearly as may be, according to the variations in the funds for its support. Where these funds are stationary, as we are taught to believe is the case in China, and as has certainly been the case in Spain, Italy, and probably most of the countries of Europe, during certain periods of their history, there the demand for labour being stationary, the command of the labourer over the means of subsistence, is comparatively very scanty, and population is observed to make no perceptible progress, and sometimes to be even diminished.

In the second place, it is a fact equally notorious, that the actual increase of the funds for the maintenance of labour does not depend simply upon the physical capacity of any particular country to produce food and other necessaries, but upon the degree of industry, intelligence and activity, with which these powers are at any particular time called forth. We observe countries, possessing every requisite for producing the necessaries and conveniences of life in abundance, sunk in a state of ignorance and indolence, from the vices of their governments, or the unfortunate constitution of their society,—and slumbering on for ages with scarcely any increase in the means of subsistence, till some fortunate event introduces a better order of things; and then, the industry of the nation being roused, and allowed to exert itself with more freedom, more ample funds for the maintenance of labour are immediately provided, and population is observed to make a sudden start forwards, at a rate quite different from that at which it had before proceeded.

This seems to have been the case with many of the countries of Europe, during some periods of their history; but is more particularly remarkable in Russia, the population of which, though very early inhabited, was so extremely low before the be-
ginning

ginning of the last century, and has proceeded with such rapid steps since, particularly since the reign of Catherine II.

It is also a fact that has often attracted observation in a review of the history of different nations, that the waste of people occasioned by the great plagues, famines and other devastations, to which the human race has been occasionally subject, has been repaired in a much shorter time than it would have been, if the population, after these devastations, had only proceeded at the same rate as before. From which it is apparent, that, after the void thus occasioned, it must have increased much faster than usual ; and the greater abundance of the funds for the maintenance of labour, which would be left to the survivors under such circumstances, indicates again the usual conjunction of a rapid increase of population with a rapid increase of the funds for its maintenance. Just after the great pestilence in the time of Edward III., a day's labour would purchase a bushel of wheat; while, immediately before, it would hardly have purchased a peck.

With regard to the minor variations in the different countries of Europe, it is an old and familiar observation, that, wherever any new channels of industry, and new sources of wealth, are opened, so as to provide the means of supporting an additional number of labourers, there, almost immediately, a stimulus is given to the population ; and it proceeds, for a time, with a vigour and celerity proportionate to the greatness and duration of the funds on which alone it can subsist.

In the third place, it is no less certain and visible, that, in a few countries where the funds for the maintenance of labour are in great abundance, the rate at which population increases is so rapid, that, if it were to continue unabated, the largest and richest territory, nay, the whole globe of the earth, would, in a few centuries, be completely possessed ; but, as the great abundance of these funds appears absolutely to depend upon the circumstance of there being an abundance of good land to be had at a very low price, it is quite clear that this state of things cannot possibly continue ; and that the funds for the maintenance of labour must, in the progress of cultivation and population, cease to increase with the same rapidity very long before they come to a stop, or before the country can be considered as fully peopled. The impossibility of the continued increase of these funds at the same rate, will be still more evident when applied to the peopled states of Europe and Asia, under any imaginable system of government : and, in reference to the peopling of the whole earth, it involves a manifest absurdity, to suppose, that a certain abundance of the funds for the maintenance of labour, which, wherever it has been found to exist, depends upon the land bearing a very great proportion to the people, should experience no change, while this proportion was gradually altering, so as ultimately to become the opposite of what it was at first.

From this slight survey of what has certainly taken place, and is actually taking place, with respect to the funds for the maintenance of labour in different countries, we conceive that the three following propositions may be stated as among the *facts* least capable of being controverted.

1. That man, like all other animals, multiplies in proportion to the means of subsistence which, under the actual circumstances in which he lives, are placed within his reach.

2. That there is a power of increase in the human race, much greater than is generally exercised, always ready to exert itself as soon as it finds an opening ; and appearing continually in sudden starts of population, whenever the funds for the maintenance of labour have experienced an increase, in whatever way this may have been occasioned.

3. That this power of increase is so great, and, in its nature, necessarily so different from any increase which can result from adding together different portions of a limited quantity of land, or gradually improving the cultivation of the whole, that the funds for the maintenance of labour cannot, under any sytsem the most favourable to human industry, be made permanently to keep pace with such an increase of population as has been observed to take place for short periods in particular countries ; and consequently, as man cannot live without food, that the superior power of population cannot be kept on a level with the funds which are to support it, without the almost constant operation of considerable *checks*, of some kind or other.

What these checks are, is the next important question ; and, keeping in mind, that it is strictly and purely a question of mere *fact*, and not of reasoning or hypothesis, let us first hear Dr Smith. In speaking of the dependence of man, like other animals, on the means of subsistence, and of the impossibility of his increasing beyond them, he observes, ' But, in civilized soci-
' ety, it is only among the inferior ranks of people, that the
' scantiness of subsistence can set limits to the further multipli-
' cation of the species ; and it can do so in no other way, than
' by destroying a great part of the children which their fruitful
' marriages produce. '

As the poverty and misery which would destroy a considerable portion of children, must necessarly be most severely felt, not only by the human beings thus suffering, but by their parents and survivors, it must be acknowledged, that such a premature mortality

tality is a very harsh leveller; and it is fortunate for the human race, that there are other ways besides this, by which population may proportion itself to the means of subsistence. Mr Malthus shows clearly, that the effects of the difficulty of providing for a family, do not appear merely in premature mortality, but in the delay of engaging in a connexion which is likely to be attended with such a consequence. And this view of the subject not only accords better with our ideas of a being who possesses the distinctive faculty of reason, but is completely confirmed by what is taking place in all the countries with which we are acquainted, where we find, that when the funds for the maintenance of labour become comparatively scanty, the marriages generally become later and less frequent.

It appears, then, without entering into any argument or detail, that the checks to population may be divided into two general classes—those which operate in *preventing the birth* of a population which cannot be supported, and those which *destroy it* after it has been brought into being; or, as Mr Malthus has called them, the *preventive* checks and the *positive* checks.

The necessary and constant operation of some checks to population, in almost all the societies with which we are acquainted, being fully established, and these checks being most clearly divisible into the two before mentioned classes, we can scarcely hesitate in determining which of them we should wish to see put in operation.

It is observed, in most countries, that in years of scarcity and dearness, the marriages are fewer than usual; and if, under all the great variations to which the increase of the means of subsistence is necessarily exposed from a variety of causes; from a plenty or scarcity of land; from a good or a bad government; from the general prevalence of intelligence and industry, or of ignorance and indolence; from the opening of new channels of commerce, or the closing of old ones, &c. &c., the population were proportioned to the actual means of subsistence, more by the prudence of the labouring classes in delaying marriage, than by the misery which produces premature mortality among their children,—it can hardly be doubted that the happiness of the mass of mankind would be decidedly improved.

It is further certain, that, under a given increase of the funds for the maintenance of labour, it is physically impossible to give to each labourer a larger share of these funds, or materially to improve his condition, without some increase of the preventive check; and consequently, that all efforts to improve the condition of the poor, that have no tendency to produce a more favourable proportion between the means of subsistence and the popu-

2

lation which is to confume them, can only be partial or temporary, and muft ultimately defeat their own object.

It follows, therefore, as a natural and neceffary conclufion, that
in order to improve the condition of the lower claffes of fociety,
to make them fuffer lefs under any diminution of the funds for
the maintenance of labour, and enjoy more under any actual
ftate of thefe funds, it fhould be the great bufinefs to difcourage helplefs and improvident habits, and to raife them as much
as poffible to the condition of beings who ‘ look before and
after.’ The caufes which principally tend to fofter helplefs, indolent and improvident habits among the lower claffes of fociety, feem to be defpotifm and ignorance, and every plan of conduct towards them which increafes their dependence, and weakens the motives to perfonal exertion. The caufes, again, which
principally tend to promote habits of induftry and prudence, feem
to be, good government and good education, and every circumftance which tends to increafe their independence and refpectability. Wherever the regifters of a country, under no particular dif-
advantages of fituation, indicate a great mortality, and the general prevalence of the check arifing from difeafe and death, over
the check arifing from prudential habits, there we almoft invariably find the people debafed by oppreffion, and funk in ignorance
and indolence. Wherever, on the contrary, in a country without
peculiar advantages of fituation, or peculiar capability of increafe,
the regifters indicate a fmall mortality, and the prevalence of the
check from prudential habits above that from premature mortality ;
there, we as conftantly find fecurity of property eftablifhed, and
fome degree of intelligence and knowledge, with a tafte for clean-
linefs and comforts, pretty generally diffufed.

Nor does experience feem to juftify the fears of thofe who
think, that one vice at leaft will increafe in proportion to the increafe of the preventive check to population. Norway, Switzerland, England and Scotland, which are moft diftinguifhed for the
fmallnefs of their mortality, and the operation of the prudential
reftraint on marriage, may be compared to advantage with other
countries, not only with regard to the general moral worth and
refpectability of their inhabitants, but with regard to the virtues
which relate to the intercourfe of the fexes. We cannot, as Mr
Malthus obferves, eftimate with tolerable accuracy the degree in
which chaftity in the fingle ftate prevails. Our general conclufions muft be founded on general refults ; and thefe are clearly
in our favour.

We appear, therefore, to be all along borne out by experience
and obfervation, both in our premifes and conclufions. From
what we fee and know, indeed, we cannot rationally expect that

the paffions of man will ever be fo completely fubjected to his reafon, as to enable him to avoid all the moral and phyfical evils which depend upon his own conduct. But this is merely faying, that perfect virtue is not to be expected on earth ; an affertion by no means new, or peculiarly applicable to the prefent difcuffion. The differences obfervable in different nations, in the preffure of the evils refulting from the tendency of the human race to increafe fafter than the means of fubfiftence, entitle us fairly to con- clude, that thofe which are in the beft ftate are ftill fufceptible of confiderable improvement ; and that the worft may at leaft be made equal to the beft. This is furely fufficient both to animate and to direct our exertions in the caufe of human happinefs ; and the direction which our efforts will receive, from thus turning our attention to the laws that relate to the increafe and decreafe of mankind, and feeing their effects exemplified in the ftate of the different nations around us, will not be into any new and fufpi- cious path, but into the plain, beaten track of morality. It will be our duty to exert ourfelves to procure the eftablifhment of juft and equal laws, which protect and give refpectability to the low- eft fubject, and fecure to each member of the community the fruits of his induftry ; to extend the benefits of education as widely as poffible, that, to the long lift of errors from paffion, may not be added the ftill longer lift of errors from ignorance ; and, in general, to difcourage indolence, improvidence, and a blind indulgence of appetite, without regard to confequences ; and to encourage induftry, prudence, and the fubjection of the paffions to the dictates of reafon. The only change, if change it can be called, which the ftudy of the laws of population can make in our duties, is, that it will lead as to apply, more fteadily than we have hitherto done, the great rules of morality to the cafe of marriage, and the direction of our charity ; but the rules themfelves, and the foundations on which they reft, of courfe remain exactly where they were before.

This appears to us to be the fubftance of what Mr Malthus has faid. Yet this theory, and thefe conclufions, fimple and con- fiftent as they appear to be, and refting, as they do all along, up- on the moft obvious and undeniable facts, are rejected by a pret- ty large clafs of religious and refpectable people, becaufe they think, that the acknowledgement of a law of increafe in the hu- man race greater than any poffible increafe of the means of fub- fiftence, is an impeachment of the power or benevolence of the Deity. Mr Ingram fays, ' that upon the firft perufal of the fenti- ments contained in the Effay, the religious mind revolts at the apparent want of intelligence and contrivance in the Author of the creation, in infufing a principle into the nature of man, which

N

it required the utmost exertion of human prudence and ingenuity to counteract. '

In answer to this, and to all similar objections, we should observe, first, that we are not permitted to reject truths, of which our senses and experience give us the firmest assurance, because they do not accord with our preconceived notions respecting the attributes of the Deity. All our evidence for the prevailing benevolence of the works of creation—all our evidence of the power of the Creator—is derived from these sources. This evidence we must not, and cannot refuse to hear, in the first instance ; and it is an after concern, to reconcile the undeniable state of the fact to the attributes which we assign to the Divinity.

But to such persons as Mr Ingram, and the class who often urge this objection, we have a further answer. We should observe, that from those who do not believe in revelation, we might expect such an objection ; but that it appears to come with peculiar inconsistency from Christians. We do not pretend to be deep theologians ; but we have always understood that the highest authorities, both in the English and Scotish church, have uniformly represented this world as a state of discipline and preparation for another ; and indeed, that this doctrine is almost universally considered as the characteristic doctrine of the New Testament.

Now, we will venture to say, that, in the whole compass of the laws of nature, not one can be pointed out, which, in so peculiar and marked a manner, accords with this view of the state of man on earth. The purpose of the earthquake, the hurricane, or the drought, by which thousands and even millions of the human race are at once overwhelmed, or left to perish in lingering want— it must be owned, is inscrutable ; particularly as we have been expressly cautioned, in scripture, not to be too ready to consider such events in the light of judgments for the offences of the persons thus suffering. Yet that these events, which are of obvious and acknowledged recurrence, should be passed over without difficulty by the Christian, and that he should be staggered by a law of nature, which eminently illustrates and confirms one of the main doctrines of his religion, is, we own, to us, quite unaccountable ; and affords a very curious instance of the inconsistency of human reason. If it be really true, as we believe it is, that this life is a state of discipline and preparation for another, is it possible that we should find any difficulty in believing that a law of nature exists peculiarly calculated to rouse the faculties, and direct the exertions of the human race, which, by its varying pressure, and the various difficulties to which it gives rise, exercises and enlarges the powers of the mind, and calls into action all the

H h 2

great

great moral virtues which dignify and adorn human nature, as necessary to human happiness; which, above all, is constantly inculcating the necessity of the subjection of the passions to the dictates of reason and religion, and which, even if vice and misery were almost banished from the earth by the efforts of human virtue, would occasion the necessity of constant watchfulness and attention to maintain and secure the happiness which had been obtained?

On the other hand, if this law does exist, as we cannot for a moment doubt, from the evidence of incontestable facts, it merely affords a striking illustration and confirmation of that view of human life which is held out to us in the Scriptures; and, instead of being objected to by the Christian, it ought to be hailed as a powerful ally; as, to us at least, it appears to be one of those natural laws discovered by human experience, which may be urged with considerable force in favour of revealed religion.

The next class of objectors consists of worldly statesmen and politicians, who, at the slightest mention of checks to population, immediately conceive that our armies will want soldiers, and our manufactures hands. To such persons, it would of course be in vain to urge, that defence is better than conquest, and that the happiness of a society is a consideration paramount to the extent of its exports. If we had no other arguments than these, we know full well that it would be useless to urge them against such objectors. But, even these persons, we think, must allow, that the power of a country, both in war and in commerce, must depend upon that part of its population which is active and efficient, not upon that which is helpless and inefficient. If it has been found by experience that one country, which has, we will say, 200,000 births in each year, does not rear so many to puberty as another country which has only 160,000, must it not be allowed, that the first is the weaker of the two? And if, in addition to the question of numerical force, we take into consideration the state of misery and depression in the first country, which must have occasioned the premature mortality, we cannot doubt that the second would be infinitely superior in the industry and energy, as well as the happiness of its inhabitants. Not only would a country, where the checks to population arise from the prudential habits of the lower classes, rather than from premature mortality, possess a greater military and manufacturing population, with the same means of subsistence, but, from the very circumstance of the country's containing this larger proportion of persons in the active periods of life, the means of subsistence would stand a much fairer chance of being increased with rapidity. This is, in fact, confirmed by experience. England, Scotland, Switzerland and Norway, where the premature checks

to population are obferved to prevail with the greateft force, increafe fafter in the funds for the maintenance of labour, and, of
courfe, in the population fupported by them, than moft of the
countries of Europe that have a larger proportion of births.

So far, therefore, is it from being true, that the increafed prudence of the poor, with regard to marriage, would be attended
with a falling off in the military and commercial population of a
country, or by any obftructions to its further increafe, as far as
our experience has hitherto gone, it muft be acknowledged that
its effects have been juft the reverfe.

We have heard it, however, afked, whether, if the advice
which inculcates an increafed prudence with regard to marriage,
were really attended to, it might not be carried too far, and materially diminifh the population of a country, or prevent its increafe ? In anfwer to this, we fhould readily allow, that the e-
vent, however improbable, was within the range of poffibility ;
but fhould add, that if fuch poffibilities were to preclude fimilar
precepts, the range of moral inftruction would be limited indeed.
It will hardly be admitted, that we fhould be deterred from enforc-
ing, with all our power, the precepts of benevolence in oppofition
to felfifhnefs, becaufe, if we really made men quite regardlefs of
their own interefts, we fhould do much more harm than good.
There is, in fuch cafes, a mean point of perfection, which it is our
duty to be conftantly aiming at ; and the circumftance of this
point being furrounded on all fides with dangers, is only according
to the analogy of all ethical experience. The fact undoubtedly is,
that, in the paft hiftory of the world, and in its actual condition,
we fee countless examples of the mifery produced by the neglect of this prudential abftinence ; and no inftance, even of the
flighteft inconvenience, from its exceffive influence. As there is,
in reality, no danger of ever making the mafs of mankind too
generous or too compaffionate, fo there is juft as little of our de-
populating the world by making them too much the creatures of reafon, and giving prudence too great a maftery over
the natural paffions and affections. The prevailing error in the
game of life is, not that we mifs the prizes through excefs of ti-
midity, but that we overlook the true ftate of the chances in our
eager and fanguine expectations of winning them. Of all the
objections that ever were made to a moralift who offered to arm
men againft the paffions that are everywhere feducing them into
mifery, the moft flattering, but, undoubtedly, the moft chimerical, is, that his reafons are fo ftrong, that if he were allowed to
diffufe them, paffion would be extinguifhed altogether, and the activity, as well as the enjoyments of man, annihilated along with
his vices.

H h 3

What

What we have now ftated is as much, we fuppofe, as the indolent ftudents, for whofe benefit it is chiefly intended, will be well able to digeft at a meal. We fhall ftop here, therefore, for the prefent ; and, if any of them are induced, by what we have faid, to venture on the perufal of Mr Malthus's entire book, we engage, for their encouragement, to help them over the ftartling paffages of it, by a fhort examination of the other objections which have been urged againft it.

THE

EDINBURGH REVIEW.

JULY, 1830.

N⁰· CII.

Art. I.—*The Law of Population : a Treatise in Six Books, in Disproof of the Superfecundity of Human Beings, and developing the real Principle of their increase.* By Michael Thomas Sadler, M.P. 2 vols. 8vo. London : 1830.

WE did not expect a good book from Mr Sadler ; and it is well that we did not ; for he has given us a very bad one. The matter of his treatise is extraordinary ; the manner more extraordinary still. His arrangement is confused, his repetitions endless, his style every thing which it ought not to be. Instead of saying what he has to say with the perspicuity, the precision, and the simplicity in which consists the eloquence proper to scientific writing, he indulges without measure in vague, bombastic declamation, made up of those fine things which boys of fifteen admire, and which every body, who is not destined to be a boy all his life, weeds vigorously out of his compositions after five-and-twenty. That portion of his two thick volumes which is not made up of statistical tables, consists principally of ejaculations, apostrophes, metaphors, similes,—all the worst of their respective kinds. His thoughts are dressed up in this shabby finery with so much profusion and so little discrimination, that they remind us of a company of wretched strolling players, who have huddled on suits of ragged and faded tinsel, taken from a common wardrobe, and fitting neither their persons nor their parts ; and who then exhibit themselves to the laughing and pitying spectators, in a state of strutting, ranting, painted, gilded beggary. ' Oh, rare Daniels !' ' Political eco- ' nomist, go and do thou likewise !' ' Hear, ye political econo- ' mists and anti-populationists !' ' Population, if not proscribed ' and worried down by the Cerberean dogs of this wretched and

' cruel system, really does press against the level of the means of
' subsistence, and still elevating that level, it continues thus
' to urge society through advancing stages, till at length the
' strong and resistless hand of necessity presses the secret spring
' of human prosperity, and the portals of Providence fly open,
' and disclose to the enraptured gaze the promised land of con-
' tented and rewarded labour.'—These are specimens, taken at
random, of Mr Sadler's eloquence. We could easily multiply
them; but our readers, we fear, are already inclined to cry for
mercy.

Much blank verse and much rhyme is also scattered through
these volumes, sometimes rightly quoted, sometimes wrongly,—
sometimes good, sometimes insufferable,—sometimes taken from
Shakspeare, and sometimes, for aught we know, Mr Sadler's
own. ' Let man,' cries the philosopher, ' take heed how he
' rashly violates his trust;' and thereupon he breaks forth into
singing as follows :

> ' What myriads wait in destiny's dark womb,
> Doubtful of life or an eternal tomb !
> 'Tis his to blot them from the book of fate,
> Or, like a second Deity, create ;
> To dry the stream of being in its source,
> Or bid it, widening, win its restless course ;
> While, earth and heaven replenishing, the flood
> Rolls to its Ocean fount, and rests in God.'

If these lines are not Mr Sadler's, we heartily beg his pardon
for our suspicion—a suspicion which, we acknowledge, ought
not to be lightly entertained of any human being. We can only
say, that we never met with them before, and that we do not
much care how long it may be before we meet with them, or
with any others like them, again.

The spirit of this work is as bad as its style. We never
met with a book which so strongly indicated that the writer was
in a good humour with himself, and in a bad humour with every
body else ;—which contained so much of that kind of reproach
which is vulgarly said to be no slander, and of that kind of
praise which is vulgarly said to be no commendation. Mr Malthus is attacked in language which it would be scarcely decent
to employ respecting Titus Oates. ' Atrocious,' ' execrable,'
' blasphemous,' and other epithets of the same kind, are poured
forth against that able, excellent, and honourable man, with a
profusion which in the early part of the work excites indignation;
but, after the first hundred pages, produces mere weariness and
nausea. In the preface, Mr Sadler excuses himself on the plea
of haste. Two-thirds of his book, he tells us, were written

in a few months. If any terms have escaped him which can be construed into personal disrespect, he shall deeply regret that he had not more time to revise them. We must inform him that the tone of his book required a very different apology;—and that a quarter of a year, though it is a short time *for* a man to be engaged in writing a book, is a very long time for a man to be in a passion.

The imputation of being in a passion Mr Sadler will not disclaim. His is a theme, he tells us, on which ' it were impious ' to be calm ;' and he boasts that ' instead of conforming to the ' candour of the present age, he has imitated the honesty of pre- ' ceding ones, in expressing himself with the utmost plainness ' and freedom throughout.' If Mr Sadler really wishes that the controversy about his new principle of population should be carried on with all the license of the seventeenth century, we can have no personal objections. We are quite as little afraid of a contest in which quarter shall be neither given nor taken as he can be. But we would advise him seriously to consider, before he publishes the promised continuation of his work, whether he be not one of that class of writers who stand peculiarly in need of the candour which he insults, and who would have most to fear from that unsparing severity which he practises and recommends.

There is only one excuse for the extreme acrimony with which this book is written, and that excuse is but a bad one. Mr Sadler imagines that the theory of Mr Malthus is inconsistent with Christianity, and even with the purer forms of Deism. Now even had this been the case, a greater degree of mildness and self-command than Mr Sadler has shown would have been becoming in a writer who had undertaken to defend the religion of charity. But in fact, the imputation which has been thrown on Mr Malthus and his followers, is so absurd as scarcely to deserve an answer. As it appears, however, in almost every page of Mr Sadler's book, we will say a few words respecting it.

Mr Sadler describes Mr Malthus's principle in the following words :—

' It pronounces that there exists an evil in the principle of population; an evil, not accidental, but inherent; not of occasional occurrence, but in perpetual operation; not light, transient, or mitigated, but productive of miseries, compared with which all those inflicted by human institutions, that is to say, by the weakness and wickedness of man, however instigated, are " light :" an evil, finally, for which there is no remedy save one, which had been long overlooked, and which is now enunciated in terms which evince any thing rather than confidence. It is a principle, moreover, preeminently bold, as well as " clear." With a presumption, to call it by no fitter name, of which it may be doubted whether literature, heathen or Christian, furnishes a parallel, it professes to trace this supposed evil to its source, " the laws of nature, which are those of God ;" thereby implying, and indeed asserting, that the law by which the Deity multiplies his offspring, and that by which he makes provision for their sustentation, are different, and, indeed, irreconcilable.'

' This theory,' he adds, ' in the plain apprehension of the ' many, lowers the character of the Deity in that attribute, which, ' as Rousseau has well observed, is the most essential to him, his ' goodness; or otherwise, impugns his wisdom.'

Now nothing is more certain than that there is physical and moral evil in the world. Whoever, therefore, believes, as we do most firmly believe, in the goodness of God, must believe that there is no incompatibility between the goodness of God and the existence of physical and moral evil. If then the goodness of God be not incompatible with the existence of physical and moral evil, on what grounds does Mr Sadler maintain that the goodness of God is incompatible with the law of population laid down by Mr Malthus?

Is there any difference between the particular form of evil which would be produced by over-population, and other forms of evil which we know to exist in the world? It is, says Mr Sadler, not a light or transient evil, but a great and permanent evil.—What then? The question of the origin of evil is a question of ay or no,—not a question of more or less. If any explanation can be found by which the slightest inconvenience ever sustained by any sentient being can be reconciled with the divine attribute of benevolence, that explanation will equally apply to the most dreadful and extensive calamities that can ever afflict the human race. The difficulty arises from an apparent contradiction in terms; and that difficulty is as complete in the case of a headach which lasts for an hour, as in the case of a pestilence which unpeoples an empire,—in the case of the gust which makes us shiver for a moment, as in the case of the hurricane in which an Armada is cast away.

It is, according to Mr Sadler, an instance of presumption unparalleled in literature, heathen or Christian, to trace an evil to ' the laws of nature, which are those of God,' as its source. Is not hydrophobia an evil? And is it not a law of nature that hydrophobia should be communicated by the bite of a mad dog? Is not malaria an evil? And is it not a law of nature, that in particular situations the human frame should be liable to malaria? We know that there is evil in the world. If it is not to be traced to the laws of nature, how did it come into the world? Is it supernatural? And if we suppose it to be supernatural, is not the

difficulty of reconciling it with the divine attributes as great as
if we suppose it to be natural? Or, rather, what do the words
natural and supernatural mean, when applied to the operations
of the supreme mind?

Mr Sadler has attempted, in another part of his work, to meet
these obvious arguments, by a distinction without a difference.

' The scourges of human existence, as necessary regulators of the numbers of mankind, it is also agreed by some, are not inconsistent with the
wisdom or benevolence of the Governor of the universe; though such
think that it is a mere after-concern to " reconcile the undeniable state of
the fact to the attributes we assign to the Deity." " The purpose of the
earthquake," say they, " the hurricane, the drought, or the famine, by
which thousands, and sometimes almost millions, of the human race, are
at once overwhelmed, or left the victims of lingering want, is certainly
inscrutable." How singular is it that a sophism like this, so false, as a
mere illustration, should pass for an argument, as it has long done! The
principle of population is declared to be naturally productive of evils to
mankind, and as having that constant and manifest tendency to increase
their numbers beyond the means of their subsistence, which has produced
the unhappy and disgusting consequences so often enumerated. This is,
then, its universal tendency or rule. But is there in Nature the same constant tendency to these earthquakes, hurricanes, droughts, and famines, by
which so many myriads, if not millions, are overwhelmed or reduced at
once to ruin? No; these awful events are strange exceptions to the ordinary course of things; their visitations are partial, and they occur at
distant intervals of time. While Religion has assigned to them a very
solemn office, Philosophy readily refers them to those great and benevolent principles of Nature by which the universe is regulated. But were
there a constantly operating tendency to these calamitous occurrences;
did we feel the earth beneath us tremulous, and giving ceaseless and certain tokens of the coming catastrophe of nature; were the hurricane heard
mustering its devastating powers, and perpetually muttering around us;
were the skies " like brass," without a cloud to produce one genial drop
to refresh the thirsty earth, and famine, consequently, visibly on the approach; I say, would such a state of things, as resulting from the constant
laws of Nature, be " reconcilable with the attributes we assign to the
Deity," or with any attributes which in these inventive days could be
assigned to him, so as to represent him as any thing but the tormentor,
rather than the kind benefactor, of his creatures? Life, in such a condition, would be like the unceasingly threatened and miserable existence of
Damocles at the table of Dionysius, and the tyrant himself the worthy
image of the deity of the anti-populationists.'

Surely this is wretched trifling. Is it on the number of bad
harvests, or of volcanic eruptions, that this great question depends? Mr Sadler's piety, it seems, would be proof against
one rainy summer, but would be overcome by three or four in
succession. On the coasts of the Mediterranean, where earth-

quakes are rare, he would be an optimist. South America would make him a sceptic, and Java a decided Manichean. To say that religion assigns a solemn office to these visitations is nothing to the purpose. Why was man so constituted as to need such warnings? It is equally unmeaning to say that philosophy refers these events to benevolent general laws of nature. In so far as the laws of nature produce evil, they are clearly not benevolent. They may produce much good. But why is this good mixed with evil? The most subtle and powerful intellects have been labouring for centuries to solve these difficulties. The true solution, we are inclined to think, is that which has been rather suggested, than developed, by Paley and Butler. But there is not one solution which will not apply quite as well to the evils of over-population as to any other evil. Many excellent people think that it is presumptuous to meddle with such high questions at all, and that, though there doubtless is an explanation, our faculties are not sufficiently enlarged to comprehend that explanation. This mode of getting rid of the difficulty, again, will apply quite as well to the evils of over-population as to any other evils. We are sure, that those who humbly confess their inability to expound the great enigma, act more rationally and more decorously than Mr Sadler, who tells us, with the utmost confidence, which are the means and which the ends,—which the exceptions and which the rules, in the government of the universe;—who consents to bear a little evil without denying the divine benevolence, but distinctly announces that a certain quantity of dry weather or stormy weather would force him to regard the Deity as the tyrant of his creatures.

The great discovery by which Mr Sadler has, as he conceives, vindicated the ways of Providence, is enounced with all the pomp of capital letters. We must particularly beg that our readers will peruse it with attention.

‘ No one fact relative to the human species is more clearly ascertained, whether by general observation or actual proof, than that their fecundity varies in different communities and countries. The principle which effects this variation, without the necessity of those cruel and unnatural expedients so frequently adverted to, constitutes what I presume to call THE LAW OF POPULATION; and that law may be thus briefly enunciated :

‘ THE PROLIFICNESS OF HUMAN BEINGS, OTHERWISE SIMILARLY CIRCUMSTANCED, VARIES INVERSELY AS THEIR NUMBERS.

‘ The preceding definition may be thus amplified and explained. Premising, as a mere truism, that marriages under precisely similar circumstances will, on the average, be equally fruitful everywhere, I proceed to state, first, that the prolificness of a given number of marriages will, all other circumstances being the same, vary in proportion to the condensation of the population, so that that prolificness shall be greatest where the numbers on an equal space are the fewest, and, on the contrary, the smallest where those numbers are the largest.'

Mr Sadler, at setting out, abuses Mr Malthus for enouncing his theory in terms taken from the exact sciences. ' Applied to ' the mensuration of human fecundity,' he tells us, ' the most ' fallacious of all things is geometrical demonstration ;' and he again informs us that those ' act an irrational and irreverent ' part who affect to measure the mighty depth of God's mercies ' by their arithmetic, and to demonstrate, by their geometrical ' ratios, that it is inadequate to receive and contain the efflux of ' that fountain of life which is in Him.'

It appears, however, that it is not to the use of mathematical words, but only to the use of those words in their right senses, that Mr Sadler objects. The law of inverse variation, or inverse proportion, is as much a part of mathematical science as the law of geometric progression. The only difference in this respect between Mr Malthus and Mr Sadler is, that Mr Malthus knows what is meant by geometric progression, and that Mr Sadler has not the faintest notion of what is meant by inverse variation. Had he understood the proposition which he has enounced with so much pomp, its ludicrous absurdity must at once have flashed on his mind.

Let it be supposed that there is a tract in the back settlements of America, or in New South Wales, equal in size to London, with only a single couple, a man and his wife, living upon it. The population of London, with its immediate suburbs, is now probably about a million and a half. The average fecundity of a marriage in London is, as Mr Sadler tells us, 2.35. How many children will the woman in the back settlements bear according to Mr Sadler's theory? The solution of the problem is easy. As the population in this tract in the back settlements to the population of London, so will be the number of children born from a marriage in London to the number of children born from the marriage of this couple in the back settlements. That is to say—

$$2 : 1,500,000 :: 2.35 : 1.762,500.$$

The lady will have 1,762,500 children : a large ' efflux of the ' fountain of life,' to borrow Mr Sadler's sonorous rhetoric, as the most philoprogenitive parent could possibly desire.

But let us, instead of putting cases of our own, look at some of those which Mr Sadler has brought forward in support of his theory. The following table, he tells us, exhibits a striking proof of the truth of his main position. It seems to us to prove only that Mr Sadler does not know what inverse proportion means.

Countries.	Inhabitants on a square mile, about	Children to a Marriage.
Cape of Good Hope .	1	5.48
North America . .	4	5.22
Russia in Europe . .	23	4.94
Denmark	73	4.89
Prussia	100	4.70
France	140	4.22
England	160	3.66

Is 1 to 160 as 3.66 to 5.48 ? If Mr Sadler's principle were just, the number of children produced by a marriage at the Cape would be not 5.48, but very near 600. Or take America and France. Is 4 to 140 as 4.22 to 5.22 ? The number of births to a marriage in North America ought, according to this proportion, to be about 150.

Mr Sadler states the law of population in England thus :—

‘ Where the inhabitants are found to be on the square mile,
From   50 to 100 (2 counties) the births to 100 marriages are 420
 —   100 to 150 (9 counties)   396
 —   150 to 200 (16 counties)   390
 —   200 to 250 (4 counties)   388
 —   250 to 300 (5 counties)   378
 —   300 to 350 (3 counties)   353
 —   500 to 600 (2 counties)   331
 —   4000, and upwards (1 county)   .   .   . 246
 ‘ Now, I think it quite reasonable to conclude, that, were there not another document in existence relative to this subject, the facts thus deduced from the census of England are fully sufficient to demonstrate the position, that the fecundity of human beings varies inversely as their numbers. How, I ask, can it be evaded ?’

What, we ask, is there to evade ? Is 246 to 420 as 50 to 4000 ? Is 331 to 396 as 100 to 500 ? If the law propounded by Mr Sadler were correct, the births to a hundred marriages in the least populous part of England, would be $\dfrac{246 \times 4000}{50}$ that is 19,680,—nearly two hundred children to every mother. But we will not carry on these calculations. The absurdity of Mr Sadler's proposition is so palpable that it is unnecessary to select particular instances. Let us see what are the extremes of population and fecundity in well-known countries. The space which Mr Sadler generally takes is a square mile. The population at the Cape of Good Hope is, according to him, one to the square mile. That of London is two hundred thousand to the square mile. The number of children at the Cape, Mr Sadler informs us, is 5.48 to a marriage. In London, he states it at 2.35 to a marriage. Now how can that of which all the variations lie between 2.35 and 5.48 vary either directly or inversely, as that which admits of all the variations between one and two hundred thousand? Mr Sadler evidently does not know the meaning of the word proportion. A million is a larger quantity than ten. A hundred is a larger quantity than five. Mr Sadler thinks, therefore, that there is no impropriety in saying that a hundred is to five, as a million is to ten, or in the inverse ratio of ten to a million. He proposes to prove that the fecundity of marriages varies in inverse proportion to the density of the population. But all that he attempts to prove is that, while the population increases from one to a hundred and sixty on the square mile, the fecundity will diminish from 5.48 to 3.66; and that again, while the population increases from one hundred and sixty to two hundred thousand on the square mile, the fecundity will diminish from 3.66 to 2.35.

The proposition which Mr Sadler enounces, without understanding the words which he uses, would indeed, if it could be proved, set us at ease as to the dangers of over-population. But it is, as we have shown, a proposition so grossly absurd, that it is difficult for any man to keep his countenance while he repeats it. The utmost that Mr Sadler has ever attempted to prove is this,—that the fecundity of the human race diminishes as population becomes more condensed,—but that the diminution of fecundity bears a very small ratio to the increase of population,—so that while the population on a square mile is multiplied two-hundred-thousand-fold, the fecundity decreases by little more than one-half.

Does this principle vindicate the honour of God? Does it hold out any new hope or comfort to man? Not at all. We pledge ourselves to show, with the utmost strictness of reasoning, from Mr Sadler's own principles, and from facts of the most notorious description, that every consequence which follows from the law of geometrical progression, laid down by Mr Malthus, will follow from the law, miscalled a law of inverse variation, which has been laid down by Mr Sadler.

London is the most thickly-peopled spot of its size in the known world. Therefore the fecundity of the population of London must, according to Mr Sadler, be less than the fecundity of human beings living on any other spot of equal size. Mr Sadler tells us, that ' the ratios of mortality are influenced by ' the different degrees in which the population is condensated; ' and that, other circumstances being similar, the relative num- ' ber of deaths in a thinly-populated, or country district, is less ' than that which takes place in towns, and in towns of a mode- ' rate size, less again than that which exists in large and popu- ' lous cities.' Therefore the mortality in London must, accord- ing to him, be greater than in other places. But though, ac- cording to Mr Sadler, the fecundity is less in London than else- where, and though the mortality is greater there than elsewhere, we find that even in London the number of births greatly ex- ceeds the number of deaths. During the ten years which ended with 1820, there were fifty thousand more baptisms than bu- rials within the bills of mortality. It follows, therefore, that, even within London itself, an increase of the population is taking place by internal propagation.

Now if the population of a place in which the fecundity is less and the mortality greater than in other places still goes on in- creasing by propagation, it follows that in other places the popu- lation will increase, and increase still faster. There is clearly nothing in Mr Sadler's boasted law of fecundity which will keep the population from multiplying till the whole earth is as thick with human beings as St Giles's parish. If Mr Sadler denies this, he must hold, that in places less thickly peopled than Lon- don, marriages may be less fruitful than in London, which is directly contrary to his own principles; or that in places less thickly peopled than London, and similarly situated, people will die faster than in London, which is again directly contrary to his own principles. Now if it follows, as it clearly does follow, from Mr Sadler's own doctrines, that the human race might be stowed together by three or four hundred to the acre, and might still, as far as the principle of propagation is concerned, go on increa- sing, what advantage, in a religious or moral point of view, has his theory over that of Mr Malthus ? The principle of Mr Mal- thus, says Mr Sadler, leads to consequences of the most fright- ful description. Be it so. But do not all these consequences spring equally from his own principle? Revealed religion con- demns Mr Malthus. Be it so. But Mr Sadler must share in the reproach of heresy. The theory of Mr Malthus represents the Deity as a Dionysius hanging the sword over the heads of his trembling slaves. Be it so. But under what rhetorical figure are we to represent the Deity of Mr Sadler?

A man who wishes to serve the cause of religion ought to he- sitate long before he stakes the truth of religion on the event of

a controversy respecting facts in the physical world. For a time
he may succeed in making a theory which he dislikes unpopular,
by persuading the public that it contradicts the Scriptures, and
is inconsistent with the attributes of the Deity. But if at last
an overwhelming force of evidence proves this maligned theory
to be true, what is the effect of the arguments by which the ob-
jector has attempted to prove that it is irreconcilable with natural and revealed religion? Merely this, to make men infidels.
Like the Israelites, in their battle with the Philistines, he has
presumptuously, and without warrant, brought down the ark of
God into the camp, as a means of ensuring victory:—and the
consequence of this profanation is, that, when the battle is lost,
the ark is taken.

In every age the Church has been cautioned against this fatal
and impious rashness by its most illustrious members,—by the
fervid Augustin, by the subtle Aquinas, by the all-accomplished
Pascal. The warning has been given in vain. That close alli-
ance which, under the disguise of the most deadly enmity, has
always subsisted between fanaticism and atheism, is still unbroken. At one time, the cry was,—' If you hold that the earth
' moves round the sun, you deny the truth of the Bible.' Popes,
conclaves, and religious orders, rose up against the Copernican
heresy. But, as Pascal said, they could not prevent the earth
from moving, or themselves from moving along with it. One
thing, however, they could do, and they did. They could teach
numbers to consider the Bible as a collection of old women's
stories, which the progress of civilisation and knowledge was re-
futing one by one. They had attempted to show that the Ptole-
maic system was as much a part of Christianity as the resurrection of the dead. Was it strange, then, that, when the Ptole-
maic system became an object of ridicule to every man of education in Catholic countries, the doctrine of the resurrection
should be in peril? In the present generation, and in our own
country, the prevailing system of geology has been, with equal
folly, attacked on the ground that it is inconsistent with the
Mosaic dates ; and here we have Mr Sadler, out of his especial
zeal for religion, first proving that the doctrine of superfecundity is irreconcilable with the goodness of God, and then laying
down principles, and stating facts, from which the doctrine of
superfecundity necessarily follows. This blundering piety reminds us of the adventures of a certain missionary, who went to
convert the inhabitants of Madagascar. The good father had an
audience of the king, and began to instruct his majesty in the
history of the human race as given in the Scriptures. ' Thus,
' sir,' said he, ' was woman made out of the rib of man, and ever

' since that time a woman has had one rib more than a man.'—
' Surely, father, you must be mistaken there,' said the king.
' Mistaken!' said the missionary. 'It is an indisputable fact. My
' faith upon it! My life upon it!' The good man had heard the
fact asserted by his nurse when he was a child,—had always considered it as a strong confirmation of the Scriptures, and fully
believed it, without having ever thought of verifying it. The
king ordered a man and woman, the leanest that could be found,
to be brought before him, and desired his spiritual instructor to
count their ribs. The father counted over and over, upward and
downward, and still found the same number in both. He then
cleared his throat, stammered, stuttered, and began to assure the
king that, though he had committed a little error in saying that a
woman had more ribs than a man, he was quite right in saying
that the first woman was made out of the rib of the first man.
' How can I tell that?' said the king. ' You come to me with a
' strange story, which you say is revealed to you from heaven. I
' have already made you confess that one half of it is a lie ; and
' how can you have the face to expect that I shall believe the
' other half?'

We have shown that Mr Sadler's theory, if it be true, is as
much a theory of superfecundity as that of Mr Malthus. But
it is not true. And from Mr Sadler's own tables we will prove
that it is not true.

The fecundity of the human race in England Mr Sadler rates
as follows :—

' Where the inhabitants are found to be on the square mile

From	50 to 100	(2 counties)	the births to 100 marriages are			420
—	100 to 150	(9 counties)	.	.	.	396
—	150 to 200	(16 counties)	.	.	.	390
—	200 to 250	(4 counties)	.	.	.	388
—	250 to 300	(5 counties)	.	.	.	378
—	300 to 350	(3 counties)	.	.	.	353
—	500 to 600	(2 counties)	.	.	.	331
—	4000 and upwards	(1 county)	.	.	.	246

Having given this table, he begins, as usual, to boast and triumph. ' Were there not another document on the subject in
' existence,' says he, ' the facts thus deduced from the census of
' England are sufficient to demonstrate the position, that the fe-
' cundity of human beings varies inversely as their numbers.'
In no case would these facts demonstrate that the fecundity of
human beings varies inversely as their numbers, in the right
sense of the words inverse variation. But certainly they would,
' if there were no other document in existence,' appear to indicate something like what Mr Sadler means by inverse variation.

Unhappily for him, however, there are other documents in existence, and he has himself furnished us with them. We will extract another of his tables:—

TABLE LXIV.

Showing the Operation of the Law of Population in the different Hundreds of the County of Lancaster.

Hundreds.	Population on each Square Mile.	Square Miles.	Population in 1821, exclusive of Towns of separate Jurisdiction.	Marriages from 1811 to 1821.	Baptisms from 1811 to 1821.	Baptisms to 100 Marriages.
Lonsdale .	96	441	42,486	3651	16,129	442
Almondness .	267	228	60,930	3670	15,228	415
Leyland . . .	354	126	44,583	2858	11,182	391
West Derby .	409	377	154,040	24,182	86,407	357
Blackburn . .	513	286	146,608	10,814	31,463	291
Salford	869	373	322,592	40,143	114,941	286

Mr Sadler rejoices much over this table. The results, he says, have surprised himself; and, indeed, as we shall show, they might well have done so.

The result of his enquiries with respect to France he presents in the following table:—

'The legitimate births are, in those departments where there are to each inhabitant

From 4 to 5 hects. (2 departs.) to every 1000 marriages, .	5130
3 to 4 . . (3 do.)	4372
2 to 3 . . (30 do.)	4250
1 to 2 . . (44 do.)	4234
.06 to 1 . . (5 do.)	4146
and .06 . . (1 do.)	2557

Then comes the shout of exultation as regularly as the *Gloria Patri* at the end of a Psalm. ' Is there any possibility of gain-' saying the conclusions these facts force upon us; namely, that ' the fecundity of marriages is regulated by the density of the ' population, and inversely to it?'

Certainly these tables, taken separately, look well for Mr Sadler's theory. He must be a bungling gamester who cannot win when he is suffered to pack the cards his own way. We must beg leave to shuffle them a little, and we will venture to pro-

mise our readers that some curious results will follow from the
operation. In nine counties of England, says Mr Sadler, in
which the population is from 100 to 150 on the square mile, the
births to 100 marriages are 396. He afterwards expresses some
doubt as to the accuracy of the documents from which this estimate has been formed, and rates the number of births as high as
414. Let him take his choice. We will allow him every advantage.

In the table which we have quoted, numbered lxiv. he tells
us that in Almondness, where the population is 267 to the square
mile, there are 415 births to 100 marriages. The population of
Almondness is twice as thick as the population of the nine
counties referred to in the other table. Yet the number of
births to a marriage is greater in Almondness than in those
counties.

Once more, he tells us, that in three counties, in which the
population was from 300 to 350 on the square mile, the births
to 100 marriages were 353. He afterwards rates them at 375.
Again we say, let him take his choice. But from his table of
the population of Lancashire it appears that, in the hundred of
Leyland, where the population is 354 to the square mile, the
number of births to 100 marriages is 391. Here again we have
the marriages becoming more fruitful as the population becomes
denser.

Let us now shuffle the censuses of England and France together. In two English counties which contain from fifty to
100 inhabitants on the square mile, the births to 100 marriages
are, according to Mr Sadler, 420. But in forty-four departments
of France, in which there are from one to two hecatares to each
inhabitant, that is to say, in which the population is from 125
to 250, or rather more, to the square mile, the number of births
to 100 marriages is 423 and a fraction.

Again, in five departments of France in which there is less
than one hecatare to each inhabitant, that is to say, in which
the population is more than 250 to the square mile, the number
of births to 100 marriages is 414 and a fraction. But in the
four counties of England in which the population is from 200
to 250 on the square mile, the number of births to 100 marriages
is, according to one of Mr Sadler's tables, only 388, and by his
very highest estimate no more than 402.

Mr Sadler gives us a long table of all the towns of England
and Ireland, which, he tells us, irrefragably demonstrates his
principle. We assert, and will prove, that these tables are alone
sufficient to upset his whole theory.

It is very true, that in the great towns the number of births to a marriage appears to be smaller than in the less populous towns. But we learn some other facts from these tables which we should be glad to know how Mr Sadler will explain. We find that the fecundity in towns of fewer than 3000 inhabitants, is actually much greater than the average fecundity of the kingdom, and that the fecundity in towns of between 3000 and 4000 inhabitants is at least as great as the average fecundity of the kingdom. The average fecundity of a marriage in towns of fewer than 3000 inhabitants is about four; in towns of between 3000 and 4000 inhabitants it is 3.60. Now the average fecundity of England, when it contained only 160 inhabitants to a square mile, and when, therefore, according to the new law of population, the fecundity must have been greater than it now is, was only, according to Mr Sadler 3.66 to a marriage. To proceed, —the fecundity of a marriage in the English towns of between 4000 and 5000 inhabitants, is stated at 3.56. But when we turn to Mr Sadler's table of the counties, we find the fecundity of a marriage in Warwickshire and Staffordshire rated at only 3.48, and in Lancashire and Surrey at only 3.41.

These facts disprove Mr Sadler's principle; and the fact on which he lays so much stress,—that the fecundity is less in the great towns than in the small towns,—does not tend in any degree to prove his principle. There is not the least reason to believe that the population is more dense, *on a given space,* in London or Manchester, than in a town of 4000 inhabitants. But it is quite certain that the population is more dense in a town of 4000 inhabitants than in Warwickshire or Lancashire. That the fecundity of Manchester is less than the fecundity of Sandwich or Guildford, is a circumstance which has nothing whatever to do with Mr Sadler's theory. But that the fecundity of Sandwich is greater than the average fecundity of Kent, —that the fecundity of Guildford is greater than the average fecundity of Surrey, as from his own tables appears to be the case,—these are facts utterly inconsistent with his theory.

We need not here examine why it is that the human race is less fruitful in great cities than in small towns or in the open country. The fact has long been notorious. We are inclined to attribute it to the same causes which tend to abridge human life in great cities,—to general sickliness and want of tone, produced by close air and sedentary employments. Thus far, and thus far only, we agree with Mr Sadler, that when population is crowded together in such masses, that the general health and energy of the frame are impaired by the condensation, and by the habits attending on the condensation, then the fecundity of

the race diminishes. But this is evidently a check of the same
class with war, pestilence, and famine. It is a check for the
operation of which Mr Malthus has allowed.

That any condensation which does not affect the general health
will affect fecundity, is not only not proved—it is disproved—
by Mr Sadler's own tables.

Mr Sadler passes on to Prussia, and sums up his information
respecting that country as follows :—

Inhabitants on a Square Mile, German.	Number of Provinces.	Births to 100 Marriages, 1754.	Births to 100 Marriages, 1784.	Births to 100 Marriages, Busching.
Under 1000	2	434	472	503
1000 to 2000	4	414	455	454
2000 to 3000	6	384	424	426
3000 to 4000	2	365	408	394

After the table comes the boast as usual :

' Thus is the law of population deduced from the registers of Prussia
also; and were the argument to pause here, it is conclusive.   The results obtained from the registers of this and the preceding countries,
exhibiting, as they do most clearly, the principle of human increase, it
is utterly impossible should have been the work of chance ; on the contrary, the regularity with which the facts class themselves in conformity
with that principle, and the striking analogy which the whole of them
bear to each other, demonstrate equally the design of Nature, and the
certainty of its accomplishment.'

We are sorry to disturb Mr Sadler's complacency. But, in
our opinion, this table completely disproves his whole principle.
If we read the columns perpendicularly indeed, they seem to be
in his favour. But how stands the case if we read horizontally?
Does Mr Sadler believe, that during the thirty years which
elapsed between 1754 and 1784, the population of Prussia had
been diminishing?   No fact in history is better ascertained than
that, during the long peace which followed the seven years' war,
it increased with great rapidity.   Indeed, if the fecundity were
what Mr Sadler states it to have been, it must have increased
with great rapidity.   Yet, the ratio of births to marriages is
greater in 1784 than in 1754, and that in every province.   It
is, therefore, perfectly clear that the fecundity does not diminish
whenever the density of the population increases.

We will try another of **Mr Sadler's** tables :

TABLE LXXXI.

Showing the Estimated Prolificness of Marriages in England, at the close of the Seventeenth Century.

Places.	Number of Inhabitants.	One Annual Marriage, to	Number of Marriages.	Children to one Marriage.	Total Number of Births.
London . . .	530,000	106	5000	4.	20,000
Large Towns .	870,000	128	6800	4.5	30,000
Small Towns and Country Places	4,100,000	141	29,200	4.8	140,160
	5,500,000	134	41,000	4.65	190,760

Standing by itself, this table, like most of the others, seems to support Mr Sadler's theory. But surely London, at the close of the seventeenth century, was far more thickly peopled than the kingdom of England now is. Yet the fecundity in London at the close of the seventeenth century was 4; and the average fecundity of the whole kingdom now is not more, according to Mr Sadler, than 3½. Then, again, the large towns in 1700 were far more thickly peopled than Westmorland and the North Riding of Yorkshire now are. Yet the fecundity in those large towns was then 4.5. And Mr Sadler tells us that it is now only 4.2 in Westmorland and the North Riding.

It is scarcely necessary to say any thing about the censuses of the Netherlands, as Mr Sadler himself confesses that there is some difficulty in reconciling them with his theory, and helps out his awkward explanation, by supposing, quite gratuitously, as it seems to us, that the official documents are inaccurate. The argument which he has drawn from the United States will detain us but for a very short time. He has not told us,—perhaps he had not the means of telling us,—what proportion the number of births in the different parts of that country bears to the number of marriages. He shows, that in the thinly-peopled states, the number of children bears a greater proportion to the number of grown-up people than in the old states; and this, he conceives, is a sufficient proof that the condensation of the population is unfavourable to fecundity. We deny the inference altogether.   Nothing can be more obvious than the explanation of the phenomenon.   The back settlements are for the most part peopled by emigration from the old states; and emigrants are almost always breeders.   They are almost always vigorous people in the prime of life.   Mr Sadler himself, in another part of his book, in which he tries, very unsuccessfully, to show that the rapid multiplication of the people of America is principally owing to emigration from Europe, states this fact in the plainest manner:

' Nothing is more certain, than that emigration is almost universally supplied by "single persons in the beginning of mature life ;" nor, secondly, that such persons, as Dr Franklin long ago asserted, " marry and raise families."

' Nor is this all.   It is not more true, that emigrants, generally speaking, consist of individuals in the prime of life, than that " they are the most active and vigorous" of that age, as Dr Seybert describes them to be.   They are, as it respects the principle at issue, a select class, even compared with that of their own age generally considered.   Their very object in leaving their native countries is to settle in life, a phrase that needs no explanation; and they do so.   No equal number of human beings, therefore, have ever given so large or rapid an increase to a community as " settlers" have invariably done.'·

It is perfectly clear that children are more numerous in the back settlements of America than in the maritime states, not because unoccupied land makes people prolific, but because the most prolific people go to the unoccupied land.

Mr Sadler having, as he conceives, fully established his theory of population by statistical evidence, proceeds to prove, ' that it ' is in unison, or rather required by the principles of physiology.' The difference between himself and his opponents he states as follows :—

' In pursuing this part of my subject, I must begin by reminding the reader of the difference between those who hold the superfecundity of mankind, and myself, in regard to those principles which will form the basis of the present argument.   They contend, that production precedes population; I, on the contrary, maintain that population precedes, and is indeed the cause of, production.   They teach, that man breeds up to the capital, or in proportion to the abundance of the food, he possesses; I assert, that he is comparatively sterile when he is wealthy, and that he breeds in proportion to his poverty; not meaning, however, by that poverty, a state of privation approaching to actual starvation, any more than, I suppose, they would contend, that extreme and culpable excess is the grand patron of population.   In a word, they hold that a state of ease and affluence is the great promoter of prolificness: I maintain that a considerable degree of labour, and even privation, is a more efficient cause of an increased degree of human fecundity.'

To prove this point, he quotes Aristotle, Hippocrates, Dr Short,

Dr Gregory, Dr Perceval, M. Villermi, Lord Bacon, and Rousseau. We will not dispute about it; for it seems quite clear to us, that if he succeeds in establishing it, he overturns his own theory. If men breed in proportion to their poverty, as he tells us here,—and at the same time breed in inverse proportion to their numbers, as he told us before, it necessarily follows, that the poverty of men must be in inverse proportion to their numbers. Inverse proportion, indeed, as we have shown, is not the phrase which expresses Mr Sadler's meaning. To speak more correctly, it follows from his two positions, that if one population be thinner than another, it will also be poorer. Is this the fact? Mr Sadler tells us, in one of those tables which we have already quoted, that in the United States, the population is four to a square mile, and the fecundity 5.22 to a marriage, and that in Russia the population is twenty-three to a square mile, and the fecundity 4.94 to a marriage. Is the North American labourer poorer than the Russian boor? If not, what becomes of Mr Sadler's argument?

The most decisive proof of Mr Sadler's theory, according to him, is that which he has kept for the last. It is derived from the registers of the English Peerage. The Peers, he says, and says truly, are the class with respect to whom we possess the most accurate statistical information.

' Touching their *number*, this has been accurately known and recorded ever since the order has existed in the country. For several centuries past, the addition to it of a single individual has been a matter of public interest and notoriety: this hereditary honour, conferring not personal dignity merely, but important privileges, and being almost always identified with great wealth and influence. The records relating to it are kept with the most scrupulous attention, not only by heirs and expectants, but they are appealed to by more distant connexions, as conferring distinction on all who can claim such affinity. Hence there are few disputes concerning successions to this rank, but such as go back to very remote periods. In later times, the marriages, births, and deaths, of the nobility, have not only been registered by and known to those personally interested, but have been published periodically, and, consequently, subject to perpetual correction and revision; while many of the most powerful motives which can influence the human mind conspire to preserve these records from the slightest falsification. Compared with these, therefore, all other registers, or reports, whether of " sworn searchers" or others, are incorrectness itself.'

Mr Sadler goes on to tell us that the Peers are a marrying class, and that their general longevity proves them to be a healthy class. Still peerages often become extinct;—and from this fact he infers, that they are a sterile class. So far, says he, from increasing in geometrical progression, they do not even keep up their numbers. ' Nature interdicts their increase.'

' Thus,' says he, ' in all ages of the world, and in every nation of it, have the highest ranks of the community been the most sterile, and the lowest the most prolific. As it respects our own country, from the lowest grade of society, the Irish peasant, to the highest, the British peer, this remains a conspicuous truth ; and the regulation of the degree of fecundity conformably to this principle, through the intermediate gradations of society, constitutes one of the features of the system developed in these pages.'

We take the issue which Mr Sadler has himself offered. We agree with him, that the registers of the English Peerage are of far higher authority than any other statistical documents. We are content that by those registers his principle should be judged. And we meet him by positively denying his facts. We assert, that the English nobles are not only not a sterile, but an eminently prolific, part of the community. Mr Sadler concludes, that they are sterile, merely because peerages often become extinct. Is this the proper way of ascertaining the point? Is it thus that he avails himself of those registers, on the accuracy and fulness of which he descants so largely? Surely his right course would have been to count the marriages, and the number of births, in the Peerage. This he has not done;—but we have done it. And what is the result ?

It appears from the last edition of Debrett's *Peerage*, published in 1828, that there were at that time 287 peers of the United Kingdom, who had been married once or oftener. The whole number of marriages contracted by these 287 peers was 333. The number of children by these marriages was 1437,—more than five to a peer,—more than 4.3 to a marriage,—more, that is to say, than the average number in those counties of England, in which, according to Mr Sadler's own statement, the fecundity is the greatest.

But this is not all. These marriages had not, in 1828, produced their full effect. Some of them had been very lately contracted. In a very large proportion of them there was every probability of additional issue. To allow for this probability, we may safely add one to the average which we have already obtained, and rate the fecundity of a noble marriage in England at 5.3 ;—higher than the fecundity which Mr Sadler assigns to the people of the United States. Even if we do not make this allowance, the average fecundity of the marriages of peers is higher by one-fifth than the average fecundity of marriages throughout the kingdom. And this is the sterile class ! This

is the class which ' nature has interdicted from increasing !' The
evidence to which Mr Sadler has himself appealed proves that
his principle is false,—utterly false,—wildly and extravagantly
false. It proves that a class, living during half of every year in the
most crowded population in the world, breeds faster than those
who live in the country,—that the class which enjoys the greatest
degree of luxury and ease, breeds faster than the class which
undergoes labour and privation. To talk a little in Mr Sadler's
style, we must own that we are ourselves surprised at the results which our examination of the peerage has brought out.
We certainly should have thought that the habits of fashionable
life, and long residence even in the most airy parts of so great
a city as London, would have been more unfavourable to the
fecundity of the higher orders than they appear to be.

Peerages, it is true, often become extinct. But it is quite clear
from what we have stated, that this is not because peeresses are
barren. There is no difficulty in discovering what the causes
really are. In the first place, most of the titles of our nobles
are limited to heirs male ; so that, though the average fecundity
of a noble marriage is upwards of 5, yet, for the purpose of keeping up a peerage, it cannot be reckoned at much more than $2\frac{1}{2}$.
Secondly, though the peers are, as Mr Sadler says, a marrying
class, the younger sons of peers are decidedly not a marrying
class ; so that a peer, though he has at least as great a chance
of having a son as his neighbours, has less chance than they
of having a collateral heir.

We have now disposed, we think, of Mr Sadler's principle of
population. Our readers must, by this time, be pretty well satisfied as to his qualifications for setting up theories of his own.
We will, therefore, present them with a few instances of the
skill and fairness which he shows when he undertakes to pull
down the theories of other men. The doctrine of Mr Malthus,
that population, if not checked by want, by vice, by excessive
mortality, or by the prudent self-denial of individuals, would increase in a geometric progression, is, in Mr Sadler's opinion, at
once false and atrocious.

' It may at once be denied,' says he, ' that human increase
' proceeds geometrically ; and for this simple but decisive reason,
' that the existence of a geometrical ratio of increase in the works
' of nature, is neither true nor possible. It would fling into utter
' confusion all order, time, magnitude, and space.'

This is as curious a specimen of reasoning as any that has
been offered to the world since the days when theories were
founded on the principle that nature abhors a vacuum. We proceed a few pages farther, however ; and we then find that geo-

metric progression is unnatural only in those cases in which Mr Malthus conceives that it exists; and that in all cases in which Mr Malthus denies the existence of a geometric ratio, nature changes sides, and adopts that ratio as the rule of increase.

Mr Malthus holds that subsistence will increase only in an arithmetical ratio. ' As far as nature has to do with the ques-' tion,' says Mr Sadler, ' men might, for instance, plant twice the ' number of peas, and breed from a double number of the same ' animals, with equal prospect of their multiplication.' Now, if Mr Sadler thinks that, as far as nature is concerned, four sheep will double as fast as two, and eight as fast as four, how can he deny that the geometrical ratio of increase does exist in the works of nature? Or has he a definition of his own for geometrical progression, as well as for inverse proportion?

Mr Malthus, and those who agree with him, have generally referred to the United States, as a country in which the human race increases in a geometrical ratio, and have fixed on twenty-five years as the term in which the population of that country doubles itself. Mr Sadler contends that it is physically impossible for a people to double in twenty-five years; nay, that thirty-five years is far too short a period,—that the Americans do not double by procreation in less than forty-seven years,— and that the rapid increase of their numbers is produced by emigration from Europe.

Emigration has certainly had some effect in increasing the population of the United States. But so great has the rate of that increase been, that after making full allowance for the effect of emigration, there will be a residue, attributable to procreation alone, amply sufficient to double the population in twenty-five years.

Mr Sadler states the results of the four censuses as follows:

' There were, of white inhabitants, in the whole of the United States in 1790, 3,093,111; in 1800, 4,309,656; in 1810, 5,862,093; and in 1820, 7,861,710. The increase, in the first term, being 39 per cent; that in the second, 36 per cent; and that in the third and last, 33 per cent. It is superfluous to say, that it is utterly impossible to deduce the geometric theory of human increase, whatever be the period of duplication, from such terms as these.'

Mr Sadler is a bad arithmetician. The increase in the last term is not, as he states it, 33 per cent, but more than 34 per cent. Now, an increase of 32 per cent in ten years, is more than sufficient to double the population in twenty-five years. And there is, we think, very strong reason to believe that the white population of the United States does increase by 32 per cent every ten years.

Our reason is this: There is in the United States a class of persons whose numbers are not increased by emigration,—the negro slaves. During the interval which elapsed between the census of 1810 and the census of 1820, the change in their numbers must have been produced by procreation, and by procreation alone. Their situation, though much happier than that of the wretched beings who cultivate the sugar plantations of Trinidad and Demerara, cannot be supposed to be more favourable to health and fecundity than that of free labourers. In 1810, the slave trade had been but recently abolished, and there were in consequence many more male than female slaves,—a circumstance, of course, very unfavourable to procreation. Slaves are perpetually passing into the class of freemen; but no freeman ever descends into servitude; so that the census will not exhibit the whole effect of the procreation which really takes place.

We find by the census of 1810, that the number of slaves in the Union was then 1,191,000. In 1820, they had increased to 1,538,000. That is to say, in ten years, they had increased 29 per cent—within three per cent of that rate of increase which would double their numbers in twenty-five years. We may, we think, fairly calculate, that if the female slaves had been as numerous as the males, and if no manumissions had taken place, the census of the slave population would have exhibited an increase of 32 per cent in ten years.

If we are right in fixing on 32 per cent as the rate at which the white population of America increases by procreation in ten years, it will follow, that, during the last ten years of the eighteenth century, nearly one-sixth of the increase was the effect of emigration; from 1800 to 1810, about one-ninth; and from 1810 to 1820, about one-seventeenth. This is what we should have expected; for it is clear that, unless the number of emigrants be constantly increasing, it must, as compared with the resident population, be relatively decreasing. The number of persons added to the population of the United States by emigration, between 1810 and 1820, would be nearly 120,000. From the data furnished by Mr Sadler himself, we should be inclined to think that this would be a fair estimate.

‘ Dr Seybert says, that the passengers to ten of the principal ports of the United States, in the year 1817, amounted to 22,235; of whom 11,977 were from Great Britain and Ireland; 4164 from Germany and Holland; 1245 from France; 58 from Italy; 2901 from the British possessions in North America; 1569 from the West Indies; and from all other countries, 321. These, however, we may conclude, with the editor of Styles's Register, were far short of the number that arrived.’

We have not the honour of knowing either Dr Seybert or the

editor of Styles's Register. We cannot, therefore, decide on
their respective claims to our confidence so peremptorily as Mr
Sadler thinks fit to do. Nor can we agree to what Mr Sadler
very gravely assigns as a reason for disbelieving Dr Seybert's
testimony. ' Such accounts,' he says, ' if not wilfully exagge-
' rated, must always fall short of the truth.' It would be a curious question of casuistry to determine what a man ought to
do in a case in which he cannot tell the truth except by being
guilty of wilful exaggeration. We will, however, suppose,
with Mr Sadler, that Dr Seybert, finding himself compelled
to choose between two sins, preferred telling a falsehood to exaggerating ; and that he has consequently underrated the number
of emigrants. We will take it at double of the Doctor's estimate,
and suppose that in 1817, 45,000 Europeans crossed to the United
States. Now, it must be remembered, that the year 1817 was
a year of the severest and most general distress over all Europe,
—a year of scarcity everywhere, and of cruel famine in some
places. There can, therefore, be no doubt that the emigration
of 1817 was very far above the average, probably more than
three times that of an ordinary year. Till the year 1815, the
war rendered it almost impossible to emigrate to the United
States either from England or from the Continent. If we suppose the average emigration of the remaining years to have been
16,000, we shall probably not be much mistaken. In 1818 and
1819, the number was certainly much beyond that average ; in
1815 and 1816, probably much below it. But even if we were
to suppose that in every year from the peace to 1820, the number of emigrants had been as high as we have supposed it to be
in 1817, the increase by procreation among the white inhabitants
of the United States would still appear to be about 30 per cent
in ten years.

Mr Sadler acknowledges that Cobbett exaggerates the number of emigrants, when he states it at 150,000 a-year. Yet even
this estimate, absurdly great as it is, would not be sufficient
to explain the increase of the population of the United States on
Mr Sadler's principles. He is, he tells us, ' convinced that dou-
' bling in 35 years is a far more rapid duplication than ever has
' taken place in that country from procreation only.' An increase of 20 per cent in ten years, by procreation, would therefore be the very utmost that he would allow to be possible. We
have already shown, by reference to the census of the slave population, that this doctrine is quite absurd. And, if we suppose it
to be sound, we shall be driven to the conclusion, that above eight
hundred thousand people emigrated from Europe to the United
States in a space of little more than five years. The whole in-

crease of the white population from 1810 to 1820, was within a few hundreds of 2,000,000. If we are to attribute to procreation only 20 per cent on the number returned by the census of 1810, we shall have about 830,000 persons to account for in some other way;—and to suppose that the emigrants who went to America between the peace of 1815 and the census of 1820, with the children who were born to them there, would make up that number, would be the height of absurdity.

We could say much more; but we think it quite unnecessary at present. We have shown that Mr Sadler is careless in the collection of facts,—that he is incapable of reasoning on facts when he has collected them,—that he does not understand the simplest terms of science,—that he has enounced a proposition of which he does not know the meaning,—that the proposition which he means to enounce, and which he tries to prove, leads directly to all those consequences which he represents as impious and immoral,—and that, from the very documents to which he has himself appealed, it may be demonstrated that his theory is false. We may, perhaps, resume the subject when his next volume appears. Meanwhile, we hope that he will delay its publication until he has learned a little arithmetic, and unlearned a great deal of eloquence.

ART. IV.—1. *An Outline of the Science of Political Economy.* By
NASSAU W. SENIOR, Esq. 8vo. London : 1836. (*Reprinted
for private circulation from the Encyclopedia Metropolitana.*)
2. *Principes Fondamentaux de l'Economie Politique, tirés de
leçons, édites et inédites, de M. N. W. Senior.* Par le Comte
JEAN ARRIVABENE. 8vo. Paris : 1836.

BEFORE proceeding to notice the valuable work of Mr Senior,
we propose to offer a few remarks on the views adopted by
some recent writers, especially in foreign countries, on the nature
and method of the science of political economy. It will be seen
how widely these views are at variance with those entertained by
the school of which Dr Adam Smith was the founder.

M. Sismondi, in his lately published *Etudes sur l'Economie
Politique,* which forms a kind of *résumé* of the scattered opinions
thrown out by him on the subject during his long literary life,
makes the following observations :—

' Society owes its first attention to the protection of its own material
interests, of its own subsistence ; and it is our object to examine what is
the line which society ought to adopt in order that those material goods
(biens matériels) which labour creates for her, may procure or maintain
the greatest amount of good for all (le plus grand bien de tous) ;—this is
what, according to the etymology of the word, we term *Political Economy,* for it is the *law* or *rule* of a family and of a state. . . . .

' The products of human labour, which represent, together with man's
subsistence, all the material *goods* which he desires to enjoy, and all
the intellectual goods which he cannot reach except by the assistance
of the former, have been called wealth. Wealth, or the theory of the
augmentation of wealth, has been regarded as the especial object of
political economy ; an object much better designated, since the times of
Aristotle, by the word *chrematistics.* We do not render our notions clearer
by disputing about words, and we should not reproduce this one if it did
not seem at the same time to mark with accuracy the cause of that false
direction which a branch of social science has followed in our time.
This science always has, and always ought to have for its subject, men
united in society. Economy, according to the proper sense of the
word, is the regulation of a family or house : political economy, the
regulation of a family applied to a state. These two great human associations, the primitive associations, form the proper object of the science.
But wealth is an attribute either of men or of things ; it is a comparative term, which has no sense, unless at the same time the object in
relation to which it is considered be clearly defined. Wealth, although
an attribute of things wholly material, is nevertheless an abstraction :
and *chrematistic* science, or the science of the increase of wealth, considering it abstractedly, and without reference to man and society, has

raised its edifice on a base wholly unsubstantial. Wealth is the product of human labour, which promises to man all the material goods which he desires to enjoy : it is the representative of all physical enjoyments, and moreover, of all the moral enjoyments which depend upon them. Very well, but for whom ? This question ought never to be lost sight of ; while, on the contrary, it scarcely ever presents itself to the contemplation of theorists. For whom ? According to the answer which we make to this question, man himself belongs to wealth, or wealth belongs to man. . . . . In our eyes—we do not hesitate to aver it—national wealth is the participation of *all* in the advantages of life. Members of society are no doubt destined to divide among themselves the product of social labour in different proportions ; but we can never call by the name of wealth that part which one of its members takes from another.'

Professor Cherbuliez of Geneva, who endeavours to establish a sort of eclecticism compounded of the notions of Sismondi and those of the English economists, expresses himself as follows :—

' Every question belonging to this science presents two faces, or rather divides itself into two distinct questions. A certain economical fact being given, we may ask what is the cause of it, and then study that cause in its different relations to the increase or diminution of national wealth. For example, the price of certain commodities has risen or fallen : is the cause to be found in the increase or diminution of the cost of production, or in a change of proportion between demand and supply ? Will there result from this cause a diminution or an increase of the general mass of wealth, or of the revenue of society, or of any division of society ? In following these researches, we consider riches and revenues objectively ; we make them the true and only substratum of science.

' But these riches are produced and consumed by men, that is, by intelligent and sentient beings, on whose happiness and moral and physical developement they act in a thousand ways. Every economical fact may then affect in various manners the happiness of those producers and consumers, whose condition, in respect of wealth, is modified directly or indirectly by it. Hence a second series of questions, in which wealth is considered subjectively, and men themselves are taken as the *substratum*.

' There is between these two points of view the same difference which exists between the *chrematistics* and *economics* of Aristotle; that is, between the art of acquiring riches, and the art of managing a household. In the first, wealth is an end ; in the latter, only a means.'*

---

* We should be glad to be informed where this use of the word *chrematistics*, so frequently employed in this controversy, and always attributed to Aristotle, is to be found in that author ? We can only recollect a passage in his remarks on Ethics, in which the χρηματιστικος βιος, or life of one devoted to the acquisition of wealth, is contrasted with the *contemplative* life ; but in that instance the word has obviously nothing to do with the sense now under consideration.

' Since the commencement of the present century, the *chrematistic* tendency has become predominant, and even exclusive, with English economists; while those of the Continent have continued to treat economical questions under their double point of view. We may therefore consider modern economists as divided into two schools, which differ much more by their tendencies than by their actual doctrines.'

After a short exposition of the character and doctrines of what he terms the Chrematistic school, especially as represented by Mr Senior, this writer thus proceeds :—

' Wealth is a means of happiness, and a means which procures almost all the rest.   In the sense which the economists and Mr Senior give to this word, is comprised almost every thing which can contribute to the happiness and to the developement, both moral and physical, of man in society.   The existence of wealth is the distinctive characteristic of the state of society, the summary of the advantages which man derives from that state.   The part of it which falls to each member of the political association gives, in general, a fair measure of the degree of security, independence, and leisure, which he is able to enjoy.   Now, security, independence, and leisure, are the essential conditions of our developement, even in a moral point of view ; consequently, the laws which regulate the distribution of wealth are also those which regulate the part which each member is to claim in the advantages of the social state, and the place which he is to occupy in the social hierarchy.   To describe the causes which directly, or indirectly, influence this distribution, is, in reality, to make a nearly complete statistical table of social happiness.   This being granted, can it be denied that there is a connexion between the description of these causes and the appreciation of their results ?   The questions— what is the end to which wealth should serve as a means ?   Is that end attained by existing laws ?   If it is not, what can the legislator do toward approaching it ?—do they not jointly present themselves to the mind of those who study economical questions, and is it not of the economist that they will demand a solution of them ?   Is it not the economist who will be best in a condition to solve them ?'—(*Bibliothèque Universelle de Génève*, Dec. 1836.)

Let us now contrast the views of these two writers with thy definition of the nature and objects of the science, as given be Mr Senior in the work before us.   We need scarcely direct our reader, with whichever party he may be disposed to agree, to admire the clearness of language, and the precise as well as comprehensive conception of the subject, which the following passage exhibits :—

' We believe that by confining our own and the reader's attention to the nature, production, and distribution of wealth, we shall produce a more clear, and complete, and instructive work than if we allowed ourselves to wander into the more interesting and more important, but far less definite fields by which the comparatively narrow path of Political

Economy is surrounded. The questions—to what extent and under what circumstances the possession of wealth is, on the whole, beneficial or injurious to its possessor, or to the society of which he is a member? What distribution of wealth is most desirable in each different state of society? And what are the means by which any given country can facilitate such a distribution?—all these are questions of great interest and difficulty, but no more form part of the science of Political Economy, in the sense in which we use that term, than navigation forms part of the science of astronomy. The principles supplied by Political Economy are indeed necessary elements in their solution, but they are not the only or even the most important elements. The writer who pursues such investigations is in fact engaged on the great science of legislation :—a science which requires a knowledge of the general principles supplied by Political Economy, but differs from it essentially in its subject, its premises, and its conclusions. The subject of legislation is not wealth, but human welfare. Its premises are drawn from an infinite variety of phenomena, supported by evidence of every degree of strength, and authorizing conclusions deserving every degree of assent, from perfect confidence to bare suspicion ; and its expounder is enabled, and even required, not merely to state certain general facts, but to urge the adoption or rejection of actual measures or trains of action.

‘ On the other hand, the subject treated by the Political Economist—using that term in the limited sense in which we apply it—is not *happiness* but *wealth ;* his premises consist of a very few general propositions, the result of observation, or of consciousness, and scarcely requiring proof, or even formal statement ; which almost every man, as soon as he hears them, admits as familiar to his thoughts, or at least as included in his previous knowledge ; and his inferences are nearly as general and, if he has reasoned correctly, as certain as his premises. Those which relate to the nature and production of wealth are universally true ; and though those which relate to the distribution of wealth are liable to be affected by the peculiar institutions of particular countries—in the case, for instance, of slavery, legal monopolies, or poor-laws—the natural state of things can be laid down as the general rule ; and the anomalies produced by particular disturbing causes can be afterwards accounted for. But his conclusions, whatever be their generality and their truth, do not authorize him in adding a single syllable of advice ; that privilege belongs to the writer or the statesman who has considered only one, though among the most important of those causes. The business of a Political Economist is neither to recommend nor to dissuade, but to state general principles which it is fatal to neglect, but neither advisable nor perhaps practicable to use as the sole or even the principal guides in the actual conduct of affairs : in the mean-time the duty of each individual writer is clear. Employed as he is upon a science in which error or even ignorance may be productive of such intense and such extensive mischief, he is bound, like a juryman, to give true deliverance according to the evidence, and to allow neither sympathy with indigence, nor disgust at profusion and avarice ;—neither reverence for existing institutions, nor detestation of existing abuses ;—neither love of popularity, nor of paradox, nor of system,—to deter him from stating what he believes to be the facts, or from drawing from those facts what appear to him to be the legitimate conclusions. To decide, in each case, how far those conclusions are to be acted upon, belongs to the art of government—an art to which Political Economy is only one of many subservient sciences ; which involves the consideration of motives, of which the desire for wealth is only one among many, and aims at objects to which the possession of wealth is only a subordinate means.'—Pp. 129, 130.

A comparison of the different views indicated by these three writers will at once guide the reader to the real point at issue. The English writers, or chrysologists, as M. Cherbuliez would call them, or followers of Dr Smith (though his own definition of Political Economy differs widely from that of his successors), define their science as that of the laws which regulate the production and distribution of wealth. Their opponents say that it both investigates those laws, and, moreover, directs the legislator how to regulate distribution, so as to secure that proportion in the enjoyment of it which is most conducive to the general welfare. The foreign school (we term them so for convenience, although there are many English authors whose views assimilate to theirs) hold, that it is the office of the political economist to point out in what way social happiness may best be attained through the medium of national wealth. Our own writers reply, that this is the province, not of the economist, but of the politician. The former ask, Whether all questions concerning the moral and physical wellbeing of man in society, as far as wealth affects it, are not closely connected with the truths of the abstract science of wealth ? The latter answer, that they are undoubtedly so connected, but that they are not a part of it. They admit that the economist may be best fitted to solve those questions, by the education which his science has given him ; but they deny that in doing so he is keeping within the bounds of that province. We contend that the study is purely a science : our opponents, that it includes the practical adaptations of the science to existing circumstances. In other words, that it is at once a science and an art. According to them, it is a *deontology :* according to us, an *ontology* only.

Thus far it is clear enough that the difference between the two schools is one of definition, or rather of method only. The English writers adhere to a precise division of labour, and circumscribe the province of the economist within narrow bounds; upon the principle that the science can never be truly serviceable as a guide and controller to practice, unless it is studied in the first instance on hypothetical assumptions, and by the *à priori* method. According to these, the business of the economist is—certain motives of action

operating on society with a certain degree of intensity being *given*
—to find the consequences, in the production and distribution of
wealth in that society. That it is the affair of the politician to
compare the consequences of this imaginary state of things with
existing phenomena, and to legislate, after allowing for the disturbances which have produced the existing variations from that standard. The foreign economists, generally speaking, seem not to
comprehend the use of the hypothetical method at all. If its conclusions appear to vary from things as they are, they conclude, not
that the science is inadequate by itself to produce good practical results, but that it is altogether faulty and erroneous. If
the economist cannot assume as ˙the basis of his calculations
Man as he is, with the tendencies and habits which the institutions of different countries have given him, and arrive at once
at the conclusion of what is best for man as he is, they seem
to think that he had better abandon the subject altogether. His
theories will not only be incomplete, they will be ' revolting,
' hard-hearted,' and we know not what besides. They dislike
the notion of treating Man as an abstraction, as if it were a degradation to him. ' On est peiné,' says M. Cherbuliez, ' de voir
' des êtres sensibles et intelligens transformés en producteurs et
' consommateurs, sans un mot qui rappelle l'influence journalière
' et puissante que cette double qualité exerce sur leur sensibilité
' et leur intelligence.' As well might we be affronted at finding
man spoken of in surgical books as a mere subject for anatomical
operations.

But the real difference between the two schools lies deeper than
the surface. However carefully the scientific economist may
avoid all hortatory language, and confine himself to the simple
exposition of principles and facts, there can be no doubt of the
one great practical conclusion to which the theories of English
writers of the school in question, however conflicting in many
points, tend with absolute unanimity. It is, That the ' laws
' which regulate the distribution of wealth between the different
' classes of society,' are principles with which it cannot be economically profitable for the legislature to intermeddle. That in
so far as the immediate productiveness of industry is concerned,
every such attempt, however insidiously or plausibly framed,
cannot but *pro tanto* diminish it. That whether the Legislature
interfere with the free use of capital by protecting duties, or
with the contracts between capitalist and labourer, by combination laws—or with the contract between landlord and tenant, by
restraints on alienation, &c.—in whatever shape, in short, the
multiform spirit of restriction may show itself, it cannot but produce precisely the same results as if the fertility of the earth, or

the productiveness of labour, had been to a certain extent diminished.

As to the ulterior utility of these restrictions, Political Economy, if limited by Mr Senior's definition, cannot pronounce whether or not it may bé advisable for a nation, under certain circumstances, to sacrifice a portion of the national wealth to ensure a better distribution of the remainder.   This is a grand question, to be solved only by one who can bring the knowledge acquired by his science to bear on an infinity of other knowledge essential to the legislator.   For example, it may be that certain restrictions on distribution, by raising up a powerful and united class of monopolists, may ensure the stability of a state, and thus, by an indirect process, even contribute to increase its wealth.   Thus, it is possible that the contrivances of corporations and apprenticeships may have caused or secured the flourishing of various commercial communities in the tumultuous periods of the middle ages ; but, in our view, it would be incorrect to say that the municipal system of Florence, or of Nuremberg was, on that account, *economically* a good one.

It is therefore clear, that a speculator might possibly agree in the definitions which writers of the English school give of the nature and scope of their science, and yet arrive at conclusions practically adverse to that system of free exchange.   He might acquiesce in the theoretical conclusion, that labour and capital are most productive when their use is unrestricted ; and yet when directing his view to existing circumstances, he might believe that the happiness of the community requires a restraint to be put on the employment of those means which are the best for increasing its collected wealth.   He might, in short, imagine that a limited production is *politically* a less evil than an unrestricted distribution.   But it so happens (and very naturally, as all who have studied the progress of any science are aware), that those who are dissatisfied with the practical results which appear most readily to follow from certain theoretical principles, invariably direct their anger against the principles themselves.   It was said long ago, that if a proposition in Euclid were adverse to the interest or cherished speculations of individuals, there would be found individuals enough to contradict it ; and even so it has proved with the modern science of Political Economy, using the word in the sense of Ricardo and Malthus.   Its opponents do not in general seek to pick holes in the logical sequence of its reasonings, or to point out fallacies in argument.   They chiefly attack it in two ways: they either endeavour to disprove it by reference to supposed experience (which cannot be done, because the conclusions of the science do not assume to be practically true in fact, but only in approximation, and consequently the imaginary contradiction may in each case be an exception only) ; or they deny the existence of the hypothetical science altogether, and set up in opposition to it a mixed mass of practical rules and opinions which may or may not be good for any thing, but are somewhat totally distinct from abstract philosophy. Thus it is that those speculators who dislike the principle of unrestricted competition, begin not by impugning the reasonings of the English school, but as it were by arraigning their competency ;—by asserting that there are material elements omitted in their conception of the science.

And the truth is, that the great principles of free exchange and natural distribution, after having had a long run of success among the philosophers of the Continent, have begun of late to wax unpopular with the more refined speculators; just as they have been put in action, by a very great practical revolution (as far as domestic commerce is concerned), in most of its states. In England, also, the economical doctrines have to contend not only with the sturdy old-fashioned opponents whom they have always found, but also with a new race of visionaries, whom the great changes of late years have called into activity ; for such changes always give birth to a wondrous variety of abortive speculations. There is at work a wide-spread dissatisfaction with the present state of society ; and a disposition to trace all the evils which afflict it to the competition of capitalists and labourers amongst themselves, and their supposed competition with each other. It is as if the philosophical world, never long contented with a simple adherence to the same system, had tried the *laissez faire* theories of Smith and Turgot to the uttermost, and had thrown them aside in mere weariness, and through a desire for new excitements. In Johnsonian phrase, Truth is a cow which will yield such people no more milk, and therefore they are gone to milk the bull. The last and greatest end of national institutions is to elevate the condition of the most numerous class in society. Freedom of exchange has not as yet (nor can it ever do so, unless assisted by very different agents) succeeded in removing those evils which continually weigh on the lowest portion of it. These speculators have therefore worked round to the conclusion that freedom of exchange is the cause of them; and every possible variety of uncouth restrictions on that freedom—all manner of interference with the independence of labour and of capital —now finds advocates, more or less visionary, among thinkers of the class to which we allude. In England, where enthusiasm is a little more tempered by plain sense, and by habits of public discussion than in other countries, they are for the most part contented with extolling poor-laws on a grand scale, and legislative interpositions between employer and labourer. In ⚹France and Germany speculations run higher; partly from that disposition to Utopianism, which nothing short of a century or two of practical public life will ever correct; partly because, in those countries, the philosophers and the million seem equally unable to get rid of the prevailing notion that government can do every thing, and ought to try its hand at every thing. M. Sismondi and other continental authorities are for returning to the systems of the middle ages;—for re-establishing guilds and apprenticeships in the towns, and breaking up large farms into little villein-tenements in the country. We have before us the work of a very honest and religious German writer (M. Bodz Reymond on the ' Increase of National and Private Poverty'), whose imagination has been heated with the prospect of sufferings and distress which no Political Economy can cure, until he imagines that Political Economy has occasioned them. He not only adopts views similar to those of M. Sismondi, but proposes, in serious earnest, a scheme for limiting the number of capitalists in each town, and in every trade, according to the number of workmen in that trade, for whom it may be found that sufficient employment now exists. The Owenites, and the Co-operatives in England, with much more logic and consistency, went a step farther. They soon found out that the right of property is the cause of all competition, and they proposed the adoption of restraints under which no accumulation of property could take place. Finally, other reasoners most correctly deduced fresh premises from these conclusions. They discovered, that this complicated net of restrictions could neither be woven nor preserved unbroken, except by the agency of some absolute controlling power; and that the power which was to exercise so unheard-of a jurisdiction could be no less than a theocracy; and hence arose the monstrous extravagances of St Simon and his disciples.

These curious speculations, which may one day afford to our posterity more serious matter for reflection than they now do to ourselves, are not within our present scope :—we are only tempted to observe how impossible it is for the advocates of restrictions on exchange to stand still, and logically to defend the ground which they have taken up against the advocates of farther restrictions. But with the justice or injustice of these views we have nothing to do. Our only object is to point out how essential it is to keep separate the theoretical from the practical part of political economy. The various sects of experimentalists, if we may so denominate those against whom we are contending, proclaim a science, or rather an art, which professes to model the whole social existence of man by

determining what portion each shall obtain of the whole social revenue. They deal not merely with the elementary principles of production and distribution, but with inventing laws to restrain that
production and apportion that distribution.   Thus defined, their
science or art must take into its cognizance an immense variety of
subjects not immediately connected with wealth or its sources. The
whole mass of motives which act on individuals and communities,
and regulate their conduct, and the conditions of their society, must
fall of necessity within its province.   But, upon the commonest
principles of the division of labour, it is obvious how much is
gained by distinguishing between the *Science* itself, and the *Art*
of adapting its conclusions to practice.   The former rests, as Mr
Senior truly says, on a few general assumptions respecting the
conduct of men under certain given circumstances.   But those
assumptions are few, and readily comprehensible and admissible
by all.   From these first principles a long train of results follows
by accurate reasoning.   But no one ever dreamt of contending
that the actual state of mankind in any civilized country precisely
resembles those given circumstances which the science, as we
have defined it, takes for its postulates. Consequently, the results,
however logically deducible, will never correspond exactly with
the phenomena which observation presents to our view.   Should
a statesman assume the conclusions of the science as principles
of government, without submitting them to the correction of
experience, strange and unforeseen errors would ensue.   In other
words, excellent economists may make bad legislators ;—' good
' tools without handles,' as was said of Turgot.   But this arises
not from the fallacious or nugatory character of the science itself,
but simply from their neglecting to allow for those disturbing
causes which affect the results of their calculations.   These it is
the province of the politician to estimate.   The man of science, as
such, must needs disregard them ; otherwise his science would
become a mere mass of fluctuating and contradictory opinions,
and could not by possibility be reduced to any system at all.
' Our relations with our fellow-men,' says M. Say (than whom no
writer has laid down better principles on this subject, although he
often forgets to act upon them), ' are so numerous and so compli-
' cated, that it is impossible to consider them all together, and in
' a single work.   It must be at once a treatise on politics, on
' public right, on individual and social ethics, and on inter-
' national law, as well as on Political Economy.   It is not by
' agglomerating the sciences that we perfect them.   They have
' all points of contact, it is true ; and the phenomena which are
' discovered by one, exercise an influence in the production of those

' which are discovered by another ; but while we point out these
' instances of contact, we must take care to distinguish the sub-
' jects of our studies.'

But to all this the opponents of the modern English school
have a general reply in the *etymology* of the words Political
Economy.   To use their favourite definition, it is to a state
what domestic economy is to a household.   Now, domestic
economy is clearly no science.   It is an art, founded on no
abstract principle, requiring a knowledge of a great variety of
individual details, and tact and judgment in the direction of
them.   Is Political Economy nothing more ?   If so, it is absurd
to dignify it by the name of a science at all ; which, nevertheless, those who employ this definition of it very jealously
contend that it is.   Then the quarrel is purely one of names.
Let it be allowed that we employ an incorrect and misleading
denomination for our science.   Its derivation, we readily con-
cede, points out rather an art than a science—the art of managing
the resources of a nation.   But that, we contend, is an art
founded on the maxims of several sciences,—of moral philosophy,
of political philosophy, and, finally, of the abstract science of
national wealth.   This last it is, to which English authors have
given the name of Political Economy.   They may have adopted
an inconvenient title.   We are quite ready to change it, provided
the world can agree on a new one.   Let it be *Chrematistics* or *Catal-
lactics*, or *Chrysology*, or any other hard word which its inventor
may succeed in making popular.   But let it be conceded that there
is such a science, by whatever name it may be called.   Let it be
acknowledged that it is a science which neither recommends to
do, or to abstain from doing ; which does not direct legislation ;
which regards Man in the abstract, and, simply as a wealth-
creating animal, laying aside for the occasion all the other tendencies of his complicated nature.   Sufficient for the economist to
establish sound principles, any departure from which can only be
justified by proving the interference of disturbing causes to render
their practical application impossible.

By observing this distinction, the study will be kept within
its legitimate province.   The German writers, although we believe that they have very imperfectly adhered to it in practice,
have found in the peculiar wealth of their language the means of
marking it by a more appropriate nomenclature than we possess.
They divide the subject into *Volkswirthschaft*, national economy ; and *Staatswirthschaft*, state economy.   The first, in our
view, is the science ; the second, the derivative art.   The first
treats of the phenomena of wealth ; the second assumes those

phenomena, and proceeds to frame rules for legislation founded upon them.

We have dwelt so long upon the topics suggested by the opening pages of Mr Senior's work, that but little space is left for detailed examination of its contents. Much of the matter which is collected in this 'Outline' is to be found in the lectures delivered by its author during the continuance of his quinquennial professorship at Oxford; after which time, by the provisions of the foundation, he was obliged to vacate the chair. We suppose that this duration of five years was allotted by the founder, under the impression that no longer reign can be expected for any theory in Political Economy; and that at the end of that period a new professor is wanted to correct the views of his predecessor. The work which stands second at the head of this article, consists of a translation of six of these lectures, with various additions from the author's hand, by the Count J. Arrivabene and M. Theodore Fix; forming a short treatise on some elementary points of the science. The translation is carefully executed; and in their preface the translators have urged on their readers, with much force, similar opinions to those which we entertain as to the necessity of keeping the scientific branch of Political Economy apart from the practical; but we fear that they will find their French readers very reluctant converts to this view of the subject.

Mr Senior arranges the contents of his 'Outline' under three heads; viz. the Nature, Production, and Distribution of Wealth. The chapter on the first necessarily consists of definitions; and his remarks on the various meanings of those controverted and equivocal terms with which economists have to deal, such as wealth, value, demand, &c., form a valuable introduction to his after enquiries. We would willingly have devoted some space to an examination of them; but we are obliged to pass over subjects which cannot be satisfactorily discussed except at considerable length.

The chapter on Production begins with the four elementary propositions on which, in the author's view, the whole science is founded. These are, in his language—

' 1. That every man desires to obtain additional wealth, with as little sacrifice as possible.

' 2. That the population of the world, or, in other words, the number of persons inhabiting it, is limited only by moral or physical evil; or by fear of a deficiency of those articles of wealth which the habits of the individuals of each class of its inhabitants lead them to require.

' 3. That the powers of labour, and the other instruments which produce wealth, may be indefinitely increased by using their products as the means of farther production.

' 4. That, agricultural skill remaining the same, additional labour employed on the land, within a given district, produces in general a less proportionate return; or, in other words, that though, with every increase of the labour bestowed, the aggregate return is increased, the increase of the return is not in proportion to the increase of the labour.'

With regard to the first of these propositions, plain as it appears, it is, as the author truly remarks, opposed to the well-known doctrine of ' over-production or general glut,' of which Malthus and Sismondi are the most distinguished supporters; and which is in fact *assumed* by most of those reasoners who complain of the defective distribution of wealth, under the system of free exchange, of whom we have spoken above.

The second of these elementary propositions is a modification of the well-known hypothesis, which passes usually under the name of Mr Malthus. How far the views of Mr Senior differ from those of the older writer, will be best understood by extracting a passage from one of his lectures delivered before the University of Oxford, together with the correspondence to which it gave rise. After stating the abbreviated proposition of Mill, ' that there is a *natural tendency* in population to increase faster ' than capital,' the Professor proceeded as follows:—

' If the present state of the world, compared with its state at our earliest record, be one of relative poverty, Mr Mill's reasoning is unanswerable. If its means of subsistence continue to bear the same proportion to the number of its inhabitants, it is clear that the increase of subsistence and of numbers has been equal. If its means of subsistence have increased much more than the number of its inhabitants, it is clear not only that Mr Mill's proposition (that there is a natural tendency in population to increase faster than capital) is false, but that the contrary proposition is true; and that the means of subsistence have a natural tendency to increase faster than population.

' Now, what is the picture presented by the earliest records of those nations which are now civilized? Or, *which is the same, what is now the state of savage nations?* A state of habitual poverty and occasional famine. A scanty population, but still scantier means of subsistence. Admitting, and it must be admitted, that in almost all countries the condition of the great body of the people is poor and miserable; yet as poverty and misery were their original inheritance, what inference can we draw from their misery as to the tendency of their numbers to increase more rapidly than their wealth? But if a single country can be found, in which there is now less poverty than is universal in a savage state, it must be true that, under the circumstances in which that country has been placed, the means of subsistence have a greater tendency to increase than the population. Now, this is the case in *every* civilized country. Even Ireland, the country most likely to afford an instance of what Mr Mill supposes to be the natural course of things, poor and populous as she is, suffers less from want, with her eight millions of people, than when her only inhabitants were a few septs of hunters and fishers. In our early history famines, and pestilences the consequences of famine, constantly recur. At present, though our numbers are trebled and quadrupled, they are unheard of. . . . If it be conceded that there exists in the human race a natural tendency to rise from barbarism to civilisation, and that the means of subsistence are proportionally more abundant in a civilized than a savage state, and *neither of these propositions can be denied*, it must follow that there is a natural tendency in subsistence to increase in a greater ratio than population.'*

To these lectures Mr Senior has annexed a correspondence between himself and Mr Malthus, which, did our limits permit us, we would willingly extract at length; especially on account of the additional light which it throws on the views of the deceased philosopher. Mr Senior commences his correspondence by a candid avowal that he had unintentionally misrepresented the opinions of Malthus, by supposing him to attach a more conclusive character to his general proposition, of the constant pressure of population for subsistence, than was in fact the case. He admits, also, that the difference respecting the word ' tendency,' is merely verbal. Using the word ' tendency,' to mean that which results from a known power in an agent to produce certain effects, the proposition may be true, That it is the tendency of population to increase faster than subsistence; and yet if we only mean that things have a tendency to happen, which we frequently see happen, in many cases it may be true that the tendency of subsistence is to increase faster than population. But he still tenders issue on the general assertion, That in point of fact the condition of the labouring classes in civilized countries does continue progressively to improve, so as to make Mr Malthus's law, although philosophically true, yet rarely worked out in reality, in consequence of the existence of other laws which counteract it.

Mr Malthus replies, in the first place, by vindicating his own use of the word tendency as the more philosophical, or which is here the same thing, the more correctly English. And here we quite agree with him. A greyhound may be held in the leash, so that a tortoise may gain ground on him in constant progression: but should we say that the tortoise had a tendency to outstrip the greyhound, or the greyhound the tortoise?

But the other question is one of more importance. It is clear that it is possible to admit philosophically the truth of Mr Malthus's general law, and yet to hold that, as in the case of the

---

* Lectures on Population.   London: 1831.

greyhound and the tortoise, the facts which pass under our eyes prove it to be counteracted by other and more powerful laws. It is possible to do this, as it is done by Mr Senior, with a full acknowledgment of the merit of the discoverer of that law ; and in the form of courteous and direct controversy. It is possible also to do it, as we had lately occasion to observe in reviewing the life of that distinguished philosopher, with every variety of calumny and misrepresentation, at one moment denying his principle, and abusing its author, and the next moment admitting it, for the purpose of endeavouring to establish exceptions to it. But we suspect that in both cases, although in a very different spirit, the practical truth of that law is seriously undervalued.

Single instances, such as those to which Mr Senior would refer us, prove nothing in the controversy between the two tendencies. If two disputants intrench themselves, the one behind the theoretical assertion that population has a tendency to increase faster than food,—the other behind its opposite, that food has a tendency to increase faster than population, no amount of examples will serve to confute either. To all that can be adduced on either side the adversary may reply, that in those cases his favourite tendency has been overruled by those checks on its operation which confessedly exist. But when the terms of dispute are changed into those of a question of fact, namely, which is found in most countries to increase the fastest, food or people, then history and observation alone can decide it. Tried by those tests, we very much doubt the truth of Mr Senior's proposition, when taken in the sense which he evidently attaches to it, viz. that, as a historical fact, food does *usually* increase faster than population in civilized countries. At least, the arguments usually adduced in its support appear to us far from convincing.

Mr Senior begins with the state of ' savage nations,' and their constant want of food. Savages—' septs of hunters and fishers,'— are of great use to political economists, as well as to political philosophers; their condition serves as a sort of zero in the thermometer of civilisation,—a point from which there is a gradual rise towards perfection. They are thus very valuable in hypothetical reasoning ; but, when history is the test by which truth is to be tried, this employment of them is unwarranted by fact. For, as far as our historical knowledge extends, we do not know a single instance of a savage tribe raising itself by unassisted efforts to a state of civilisation. This has always been effected by foreign emigration from a more civilized state. And, in this case, Mr Senior's general proposition may be true ; and yet do nothing towards proving his argument. A party of colonists, driven by the pressure of population from their own ancient seats, arrives in a region inhabited only by savages in want of every thing. By applying the accumulated knowledge which they bring with them to the virgin soil of this tract, they rise rapidly to a degree of prosperity in which a very considerable share of produce falls to the lot of each. Thus far there is no interruption to the law of Malthus ; for the people thus circumstanced, *i. e.* the colonists, and not the savages, are at the first link of the series of cause and effect which he describes. By and by their civilisation increases ; ranks are formed amongst them; rent arises; and a large share of surplus produce falls to the lot of a favoured few : but productiveness diminishes, and the share obtained by each of the lower class is smaller than before. This we contend to be 'historically, as well as theoretically probable : that, in all likelihood there has been a point in the past life of most nations, at which the *historical maximum* of food has fallen to the lot of each individual; and that with the increase of civilisation, his share has on the whole diminished, even in the happiest countries, by the pressure of population, and the necessity of resorting to inferior soils. Any one will see that Mr Senior's reasoning proves nothing against the probability as well as possibility of this hypothesis. It may thus be true, that the amount of food now shared by each is greater than that which falls to the lot of individuals in ' septs of hunters and fishers ;' and nevertheless that, even in his own sense, the tendency of the increase of subsistence has not been to outstrip that of population. He founds his doctrine on the two principles—that ' there exists in ' the human race a natural tendency to rise from *barbarism* to ' civilisation,' and that ' the means of subsistence are proportion- ' ally more abundant in a civilized than in a *savage* state.' Using, as he does, the words ' savage' and ' barbarous' as synonymous, we deny his first proposition, *modo et forma*, in the sense which he attaches to it ; that is, we deny that it is in the usual order of things for a people to rise out of the state of savage penury into civilisation *without the importation of foreign knowledge and industry ;* and that this aid entirely alters the conditions of the reasoning.

But, besides the argument drawn from the savage state, there is another to which Mr Senior, in common with the less reasonable opponents of Malthus, repeatedly resorts. Famines were common a few centuries ago ; famines are now unknown ; therefore the average proportion of food which falls to the lot of each individual must be greater now than a few centuries ago. When stated thus, the argument appears to us to show its own inconclusiveness. Famines, such as are read of in the annals of all

European countries, but now rarely experienced in any, arose partly from want of knowledge and skill in the economical management of the fruits of the earth, and in a still greater degree, from absence of information and difficulty of transport, increased as they were by political incumbrances of every description. In France, even up to the Revolution, it not unfrequently happened that the labourers of one province were well-nigh starving whilst those of its neighbour were enjoying superfluous abundance. The same causes operated to a much greater degree at remoter periods. But, because the peasant in the reign of Edward III. or IV. ran the risk of a famine once in five or ten years, it does not follow that his average annual share of the fruits of the earth might not be greater than that of his descendant under Queen Victoria.

If we descend to times in which we are aided by historical knowledge, proof seems rather to accumulate against Mr Senior's proposition. It is *said* that, from the year 1720 to 1750 (a period, by the way, during which the population of England was nearly stationary), the agricultural labourer could earn a peck of wheat a-day, and that at present he can only earn five-sixths of a peck, or less.* We are not much disposed to rely on such statistical information as we possess for the construction of tables which can fairly represent the average situation of the labourer at a particular period; but, in the absence of all contradiction, the evidence in favour of 'this result may, at least, be received as highly probable. Mr Hallam (in his 'Constitutional History,' if we are not mistaken) expresses an opinion that the reigns of George I. and II. present, on the whole, the most prosperous period in the history of the lower classes. It is undoubtedly true, as Ricardo and others have pointed out, that, since that time, the

---

* A very different conclusion would follow, no doubt, from some premises of Mr Senior's. He says (p. 187), that during a period in which the population of England has about doubled, the produce of the land has *certainly* tripled, *probably* quadrupled. Now since, in the same period, we have changed from exporters to importers of raw produce (to some extent, including imports from Ireland), it would follow, on the last supposition, if we are to take the words literally, that every John Bull of the present day eats *more than twice as much* as his grandfather Bull in the reign of George II.—ἥμεις τοι πατέρων μεν' ἀμείνονες εὐχόμεθ' εἶναι.

But after making every allowance for the increased quantity of vegetable produce which goes to improve the quality of meat, and possibly for a greater rate of increase in that portion of our agricultural produce which does not consist of mere ' *munitions de bouche*,' either supposition seems scarcely credible.

improvements in manufactures and communication have enabled the labourer, by the sacrifice of a smaller part of his wages, to obtain a larger amount of wrought goods, of foreign articles of comfort, and, in some districts, of fuel; and this must be taken as a partial set-off against the fall in wages as estimated in corn. But every one knows how small a proportion of the receipts of a labouring family is thus expended; and when we reflect on the enormous increase which has taken place during the same period in the productiveness of labour, and in all outward tokens of civilisation, the fact that real wages have remained stationary, at best seems strangely adverse to the theories of Mr Senior.

Passing over a long period of fluctuations, we find, if the evidence is to be believed, that in the reigns of Edward IV. and Henry VII. the labourer could earn two pecks of wheat a-day, or more than double his present wages. We may, no doubt, have considerable hesitation in receiving such a statement on such evidence as can be now procured; and we may also argue, as Mr Malthus has done, that, for various reasons, it is probable that this was a period of unusual prosperity for the lower orders. But still, with such a statement well known and undisproved, surely a writer who can affirm that, even in civilized England, ' the ' tendency of subsistence has been to increase faster than popula- ' tion,' is a bolder theorist than Malthus in his boldest day.

The mere historical fact of emigration furnishes the best answer to such speculations, when the ' law' of Malthus is limited, as it ought, of course, to be, to the case of each individual country.

' If food had increased faster than population,' says the latter writer, in his answer to Mr Senior, ' would the earth have been overspread with people since the Flood? Would the great migrations and movements of nations of which we have read have ever taken place? Would the shepherds of Asia have been engaged in such a constant struggle for room and food? Would the northern nations have ever overrun the Roman empire of the west? Would the civilized Greeks have been obliged to send out numerous colonies? Would these colonies have increased with great rapidity for a certain period, and then have become comparatively stationary? Would history, in short, have been at all what it is? America is by no means the only instance of the knowledge of an old state being applied to the comparatively unoccupied land of a new one. And in all instances of this kind, where the food has once been abundant, an actual increase of population faster than food is not only probable, but absolutely certain. In fact, such countries never could be well peopled if this did not take place. In old states the relative increase of population and food has always been found to be practically very variable. It is no doubt true, that in every stage of society there have been some nations where, from ignorance and want of foresight, the labouring classes have lived very miserably ; and both the food and population have been nearly stationary long before the resources of the soil had approached towards exhaustion. Of these nations, it might safely have been predicted, that in the progress of civilisation and improvement a period would occur when food would increase faster than population. On the other hand, if, from favourable circumstances at any time, the people of a country were very abundantly supplied, it might as safely be predicted, that in their progress towards a full population, a period would occur when population would increase faster than food. It is absolutely necessary, therefore, to know the actual condition in which a people is living in regard to subsistence, before we can say whether food or population is likely to increase the fastest. And this condition is certainly not determined exclusively by the state of civilisation and population, but is very different in the same nation at different times; and sometimes food is comparatively more abundant at an early period, and sometimes at a later period. . . . . . . Notwithstanding the poverty and misery of Ireland at an early period, I am strongly disposed to believe, that about the time when Arthur Young made his tour in that country (1776 to 1778), food was decidedly more abundant than it has been of late years. With regard to what may be called the present state of the nations of the Continent, many of them seem to have increased their food very rapidly since the Revolutionary war ; *and this increase has been followed by so very rapid an increase of population, that it seems quite impossible it should continue.* There is some reason, indeed, to think, from the accounts of Mr Jacob, that population is now increasing faster than food. It appears, then, that it cannot safely be assumed as a fact that food has generally increased faster than population.'

We have extracted this passage from the correspondence published in the Appendix to Mr Senior's 'Lectures,' not merely with a view of giving the last suggestions of Mr Malthus on a subject which has become so singularly identified with his name, but also to point out one or two instances of that practical sagacity which, in our opinion, characterised him far more remarkably than any skill in hypothetical argument. It is too well known to all of us how much confirmation has been afforded to his views respecting Ireland (which, a few years ago, were by no means popular with economists) by the Report of the Poor-law Commissioners for that country. And, with respect to the prediction contained in the last words, we have been forcibly struck by its absolute verification in the recent returns of population of the Prussian monarchy, as they have been carefully analyzed by M. Hoffmann, Director of the Statistical Bureau of Berlin. Our extracts are from a translation of M. Hoffmann's paper, published by the ' Sta' tistical Society of London,' in the first number of its *Transactions*. We shall briefly exhibit the principal facts, and proceed to consider one or two obvious inferences; premising only that Prussia is, among all European countries, that in which population increased most rapidly for some years after the peace of 1815.

	Births.	Deaths.
1820–22	1,491,520	899,006
1823–25	1,527,677	964,773
1826–28	1,515,805	1,093,597
1829–31	1,483,286	1,241,622
1832–34	1,574,729	1,258,211

In the first three years, the population increased by 600,000 souls in round numbers; in the last three years, by little more than 300,000. But this diminished ratio of progression is not occasioned only by a diminution of births; the manner in which too rapid increase is generally checked in flourishing countries. It is occasioned, in part, by a *great and steady increase of mortality.*

On an average of 1,000,000, living at the same period, there were born annually, in 1820–22, ... 43,709
There died, ... 26,346
On the same number there were born annually, in 1832–34,—
39,595
There died, ... 31,637
If we had made a comparison with the years 1829–31, the result would have been still more unfavourable; but the last of these was the *cholera* year. And although the whole number of deaths returned as having been occasioned by that disorder was little more than 30,000 for the whole Prussian dominions, yet it is probable that a much larger share in the increased mortality at that period should in fairness be set down to its direct or secondary influence.

But, with this exception, we are not allowed to account for any part of this increased mortality by means of supposed epidemics; or by imagining new and strange variations in the common order of things. The Government returns of Prussia comprise a very careful classification of the causes of death. Now, M. Hoffmann, who evidently has no Malthusian theory in his head, after examining these returns with a view to some medical solution of the phenomenon, finding that no particular disease appears to have materially outstripped the rest, comes to the alarming conclusion, that ' in the last six years it is evident that there ' was a greater activity in ALL the causes of death, *and therefore* ' *there must have existed a general and powerfully active cause by* ' *which this remarkable phenomenon was produced.*'

An increase in the malignity of all the ordinary causes of death at once, would be assuredly unaccountable on any supposition within the power of human understanding, except one—that of a deterioration in the condition of the body of the people. Now, as there is no proof that the earth during this period has been less than usually productive; [on the contrary, the harvests from 1829 to 1834 inclusive were, we believe, on the Continent as well as among ourselves, at least of an average description,] we are compelled to resort to the only remaining theory, and to attribute this deterioration to some causes existing in the state of society.

Prussia is a country possessing a large extent of waste and half cultivated land, but, generally speaking, with few advantages of soil or climate; although Saxony, Silesia, and the Rhenish provinces furnish, no doubt, favourable exceptions. Her peasantry are a hardy and laborious race, but content to subsist, as the children of so poor a soil, on very scanty means of existence. The war, in the sufferings of which she partook in an extraordinary degree, for a long time retarded the developement both of her wealth and her population. When that restraining cause was removed, both took a sudden start; and, at the very same period, the substitution of fixed annual-rents for the feudal services of former times, materially changed the condition both of landlords and peasantry. It encouraged the former to attempt extended ameliorations in the cultivation of their land; and it gave to the latter a security and a freedom which enabled them to make use of their industry on better terms. Hence, during the first years of the peace, the numbers of the people increased, and fresh land was probably taken into cultivation, with a rapidity rather American than European; and it may be presumed that, for some short time, subsistence advanced even in a greater ratio than population. But this did not long continue; the inevitable necessity of *resorting to poorer soils,* in a community almost wholly agricultural, produced those results which theory and experience, slighted as they are by presumptuous speculators in all countries, combine to indicate. The peasants probably found their industry less efficient: their condition began to grow worse, while their numbers still continued to advance. Mr Jacob's Report on the Corn Trade furnished to Mr Malthus strong presumption of the hard fare and poor circumstances of the labouring classes in Prussia fifteen years ago; and the great increase of potato consumption about the same period, contributed, no doubt, at once to the excess of population and to the mortality which since has checked, by establishing the lowest standard of subsistence. It must have seemed but too likely, to every one acquainted with their real condition at that time, that if the then ratio of increase continued much longer, it would be checked at last by positive causes. And the returns before us show conclusively to our minds, that the limit has been reached. Increased mortality begins to prove that the increase of numbers has exceeded that rate beyond which the iron law of necessity ordains that no increase shall be unattended by suffering. In the fluctuation of events, we may undoubtedly expect that some new set of causes will in time give increased productiveness to Prussian labour. This is the most desirable remedy for the temporary distress which we have described; and if the labouring classes take advantage of such a period of sunshine, to raise, by their own exertions, the standard of comfort and subsistence among them, the nation will have advanced one step in real prosperity ; if not, the same vicissitudes with those which we are now witnessing will recur again.

If we possessed equally accurate accounts of the course of population in other states similarly circumstanced with Prussia, we have little doubt that they would exhibit similar results : they would probably show that the extraordinary progress which began about the period of the peace of 1815 has not maintained itself steadily ; and that the diminished ratio in these latter years has been owing, not to a diminished number of births only, but to an increased mortality,—proving a temporary deterioration in national circumstances. There might be found exceptions to this rule in countries where, as in England, manufacturing industry has been rendered more productive by improvements in machinery; or where, as in parts of Austria, agricultural industry has perhaps lost none of its productiveness, by reason of the vast extent of fertile land still uncultivated, or scarcely cultivated. Which way the balance would incline, we do not pretend to decide ; but are strongly impressed with the opinion, that in a great part of Europe the last ten years have been an epoch of retrogression in the oscillating course of events, as far as the prosperity of the lower classes is concerned.

Political Economy, it has been truly said, is a science which conducts us, not to facts, but to tendencies, or approximations; and we readily admit that the law of Malthus is often and extensively counteracted by those advances in the productiveness of labour which result from improvements in science and civilisation. If so, we may be asked, Why argue against the validity of Mr Senior's proposition ? Because, we answer, there is at present, in our opinion, a tendency to rely on that increased productiveness of labour as a far more permanent and effective counter-agent than it will eventually be found. It is not at all surprising that such should be the case. The doctrine of population is, in Political Economy, what that of original sin is in theology,—offensive to philosophical pride, and irksome to sanguine temperaments; and hence the endless attempts which are made to contradict or to evade it. It is humiliating to feel that society must rely on the slow and painful process of moral restraint as the only corrective of a necessary evil. It disappoints our benevolent anticipations to find that the poorer classes among us partake so little in all the miracles of our advancing civilisation. We prefer to be told that there are extrinsic causes at work, which promise to render the ancient law of our nature a mere philosophical curiosity—a theorem without application;—that machinery and science, and facilities of communication, are outstripping the rapid march of numbers, and rendering our sage apprehensions wholly imaginary. The extraordinary advance of England in these respects, in the course of the last few years, has no doubt had an effect in lessening the practical belief in economical doctrines. Nay, so easily are men turned from their principles by the most partial observation, that we believe the mere absorption of our pauper population through the effect of the New Law has turned some Malthusians into apostates from their prophet. But if society has a power to modify, in some degree, its own future destinies by means of education, then these views, if mistaken, as we believe them to be, are pregnant with real danger. ' In discussing our ' future progress of improvement'—we quote once more the Letter from which our last extract was drawn—' it cannot but lead ' to error, to lay down positions calculated to direct the attention ' toward means which must of necessity be inefficient; while the ' nature of the difficulty to be contended with, and the only ' efficient means of contending with it successfully, and of im- ' proving the progress of society, are kept in the background. ' Your position, that food has a tendency to increase faster than ' population, appears to me to be open to this objection, and ' therefore I cannot approve of it.'

After discussing the two first of his elementary laws, Mr Senior proceeds to complete the second division of his labours by defining and explaining Production. This is one of the most masterly chapters of the work; but we can do no more than refer our readers to it; as it is much too tersely written to admit of farther condensation. The instruments of production he divides into labour, natural agents, and ' abstinence;' *i. e.* ' the conduct ' of a person who either abstains from the unproductive use of ' what he can command, or designedly prefers the production of ' remote to that of immediate results.' Abstinence, in short, is a new name for that course of conduct of which the result is *capital,* ' and which stands in the same relation to profit as labour ' does to wages.' It is, as its inventor admits, not a very accurate denomination; but it would be difficult to find a better; and considering the very narrow sense in which the term capital is usually employed, it appears almost a necessary importation into the language of the science. Its chief value, we may observe, appears in the discussion (p. 175) respecting ' cost of pro- ' duction.' According to the third ' elementary proposition,' it is by the use of abstinence that ' labour and the other instruments ' which produce wealth may be indefinitely increased.'

The author next proceeds to illustrate that fundamental difference between the effectiveness of the three agents of production, as applied to manufactures or to agriculture, on which his fourth elementary proposition rests. This difference consists, in the first place, in the power ' which agricultural industry pos- ' sesses, and manufacturing industry does not possess, of obtain- ' ing an additional product from the same materials :' Secondly, in the power which manufacturing industry possesses of obtaining an increase of produce by a less proportional increase of labour and capital; while agricultural industry, on the other hand, not only does not possess this power, but does, in fact, obtain a diminished return from every fresh application of labour and capital—skill, of course, in both cases remaining the same. On this last proposition is founded, as all students in the science are well aware, the theory of Rent.

What the theory of population is in one branch of the science, the theory of Rent, as arising from the diminishing efficiency of the powers of nature, is in another;—a *lapis offensionis,* startling and offending many ; partly from the exaggerated results which, undoubtedly, Mr Ricardo and his followers have drawn from it ; and partly from the apparent contradiction which it offers to phenomena familiar to most observers. Mr Senior, we think, has treated this difficult part of his subject with great judgment and acuteness ; and we know of no writer who has so ably pointed out the mode of reconciling the abstract theory of a relative rise of rent, with the fact of a positive rise of rent from increased productiveness of labour,—such as has taken place so extensively in England.

In proceeding to consider the subject of the distribution of wealth, Mr Senior begins by pointing out a deficiency in the common language of the science, which he endeavours to correct, as far as is necessary for the purpose of his discussion ; and in doing so he does, in fact, lay the foundation of a very different phraseology from that now in use, which he *partly* adopts.

' According to the usual language of political economists, labour, capital, and land are the three instruments of production; labourers, capitalists, and landlords are the three classes of producers ; and the whole produce is divided into wages, profit, and rent. . . . . It appears to us, that, to have a nomenclature which should fully and precisely indicate the facts of the case, no less than twelve distinct terms would be necessary. For each class there ought to be a name for the instrument employed or exercised ; a name for the class of persons who employ or exercise it ; a name for the act of employing or exercising it ; and a name for the share of the produce by which that act is remunerated.'

We may condense Mr Senior's proposals for completing this nomenclature into a sort of tabular form ; leaving a blank for one term in the series, which our language does not furnish.

Instrument.	Powers of mind and body.	Capital.	Natural agent.
Class.	Labourer.	Capitalist.	Landlord.
Act.	Labour.	Abstinence.	
Reward.	Wages.	Profit.	Rent.

But the meaning in which some of these terms are employed by Mr Senior, differs both from their popular signification, and from that which is usually given to them by scientific writers. To begin with wages. The whole reward of a labourer, except so far as he brings capital of his own to aid his exertions, and derives profit from its use, is commonly comprehended under this appellation ; but Dr Smith, in that well-known and popular chapter of his book which treats of the different returns to labour and capital in different employments, points out several causes which produce an inequality of pecuniary gain to the labourer in his respective occupations. Now, part of this apparent inequality is resolvable into the fact, that in some occupations the labourer advances much capital, while in others he advances little or none ; and that all the returns to his capital, as well as his labour, are lumped together under the current title of wages. The education of a skilled labourer is, of course, his capital, and the profit forms an important part of his nominal wages ; just as the nominal wages of a physician or a lawyer comprehend profit on the capital invested by each in the necessary appendages of their profession,—in a carriage or a clerk. Thus far Mr Senior agrees with former authorities. But he carries his analysis of the component parts of wages much farther. In his technical sense, ' wages ' appear to mean nothing more than the average reward which can be earned by a day-labourer in the most ordinary employment. All that may be earned by a highly paid class, or individual, beyond this amount, he would rank as profit or as rent. And as his definition of profit does not materially differ from those already received, he is of course obliged to give to rent a new and very extended signification, as will appear from the following passages :

'Land, though the principal, is not the only natural agent which can be appropriated. The mere knowledge of the operations of nature, as long as the use of that knowledge can be confined either by secrecy or by law, creates a revenue to its possessor analogous to the rent of land. The payment made by a manufacturer to a patentee for the privilege of using the patent process, is usually termed in the language of commerce a rent ; and under the same head must be ranked all the peculiar advantages of situation or connexion, and all extraordinary qualities of body or mind. The surplus revenue which they occasion beyond wages and profits, is a revenue for which no additional sacrifice has been made. The proprietor of these advantages differs from a landlord only in the circumstance that he cannot in general let them out to be used by another, and must consequently either let them remain useless or turn them to account himself. . . . . . If, therefore, the established division is adhered to, and all that is produced is to be divided into rent, profit, and wages—and certainly that appears to be the most convenient classification: —and if wages and profits are to be considered as the reward of peculiar sacrifices—the former the remuneration for labour, and the latter for abstinence from immediate enjoyment,—it is clear that under the term ' rent ' must be included all that is obtained without any sacrifice ; or, *which is the same thing*, beyond the remuneration for that sacrifice ;—all that nature or fortune bestows, either without any exertion on the part of the recipient, or in addition to the average remuneration for the exercise of industry, or the employment of capital.'—Pp. 166, 167.

It follows naturally from this definition, that any remuneration obtained by extraordinary talents (either in the use of capital or of labour, we suppose), is in his view a rent. The skill acquired through education is of course capital, the result of previous abstinence ; but the genius or aptitude which makes one man better able to use that skill to purpose than another, is an ' appro- ' priated natural agent.'

' Sir Walter Scott could write a volume with the labour of about three hours a-day for a month, and for so doing received L.500 or L.1000. An ordinary writer, with equal application, would find it difficult to produce a volume in three months, and still more difficult to sell it for L.50. Is then the extraordinary remuneration of the labourer, which is assisted by extraordinary talents, to be termed rent or wages ? It originates in the bounty of nature ; so far it seems to be rent. It is to be obtained only on the condition of undergoing labour ; so far it seems to be wages. It might be termed, with equal correctness, rent, which can be received only by a labourer, or wages, which can be received only by the proprietor of a natural agent. But as it is clearly a surplus, the labour having been previously paid for by average wages, and that surplus the spontaneous gift of nature, we have thought it most convenient to term it *rent.*'—P. 182.

And he proceeds to compare it to the gain of a miner seeking for copper who should come on an equally fertile vein of silver; ' or of the holders of black cloth on the decease of one of the ' Royal Family;' both of which he would take from the category of profit to place within that of rent. So again in the following passage :

' According to our nomenclature, a very small portion of the earnings of the physician or of the lawyer can be called wages. Forty pounds a-year would probably pay all the labour that either of them undergoes in order to make, we will say, L.4000 a-year. Of the remaining L.3960, probably L.3000 may in each case be considered as *rent,* as the result of extraordinary talent or good fortune. The rest is profit on their re- spective capitals; capitals partly consisting of knowledge, and of moral and intellectual habits, acquired by much previous expense and labour, and partly of connexion and reputation, acquired during years of proba- tion, while their fees were inadequate to their support.'—P. 184.

The phrase ' appropriated natural agent,' which Mr Senior has borrowed from former writers, and adapted to a new purpose, appears scarcely accurate, if closely examined; for the strength of an ordinary labourer is clearly as much an ' appropriated na- ' tural agent' as the talents of a Scott. But, regarding this as a mere verbal objection, we are willing to waive it. Now, in the first place, it is obvious that, under this nomencla- ture, all that in common language is termed *monopoly profit,* is in future to be ranked as *rent.* So, of course, ought the high profits or high wages secured by individuals who embark in occupations which, from peculiar circumstances, are not sought after with the same intensity of competition which the actual return to capital invested in them would warrant. The first of Dr Smith's well-known causes ' of variation in profits and ' wages,'—namely, ' the agreeableness or disagreeableness of dif- ' ferent occupations,'—ought rather to be called a cause creating a rent in some occupations. For it is clear that the extra profits realized by one who undertakes an occupation which others will not undertake, must be specifically similar to those realized in one which others *cannot* undertake, either from natural or legal difficulties. The superior disagreeableness of the business of a common informer, or an executioner, is a ' natural agent,' which these personages have ' appropriated;' just as a newly discovered power of nature is appropriated by a patentee. And Mr Senior ought, in consistency, to have called its reward a rent. This he has not done; adopting, in that case, Dr Smith's denomina- tion of extra profit or wages. This can only have been from the consciousness that pursuing his own nomenclature to the utmost would have the appearance of a curious over-refining on established language. But if adopted in part, it ought, for the sake of clearness, to be adopted altogether. Nay, he should have gone farther still. The wages of labourers in some countries—say India—are nearly as low as they can be : and so are their productive powers. The wages of the Pole—the Frenchman—the Englishman—rise by gradation above these : and so do also their productive powers. Their superior skill and energy, as well as the favourable circumstances which contribute to aid them, are ' appropriated natural agents.' Ought not the excess of remuneration obtained by these labourers respectively above the Hindoo to be termed ' rent,' as much as the excess of the gains of a Halford above those of a parish doctor ?

In the next place, it will be seen (by the example of black cloth), that fortuitous contingencies, which may raise for a time the rate of profit, are considered by him as affording a rent. Now, here we cannot but think his nomenclature not only too refined, but somewhat misleading. The fact is, that these contingencies do enter for something, although for very little, into the calculations of those who are about to undertake any business ; and are hence a portion of the causes which produce the ordinary rate of profit in that business. Thus the high gain of a miner who strikes on a vein of more valuable metal, or of a holder of black cloth on a royal decease, which Mr Senior regards as rent, we should rather consider as entering into the average return to capital in those two employments. At another time the miner may be working for a long time at a dead loss ; and it may so happen that a general mourning is not proclaimed for several years together. The extra profits obtained on the occurrence of the favourable contingency may do no more than balance the loss sustained through the unfavourable. Again, if the gains of those few who make more than average profits in any employment, are all to be termed 'rent' (and any one who follows out Mr Senior's reasoning will see that they must be so), the common doctrine of the average equality of profits should seem to be founded altogether on a misnomer. He says, as we have seen, that all that is obtained without any sacrifice, is ' the same thing ' with all that is obtained ' beyond *the* remuneration for that sa-' crifice,'—meaning, we presume, the *average* remuneration ; and, consequently, that if the first be rent, the second is so likewise. But what is the meaning of the phrase ' average remuneration,' or ' average profit' ? Does not the very phrase imply that some profit is above the average ? The common profits in a trade are said to be at twelve per cent when A realizes fifteen, and B, with the same amount of capital, realizes nine. According to Mr Senior, A's extra three per cent is not profit at all, but rent. Then, twelve per cent is not the average profit, but the highest that can be made. By the mere application of unusual abilities, and readiness in the pursuit of advantages, to the ordinary processes of retail trade, Mr Morrison—so well known in the mercantile world—has been enabled to realize large profits, and eventually an enormous fortune. According to Mr Senior's nomenclature, Mr Morrison's abilities must have yielded him a ' rent,' as much as Sir Walter Scott's. But Mr Morrison's success must necessarily have impoverished many competitors, just as Sir W. Scott may have driven many a Leadenhall-Street artisan out of the market. And unless Mr Morrison's gains have been so incredibly immense as to raise the average rate of retail profits all over the country during the period of his operations, it is clear that some other traders must have remained as far below the average as he has soared above it. Why should their inferior gains be termed ' profit,' and his partly ' profit' and partly ' rent'?

And if such a nomenclature is fallacious in the case of ordinary trades, it must be equally so, although less obviously, in respect of those which partake more of the nature of a lottery. It is one of Dr Smith's principles, that enormous prizes tend to fix the rate of profits or wages even below the average. The learned professions, for instance, ' attract competition, not so much in proportion to ' the real value of the contingency, as to the excess of the possible ' return over the certain outlay;' and, consequently, it is possible that the whole revenue of all three may not be sufficient to replace the capital employed, and afford the wages of a day-labourer to every member of them in addition. Such, at least, is unquestionably the case in the legal profession; although Mr Senior, with that love of paradox which he occasionally evinces, will have it that it is less of a lottery than the church. Now, the profession to which Sir Walter Scott belonged is far more hazardous than any of the three. Where there is one Sir Walter Scott, there are perhaps a few hundred individuals who obtain prizes of more or less value; there are perhaps three or four thousand who gain a bare subsistence; and perhaps twice as many who continue to present the public with their lucubrations at a dead loss. Were the whole revenue of a Scott and all his successful brethren divided equally among the tribe of authors, they would undoubtedly remain the worst paid craft in Christendom.

This being the case, we cannot see any necessity for ranking those extra gains of individual labourers as rent, which, if divided among the whole body of labourers in that employment, might not raise their average reward even above that low remuneration which alone receives the name of wages from Mr Senior. And, lastly, his definition of rent, as is confessed by himself, excludes a condition which enters into all our ordinary notions of it ;—namely, that it is something obtained by a proprietor for the use of his property, independent of his own exertions. A landowner cultivating his own soil does indeed obtain his surplus produce by his own labour; but if he were to let that soil to another, he would obtain the same surplus produce; whereas an artist, or an author, depends wholly on his own talents for his surplus remuneration.

On the whole, therefore, admitting the ingenuity of Mr Senior's nomenclature, we cannot but think that the inconvenience he incurs, by classing under the same name things so widely different, overbalances any superior clearness which he may expect to attain by it; especially in a work professedly popular and elementary. We do not know that any shorter or plainer road is gained to the valuable conclusions of the science by establishing wages at an uniform standard as the remuneration of mere ordinary labour, or by denying the name of profits to all, that, from whatever cause, exceeds the average. We prefer to retain for rent its usual limited signification; and allow that wages and profits are liable to extensive variations, both in the amount obtained by different classes and by different individuals.

We regret that our limits have obliged us to exhibit so imperfect a view of the contents of this valuable treatise. Or, perhaps, we ought rather to reproach ourselves for having been tempted into incidental discussions on minor points, instead of employing our space more usefully in presenting a condensed view of its general character. But this is the less a matter of regret, because we hope on some future occasion to have the author's views developed in a fuller and completer shape. Devoted as he is to his science, we cannot suppose that he means to confine himself, as he has lately done, to the practical labour of furnishing valuable hints for public measures. Without undervaluing the assistance which he has rendered in this way, we trust he will not forget the claim which abstract science has upon him still, as one especially able to correct its hypothetical results, by his own extensive practical knowledge : indeed, the specimen before us differs from all other elementary treatises on the subject with which we are acquainted, less by the depth of its theoretical views than by the peculiar manner in which observation and experience are brought to bear upon them, without any of that exclusive arrogance with which theory and practice are wont to maintain their respective independence. It is at once philosophical and popular; presenting throughout a remarkable specimen of clearness, simplicity, and condensation of language, applied to subjects which it is often difficult to treat without harshness and obscurity.

ON NATIONAL ECONOMY.

No. III.

MISS MARTINEAU'S "COUSIN MARSHALL"—"THE PREVENTIVE CHECK."

THE *Westminster Review*, in speaking of one of Miss Martineau's little books, bursts forth into the following exclamation:

" What a country is England! where a young lady may put forth a book like this, quietly, modestly, and without the apparent consciousness of doing any extraordinary act; and, what is more, where others see as little to be surprised at in the circumstance, and receive the boon with the indifference of any ordinary courtesy!"

This flourish we feel a strong inclination to parody. Our own reflections, after reading " *Cousin Marshall,*" though of a different cast, yet fell into a very similar form. We could not help saying to ourselves —

" What a frightful delusion is this, called, by its admirers, Political Economy, which can lead a young lady to put forth a book like this! — a book written by a *woman* against the *poor* — a book written by a *young woman* against *marriage!* And what is more, where a long tirade against all charity, and an elaborate defence of the closest selfishness, is received with acclamation by those who profess themselves the friends of the people and the advocates of the distressed."

In another point of view, too, we might fairly express amazement at the delight with which Miss Martineau's tracts are received, if we could be surprised at any thing from a " *political economist.*" These gentry are ever complimenting each other, and the whole class to which they belong, as the only men who know how to reason logically on the management of a country. The contempt which they uniformly express for the minds and arguments of those who receive not their fancies, is often ludicrous, sometimes irritating. And yet, in the present case, their warmest and most unqualified approbation is unhesitatingly given to a tissue of reasonings, which would disgrace the third class of any ladies' boarding-school of decent character, in these days of improved female education.

What, for instance, would any pro-

perly-qualified " English teacher " say to such a specimen of logic as that which forms the main substance and staple of *Cousin Marshall?* The narrative gives us some lively, but rather overdrawn sketches, of workhouse grievances, and other mal-administrations of the poor-laws. The conclusion drawn from these sketches, in the doctrinal parts of the book, is, that the poor-laws should be *wholly abolished! entirely swept away!!*

Try the same argument on the Court of Chancery. No one doubts that great grievances exist in that court, and not less under a Brougham than under an Eldon. Property has been wasted in useless disputes; hearts have been broken by endless delay; *therefore,* according to Miss Martineau's exquisite logic, it would be better at once *wholly to abolish the Court of Chancery,* and let the lieges, if they will get into disputes about their property, settle those disputes by fisty-cuffs, or ask for a " writ of helter-skelter."

Or who, again, of higher intellect than some village overseer, grumbling out his weekly complaint, " the more you give, the more you may," would dream of seriously urging the insufficiency of a charity *to do every thing,* as an argument against *doing any thing?* And yet this " *skilful dialectician,*" as one of her admirers calls her, gravely puts this forward, once and again, as a conclusive argument! Lying-in charities are vehemently denounced, as among " the worst in existence" of all public institutions. And what is a chief objection to them?

" It is dreadful to see the numbers of poor women disappointed of a reception at the last moment, and totally unprovided. The more are admitted, the more are thus disappointed." p. 37.

So that, if you have a lying-in hospital in an indigent neighbourhood, with fifty beds, and you find that the applications would fill a hundred, the remedy is, not to enlarge it, but *to pull it down!*

Arguing in a similar manner, of distributions of coals and blankets in winter, we are taught to believe that such distributions are actually wicked and inhuman.

" If I were you, I would explain to my neighbours, that, finding this mode of charity *creates more misery than it relieves*, I should discontinue it. • • The more support you offer them, the more surprisingly they will increase." p. 117.

How the gift of coals and blankets to a poor family at Christmas should " create misery," does not, at first sight, appear very obvious. But Miss M. has a reason ready for this :

" The beggars are brought by your master's charity-purse. I reckon, from what I have seen here, that every blanket given away brings two naked people, and every bushel of coals, a family that wants to be warmed." p. 89.

The *Arabian Nights' Entertainments* are dry matter of fact compared with this. Whole families moving from one part of the country to another, abandoning their parishes and settlements, for the chance of a blanket and a bushel of coals when the winter comes round ! And villages, where the cottages stand empty in such abundance, that new-comers, in any number, can find dwellings all ready to their hands ! Where has this young woman lived all her days ?

It probably would be too great a tax upon Miss M.'s logical and reflective powers, to ask her whether, if a pauper, by coming from Berkshire into Hants, "*increased* the misery" in the latter, he did not also equally *diminish* the misery in the former ? The mere moving about of the poor in search of compassion, even were it true to any extent, is not an " increase of misery" to the country at large ; but the right way to end all dispute about " bringing naked people" into parishes, is not to starve them every where alike, but to cherish them every where alike, and then they will not "swarm after a charity-purse."

But if we were to follow Miss M. through all her chimeras and causes of alarm, we might write a book at least as large as her own. Her greatest horror is, of course, the perverse folly of the poor in marrying ! and nothing can exceed the absurdity of some of the motives she assigns for the marriages of the poor. Lying-in hospitals are denounced as "causing misery," just as much as the distribution of

coals and blankets ; and then it is asked —

" What else could be expected, under so direct a bounty on improvidence, under so high a premium on population ?" p. 37.

So that this young lady evidently takes it for granted, that many people marry principally, or solely, in order to have the happiness of lying-in in an hospital ! ! !

In another place she equally condemns alms-houses.

" They are very bad things. Only consider the number of young people that marry, under the expectation of getting their helpless parents maintained by the public." p. 42.

And as alms-houses are not to be built, lest the young folks should marry, so, in another place, the cottage system is condemned, and for the same reason — " Under no system does population increase more rapidly." Now what is meant by "the cottage system" is merely this, that every poor agricultural labourer should have his own little dwelling ; and also, if possible, his own garden. In many districts, it is well known, two or three families are at present crammed into one cottage, and twelve or fourteen persons, grown or growing up, are forced to sleep in two small rooms. This is the system which this young lady would wish to have kept up, because, forsooth, if men were allowed to have cottages, they would soon want wives and children ! " Under no system does population increase more rapidly !" Delicate creature !

The truth is, that there is nothing here but a very old story. The feelings of these political economists towards the people, are just the same as those entertained three thousand years ago by Pharaoh towards the children of Israel. The cry is just the same : " Come now, let us deal *wisely* with the people, *lest they multiply upon us.*" And there are those among ourselves, who, if they dare, would gladly employ the same means with those adopted by Pharaoh. Dean Swift's plan, however, of making pork of the young ones, was preferable, in many points of view, to the Egyptian method.

But, by whatever means it may be brought about, Miss Martineau agrees with the Edinburgh professor, that nothing but " *a limitation of numbers*" will save the country. And so said Pharaoh.

It is true, that neither Miss Martineau, nor Dr. Chalmers, nor any of the leading writers of that party, have yet dared to propose to the world—or, probably, even to confess to themselves, —the ultimate lengths to which their system would carry them. But half measures will not do : they may as well speak out at once. We tell them, without doubt or hesitation, that not only is their whole system *based upon untruth and mistatement of fact*, but that *the remedy they propose is wholly insufficient to meet the evil* which they profess to have discovered. And upon these two points we shall trouble Miss Martineau with a few observations.

I. Then, we must tell her, in the plainest terms, that THE EVIL of which she stands in so much dread, is WHOLLY THE CREATURE OF HER OWN IMAGINATION; aided, probably, by the absurd exaggerations of Malthus, Chalmers, and others. This supposed evil is the growth of pauperism, the decline of the wealth of the nation, the gradual absorption of property in the support of the poor, ending, of course, in universal poverty and distress at the last. This is the ever-recurring burden of her song.

" Distress is more prevalent than ever, and goes on to increase every year. The failure of British benevolence, vast as it is in amount, has hitherto been complete." p. 39.

" The wonder is, how the pauper system has failed to swallow up all our resources, and make us a nation of paupers. But to this condition we shall infallibly be brought, unless we take speedy means to stop ourselves." p. 49.

" In a few years more, the profits of all kind of property will be absorbed by the increasing rates, and capital will therefore cease to be invested; land will be let out of cultivation, manufactures will cease, and the nation become one vast congregation of paupers." p. 49.

" Our pauper-list is swelled, year by year; it grows at both ends. Paupers multiply their own numbers as fast as they can, and rate-payers sink down into rate-receivers." p. 111.

" We are now borne down, we shall soon be crushed by the weight of our burdens." p. 121.

" The proportion of the indigent to the rest of the population having increased from age to age." p. 130.

" If not adopted speedily, all measures will be too late to prevent the universal pre valence of poverty in this kingdom ; the legal provision for the indigent now operating the extinction of our national resources, at a perpetually increasing rate." p. 132.

It requires a strong belief in the infatuation of these people, to prevent our charging them with downright effrontery. For what but either the one or the other can produce such assertions as these? To represent the poor as perpetually encroaching on the property of the rich, and as encroaching at so rapid a rate as to threaten the entire annihilation of all capital ; and to state these things with their eyes open, and with the power of comparing and judging of things around them, is certainly one of the most astounding attempts that has ever been made, upon the credulity of the public.

The poor are said to be preying upon the rich at so rapid a rate as to threaten the entire absorption of all property, if the present state of things shall be allowed to continue much longer. Such is the statement. Now what is the fact?

Notoriously, undeniably, beyond all question, *just the contrary !* If there be any one thing clearer than another, it is this, that for many years past the rich have been growing richer, and the poor growing poorer; and both in a ratio quite inconsistent with the peace and happiness of the community.

In fact, the accumulations of the rich, during the last thirty years, have been so vast, as almost to stagger credibility. Look, in the first place, at the national debt; six hundred millions of which, or three-fourths of the whole, have been accumulated since the end of the last century, and that by the savings of the surplus wealth of those whose means exceeded their wants. An equal sum, or even more, has been expended upon new canals, roads, docks, and other useful works; all yielding a return to the investing parties, and all coming under the same description of *accumulated wealth.* And if we look at the rent-rolls of our landed proprietors, we find little indeed of that dwindling away under the encroachments of the poor which Miss M. so pathetically describes. A statement, apparently well founded, now lies before us, published in 1783, of the rentals of the estates of the seven most wealthy British peers at that period. The aggregate of the whole seven fell short of 400,000*l.* a-year. No one at all acquainted with the subject, would now estimate the united incomes of the same noble families at less than *a million* per annum. The "extinction of their resources," which Miss M. so feelingly prognosticates, has not, then, made much progress, at least during the past fifty years.

But we must advance a step further, and grapple at once with the main proposition of this part of the subject. Miss Martineau asserts that the poor-laws produce nothing but increasing misery; and she even ventures explicitly to affirm, that " the *proportion* of the indigent to the rest of the population has *increased* from age to age;" and that " the legal provision for the indigent is now operating the extinction of our national resources, at a perpetually increasing rate." p. 132.

Now, in reply to these assertions, we are compelled to say, as in the case of Dr. Chalmers, that they are not only *not true*, but that they are *directly opposed to the truth.* Not only do they not state facts correctly, but they state what is exactly the reverse of the facts; the simple truth being, that instead of pauperism, indigence, and their concomitant expenditure being ever on the *increase*, they have for centuries past, and do still, exhibit a continually progressive *diminution*.

It is certainly more than could have been expected, that we should be able, at the present moment, to make and support such an assertion as this. True, the two elements of a national provision for the poor, and an increasing population, have been steadily at work, advancing the state of society and diminishing poverty. But the disciples of Adam Smith have also been at work for more than thirty years, in earnest counteraction of the beneficent tendency of these two great ameliorating causes. By preaching up the advantage of large farms; by turning thousands of little farmers upon the world; by demolishing cottages; by enclosing commons; and by forcibly compelling the labouring man to go to the overseer, even when work was ready for him, and he willing to work;—they have certainly done all that was possible for man to do towards rendering pauperism, among the agricultural labourers, all but universal.

In like manner have the same parties been working, without ceasing, against the other great branch of national industry. Finding that the labourer at Lyons was only paid 8*d.* or 9*d.* a-day, they never rested until by " free trade" they had opened a direct competition between that town and Macclesfield. By this scheme they have reduced the wages of a Macclesfield weaver, in ten years, from 18*s.* to 7*s.* 6*d.* a-week. One natural consequence is, that, striving for bread for their families, two men will now do (working fourteen hours a-day) as much work as, in 1819, three were accustomed to do. Of course, the third man may now go to the overseer; and then we have endless complaints of " surplus population" and " increasing pauperism."

Under all these circumstances it may well be matter of wonder, that the poor-rates of England have not, of late years, most rapidly increased. Still, however, they have not. Still, in the midst of all this misery, caused, as it is, not by the poor-laws, but by the political economists, the enemies of the poor-laws,—we are able to meet Dr. Chalmers, Miss Martineau, and the rest, and fearlessly to assert, that it is *not true* that " the proportion of the indigent to the rest of the population has increased from age to age." That the poor-rates may have increased, or that the persons relieved may have increased, *positively*, is doubtless true: but Miss Martineau states the question fairly, which is, have they increased *in proportion to the rest of the population?* The true answer to this is, No!

In 1673, we learn from Davenant, that the number of paupers was 1,330,000; in 1700, they were stated by Braddon at 1,200,000; in 1735, Samuel Webber calculates them at 1,400,000.

Now the population was, in 1680, 5,500,000; in 1700, 5,475,000; in 1740, 6,074,000. The indigent, then, were in the proportion of about 22 or 23 in every 100, at the period in question.

In 1803, the numbers of paupers had fallen to 1,039,716, according to the official reports; but the population had grown to be 9,168,000. The indigent, therefore, were now only in the proportion of 11 or 12 in every 100. In 1815, the reported number of paupers was 895,336; but the population was then 11,360,505. The indigent have, therefore, decreased to the proportion of only *eight* in every hundred.

One word of explanation must be interposed in this place. The real amount of pauperism is over-estimated, if we take any one of these amounts as its true representation. The practice of setting down as a pauper every one who, on an emergency, and for once, receives a trifle as casual relief, always swells the account far beyond the truth. But this practice prevails as much now as ever. We are, therefore, quite entitled to use the facts as we find them; and to assert from those facts, that the proportion of the indigent, instead of augmenting, has diminished, within the last century, nearly *two-thirds*.

But we must speak of it in another point of view; the question of pauperism, as either *increasing* or *diminishing*, concerns not only those who *receive* relief, but also those who *pay* it. Is it an increasing burden or not, as compared with the nation's augmented power to bear it? Our answer is, it is a greatly diminishing charge, considered in this point of view.

Compare its gradual increase with the contemporaneous increase of the national revenue. In 1601, the revenue was 607,995*l.*, the poor-rate 200,000*l.*; being nearly equal to *one-third*.

In 1700 the revenue had risen to 3,895,205*l.*, but the poor-rate only to 1,000,000*l.*; being little more than *one-fourth*.

In 1760 the revenue was 8,800,000*l.*, but the poor-rate had only advanced to 1,500,000*l.*; being now scarcely more than *one-sixth*.

In 1803 the revenue was 38,401,738*l.*, the poor-rate having risen to 4,077,891*l.*, or rather less than *one-ninth*.

In 1825 the revenue was 55,835,626*l.*, the poor-rate being 5,734,216*l.*, or little more than *one-tenth*.

Such has been the relative progress, on the one hand of the national resources, as indicated by revenue, and on the other, of the sum required for the indigent poor; the latter, as we have seen, being perpetually diminishing, as weighed against the former.

Or we may institute another comparison, and see how the progressive augmentation of the foreign trade of the country has accompanied and outstripped the claims of the poor.

In 1673 our exports amounted to 2,043,043*l.*, and our poor-rates to 840,000*l.*; the proportion being somewhat more than *one-third*.

In 1698 our exports were 3,525,907*l.*, and our poor-rates 819,000*l.*; or less than *one-fourth*.

In 1700 our exports had advanced to 6,045,432*l.*, but the poor-rates only to 1,000,000*l.*; or less than *a sixth*.

In 1776 our exports were 14,755,699*l.* and our poor-rates 2,000,000*l.*; or less than *one-seventh*.

In 1814 the exports had reached 50,624,229*l.*, and the poor-rates to 6,294,584*l.*; or about *one-eighth*.

And in 1825 the exports were 60,898,721*l.*, while the poor-rates were 5,734,216*l.*; or less than *one-tenth*.

Thus, while Miss Martineau assures us, that if the poor-laws be maintained, " manufactures will be discontinued, and commerce will cease" (p. 49), the historic fact stands on record against her, that, after the experience of more than two centuries, it is found that our foreign trade, which at the commencement of the period did not exceed thrice the amount paid to our paupers, has constantly outstripped it in the advance which each have experienced, and is now *tenfold*, in place of being *threefold* the amount required by the indigent poor.

So much for the dreams and fancies constantly put forward by these people, touching the dreadful growth of pauperism. Like all their other statements of fact, they turn out to be nothing but fiction; the real truth being, that these gentry find it far more easy and convenient to invent the facts required, in their closets, than to search for them in historic or statistic records; where, indeed, they would never find any thing to answer their purpose.

But we must now proceed to the remaining branch of the subject; which concerns,—

II. The entire inefficiency and inutility of the remedies proposed.

The *evil* which she imagines to exist (and it exists only in imagination), is " a disproportion of numbers to the means of subsistence." Population has been too much encouraged, and thus a most dreadful " multiplication of consumers" has taken place.

The *remedy* she proposes is " a limitation of numbers," a " proportioning the number of consumers to the subsistence fund." To do this, " all encouragements to the increase of population should be withdrawn, and every sanction given to the preventive check." With which view she proposes,

1. "To enact that no child born from any marriage taking place within a year from the date of the law, and no illegitimate child born within two years from the same date, shall ever be entitled to parish assistance." In other words, to

abolish the poor-laws *in toto*, substituting nothing in their room ; and only allowing the poor now in existence to enjoy their rights for their own lives.

2. To abolish all alms-houses, all foundling-hospitals, and, we suppose, all orphan-asylums, all lying-in-charities, all infirmaries, and all schools in which maintenance as well as education is provided.

A most sweet and tender-hearted young lady, this, truly ! A few trifling objections, however, occur to us, as worth a short consideration, before a change so sweeping be seriously determined upon. For this plan appears to us to be,

1. *Altogether unphilosophical.*

2. *Opposed to all experience.*

3. *Unpracticable, cruel, and inconsistent with her own admissions.*

4. *An unjust denial of the clearest rights of the poor.*

5. *Necessarily productive of the grossest immorality.*

First, we say that this scheme is *altogether unphilosophical*. It is so, whether considered in a moral or in a physiological point of view.

In a moral point of view, if the evil really were, as Miss Martineau supposes, that the people marry too recklessly and increase too rapidly, would not common sense tell us, that the most efficacious way of working their improvement in this respect would be, to do all we could to elevate, not to depress them? The cottage system, which Miss M. utterly condemns, does this. It gives hope and courage to the labourer; it places comfort and independence within his reach : he learns to respect himself; he wishes to have a wife and family worthy of his regard ; and he is not likely to rush into a precipitous engagement. Miss M. herself can see this, and yet misapplies it. Her hero says—

" I know an industrious young man, a shopkeeper, who has been attached for years, but who will not marry till his circumstances justify it : half-a-dozen vagabond paupers have been married in his parish during the time that he has been waiting." p. 53.

And yet, seeing this, Miss M. still supposes, that to deprive the poor of all their present legal rights, and of nearly all their aids from charity, would be the way to elevate their character. To make a man desperate, to make him reckless, is the way, according to this young lady, to teach him carefulness and self-respect ! She argues thus, too, with the case of Ireland before her eyes, in which no poor-laws tend to increase population; and in which those other nuisances, alms-houses, infirmaries, and asylums, are but little known. Are the poor Irish noted for their caution in avoiding hasty marriages ? Does the preventive check operate as Miss M. would have it, in that country ?

But Miss M. is equally wrong in her view of the physiology of the case. She adopts most implicitly the Malthusian fancy, that people always breed up to food, and that the more food the more children; whereas, the truth is exactly the reverse. Speaking generally, a population always increases the more or less rapidly in proportion to the larger or smaller amount of poverty that exists amongst it. This fact thrusts itself upon our notice wherever we turn our view. The Irish cottager, to whom we have just alluded, is a well-known instance of it: he is poor enough, we suppose, for Miss M. herself; indeed, except the English cottager is to be actually starved, we do not see how he can well be made poorer; and yet the Irish cottager's prolificness is too proverbial for us to dwell upon. We merely allude to it in passing, to shew that the notion of starving people into a slow rate of increase is about the most absurd fancy that could possibly enter into a human brain.

The same rule, however, prevails every where. We might fill a volume with the proofs of it, but we will merely instance one or two facts which lie close at hand.

In the metropolis we have poor districts, and others comparatively rich. The poorest section is that called the Tower Hamlets, containing Spitalfields, Bethnal Green, and other parishes filled with labouring poor; and the population abstract of 1821 tells us, that in ten years preceding, there had been, in this district, 23,391 marriages and 69,198 births, being nearly three births to a marriage.

The same abstract informs us, that in Westminster, the abode of wealth and abundance, there were, in the same period, 28,830 marriages, and only 49,270 births, or less than two births to a marriage : — five thousand more marriages than in the poorer district, and yet twenty thousand less births !

In like manner, in wealthy and luxurious Bath, there were, in ten years,

4136 marriages, and only 9061 births, or little more than two births to each. In Nottingham there were, in the same ten years, 4064 marriages and 11,941 births: — seventy less marriages, and yet nearly three thousand more births.

We take these instances merely because they lie close at hand, and seem to be fair instances for comparison. Were we to go to Galway, or the poorer districts of Scotland, where poverty reigns even more than in Spitalfields, we should find the average to be four or five, or even six to a marriage; and we should also find marriage to be universal.

So much for the *philosophy* of Miss Martineau's scheme, for checking the increase of population by starving the poor.

Secondly, however, we object, that this scheme sets at nought all the lessons of *experience*, and disregards the best-established *facts*.

The idea is, that poor-laws, and alms-houses, and infirmaries, are " encouragements to the increase of population." They are all, therefore, to be removed, in order that the " preventive check" may come into full operation; and so the people may cease to marry, and no longer increase so alarmingly.

But before all this ingenious speculation be received and acted upon, may it not be as well to ask, how this " preventive check" has been found to operate in those parts of the kingdom where the poor-laws do not prevail? Surely nothing could be more natural than this inquiry.

England has increased in population, within the last century, more than 100 per cent. In 1740 its numbers were 6,064,000; in 1831 they were 13,894,574. But this vast increase is mainly attributed by Miss Martineau to the " encouragements held out,"— to the " high premium on population given,"— by our poor-laws, alms-houses, infirmaries, &c.

How fares it, then, with the other divisions of the United Kingdom, Ireland and Scotland, where these mischievous "encouragements" and " premiums" are unknown?

Ireland, in 1733, had a population of 2,015,229; but in 1831 she numbered 7,734,365, having nearly quadrupled her numbers in about the same space of time in which the English population had been little more than doubled.

Where, then, was the efficacy of the " preventive check" in Ireland? And how was it, that, with all England's mischievous "premiums" and "encouragements" for population, poor Ireland, with the " preventive check" in full force, left her so far behind in the race of increase?

But we shall be told, probably, that the Irish are a hasty, reckless, improvident people; and that no fair argument can be drawn from their case, as compared with the more civilised and better educated peasantry of England. We turn to Scotland, then, which is open to no objection of this sort. Her sons are cautious, frugal, industrious, and exactly fitted to exhibit the "preventive check" in its best light, and most efficient operation. Scotland, too, has abolished her poor-laws, though they exist as a dead letter; nor is she overrun with those terrible alms-houses, asylums, infirmaries, &c., which so fearfully "encourage population" in England. Scotland, then, must surely be accepted by Miss Martineau as a fair illustration of the point before us. Now, how stands the case as respects Scotland, when compared with England?

England reckoned, in 1801, a population of 8,872,980; in 1831 that population had increased to 13,894,574, being an augmentation of about 57 per cent.

The population of Scotland, in 1801, was 1,599,068; in 1831 it had grown to be 2,365,807, being an increase of about 48 per cent.

A difference of 9 per cent in thirty years, or between an increase of 48 and one of 57 per cent, would certainly leave the famous " preventive check" very little to boast of. But before we admit even that, one small point has to be taken into account.

The people of Ireland and of Scotland are constantly streaming into England in great numbers, and settling there; but the people of England, except in solitary instances, do not remove into either Ireland or Scotland. All our great towns — London, Manchester, Liverpool—abound with Irishmen and Scotchmen. Reckoning their wives and children, 100,000 would be a low calculation of the Irish population of London alone. The Scotch immigrants are of a better class; but, especially in London and Liverpool, they are very numerous : there are even many churches, in both these places, for Scotchmen alone.

If, then, we allowed, out of the whole population of England, no more than 300,000 for all the settlers, both from Ireland, Scotland, and every other country, we should then reduce the English increase in thirty years to less than 54 per cent. And if we suppose only 100,000 of these to be from Scotland, the growth of the population of Caledonia, within the same thirty years, must have exceeded 54 per cent.

What has become, then, of the virtue of the "preventive check !" How is it, that with every possible advantage for its operation, in clime, and soil, and national temperament, the result of the whole appears to be absolutely nothing ? Nothing ! we repeat,—since this horrid "increase of numbers," which so frights Miss Martineau from her propriety, seems to go on just as fearfully in the absence, as in the presence, of poor-laws and public charities !

But, *thirdly,* that the scheme now before us is *impracticable, cruel,* and full of *inconsistency,* must be apparent to every one who looks at it with any other than an economist's eye.

It is especially impracticable in England, above all countries on the face of the earth. Were the people distributed over the land, every one possessing his own little plot of ground, as in Flanders, or in Jersey, there might be some chance of giving the scheme at least a fair trial. But England is in a highly artificial state; her landed proprietors, acting under the instigation of Adam Smith, have pulled down the cottages, torn up the gardens, enclosed the commons, and crowded the agricultural population together, at the rate of a hundred persons in a row of eight or nine dirty hovels. The farmer, with diminishing means and falling prices, turns to his wages, as the item of expenditure which he can most easily reduce; and he does very soon reduce his labourers to bread and water, rags, and misery. Only one stay remains to keep the framework of society together; and that stay is *the poor-law.* The labourer must not be *starved;* happen what may, the law declares that he must be fed. He relies upon this; he is not happy or content, but he bears his misery as well as he can. But pass the law which Miss M. recommends, and in five years we shall have in every parish, some infants who are doomed by statute to actual starvation. The harvest is over, half the labourers

of a parish are thrown out of work; the overseer asks, What are the ages of your children ? Two and three years, is the answer. Oh! then we know nothing of them; they were born after the new act came in force : there are two shillings for yourself and your wife —take them, and be glad you can get that. Does Miss Martineau think that this would be borne? Does she intend or wish that it should be borne ?

But in little more than twenty years, even supposing the first step to be got over, we should have a whole population of young men, all equally without the pale of the law. What does Miss Martineau think would be done with these? The Irish "surplus population" pours itself into England; where shall the English "surplus" betake itself? There is no way open for it. Henry VIII. abolished the monasteries, — the poor-laws of his time, and 70,000 victims were devoured by the gallows in a few years after. To restore peace to the country, the rights of the poor were recognised, and order resumed its sway. Abolish these rights a second time, and if the government proved strong enough to enforce its mandates, not twice nor thrice 70,000 would be the limit of the numbers which the scaffold must destroy within the next twenty years. But no government could, at this time of day, enforce such a law: the thing is altogether *impracticable.*

But Miss Martineau herself admits the occurrence of other cases of difficulty, " when many hundreds are turned off at once from the public works ;" and yet, conscious as she is of these things, she makes no provision against their occurrence. Her repeal of the poor-laws is complete and final— no fragment is left. What, then, does she herself intend should be done, if her poor-law repeal could pass in 1833, and a sudden glut should stop half the mills of Leeds or Manchester in 1855 ? All the work-people, from twenty years and downwards, would then be doomed to downright starvation; for, according to her plan, no public relief *could* be legally given to them. But does she suppose that the people would lie down and die ? Does she propose that they should do so ? No, no ; the whole thing is *impracticable!*

And it is as *cruel* as it is impracticable, and as *inconsistent* with her own professions. She not only abolishes the poor-laws entirely, letting them expire with the existing race of poor, but she is as decidedly opposed to alms-houses, telling us, that " it should be as universal a rule that working-men should support their parents, as that they should support their children."

But then we must not forget her " preventive check," which, if it means any thing, means that no man should marry without a certainty of being able to support all the family, however numerous, that he may happen to have.

Now it happens to be upon record, that when as many as 101 agricultural labourers were captured and imprisoned, in Wiltshire, on a riot for a rise of wages, in 1830, it was found that 80 out of the 101 were in the receipt of wages only amounting to from 2s. 6d. to 7s. per week each. All these men, we may suppose, were by Miss Martineau's rule prohibited from marriage ; at least, if men earning five or six shillings a-week are at liberty to marry, we know not what " the preventive check" means.

But if these eighty men were not to marry, how were they to have those children who, on Miss Martineau's scheme, were to feel bound to support them in their old age ? No ! they must not marry—they are debarred all connubial and paternal pleasures and feelings—they are to labour in helpless, hopeless solitude, till old age comes upon them, and then they are to find the poor-laws abolished, the alms-houses pulled down, and are to be told, in grave and serious mockery, that their children ought to support them ! Such is the compassion, and such is the *consistency* of a *political economist !*

We see but one way out of this difficulty. Poor-laws and public asylums are to be abolished ; and the aged poor are to look for support in their declining years to their children, and to them alone. And yet, at the same time, the preventive check is to be called into full operation, the sole object of which is, to hinder a large part of the people from having any children ! What remains, then, to be done, but to adopt the method now in use in some of the eastern nations, and to have our aged poor despatched out of the way, when they get past their labour. In fact, so obviously does this result follow, that we lately heard a country gentleman remarking to the clergyman of the parish, that as he was, according to

Miss M.'s plan, to be the promulgator and expounder of the new system, from his pulpit, it would also be advisable that he should complete his duty, by providing a proper exit for these unhappy aged members. For this end, his friend suggested that a large hammer might be suspended in the belfry of every church ; so that those aged poor who were past labour, and who had no children to support them, might be brought in due form to church, there to be legally knocked on the head, and forthwith interred out of the way !

Fourthly, however, this scheme is grossly *unjust,* and a manifest infringement of the rights of the poor.

Miss Martineau would almost persuade us, that a man who is poor has no right to *exist.* Locke, however, was of another opinion. " Reason," he says, " tells us, that all men have a right to their subsistence ; and, consequently, to meat and drink, and such other things as nature affords for their preservation." He also tells us, that " God has not left one man so to the mercy of another that he may starve him if he please. God, the Lord and Father of all, has given no one of his children such a property in his peculiar portion of the things of this world, but that he has given his needy brother *a right* to the surplusage of his goods ; so that it cannot justly be denied him when his pressing wants call for it."

And Paley also insists on " the *reasonableness* of the law, which has subjected all the estates and fortunes of the kingdom to the maintenance of the poor ;" and which, he tells us, " is not a new burden, laid upon private property by the mere strength of an arbitrary law, but it is the voice of *reason and nature,* acknowledged and enforced by the wisdom and power of the legislature."

This natural right of the man starving with hunger, over the " surplusage" of his neighbour's food, is recognised and formed into a system by our English poor-law. The poor man, thus provided for by the law, may no longer take his neighbour's goods, whatever be his own necessity. But abolish this legal provision, and immediately the *natural right,* recognised by Puffendorf, and all the leading jurists, of the starving man, to help himself rather than to die, revives in its original force. That the whole security, therefore, of property, rests upon this broad basis of the recognition of the rights of the poor, must be, one would think, sufficiently plain.

But not only have the poor this *natural right*, which is precedent to and above all laws; but they have also a further right, given them by the law itself.

Time was, when a third part of the land of England was held by the church, and most of it in trust for the poor. The church was plundered by the existing government of the greater part of these possessions; and the poor, heretofore supported by the monasteries, became so formidable both from their numbers and their desperation, that after divers useless attempts to crush them or keep them quiet, the poor-law was adopted, as the only effectual means of restoring peace or securing property. This answered its end; and property has, since then, been quietly enjoyed by the middling and higher classes. And every estate which has been acquired during the last three centuries, has been acquired with this great legal rent-charge fastened upon it,—the maintenance of the indigent poor.

The proposal now is, that a legislature composed entirely of persons of property, and elected entirely by persons of some property, shall at once put an end to this great rent-charge, and abolish for ever the legal rights of those who are without property. A more decided or wholesale robbery and confiscation could hardly be proposed. Were the poor to meet in their assembled millions, and determine to resume the estates formerly left them, and now held by the houses of Russell, Howard, and others; or to throw open again the commons, of which the rich have more recently deprived them; this would, of course, be designated as revolutionary plunder and rebellion. But that the rich should decide, by their thousands, to rid themselves of that legal and established claim upon all the property of the country, of which the poor have been possessed for more than three centuries, and to which their right is far clearer than that of many a noble to his wide-spread domains; —that such a scheme as this should be seriously entertained and deliberately adopted, would be called, we suppose, *wise and enlightened legislation!*

But Miss Martineau adds, that "if the plea of right to subsistence be grounded

on the faults of national institutions, the right ought rather to be superseded by the rectification of those institutions, than admitted at the cost of perpetuating an institution more hurtful than all the others combined."

We have not spoken of " the faults of national institutions," but if we had placed the question on that ground, our rejoinder to Miss M. would have been obvious; — Rectify your " faults" *first.* Place the poor in that predicament in which they ought to stand; and do this *before* you take away their present rights. But Miss M. proposes nothing of this kind; her plan is *first* to take away the poor man's right of relief, and *then* to consider his grievances at some future and more convenient period.

But we allude not to " the faults of political institutions." Our plea is much simpler. We say that the poor man had certain properties, certain possessions: these you have taken away; — your dukes and earls enjoy his lands, and your gentry have divided among them his commons. All these have been held, and most of them for three hundred years, upon the stipulated tenure that the poor were to be maintained. If your lords and gentry would now wish to be off their bargain, let them throw up the lands, and let the poor again enter into possession of them. But to hold the estate, and yet to refuse to pay its ancient rent-charges, would be barefaced, flagrant, audacious robbery. No one's property would be safe, no one's property ought to be safe, if such iniquity could be quietly committed.

Fifthly: Last of all, however, we must speak of the *grossly immoral tendency* of the whole scheme.

The main object kept in view, both by the reverend doctor and the young lady, is neither more nor less than the prevention of marriage. The " preventive check," says the doctor, is our only hope; the " preventive check," says the young lady, is our main reliance. And what is this " preventive check?" It is the fear of starvation, operating to deter men from marrying. And this, by the most extraordinary abuse and perversion of language that ever fell from the lips or the pen of man, is called " *moral* restraint!"

Morality, connected with a repudiation of marriage! One might be contented with dismissing this folly at once, as a downright contradiction in terms; but we will make one or two remarks, and then leave the subject.

Morality and marriage must ever subsist in a state in correlative proportions. To decrease the prevalence of marriage is to increase the prevalence of immorality. This the whole experience of mankind informs us.

What makes the Irish, semi-barbarous as they seem in other matters, and apt to the deepest crimes—what makes them rank among the most exemplary nations in all that concerns the commerce of the sexes? The universality of marriage, the entire absence of " the preventive check."

The same observation applies to America; the late observer of which, Mrs. Trollope, is constantly tempted to ridicule the excessive modesty and propriety of manner of the females. Here, too, the "preventive check" is almost entirely unknown; marriages being universal at a very early age.

But we will allow the existence, to a limited extent, of this falsely-called " moral restraint," in London;—and there we immediately find its necessary concomitant; to wit, about 30,000 prostitutes.

In France, too, the preventive check has considerable sway; and there we find, as a natural consequence, that the illegitimate births are rapidly increasing, and bid fair to exceed in number those of wedlock.

In fact, the grand mistake committed by both the young lady and the reverend divine in this matter, as in all other parts of the question, is this,—that they theorise instead of consulting facts and human nature. In this way they seem to take for granted, that if they can but stop marriages from going on, all will be right; whereas, no more speedy or effectual method can possibly be adopted for demoralizing and breaking up a community. The natural appetites and passions of men are not to be extinguished, or placed under ban, by an act of parliament. Eighty, as we have already seen, of the hundred and one poor rioters of Wiltshire, would be condemned, by Dr. Chalmers and Miss Martineau's plan, to help-less, hopeless celibacy. Seriously, then, does the reverend doctor suppose that any thing like *morality* would have been left, or that even the least vestige of decency would have remained, in the parish to which they belonged?

We have already prostitution enough, and far too much, in England; and far, far too much of infanticide, and even still worse crimes. Does Dr. Chalmers suppose, that the married men of the community are the authors of all these abominations? No, truly! it is to his favourite "preventive check" that we owe nineteen-twentieths of them.

And yet how small is the actual amount of this falsely-called " moral restraint" that really exists among us. Mr. Sadler has most clearly shewn, that were all the men in England to marry at the age of twenty-three, 169 would be the annual number of marriages out of every 20,000 of the population. He has also shewn, that 165 of these do actually marry year by year; four only remaining as the proportion deterred, *either* by " the preventive check," or by some other causes.

If, then, with only this very trifling operation of the favourite " moral restraint," we still find so much immorality prevail among us, what might be anticipated from that more extensive influence which the reverend doctor would wish to give it? What, but a state of things resembling Paris? what, but a rapid demoralization and decay of the whole fabric of society?

In behalf, then, of public morals, we object, with the strongest abhorrence, to all resort to this favourite project of " the preventive check." But we have also shewn that the measure by which this said " preventive check" is proposed to be called into operation,—a repeal of the poor-laws,—would be grossly unjust and oppressive. Also, that it would be impracticable, from its cruelty. Also, that it may be seen in the experience of Scotland and Ireland, that as a check upon human increase, it would be wholly ineffectual. And, further, that the assumption on which it rests, of poverty being a check upon the growth of a population, is entirely and grossly unphilosophical.

ART. II.—*On Political Economy, in Connexion with the Moral State and Moral Prospects of Society.* By Thomas Chalmers, D.D., Professor of Divinity in the University of Edinburgh. Glasgow. 8vo. 1832.

AS a preacher, a Christian pastor, a man of enlightened virtue and untiring benevolence, there is perhaps no one who occupies a more elevated place in the estimation of the public, or for whom we wish to be considered as entertaining deeper respect and veneration than Dr. Chalmers; but we cannot pretend to rate him so highly as a political arithmetician. It must have been remarked by all who are acquainted with his various productions, that the mind of this eloquent person is deeply imbued with one strong master-principle, eminently suited to the station and professional calling which he has so long adorned —a sincere, earnest, ardent spirit of Christian charity, and a vivid sense of the supreme efficacy of religion in promoting the happiness of mankind. But it is the very intense and absorbing character of this feeling which, by leaving no room for other impressions, and shutting out every minor consideration, unfits him for an umpire in all those mixed questions as to the influence of other and more trivial circumstances on human welfare, which it is the province of the economist to determine.

We shall not be suspected of undervaluing the efficacy of a Christian education, when we hesitate to believe that this is the only desideratum in our civic and national economy, or the only remedy for the existing evils of our social condition capable of affording us the least glimpse of hope. Acknowledging the paramount importance of those objects which it is the duty as well as the happiness of this eminent divine to promote with all his strength, and mind, and eloquence, we yet cannot renounce, like him, the aid of other measures

measures for removing that greatest blot of the present day, the depressed condition of the body of the population in this and one or two of the equally old and densely peopled states of Europe. And the conviction we entertain of the existence of other resources, not so utterly valueless for the advancement of this object as Dr. Chalmers believes, is the more gratifying, in that the pressure of the existing misery has at length reached an alarming crisis—while the proposed panacea of moral and religious culture can operate but very slowly and gradually—must, indeed, by the confession of its most sanguine advocates, require many lustres, if not generations, to produce any very general or effectual improvement.

Our readers are already acquainted with some of the tenets of Dr. Chalmers on the subject of pauperism—his inveterate hostility to everything of the nature of a public provision for the poor—his adhesion to the Malthusian theory of population, and the Malthusian remedy for its apparent excess, ' the prudential check '—which check is always spoken of by both professors as το καλον, the essence of virtue, the great end and object of moral instruction and religious sanction. This prepossession it is which forms the substratum of the entire system of political economy contained in the volume before us. The one main principle to which every argument on every subject is there referred, and by which every question is decided, is the Malthusian axiom, that the tendency of population to increase is so much greater than that of subsistence, that no relief can be afforded to the constant pressure of numbers against food by any measures tending to augment the quantity of food ; since the numbers are sure to take a proportionate start and to be quickly brought up again to ' the limit of possible subsistence,' and only ' a more unmanageable mass of misery produced.' (p. 318.) From this axiom the obvious deduction is, that all enlargements of the means of subsistence do more harm than good—that all improvements in agriculture, or any other branch of production, are rather of the nature of curses than benefits—and that our efforts should be turned from vain and hurtful attempts at increasing the quantity of human subsistence to the one solitary object of checking the increase of the persons to be subsisted ! Upon this basis then, and with the aid of a license not uncommon with the economists, but which none has ever carried to so unconscionable a length as Dr. Chalmers—that of assuming ultimate effects to be constantly present, and what is true in periods of indefinite duration to be true at all times and in every particular instance—he proceeds to construct a series of propositions on the causes which influence the wealth
and

and happiness of nations, not a little startling in many points, we suspect, to sober and practical people.

For example, it has been generally believed hitherto, that indirect taxation falls, for the most part, on the consumers of the taxed commodities, through all classes of society ; but *nous avons changè tout cela,* and it is maintained by Dr. Chalmers, that the landlords alone pay all taxes, direct and indirect, assessed and income taxes, customs and excise. And this he demonstrates in manner following :—Every impost laid upon the labouring class, or the articles which they consume, is immediately shifted upon their employers through a rise of wages; since it follows necessarily from the Malthusian axiom on population, that the wages of labour must always be at the minimum compatible with the standard of subsistence recognized by the labouring class ; and as that standard is not altered by the imposition or removal of a tax, population immediately enlarges or contracts itself, and wages rise or fall in proportion. (p. 270.) Capitalists in turn cannot pay any tax out of their profits, because ' like the labourers, they have the power of indemnifying themselves' by diminishing the supply of capital, and consequently raising prices upon their customers. And for this the recipe is very simple and easy of execution, and one, we venture to say, much resorted to of late, namely, *to spend more than their income,* and live upon their capital, until they have reduced its plethoric excess, and so raised the rate of profit to the desired amount. If, for instance, a tax of ten per cent. were laid upon profits, threatening to cut down the income of capitalists in that proportion, they have only, says Dr. Chalmers, to go on spending their former income, to secure their getting it, through the rise of prices consequent on diminished production. (pp. 273-276.) This, we need not observe, is a charming discovery for the capitalists, especially in these hard times. *Crede quod habes, et habes.* If they wish for large profits (as which of them does not ?) they have only to live as if they made them, and lo ! their profits rise exactly to meet their expenditure ! Fortunatus's wishing-cap is in their hands. But if the taxes cannot be taken out of either *wages* or *profits,* there remain only *rents* from which they can proceed ; and *thus* the landlords are proved to be really the sole tax-payers in the community.

Our author very candidly observes, that, however certain this fact may be, few people are aware of it ; and it is difficult to make the vulgar, in their ' ignorant impatience of taxation,' sufficiently thankful to the landed interest for defraying all the national burdens ; so that it would be infinitely better to commute all taxes whatsoever for one upon the net rent of land. There is one little difficulty, to be sure, in the way of the execution of this proposal—
posal—

posal—*viz.,* that *the amount of taxes to be levied reaches near
sixty millions,* while *the entire rental of the land of the three king
doms does not probably exceed forty ;* but this is a trifle, for the
necessary consequence, according to Dr. Chalmers, of such a
commutation would be, a rise of rents and a fall of prices far
more than sufficient to compensate the landowners, not only for
the absorption of all their present rental, but also the odd twenty
millions beyond it for which they would be assessed by the tax-
gatherer ! Lest we should be suspected of exaggeration, we
quote a few of the passages in which these peculiar doctrines and
novel proposals are embodied. For example—

' It were no small advantage if landlords were made to bear the
whole burdens of the state ostensibly, as they do really ; that the
importance, the paramount importance, of landed wealth and the landed
interest might stand forth, nakedly and without disguise, to the recognition of all men. So that it were well for them, if compelled, even
though against their will, to pay all taxes.' (p. 301.) ' They would
by this lose nothing, and besides have a clear and unencumbered
gain from all the enlargement that would take place in husbandry.
. . . . The change that we venture to recommend would spread an
augmented richness and value over the whole of their property. It
were for their incalculable benefit, could they only be made to perceive
it, that all taxes were commuted into a territorial impost. . . . . This
is the way to reconcile the necessary support of government with the
utmost demands of liberalism ; and in these days of fearful conflict
between the two elements of order and liberty, we believe that nothing
could more effectually harmonise them than this discharge of the
general community from all the burdens of the state, along with the
distinct and total imposition of them on the proprietors of the soil.
We want the whole weight of our taxation to lie upon them visibly,
even as we think it lies upon them virtually and substantially. They
would be indemnified by the cheapening of all commodities, consequent on the removal of the present duties, and, more than indemnified, they would be rewarded and enriched by the new rents yielded
to them from the enlargement of the agriculture.'—p. 307-309.

Nay, so inexhaustible is this source of national revenue in our
author's opinion, that his chief regret is, that too little of the produce of the land is at present appropriated by government for the
support of public functionaries, and that ' the *mere proprietors,*
the *fruges consumere nati,* are allowed to reserve too much of it.'
(p. 349.) He would adopt ' a more severe taxation than our
politicians of the present day have the courage to propose ;' ' a
more fully equipped and better-paid agency in all the departments
of national usefulness.' (p. 372.) To be sure, as some little
compensation to the landowners, he speaks of the extra-taxation
being laid out in ' a liberal provision in all the branches of the
public

public service for their younger sons—whether in the law, or in the church, or in the colleges, or in the army, or in any other well-appointed establishment, kept up for the good of the nation.'

' Under this arrangement, we should combine, with a provision for the younger branches of families, a greater efficiency and amount of public service ; a remedy against the destitution of younger children, and withal a better-served nation.'   In this way, ' through the organ of government, each estate may be looked upon as loaded with jointures for the sake of the younger members of families ; who, at the same time, instead of simple receivers, have to labour, in some vocation or other, for the benefit of the community.   And, believing, as we do, that the real incidence of taxes is on land, we would enlist all the forces of natural sentiment and affection on the side of a larger revenue to government, and a larger allowance to public functionaries of all orders.'—p. 373.

However, the landlords are not to get their money back on too easy terms, for—

' It will not for a moment be imagined that while we would apportion a much larger amount of the nation's wealth to the objects of public service, we contend for any hereditary or family right to that portion, on the part of the younger brothers of our aristocracy.   It should lie open to the competition of all the worth and talent which may exist in any quarter of society.   In the exercise of a *virtuous* patronage, it should always be disposed of to those who can give the largest return for it, in the value of their services. . . . . And we contend for no more, in behalf of the younger sons, than that they should be admitted on equal terms to the competitions of this then larger and wealthier preferment, along with men of the requisite intelligence and accomplishment from all other classes of the community.'

We fear there will be many parents whose ' feelings of natural affection ' will be inclined to prefer the vulgar mode of providing for their younger children by direct legal settlement, to the scheme Dr. Chalmers is kind enough to propose to them, of transferring a large portion of their estates to government, to be subsequently contended for by their sons in common with all other classes of the community.   Even this boon will hardly reconcile the landed proprietors of Britain to take upon themselves the entire taxation of the realm.

That there is some truth, mixed with a great deal of error, in the novel opinions and arguments of Dr. Chalmers, we willingly admit; though we are compelled to add that as what is new in them is not true, so what is true is not new.   The error will be found uniformly to have its root in that strong impression, already adverted to, of the impossibility of preventing the direful pressure of population against food, except by a restraint upon

marriage,

marriage, successfully inculcated upon the people as the very essence of morality and religion, by every pastor and instructor in the land. Fraught with this one prevailing idea, the imagination of the learned Doctor sees in every improvement of the condition of the lower classes but an opening for the generation of a greater mass of future misery; and, running through the catalogue of economical remedies proposed by other writers or statesmen for the evils of that condition, he rejects them all as ultimately pernicious, *for the very reason that they are immediately beneficial!* We will take a brief view of his labours in this course.

The work, very properly, begins by calling attention to the circumstances which influence the supply of *food* to a community, as the pivot upon which turn all questions relating to its economical condition. He proves (by the same argument we employed in a former Number) how inconsistent with fact is the assertion of those who babble about ' the decreasing fertility of the soil to which cultivation descends' necessarily occasioning a deterioration in the circumstances of the human race. He shows that every improvement, not in agriculture only, but also in manufacturing labour and in commercial communications, allows an extension of cultivation over fresh soils, less fertile or accessible, less valuable, in short, than those already entered on, and a larger expenditure of labour and capital on the latter without any falling off in their returns,—in the quaint, but expressive, phrase of our author,— ' brings both a broader belt and a deeper stratum of land under the plough.' But, though bold enough to desert his oracle, Mr. Malthus, on this point, he cannot get clear of the unfortunate prepossession with which the ' theory of population' has inoculated him. Even while acknowledging, in so many words, that as the skill and knowledge of man increase, he is enabled to obtain from the poorer soils a more liberal subsistence than he could extract from the richest at the earlier stages of his history, the Doctor sees not in this fact, coupled with the equally undeniable one, that but a fraction even of the very richest soils of the globe are yet brought under cultivation, anything to absolve mankind from taking a *more* anxious care to prevent the growth of their numbers *now* than they have hitherto taken; but struck by the fancied vision of an ultimate limit to the quantity of food which the globe can be made to produce, he calls on us, as if the enemy were at the gates, to abandon all other considerations,—to take no thought about the means, possibly in our power, for keeping our subsistence, for a time, at least, perhaps for ever, on a level with our wants,—but to apply all our energies to the great object of retarding the increase of our numbers! As if it were enough to prove our means to be

limited,

limited, to make it clear that we ought to refrain from employing them as far as they will go ! By this rule, since life will, alas ! have an end, we ought on no account to prolong it. Man can never be made perfect; how wrong then to attempt his improvement ! Happiness, like population, has an ultimate limit; we had better be content with misery ! In one instance the rule does hold good. There is a term to the patience of the public ; and we warn the anti-populationists that, if they value their reputation for sanity, they would do well to refrain from provoking it any further.

It is, indeed, an extraordinary *monomania* which affects these gentlemen. The idea of an ultimate limit to the globe's possible productiveness tyrannizes over their imaginations, and gives rise to the strangest opinions and rules of conduct. Dr. Chalmers overtops them all: his whole soul is absorbed by the frightful prospect of the time when every rood of soil on the face of the earth shall maintain its full complement of human beings, and it will be impossible for one additional individual

—— ' quocunque loco, quocunque recessu,
Unius sese dominum fecisse lacertæ.'

Like Alexander, the Professor

' Frets at the pigmy limits of the globe—'
' Æstuat, infelix, angusto limite mundi.'

It might be enough to laugh at this preposterous fallacy. But since it is, *mirabile dictu !* the fundamental axiom from which all the propositions of Dr. Chalmers are directly and specifically deduced, we think it but fair to give the principal parts of the passage in which he conceives himself to have established its truth, and analyze the value of his argument, or, rather, for that is its true name, his assumption. In spite of the increasing powers of man to extract subsistence from the less naturally fertile soils,

' Yet it must be quite evident,' he says, ' that whether in single countries, or in the whole world, this is a process which cannot go on indefinitely. The time may be indefinitely distant, and, indeed, may never come, when the absolute and impassable barrier shall at length be arrived at.' [With submission to his abler logic, we should presume to conclude from this that the process *can* 'go on indefinitely.'] ' To be satisfied that there is such a barrier, one has only to look to the extent and quality of the land in any region of the earth. . . . As sure as every country has its limit, and every continent its shore, we must acquiesce in it as one of the stern necessities of our condition, that the earth we tread upon can only be made to yield a limited produce, and so to sustain a limited population. . . . It seems very generally admitted that *should it ever come to this*, the population brought to a stand-still in respect of numbers, must either have to encounter
great

great positive distress, or must anticipate this distress by a preventive regimen. . . . But then the imagination of many is, that not until the world be fully cultivated and fully peopled, shall we have any practical interest in the question. They seem to think of the doctrine of Malthus, that the consideration of it may, with all safety, be postponed, till the agriculture of every country and every clime shall have been carried to its extreme perfection ; and that, meanwhile, population may proceed as rapidly and recklessly as it may.'

We acknowledge ourselves of the number of those who think that until we have approached somewhat nearer the utmost limit of the globe's capabilities for supporting us than the immeasurable distance which at present divides us from it, we may safely leave the progress of population to the laws which nature has established, uninterfered with by artificial ' checks' or stimulants; and that sapient calculations, as to the extreme number of myriads of human beings that might find elbow-room on the globe without pushing each other into the sea (a consideration which our author seriously moots), have no more rational bearing on our actual situation, and the most fitting line of conduct for us to adopt in the present day, than the old scholastic problem as to how many angels can dance on the point of a needle. If we saw the owner and sole occupier of an extensive estate cultivate only the single field which immediately adjoined his habitation, and, though complaining bitterly of his straitened circumstances and want of the necessaries of life, yet refuse to send his plough into the more distant fields belonging to him, on the alleged ground that there was an *ultimate limit* to his property, and that, *therefore*, it was incumbent on him to pinch his appetites, and limit his desires to what he could contrive to grow on his home field,—if under this impression he was to refrain from marriage, and deny himself the society of his family and friends, though sorely against his natural tastes,—should we not pronounce him a hypochondriac, if not a lunatic ? But in what particular would such a fantasy differ from that of a writer who proclaims a pressing necessity for every nation of the earth to guard carefully, by restraints upon marriage, against any increase of their numbers, beyond what the limited territory they happen to occupy will support,—at a time when but a fractional portion of the earth's surface is yet cultivated at all, and that very imperfectly —when myriads of acres of the richest soil, in the finest climates, are yet covered with forests or jungle, and tenanted but by reptiles and brutes ? And be it remarked, that in this comparison we have greatly favoured the Malthusian disciple, because the hypochondriac has, perhaps, a right to look forward to a fixed ultimate limit to the possible produce of his estate ; whereas the limit of the potential produce of the globe is indefinite—the productive

powers

powers of man being unlimited, and continuing to augment, at the same time that the area on which he exercises them is, if he but wills it, enlarged.

Dr. Chalmers does not allude to that exquisite proposition in which it was arithmetically and mathematically demonstrated, that while man, who, on the highest estimate, but doubles his numbers in twenty-five years, multiplies in a *geometrical* ratio, the multiplication of wheat, which increases from ten to sixty fold in one year, proceeds only in an *arithmetical* ratio. We must believe, however, that he had been studying it when he asserted, that ' no human skill or labour could make the produce of the soil increase at the rate at which population *would* increase.' We see a direct practical contradiction to this bold assertion in numerous points—in America, north and south, New South Wales, &c., where no artificial checks are in operation, where population has its full swing, and the only want experienced is that of *men*, to develope by their labour the infinite capacity of the soil, and to consume the abundance with which it is ready to reward their lightest efforts. The Malthusian philosophy would not obtain credit for an hour there. And ought not this consideration alone to convince its propagators, that the redundancy which affrights them is local, not general, and to be cured far more easily and with a happier result, by a spreading of the local excess, as fast as it appears, over ' fresh soils and pastures ever new,' than by putting matrimony in *taboo?*

These spots form really ' the extreme margin of cultivation,' where the question is to be solved, and the lesson learnt of the comparative tendencies to increase of subsistence and population— not the belts of poor land in England or the Netherlands, which the purely local circumstances of demand and supply of food, under the influence of monopolies, poor laws, and a complicated and highly artificial state of society, cause to be, from time to time, taken under the plough. But the fact is, that except in the passage we have just quoted, where the capacity of the world at large to supply mankind with sustenance, is handled, as we think we have shown, in no very lucid or logical manner, and a short subsequent chapter on emigration, which we shall presently notice, Dr. Chalmers, throughout his work, like his predecessor and master, Malthus, confines his view to a limited territory,—in truth, though not avowedly, to the British islands alone; and finding a slowly receding barrier to the safe extension of population within those limits, shuts his eyes to the facility of overstepping them, and sails away in proud and triumphant conviction of the solidity of the sieve in which he proposes to navigate the ocean of political economy. In fact, however, the learned divine should have spared himself the trouble of writing any further than his first chapter; for

for in the one assumption therein laid down, he has settled the whole question. If it is once established as a fundamental proposition, that ' food *cannot* be made to increase so fast as population,' it is surely a waste of time to go on to indite a volume, for the sake of proving that neither home nor foreign colonization—nor remission of taxes—nor extension of trade—nor a more equal distribution of property—nor the cottage and cow system—nor a poor law—can so accelerate the increase of food as to make it keep pace with population. Our author, however, sees not this ; but having first, in the short paragraph we have quoted, begged the question in the lump, proceeds with great gravity, and much labour, and an infinite expenditure of eloquent language, by parading this postulate over and over again, in an endless variety of brilliant phrases,—to ' demonstrate' it in detail!

The first windmill attacked is home-colonization. One touch of his magic lance of course overthrows this project ; for if the whole globe is too narrow for the supply of our increasing wants, so *à fortiori* must be our little speck of an island. The object of the next encounter is the supposed increase of employment to be obtained by an extension of trade. And here the Doctor discovers something very like ' a mare's nest,'—the principle, namely, that ' employment is productive of nothing but its own produce.' ' All,' he says, ' that a stocking-maker contributes to society is simply *stockings*.'—(p. 49.) And the same is true (strange as it may sound) with every branch of manufactures and commerce. ' None of these add anything to the means of subsistence at the disposal of the community, which would remain the same though they were all put a stop to.' Now the first of these propositions will be disputed by none. But the corollary which follows is not by any means a necessary consequence. Manufactures and commerce, it is true, only produce commodities of secondary importance, since they are not essential to the support of man ; and, in a late article, we have ourselves endeavoured to call attention to the fact of the subordinate rank which these employments occupy, as compared with agriculture, by which we are supplied with the first necessaries of life. So long as there is an abundance of these, the mass of the community must always be in comfortable circumstances ; even though there should be a comparative deficiency in their supply of manufactures and articles of luxury. But no abundance of the latter class of objects can at all compensate for a falling off in the production of food. On the contrary, such objects could in that case only encumber the market, the comparative scarcity and dearness of necessaries leaving the great body of consumers nothing to throw away upon superfluities.

Still,

Still, though considering it highly important that this broad distinction should be recognized between the two great classes of productions, necessaries and luxuries, we are far from stretching the argument to the length of declaring, that manufactures and commerce are of trifling importance, and might be put a stop to without any serious loss to society,—or that their increase is not productive of essential advantages. The stocking-trade, we willingly allow, produces only stockings ; the clothing-trade, cloth ; the wine-trade, wine ; and so on. But just as ' trifles make the sum of human things,' so, in the aggregate, these several branches of trade produce all that there is in the country of wealth, comfort, splendour, taste, civilization—all that distinguishes us from a horde of barbarians, clothed in skins, and tolerably provided with coarse food. Moreover, the extension of commerce and manufactures reacts upon agriculture, and tends to increase the production of food. Our author admits that this was the case throughout Europe at the termination of the middle ages ; and himself, in an able sketch after Adam Smith and Robertson, traces the economic change which then took place, in virtue of the new tastes and habits inspired in the owners and cultivators of the soil, by the presentation to their notice of those articles of splendour and luxury, which manufactures had produced and commerce brought to their doors. But he denies that the further extension of the arts of luxury can have any effect in the present day on agriculture. We think he is both inconsistent and wrong, for the stimulus is enduring. It is a constant principle of human nature, that our wants increase with the means of gratifying them. And well is it that we are so constituted. Were man the sober, chastened, and easily contented animal, which moralists have sometimes, with false views of human welfare, attempted to make him —did a mere shelter from the weather, and a sufficiency of wholesome. food and coarse clothing, satisfy his wishes, ' content to dwell in decencies for ever,' his species would probably have forever remained in a condition little superior to that of the cattle he has domesticated. Art, science, literature,—all the pleasures of refinement, taste, and intellectual occupation, would have been unknown; more than this—the ingenuity by which the gifts of nature and the enjoyments of mere animal existence are multiplied and heightened, would never have been called into action, and the prospect which, in spite of local and temporary checks, seems to us continually brightening, of a progressive and indefinite amelioration in the circumstances of mankind, would have been closed at once. But it is not so. Every augmentation in the number and variety of the means of human gratification has the certain effect of increasing the number of human wants and desires, and of stimulating industry and ingenuity to satisfy them by increased labour or skill in the production of those commodities, by exchange for which the desired objects may be obtained. Even if we admitted, which we are far from doing, that the improvement of our manufactures and the increase of our foreign and internal trade have no stimulating influence on our native agriculture, and, therefore, add nothing to our home supplies of food—yet it is impossible to deny that by offering novel and varied gratifications to the inhabitants of other countries, more fertile and less highly cultivated than our own, we must and do excite them to greater industry and energy in the creation of those agricultural products of which we stand in need. Should this operation likewise be too slow in its progress, and neither the advance of our own agriculture nor that of the foreign grower fully supply the demand of our increasing population for food, there remains the simple and obvious resource,—which our author's favourite prejudice alone hinders him from perceiving,—of enlarging the area of our own cultivation—of employing our own surplus labour and capital in raising the required food from the fertile soil of our colonies,—considering them, as we have a right to do, in the light of mere outlying portions of British territory. By the adoption of this resource, our agriculture, our manufactures, and our commerce might continue to extend themselves and mutually stimulate each other's increase, their joint progress effecting a continuous amelioration in our social condition, without any perceivable limit or hindrance to the process, but such as could proceed from wanton error and mismanagement alone.

All this, however, would by no means suit Dr. Chalmers's views. Therefore having disposed of trade, he goes on to consider whether the increase of *capital* holds out any promise of relief. This, of course, is easily negatived by virtue of the assumption upon which he set out: for *within a territory of limited extent and fertility*, where all but the very inferior qualities of land are already cultivated, the profits of capital must be kept down by the slow rate at which improvements in the productive powers of agriculture proceed; and this low rate of profit must check, in turn, the accumulation of capital. *Why* we are to confine our view of the field for the employment of capital within such narrow limits, is not mooted; but it is clear that such a limitation is purely imaginary, and that ' the margin of separation between the cultivated and uncultivated land,' the place to which Dr. Chalmers professes to bring all his propositions to be tested, may be indefinitely removed by the judicious outlay of capital upon some of the millions of acres of yet virgin land within our reach, without any

falling

falling off in the profit derivable, but much more probably with a great increase, as is shown by the high rate of interest in all colonies and newly-cultivated countries. Standing, however, upon his narrow and ' slowly receding margin,' with the same faith as if he were fixed upon a rock of adamant, the Professor of Divinity triumphantly oraculizes in the following manner, *e. g.*—

' When the progress of agriculture becomes slow or difficult, or, most of all, when it touches upon the extreme limit, then the impotency of accumulation on the part of capitalists must be severely felt. Each new investiture, in fact, will then be followed up by an adverse re-action or recoil upon themselves. As they grow in capital, they will decline in revenue. There is no escaping from this consequence. . . . Capital is thus hemmed in on all sides by a slowly-receding boundary, which it cannot overpass ; and beyond which, if it attempt to enlarge itself, it is broken into surges at the barrier by which it is surrounded.' —p. 105.

We need scarcely repeat that there is no such extreme limit to agriculture, except the distant and indefinite limit to the capacity of the globe, to which we are probably no nearer now, than we were five thousand years ago. Bound within the necromantic circle which Malthus has forbidden him to dream of overstepping, the doctor's predicament reminds us of the poor bird, whom a conjuror persuades that he has fastened him down to a table, by drawing a chalk line upon the board on which he rests his head.

' The next resource which dazzles the imagination of philan-thropists and statesmen, is foreign trade. This is held to be a fountain-head of wealth and employment, which in the eyes of many are altogether indefinite.' So says Dr. Chalmers, and forthwith proceeds to break a spear against this doctrine, taking first the case of a country which imports no food. He combats, as before, ' the delusion' that anything else accrues from foreign trade to a nation, ' beyond a slight increase of enjoyment, the substitution of one luxury for another.'

' There is mysticism in the assertion that the wine-trade of Portugal confers any other benefit on the nation, than simply the benefit of wine, or the West India trade, than sugar and coffee, or the China trade, than tea. The East and West Indies are regarded as the two hands of the empire ; and the imagination is, that were our connexion with these destroyed, Britain would suffer as much as from the lopping off of two hands, or, in other words, would be shorn of its strength and its capacity for action, in virtue of this sore mutilation. It would positively be shorn of nothing but its sugar and tea !' . . . . ' Should we consent to forego these enjoyments, then, at the bidding of our will, the whole strength at present embarked in the service of pro-curing them, would be transferred to other services ; to the extension

of

of home-trade—to the enlargement of our national establishments—to the service of defence, or conquests, or scientific research, or Christian philanthropy.'—p. 191.

This is quite M. Purgon in the ' Malade Imaginaire '—' Vous avez la un œil droit, que je me ferais crever si j'étais en votre place. Ne voyez-vous pas qu'il incommode l'autre, *et lui dérobe sa nourriture?* Croyez-moi, faites-vous le crever au plutôt, vous en verrez plus clair de l'œil gauche.' But Argan's answer, ' Cela n'est pas pressè,' will be that probably of our merchants to the assurance of Dr. Chalmers, that ' our commerce, though lopped off by the hand of violence, would leave untouched the strength and stamina of the nation.' (p. 228.) ' It would be as great and flourishing a community as before—as competent to all the purposes of defence and national independence ; and, *though shorn of her commerce and colonies*, though bereft of these showy appendages, as available, and, we think, *more so*, for all the dearest objects of patriotism.' (p. 230.)   These doctrines, we fear, will not be more popular on 'Change, than will be the proposal to commute all the taxes for one upon rent, in Parliament.   Whether in time Dr. Chalmers's eloquence will persuade us to realize his Utopia of a ' self-contained' nation,—producing all it consumes within its own limits, shutting itself out from all communication with the rest of the world, and sedulously keeping down its population by ' virtuous efforts,' considerably within the number which its internal resources are calculated to maintain in plenty,—we know not.   This, however, we know, that if our first parents had acted on these principles, their descendants would never have spread beyond the boundaries of Mesopotamia.

Our attention is next called to the case of a country which imports agricultural produce.   The doctor begins with drawing a distinction between the ' natural' population of a country, that which is chiefly supported on food the produce of its own soil, and the ' excrescent' portion of its population, which, when a country possesses any superior advantages for manufactures or commerce over its neighbours, is maintained chiefly on food imported from thence in exchange for its labour in those capacities.   This is all right enough : we do not, however, agree with our author, when he deprecates this ' enlargement of our population beyond the limits of our own agricultural basis,' and says—

' The only effect is to foster an excrescence, which, if not mortal to us as to other commercial states, is just because, with the uttermost of our false and foolish ambition, we cannot overstretch the foreign trade, so far as they did, beyond the limits of the home agriculture.   By thus seeking to enlarge our pedestal, we make it
greatly

greatly more tottering and precarious than before; for, like the feet of Nebuchadnezzar's image, it is composed of different materials, partly of clay and partly of iron. The fabric bulges, as it were, into greater dimensions than before; but while its original foundation is of rock, the projecting parts are propped upon quicksands; for the sake of lodging a few additional inmates in which, we would lay the pain of a felt insecurity, if not an actual hazard, upon all the family. We rejoice in the luxuriance of a rank and unwholesome overgrowth; and, mistaking bulk for solidity, do we congratulate ourselves on the formation of an excrescence, which should rather be viewed as the blot and distemper of our nation.'—p. 231.

We have quoted this passage at length both as a specimen of Dr. Chalmers's peculiarity of style, and because there is an apparent plausibility in the argument it contains against the allowing, if we could help it, any increase of our population beyond what our own soils will supply. But, in the first place, not being believers in the efficacy of the Malthusian specific, we do not admit that we have the power of trimming and squaring our population as we may think fit; and, when at any time they have increased, or threaten to do so, beyond what the agricultural produce of our own soils will support, it is surely better to allow the surplus to maintain themselves in independence by working up manufactured commodities which they can exchange with foreigners for the food they require — than, by prohibiting or throwing restrictions in the way of such an exchange, to drive them to consume, *in unproductive pauperism,* a portion of our home-growth, already, by the supposition, but barely sufficient for the remainder of the population. Secondly, our author's argument, which is only the old one, (dressed up in a new and more flowery fashion,) of the danger of depending for a portion of our food on foreigners—even if conceded with regard to them, is not applicable to the principle of *colonial* supply. It is not considered unwise to allow the growth of an ' excrescent ' population in Middlesex or Birmingham, beyond what the county or parish could sustain; or to encourage the dependence of numerous families in Lancashire upon provisions imported from Ireland. Nor can we see that it would be a whit more imprudent to extend the division of labour in the same manner throughout the empire at large, and to employ our Canadian fellow-subjects in growing on their rich soils the corn which is needed for the support of a portion of our English or Scotch population, who are in their turn occupied in availing themselves of the peculiar advantages this country possesses in its coal and iron, mechanical inventions, manufacturing establishments, and consummate skill, in producing articles of clothing, utensils, or luxuries for the use of the Canadians. Our author

author commits a strange blunder when, in order to strengthen his argument, he endeavours to show that ' a given excrescent population betokens only half the amount of wealth or resources in a country which an equal natural population does.' (p. 234.) We have not room for the entire quotation, which, like most of his demonstrations, is rather prolix—but the *given* ' natural ' population is reckoned by him twice over, once as a body of manufacturers and once as agriculturists, so that no wonder it appears to be double the given ' excrescent' population, which is only counted once. He proves, in short, that an artisan supported on home-grown food creates double the amount of wealth that is created by an artisan maintained on foreign-grown food, by reckoning as the creation of the former the produce of the agriculturist who feeds him—that is, of a *second* workman. By the same rule a man who, before the division of labour, spent half his time in providing himself with food and the other half in procuring clothing, was twice as productive as when, in the progress of improvement, he spends his whole time in one occupation alone, as growing food, and provides himself with clothing by exchange with another whose labour is equally confined to the production of that class of commodities.

In spite of this, Dr. Chalmers is by no means favourable to restrictions on the importation of foreign corn, but acknowledges that

' to this quarter we may look for a certain stretch or enlargement of external resources, whereby room and sustenance would be afforded for a greater number of families than we can now accommodate. Yet, after all, like every other augmentation in the outward means of support, it would but afford a temporary relief to the pressure under which we are at present labouring. As is usual with every increase, from whatever quarter of the means of subsistence, it would be speedily followed up by a multiplication of our numbers, and so land us in a larger, but not on that account a better-conditioned community than before. . . . . It is not by means of economic enlargements, but of moral principles and restraints, that the problem of our difficulties is at length to be fully and satisfactorily resolved. No possible enlargement from without will ever suffice for the increasing wants of a recklessly increasing population. We look for our coming deliverance in a moral change, and not in any or in all of those economic changes put together, which form the great panacea of so many of our statesmen. Without the prudence and virtue of our common people, we shall only have a bulkier, but withal as wretched and distempered, a community as ever.'—p. 239.

In short, the burden of the song—the assumed disease and the specific, the bugbear and the exorcism, are introduced to solve this question as well as the rest.

The next resource whose futility is demonstrated by the same logic,

logic, is the remission of taxes, which, far from being any gain to the working or middle classes, it is declared, would only be ' a sacrifice of the public good to the splendour and effeminacy of the upper orders of society ; . . . . that the landed and the funded aristocracy may be more delicately regaled or more magnificently attired and attended.' (p. 260.) We have already shown by what process of reasoning the author thinks he has proved that all taxation, whether laid on income or on commodities is resolvable in its effects into a tax on the net rent of land ;—namely, by the hypothesis, that both capital and population are possessed of such extraordinary elasticity, as to maintain profits and wages always at a minimum, so that ' any remission of taxes which bear upon the maintenance or employment of the industrious would be but the *momentary* loosening of a bondage, immediately followed up by a growth which will cause the pressure to be sensibly and really as great as before.' (p. 298.) And in the same manner, were any additional impost laid on the industrious classes, they would be *speedily* ' *compensated by* ' (what think ye ?) ' *a gradual process of decay !* ' ' Through this we should be at length landed in a smaller society, and a smaller capital for conducting its business than before.' Our author admits, that this *compensatory* process would be ' a melancholy one '—that ' taxes on industry and capital *do* operate just as a blight on the quality of the soil '—that ' it is only by a lessening of the country's food, and through a midway passage of penury and distress, they lead to a lessening both of capital and population ; ' while a removal of taxes from the industrious classes to the landed and monied, *would* cause ' a subsequent enlargement of the wealth of the former classes, *until* they were overtaken by the increase of capital and population.' (p. 300.) In other words, taxes on the industrious, it is acknowledged, *are* paid by them *until* they are starved and ruined into absolute insolvency ; and the remission of such taxes *would* proportionately raise both profits and wages, until both capitalists and labourers had, ' in the heyday of their prosperity,' *so multiplied their wealth and numbers,* as by the effect of competition once more to lower the returns to them ! And *these* are the grounds upon which, in the same page, it is asserted, that the direction of taxation is a matter of indifference—that all taxes are paid by the landlords alone, and none by the other classes of society, who are accused of entertaining ' a misplaced antipathy to taxation,' and a doltish ignorance of the advantages that accrue to them from every increase of the public burthens !

The fallacy by which our author is led into such gross inconsistencies evidently lies in his assumption of ultimate for immediate effects, jumping over the intermediate processes of decay or
prosperity,

prosperity, by which he believes the supply of capital and labour to be contracted or expanded on the imposition or removal of a tax, as ' ephemeral,' and not worth taking into account. These processes, the ' consummation ' of which is by him supposed to be instantaneous, *can*, however, in truth only be arrived at, with regard to *labour*, after the lapse of a generation *at least*, but in all probability never, owing to the interference of the numerous disturbing causes which so long a period of time always introduces. And this is upon his own hypothesis of a limited agricultural area. With the unlimited field for the utilization of labour and capital which the world really affords, there is evidently no tendency whatever in the increase of either to bring about a reduction in their remuneration.

The subject next considered is tithes ; and we are happy to be able to coincide in much of what the doctor urges, in impressive and forcible language, upon this topic. He denounces them, to be sure, in their present form, as ' an incubus on agriculture,' preventing a wide enlargement of the field of cultivation ; and is clear that they should be commuted for a rent-charge, or for land, in which case they would be precisely on the footing of rent— and all the vast benefits of a church establishment would be placed in security at no expense or sacrifice whatever to the community. We do not think it necessary to enter into this part of the subject here :—it is one that could not be adequately discussed in a short space—but we are happy to quote the following just and sagacious general remarks of a Presbyterian bystander :—

' The support of a priesthood has been set in opposition to the general comfort of families. Its only opposition is to the greater wealth and luxury of landlords. The men who do something are eyed with jealousy, because in possession of an interest and a property, which, if not theirs, would but serve to enlarge the affluence and useless splendour of the men who do nothing. Never were the feelings of generous and high-minded patriotism more egregiously misplaced, or the public good more in danger of being sacrificed to the mere semblance of a principle. We often hear of the omnipotence of truth ; and that the prejudice of many ages, the deep-laid institutions of many centuries, must, at length, give way before it. If the ecclesiastical establishments of our land shall be of the number which are destined to fall, and that because the temporalities which belong to them have been pronounced, by the oracles of our day, as an oppression and a burden on the general population, then, instead of truth being their judge or their executioner, they shall have fallen at the hand of cunning and deceitful witnesses—they shall have perished in the midst of strong delusion, at the mandate, and by the authority, of a lie.

' When power gets into the hands of the multitude, the danger is, that it may be exercised not for guidance, but for destruction. They
generally

generally act by impulse, and not by discernment: and, if only possessed with the idea, or rather with the watch-word, that the church is an incubus on the prosperity of the nation—no voice of wisdom will arrest the determination of sweeping it utterly away. We hold that a church establishment is the most effective of all machines for the moral instruction of the people ; and, that, if once taken down, there is no other instrumentality by which it can adequately be replaced. We are aware that it may be feebly, and even corruptly, administered ; but the way to rectify this, is, not to demolish the apparatus, but to direct its movements. We should hail the ascendency of the popular will, if it proceeded on this distinction ; and, instead of deprecating, should rejoice in the liberalism of the present day, did it but know how to modify so as not to extinguish. It is because democracy, instead of a regulating power, is a sweeping whirlwind, that we dread its encroachments. It is hers, not with skilful fingers to frame and adapt the machinery of our institutions ; but with the force of an uplifted arm, to inflict upon them the blow of extermination. Whatever the coming changes in the state of our society may be, there is none that would more fatally speed the disorganization and downfall of this great kingdom, than if a hand of violence were put forth on the rights and revenues of the church of England. Even with the present distribution of her wealth, it will be found, that the income of her higher, as well as humbler clergy, has been vastly overrated ; and nothing, we believe, would contribute more to soften the prejudices of the nation against this venerable hierarchy, than a full exposure of all her temporalities, grounded on the strictest and most minute inquiry. And, certain it is, that, with the best possible distribution of this wealth, it will be found hardly commensurate to the moral and spiritual wants of the now greatly increased population. If all pluralities were abolished, and the enormous overgrown towns and cities of the land were adequately provided with churches, it would be found, that the whole of the existing revenues would hardly suffice for a requisite number even of *merely working ecclesiastics.* We cannot imagine a policy more ruinous, than that which would impair the maintenance of a church that has so long been illustrious for its learning, and that promises now to be the dispenser of greater blessings to the people, than at any former period of its history, by the undoubted increase of its public virtue and its piety.'

We are surprised that Dr. Chalmers should adopt that silly cant phrase of ' working clergy'—as if a faithful bishop were not in truth a more hardly-worked man than any parish priest in his diocese ;—but making allowance for this slip, the passage which we have quoted appears to us well worthy of careful meditation.

We next arrive at a discussion of the question, whether the interests of a community can be advanced by a greater or less subdivision of its landed property, through the laws of inheritance. Our author's opinion rests upon the peculiar theory he espouses
on

on the incidence of taxation ; and indeed his reasonings tend to make it appear the perfection of policy, for the government of a country to be its sole landlord, with a dependent aristocracy of placemen and *gens de bureau.* We heartily agree with him in deprecating a minute subdivision of landed property, ' in which case there would be few, if any, of the landed proprietors that could command any of the higher enjoyments of life,' and in the belief, that ' in virtue of elegance, luxury, and leisure, being an inheritance, there is a blessing in the present system of things to the whole mass of society ;' that ' from this higher galaxy of rank and fortune, there are droppings, as it were, of a bland and benignant influence on the general platform of humanity.' But ' why mistake reverse of wrong for right ?' why forget that the sole choice does not lie between two extremes ? Because an agrarian partition of the land would be an injury to all classes, it does not follow that the smaller the number of landed proprietors the better. He recommends, that ' instead of *letting down the peerage of our realms to the external condition of our peasantry,* we should rather go forth among the peasantry, and pour such a moral lustre over them, as might equalize them, either to peers or princes, in all the loftiest attributes of humanity.'—(p. 370.) This, with reverence, is the figure of speech styled flummery. It is not thus that the great question is to be argued, as to where lies the happy medium between the extremes of subdivision and concentration of landed proprietorship, and by what modification of the laws of inheritance it is to be secured. We have not space here even to touch upon this subject, but it must be obvious to all, that if there are great evils in the agrarianism of France, there are likewise some attendant on the excessive accumulation of landed property into few hands, which has been in gradual progress in this country during the past century, to the almost complete extinction of those two most valuable classes, which once formed the staple of English society, the minor resident country-gentleman and the independent yeoman.

The last (but one) of all the expedients for restoring the distempered community to health, which our author discusses and dismisses as inefficacious, is emigration. Now we submit that he would have acted more wisely, by taking this *first,* because the arguments by which he has attempted to prove the inadequacy of every other resource, whether increase of employment, of commerce, of capital, or the remission of taxes and of tithes, were all based on the assumption of a necessarily limited area, whence our increasing population could supply themselves with food ; and it, therefore, surely behoved him to begin by proving the existence of such a limitation, and the impossibility of widening it by emigration.

gration. The fact, however, is, as indeed we have already made it appear, that his entire work, precisely like that of his great master, Malthus, with the exception of this very scanty chapter on emigration, has reference only to a country absolutely limited, in its supply of food and the disposal of its population, to its own soils, and those already in a high state of culture. When such a country can be pointed out to us, we may think it worth while to enter more at large than we have done into the arguments with which the doctor has been labouring to destroy shadows of his own creation.

Let us now see in what manner, when obliged at length to face the question of emigration, and acknowledge that no country, least of all this, is surrounded by an ·impassable wall, he contrives to avoid perceiving the clue it affords to all the embarrassments which the assumption of a limited area has enabled him to draw around a labouring population given to the heinous offence of ' marrying and being given in marriage' without an accurate previous calculation of all the circumstances likely to affect the demand and supply of labour in the course of the ensuing generation.

' When the agriculture of a country arrives at its limit, there is a pressure that would not be felt, but for the tendency of the population to increase. But long before this limit is reached, is the pressure felt ; because the tendency to an increase in the population exceeds the rate of enlargement in the agriculture.'

Agreed ; and now for the conclusion from these premises :—

' The probability, then, is, that even emigration will not eventually alleviate the distresses of our land. The same cause which outstrips the enlargement within, may also outstrip the efflux abroad.'—p. 379.

Was there ever such a *non sequitur?* Is it not like saying, that because a man is thirsty, the probability is, he would drink the Tweed dry ; or that it were vain to give liberty to a captive, because the same cause which makes him find his cell too confined for his wishes, will lead him, like Alexander, to think the world all too narrow likewise ! The limit to the agriculture of a country, under the circumstances of Great Britain, is a receding, not a stationary limit. Granting that it recedes less slowly than the population increases, and that there is a consequent pressure, is there any reason to presume from this that the pressure would continue, if the whole uncultivated world were opened to the agriculture of the same population ? But our author says, ' the question may be made a matter of computation.' Certainly it may ; and we wish he had attempted the calculation—not by a piece of mathematical jargon, about ' geometrical and arithmetical ratios,' as imposing and almost as correct as Mr. Jenkinson's discourse upon cosmogony

in

in the Vicar of Wakefield,—but by a fair estimate of the quantity of cultivable soil at our disposal on the surface of the globe, and of the millions which it would maintain in comfort. Nothing of this sort has been attempted by our author. We will, however, endeavour by a brief sketch to supply his deficiency.

The extent of *land* in our colonial territory of North America, including the British provinces, Hudson's Bay territory, and Western or Indian territory, but exclusive of the North Polar region, reaches, according to Mr. Bouchette, to about 2,700,000 square miles. But if we reckon only the one million of square miles which lie south of the latitude of London, this will give us a surface *eight times as large as that of all the British islands,* and not a whit inferior to them in climate or, it is believed, in soil. With regard to the Cape and Australia, so little is known of the interior of these two great continents, that it is difficult to form any judgment as to the extent of land at our disposal in them. But if we only count upon a belt of land averaging a hundred miles in depth from those parts of their sea-coasts which we have surveyed and taken possession of, this will give us in these two quarters of the globe a surface of more than twenty millions of square miles. Here then, without going further, is an area of twenty-one millions of square miles, the population of which at present is a mere fraction, not worth speaking of. Now the actual population of Great Britain and Ireland is about two hundred and five to the square mile, and supposing one-fortieth to be ' excrescent,' or supported on foreign-grown food, it will appear that every square mile in the British kingdoms, deficient as is our agriculture in many districts, especially throughout Ireland, supports two hundred souls. We have no reason to suppose the proportion of cultivable to non-cultivable surface to be less in our colonies than at home. We know, indeed, many of their extensive savannahs and primeval forests to be more fertile than our very best soils in Britain, and able to bear many repeated croppings without manure. But allow that they are, on an average, only equal in fertility, and it will be seen that the application of our yet very imperfect agricultural processes to our colonial soils would provide support for at least 4,200,000,000 of persons at the present British standard of maintenance, or about one hundred and seventy times our present numbers ; so that if our increase were to continue at the rate of a doubling in fifty years, which it has pretty steadily maintained during the present century, (under the stimulating influence in England of a badly-administered poor-law, offering a direct premium to parents on the birth of every additional child,) nearly *four centuries* must pass away before there could be a greater scarcity of food felt than at present, even upon the

the incredible supposition, that our agricultural skill should in the mean time remain unimproved. We may therefore feel ourselves tolerably safe as yet.

If it be asked what room there is for a similar development of the other nations of the earth, we answer, first, that there is but too much reason to fear that their misgovernment, disturbances, want of security for property, and frequent exposure to the scourges of war, pestilence, and famine, will yet for many generations to come prevent their making much progress in population. But should a more favourable state of things turn up, Europe alone has, we are convinced, a sufficiency of surface-soils to support, if duly cultivated, a hundred times her present population; and in Asia, Africa, and the two Americas, with the exception of a small part of China and India, the resources of the soil are as yet hardly entered upon. Look, for example, at the almost boundless plains of South America, which intervene between the Andes and the Atlantic—plains chiefly composed of deep alluvial soil, fertilized and intersected in every direction by the most magnificent navigable rivers and a rich maze of tributaries. Look at Asia Minor, Persia, Central Asia, and the vast extent of Asiatic Russia,—can it be doubted that these districts, under a government which protected industry from unjust exaction, would afford sustenance to very many times their present number of inhabitants? Of the capabilities of Northern Africa for colonization, an experiment is now, we hope, in course of trial. It is known that a great extent of its surface was once highly cultivated, and supported a dense population; and we can see no reason for doubting that, with the aid of modern skill and science, it might again be brought to at least an equal state of fertility. Of the central parts of that vast continent, south of the Sandy Desert, too little is known for us to speak with any confidence of its resources; but harassed and brutalized as its inhabitants are, for the most part, by the odious traffic in slaves, oppressed by predatory tribes, and subjected to the tyranny of atrocious despots, it is impossible to believe that their numbers have as yet made anything like an approach to the limits of the capacity of the country for their support. So far, therefore, from its being true, that the population either of the British kingdoms, or of the world at large, is already as numerous as can be maintained off the soils which are at their disposal, we believe it does not reach the one-thousandth part of the number which these soils would feed, were the agricultural skill, and science, and other resources which the most advanced among the nations even now possess, judiciously applied to their cultivation; and we can see nothing to prevent those resources being, in the course of time, themselves multiplied a thousand-fold by future discoveries

and

and improvements.   It has been calculated, that one square mile now may be made to maintain as many human beings as could live upon a thousand square miles of hunting ground, in an age when man lived by the chase alone.   Can we presume to assert, that in the progress of husbandry, agricultural chemistry, and vegetable and animal physiology, other improvements may not carry us as far forward again, so that, if need were, even the thousandth part of a square mile might support as many as the mile does now? Strange as this may sound in the present state of our knowledge, things that sounded as strange to our forefathers have already been brought about.

But it is said, we *must* be brought to a stand-still *at length*, for the surface of the globe will afford elbow-room for but a limited number!   Dr. Chalmers seriously adduces this ultimate prospect as an argument, and shudders at the risk of men becoming as thickly packed ' as mites in a cheese!' Now, in the first place, the predicted calamity does not appear to us so very fearful—the mites, for aught we can see, have a very happy time of it.   In the next, we submit, that when there appears any near prospect of such an over-peopling as that—of a deficiency of standing-room for the inhabitants of the world—it may be time to consider the propriety of crying ' hold hard' to the young men and maidens who are rashly inclining to be connubial.   And it ought to relieve the anxiety of these philosophers for the fate of such as may have their lot cast in those distant times, that in the works of Mr. Malthus and Dr. Chalmers, of which doubtless that remote posterity will possess the ten-thousandth edition, they are provided with a specific—*infallible*, by their account, in its effect of ' upholding a well-conditioned state of society,' by checking the rate of increase at any point where it may be considered desirable— within ' the limit' of comfortable arm's length for example, or the proportion of square feet of stowage that is allowed to each individual on board a man-of-war!   The very confidence the Malthusians possess in the excellence of their specific ought to be enough to convince them, that no ultimate injury need be apprehended from the over-increase of population, with so obvious and easy a resource at hand.   But to persuade us to have recourse to it now, is indeed right midsummer madness—the *ne plus ultra* of moonstruck, Laputan philosophy.   Some member lately objected in the House of Commons to any reduction in the duty on coals exported, on the ground that we ought to husband our stock, since it is limited, and, according to the calculation of experienced geologists, not more than enough to last us, at our present rate of consumption, about 6600 years!   We should take this ' prudential' gentleman to be a Malthusian philosopher.   And our only wonder

is,

is, that these expansive philanthropists—who would starve the present race of man in their benevolent care for the comfort of his posterity in the hundredth generation—do not likewise preach a crusade against artificial fires, as robbing the atmosphere of its oxygen ; stint us of spring water, lest we drink the heavens dry, or shrink the level of the ocean ; and call for a prohibition of dark colours, as tending by their absorption to exhaust the sun of his light. Air, light, and water—like the food-producing powers of the earth—have their ultimate limits ; and we are about as near to the one as to the others.

But Dr. Chalmers has an objection to emigration peculiar to himself, and strongly characteristic of his style of reasoning. ' Emigration is *injurious,* in spite of *its effects in relieving the evils of a crowded population, because* it stimulates population.' Still if, at the same time that it stimulates the growth of population, it prevents all that is evil in that increase, where is the harm of such stimulus, allowing that it is one ? But indeed, by our author's argument, it only stimulates population by increasing the comforts of life, and affording the means of plentiful subsistence to greater numbers ; and if this be an evil, we are ready to face it, exclaiming, ' Evil, be thou our good!' On this ground, every invention tending to enlarge the powers of mankind for procuring subsistence or additional comforts, is a horrid mischief, to be deprecated and avoided with especial caution. The system of turnip husbandry and other late advances made in this country in agriculture admitted of the support of a larger population, and consequently encouraged its growth ; these, therefore, come under Dr. Chalmers's ban. The labours of the Board of Agriculture must, in his eyes, be pestilent ; nay, the very invention of agriculture itself, as well as all its subsequent improvements, should, in consistency, be stigmatized by him as an evil of the first magnitude. It was, to the full as much as emigration can be, ' a bounty on the multiplication of the species.' Mankind, therefore, has been all along under a grievous mistake in supposing gratitude due to those who have multiplied the productions of the earth. Mr. Coke and Mr. Curwen are plotters of evil, Ceres was the incarnation of a malevolent principle, and Triptolemus the true arch-enemy of his race !

If there is any one desire or design more manifest than another throughout the works of nature, or more worthy of the benevolence of nature's great Author, it is that there should be the utmost possible multiplication of beings endowed with life and capacity for enjoyment. We do not see that nature has contented herself with establishing little groups of organized beings in snug corners, to thrive there in security and content, through a nice adjustment of
their

their numbers to the food within their reach;—whether proceeding from a mysterious adaptation of their procreative powers to their numerical state, as in Mr. Sadler's gratuitous hypothesis,—or, from a self-regulating power, dictated by instinct, or prudential intelligence, according to Mr. Malthus's equally unnecessary suggestion. No! abundance, extension, multiplication, competition for room, is the order of creation; and the only limit to the increase of each species, the mutual pressure of numbers on each other. But, if there is any one species of the animate world, whose multiplication we may venture to suppose an especial object of the Divine regard, can it be other than that which alone of all He has endowed with a particle of His spirit—with intellect, reason, speech, the faculty of *improvement*, and *an immortal·soul?* Whilst every other species is taught to spread and multiply as widely as its relative powers allow, is MAN alone, though conscious of his sovereignty over all the rest of living creation, to confine himself carefully within a limited area,—alone to apply his energies to *prevent* the increase of his numbers, the enlargement of his resources, and the extension of his dominion? How blinded to the ONE GRAND OBJECT OF CREATION must he be, who would so limit the expansion, and annihilate the bright future of his race!

Our author is wrong when he asserts of emigration, that ' the longer it is prosecuted the more impracticable it becomes.' (p. 381.) On the contrary, experience has always proved, that it is the first commencement of a colony which alone presents any serious difficulties, and that the further its settlement advances, the more easily may it be extended. Even Mr. Malthus admits this; and that it must be so is obvious enough. Again, Dr. Chalmers errs sadly when he assumes that emigration can only take place as a consequence of ' extreme general destitution and distress,' and that, on this account, the continual spreading of population must be a process of continual suffering. It is quite sufficient that there should be a certain preponderance of wealth, comforts, or enjoyment of any kind, to be met with abroad, to tempt to a continual efflux, provided the means are not wanting, and the institutions of society do not interfere as a check. It is not ' the experience of great distress and destitution ' which causes the annual flitting of thousands from the eastern states of America to the western. It is not merely the most wretched among our paupers who can be persuaded ' to forego all the recollections of their boyhood, the scene and the dwelling-place of their dearest intimacies,' by migrating to Canada or Australia. On the contrary, it is notorious that capitalists, persons possessed of thousands, are continually moving off to settle there. And, if a double

profit

profit overcomes the repugnance to ' voluntary exile ' in the wealthy capitalist, will not a double wage do as much for the labouring class ?   Their condition in the mother country may be *good ;* and yet to induce them to remove to the colony, it may be sufficient that they have a prospect of its there being *better*—perhaps twice —perhaps ten times as *good.*

But, may we not turn the tables upon those who would substitute for the natural, ancient, and easy resource of emigration in the case of a state which is, or threatens to be, crowded, an unnatural, and we believe, impracticable, restraint upon marriage ?   When they urge that it must be ' no light evil ' from which the emigrant makes his escape, may we not retort, that it is no inconsiderable sacrifice to forego the *domus et placens uxor*—the sweets of domestic happiness—the pleasures of marital and paternal affection ?   While they accuse the advocate for emigration of urging the poor to break the natural ties of home and kindred, they are themselves striving to prevent the formation of those ties which are of all the strongest, the most virtuous, and the most joy-dispensing—those of the father and the husband.   If the emigrant quits his parental roof, the wound soon heals, for it is in the course of nature that he should do so, and he exchanges for it a roof-tree and a family of his own, *of which the Malthusians would deprive him.*   In fact, their scheme is merely to substitute one privation for another, a greater for a less, with the additional disadvantage of a general narrowing of the numbers of mankind, and the aggregate happiness, through the selfish desire of a few to monopolize the bounties provided by nature for the whole race, and a sordid and short-sighted doubt of their sufficiency.   The conduct recommended by these writers as the acme of human virtue, and the great end of Christian instruction, is, in fact, precisely that of the man in the parable who wrapped his talent in a napkin, instead of putting it out where it might multiply.

The last expedient of which Dr. Chalmers professes to demonstrate the inefficacy, is a legal provision for the poor.   Our readers are already aware of the deeply-rooted hostility he has always manifested to such an institution—an hostility which, like all his other economical errors, springs directly from the unhappy and unreasonable persuasion of the want of room for man upon the earth.   We have lately said so much upon this subject that we shall abstain from further comment on his mistaken preference of what he calls ' the ministrations of spontaneous and individual benevolence,—the fortuitous and free gratuities of the philanthropist,'—that is, in plain words, a system of mendicity and vagrancy, over one of regulated and legalized relief: but, passing this, and other propositions, which he reiterates as if they had not been

over and over again exposed and refuted—such as the bold assertions, in the face of the contrast presented on all these points by
Ireland and England,—the one with, the other without a poor
law—that an institution of that nature *necessarily* impoverishes a
country!—deepens the wretchedness of the peasantry!—deadens
charity!—and destroys the security of property!—we will merely
notice one fatal mistake which alone would render Dr. Chalmers
incompetent to reason on the subject: we speak of his imagining
a poor law to be merely ' legalized or compulsory *charity.*'

' The virtue of humanity ought never to have been legalized, but left
to the spontaneous workings of man's own willing and compassionate
nature. Justice, with its precise boundary and well-defined rights, is
the fit subject for the enactments of the statute-book ; but nothing can
be more hurtful than thus to bring the terms or the ministrations of
benevolence under the bidding of authority.'—p. 415.

The truth, however, on the contrary is, that the poor have a
decided claim, in justice, to a support from off the land on which
Providence has placed them, if that land is capable of affording it
to their exertions. Such a provision, therefore, instead of being
a matter of charity and benevolence, ' a thing of love, not law,' is
but the legal concession of a right antecedent even to that of the
owners of the soil—a divine right—a right based on the eternal
and immutable principles of intuitive justice. And its necessity
may be equally proved on less high grounds. The only mode
of preserving the peace of society, is to afford to every one suffering the extremity of want, some resource short of plunder and
violence. The expediency of a poor law, as a mere measure of
preventive police, may be easily demonstrated. It is in truth called
for as imperatively by policy as by humanity, and by justice still
more clearly than by either.

Dr. Chalmers, however, is only consistent in his opposition to
it. Under the assumption on which he reasons, of its being impossible to keep subsistence level with population, he is quite
right. Only he should not have stopped short of the conclusion to
which his premises will necessarily conduct him—the propriety of
passing a law to put out of their misery, at once, those ' for whom
there is no room on the earth ;' seeing that they must perish by
inches, and during this process inflict much evil on the rest of
society by encroaching on the bare sufficiency it possesses for its
own wants. Private charity is quite as injurious and as nugatory
in this light, as a poor law. It can only relieve one individual at
the expense of another; and we refer the doctor to Mr. Malthus
himself, who declares expressly, what indeed is a necessary consequence of his principle, that a poor man cannot by charity be
enabled to live better than before, without proportionately de-
pressing

pressing others of the same class.* We submit, therefore, that the true policy deducible from the Malthusian premises, is, that we should not merely abolish the poor laws, but go on to despatch the surplus population as fast as it appears. Malthus was decidedly wrong in hesitating to follow his principle up to its full extent. He contents himself with recommending that relief should be administered ' sparingly.' This is execution by slow torture. Dr. Chalmers, on the other hand, dwells with delight on the ' fullness of relief' afforded by spontaneous charity, forgetful that, on his own principle of a limited quantity of food, what is given to beggar Paul, must be taken from labourer Peter. This slight discrepancy between the professors is, however, no more than what has often appeared in the modes of ' fortuitous and free philanthropy' of other ages—

> ' God cannot love, says Blunt, with tearless eyes,
> The wretch he starves,—and piously denies.
> While the good bishop, with indulgent air,
> Admits and leaves them Providence's care.'

Having thus gone through the whole list of political expedients for securing the well-being of the community, and ' demonstrated their futility' in succession, by help of the postulate which declared it from the first,—our author brings us in triumph to the ' *argal*' at which he has been all along straining, viz. that since nothing can make food keep pace with population, all our efforts should be turned to make population keep pace with food ; and the only specific for this is ' prudential restraint upon marriage,' self-imposed by each individual, and inculcated by a Christian education.

Now we will not yield even to Dr. Chalmers, in a fervent zeal for the spread of ' moral and Christian education.' We need scarcely say, that we agree wholly with him in the vast benefits derivable from national endowments for this purpose. But we cannot agree in the opinion, that it is any part of the duty of a moral and Christian pastor, to interfere with the dictates of nature, as to the proper period for marriage. We do not, in short, recognise any necessary connexion between religion and celibacy—virtue and abstinence from wedlock. We desire general education as a means, not of proportioning the numbers of mankind to their food, but of providing them with that intellectual alimen which, at the same time that it enlightens them on their true physical interests, adds to their mental and social gratifications ; and while affording them the prospect of eternal happiness in another world, equally assists them to secure their welfare in the present. None shall go beyond us in anxiety to inculcate universally the

---

* Book iii. chap. 4.

principles

principles of ' prudence and foresight.' We only differ from our author as to the true application of those principles, which we should prefer directing towards the means of procuring a sufficiency for the maintenance of a family in respectability and comfort, rather than towards the avoidance of the burthen of a family, lest their maintenance should not be procurable. We know where it is said, ' He feedeth the ravens who call upon him.' And, though blaming as much as any an indolent and careless reliance on Providence,—though assenting, in its *moral* sense, to the truth of ' Aide-toi, le ciel t'aidera,'—the ' prudence' that we recommend, is an active, not a negative one—a judicious struggle against threatening evils, not a cowardly and Fabian retreat before them— a determination to push back by all imaginable means the apparent barrier to our onward progress, not a timid shrinking within ourselves, lest we haply receive a rub or two against it. And since we are quite confident that the barrier is in truth imaginary, or rather conventional, the offspring of our voluntary arrangements, and to be kept at any distance we please—that

——' spatium Natura beatis
Omnibus esse dedit, si quis cognoverit uti'—

that the foresight of the members of a civilized community, judiciously directed, and uninterfered with by mistaken laws or officious advice, will enable them to procure a plentiful subsistence for all their possible numbers, either from within or without the geographical limits of the district they at present inhabit—we do think it no part of the duty of a Christian minister, to endeavour to give a different direction to the ' prudence and foresight' of his fellow-citizens, and we are quite sure, that by so doing, he will only be fighting against nature, and must do far more harm than good. By discouraging matrimony, he will probably but encourage illicit indulgence—

' Naturam expellas furcâ tamen usque recurret;'—

at the very best, he enforces a needless amount of privation, and checks the production of a large increase of human happiness.

The moral tendency, indeed, of this doctrine, we consider indescribably pernicious. By holding out to all, that improvements of any kind are useless, and even mischievous, for that ' every enlargement of our resources only tends to land us in a larger, it is true, but a more straitened population,' it directly discourages all attempts at the amelioration of our condition, whether public or private ; and fosters in all classes a selfish and apathetic indolence, a mean distrust of our own powers, instead of that confident resolution to employ them to the utmost, which, under fair play, is almost certain of overcoming every obstacle. We need

no

no stronger illustration of the proof of this than the book we are reviewing. Here are half-a-dozen resources canvassed for raising the condition of the body of the population—each of them is *admitted* to be more or less efficacious towards that end, but because it is assumed that there is an ultimate limit to the efficacy of each, they are all dismissed as unprofitable, deceptive, and even hurtful, and we are gravely told to cease our efforts for enlarging our resources, and direct them wholly to limiting our wants !

Again : by this doctrine the wealthy and the powerful are completely absolved from the duty of contributing to relieve the distresses of their poorer neighbours, either by direct charity, or a just and wise attention to the economical means for improving their condition ; since all such attempts are declared to be not only fruitless but mischievous. It absolutely frees a government from all responsibility for the sufferings of the mass of the community, by throwing the blame entirely on *Nature* and the improvidence of the poor themselves, and declaring the evil to admit of no remedy from any possible exertions of the legislature. We cannot imagine any theory more destructive than this would be, were it generally received, whether among the higher and more powerful, or the lower classes themselves ; and we must consider those who labour to propagate it, though including, we are well aware, many of the most ardent and benevolent philanthropists of the age, to be, unconsciously, the enemies of their kind.

We hope Dr. Chalmers, in particular, will pardon the freedom of our remarks. We cannot sit by in silence and see the weight of his authority and the force of his eloquence exerted on the side of what we consider a most portentous and abominable doctrine. We implore him to re-consider his opinions. The welfare of existing millions—the existence of future myriads, depends on the destruction of the miserable sophism, which lies at the bottom of his whole economical system.

REFLECTIONS ON THE THEORY OF POPULATION.

THE facts and reasonings on which the theory of population, as illustrated by Malthus, is founded, admit of very brief explanation. The increase of the human species is necessarily limited by that of the means of subsistence. Any increase which exceeds this limit must be productive of poverty, vice, disease, and death. We are taught by experience, that the productive powers of the earth acknowledge at least a practical limitation: that if the utmost point of its possible fertility cannot be speculatively assigned, we are authorised to say that the practical increase will fall within certain limits easily assignable; and that, looking to the same experience, which is the only safe guide in questions of this kind, we cannot fail to perceive, that the constant energy of the principle of population far surpasses the limits of agricultural improvement; and that the necessary and unalterable relations are sustained in practice, either by moral restraint alone, which anticipates and prevents the horrors arising out of any great inequality, or by that sweeping and resistless misery by which nature is avenged for every flagrant contempt of her immutable ordinations.

To prove that his theory is not the gratuitous produce of a gloomy imagination, Mr Malthus refers to the incontestible fact, that the population of British America doubled itself, under many and formidable inconveniences, in the space of twenty-five years: and justly assuming that this is the narrowest limit which can be assigned to the undisturbed energy of this productive power, he asks, in which of the civilized countries of Europe the most vigorous efforts of industry and of science could, within the same short period, double the actual produce of agriculture? Even if this could be done *once*, could it be repeated? Could the same series be continued for centuries to come, even if every inch of European territory were improved to the fertility of the most cultivated garden? Every man of sense will at once answer in the negative. The result is, that the principle of population, not at any future and distant period, but in our own days, as well as in ages that are

past, has been restrained in its natural tendency to transcend the limits of subsistence, by some rigorous and efficient check,—by some moral impediment, which has prevented the existence of a surplus population, doomed to misery and destruction,—or by some fearful visitation, which, when the inexorable laws of the physical world have once been transgressed, has swept the helpless sufferers from the face of that earth which ever groans with the vice and misery of its inhabitants.

Such is a very general outline of the theory of population,—a theory not founded on any remote or uncertain facts, or on a series of hypothetical statements, but established out of the materials which the most common experience supplies, and by a much shorter process of deduction than is usually required to establish the truths of science.

The conclusions from the general principle thus laid down are of infinite importance to the right understanding of some of the most momentous questions of interior police. If it be true that population has a natural tendency to increase in a more rapid ratio than the means of subsistence, it is obvious that all legislative encouragements to such increase are at best superfluous; but if it be also true that a surplus population, when once called into being by a system of mistaken policy, can be brought down to the inevitable limits which nature has ordained by devouring misery alone, it follows, that all such measures are in the highest degree cruel and impolitic. Let government occupy itself in its legitimate function of extending the resources of the country, by protecting industry in its operation and rewards; an increase of population will surely follow the increased means of providing for it; but let no legislature attempt to invert the natural course of policy by the encouragement of early marriages,—by bestowing premiums and immunities, honours and distinctions, which only give a superfluous and fatal activity to a spring already too powerful for human prudence and self-control.

The same principle involves the clear and unqualified condemnation of poor laws, so far as they not only provide for existing and inevitable misery, but tend to increase its amount by encouraging the growth of population. Private charity, so respectable in its

2 D

motive, so pure in its exercise, so beneficial both to the donor and receiver, so free from all objections in point of policy to which a compulsory system is exposed, might be found adequate to the relief of all real and inevitable calamity ; and the existence of legal provisions for the support of the poor is therefore without defence, upon the principles of true philosophy. But the questions about the original formation of such establishments, and their continuance when once formed, and interwoven with a vicious system of public morals, are quite distinct. It by no means follows that we are bound instantly to destroy whatever we should have refused, in the first instance, to construct. A tenderness to human suffering often exacts of philosophy great deference even to the most impolitic and barbarous institutions. It is strange, that amid the acknowledged and intolerable evils of the poor laws, which have now excited one universal murmur of condolence and despair, so few should be disposed to recognise the true source of the calamity in the opposition of the principle of policy on which these laws are founded, to the immutable ordinances of nature : that so many intelligent persons should yet stubbornly look to the detail of regulation, instead of turning their eyes to the great and palpable vice of the entire system : that the insanity of that law, which assumes the unlimited abundance of the materials of labour and the means of subsistence, in the midst of the most cogent and touching evidence of their deficiency, should yet be disputed : and that the man who has vigorously and fearlessly unmasked the fatal delusion, should be rewarded with unsparing insolence, and branded as the enemy of his species. It is *not* the object of Mr Malthus at once to sweep away the poor laws, and to abandon the floating mass of wretchedness which they have created to unpitied destruction : but he has pointed out the true source of the overwhelming calamity ; he has cleared the great principle of all such establishments from the mist of prejudice in which it has been immemorially involved ; he has shown, not with what unsparing havoc a pretended reformation ought to be accomplished, but *in what direction* all practicable improvements ought to be attempted. With a just and

philosophical rigour, he has deprived the ordinary tamperers with the most delicate subjects of domestic administration of their childish plausibilities for concealing the truth from a misguided public ; he has developed the true source and fatal magnitude of the evil, and prepared the way for an efficient remedy, which philosophy may indeed prescribe, but time alone can accomplish. This is all that, in such perplexed problems, science can do for humanity.

Intimately connected with the theory of population is the question of the corn laws, which has long divided the most able and enlightened political economists. This momentous discussion has hitherto been conducted too much on the ground of minute and trifling details, and without that steady regard to general principles, which alone can lead to a satisfactory solution of the difficult problem.

The increase of population in any community becomes, in the present circumstances of Europe, independent of the supply of food afforded by the improved agriculture of that particular state ; the demands of commerce for labour, with the facility of a foreign supply of grain, might, but for legislative interference, create the most appaling disproportions. The agriculture of a civilized state cannot, for obvious reasons, sustain a fair competition in the general market with that of semi-barbarous nations ; it will therefore, in the natural course of events, be neglected, and the population must, of course, become dependent on foreign states for subsistence. Such is the inevitable course of that state of society in which we live, unless arrested by the interposition of the laws ; the same impulse of resistless competition—the same pressure of severe discouragement, which have annihilated the once thriving manufactures, and swept away the commerce of flourishing states, will extinguish also that manufacture of food, which, like all others, thrives only by encouragement and reward. It is true indeed, that a fatal crisis has never yet arrived to any state so as to leave its fields desolate in the abandonment of its agriculture ; for the rapid and unequal growth of commerce and manufactures, which can alone hasten such a catastrophe, is comparatively recent in the history of the world ; and the calamity of agricultural desolation has been averted by the operation of private interests, demanding and receiving the protection of the laws,—interests which, however selfish in their origin, have in this, as in many other cases, wrought in strict subservience to the public prosperity. But even this constant and powerful instinct has not saved England from occasional and severe agricultural derangements, which, in many possible combinations of European policy, might have left her without resources to propitiate a starving population, and avert the horrors of insurrection. Those who have studied the science of political economy, not merely in its metaphysical details, but in its higher moral bearings, know that the mere accumulation of wealth, although an important, is not the exclusive object of its researches ; that there are cases in which its most imperative maxims of a class, strictly economical, must be subordinated to the demands of a higher and more interesting policy ; and that where national honour, tranquillity, or security is concerned, the most legitimate theory for the mere increase of wealth must, without scruple, be surrendered. It was thus that the legislature interposed by means of the navigation laws ; and by circumscribing its shipping market to the commerce of England, made a sacrifice of profit to security and strength, which has commanded the gratitude of England, and the applauding envy of mankind. The principle of that entire freedom which distinguishes the liberal commercial policy of modern times is indeed sacred in every case which falls within its legitimate application—in every case where the question is singly about the accumulation of wealth, and where the sure sagacity of private interest will triumph over the presumptuous empiricism of legislation,—in every case where those objects alone are at stake, which address themselves to the unerring instinct of that private cupidity from which alone the principle derives its application and its force ; but it is weak and unphilosophical to appeal to this maxim for the solution of cases which involve higher elements than the principle itself is intended to embrace, and which can be resolved only by a wider range of comparison, and larger and higher views of policy. The question is not, whether corn may be bought cheaper under

an unrestricted freedom of trade than with the incumbrance of corn laws ? or, whether an enhancement of the price of grain does not operate on the price of labour, the state of manufactures, and the course of foreign trade ? no man who understands even the elements of political economy can hesitate for a moment as to any of these propositions. But the important matters truly at issue are—whether, under the visible preponderance of manufacturing and commercial enterprise in a state which is excluded by opulence, by taxation, by the accumulated pressure of natural and artificial burdens, from all agricultural competition with the frugal poverty of other nations, agriculture will not inevitably decline, and a fatal disproportion be created betwixt the population and the produce of that particular state ? Whether this disproportion will not, unless the legislature interfere, naturally increase till a state of dependence be created not less artificial than formidable ? And whether it be not the office of a high and presiding policy to interpose before the mischief of the system be consummated ? and by the steady sacrifice of some portion of wealth, and amid the temporary struggles of a vivacious, and already luxuriant, commerce, restore the great and salutary proportions of nature, which never intended that the population of a mighty empire should repose for subsistence on the precarious fertility, or still more precarious policy, of neighbouring states, to whom she stands jealously opposed by the very tenure of her greatness.

Such is a specimen of the important applications of which the theory of population is susceptible—a theory which indeed affects, more or less, almost every great question of domestic policy. Those who calumniate the philosophy which they do not understand, have many expedients, indeed, to provide for any excess of population. They propose the cultivation of waste lands ; they hold out the cheering prospect of emigration ; they cannot believe that the world is not large enough to afford, in some corner, an asylum for human folly. Can such reasoners forget, that the additional cultivation, which is profitable, will surely be attempted ? and that the fact of its not having been hitherto undertaken, affords conclusive evidence, that hitherto it would not have been beneficial—that the same argument applies to the toils, the perils, the repulsive uncertainties of emigration—that if either enterprise would repay the danger and toil which it demands, it would undoubtedly be hazarded—and if it would not, that the inevitable failure of the experiment just presents one shape of that *misery* in which a redundant population is extinguished, and which it is the object of every enlightened friend of humanity to avert. The precarious resources of waste lands, and Transatlantic wilds are to be explored, not as affording an outlet to any excess of population which may be created, or an invitation to the imprudence which calls it into existence ; but an ample field to enterprise and labour which, when crowned with success, will assuredly find a progeny to participate in the fruits. The order of nature and the voice of wisdom demanded that the creation of that abundance, which can alone avert misery in all its forms, should precede the existence of the population which is to consume it.

The theory of population has been misrepresented as repugnant to the best feelings, and finest impulses of our nature—propitious to the schemes of despotism—and insulting to the dignity of the species.

Is that philosophy then at variance with the dearest and noblest of the passions, which would guard its virtuous gratifications from the pangs of embittering remorse—the countless ills of hopeless and fatal poverty ? The enlightened moralist and statesman, far from discountenancing the pure and virtuous union of the sexes, is ambitious to provide for the dignity and stability of the endearing attachment—to avert from the most sacred retreat of mortal felicity, the canker of care and sorrow, before which enjoyment withers away, and the ardour of passion slowly but surely expires. It is the fatal prerogative of human folly to levy war upon the bounty of nature, and perversely to extract from the richest blessings of Providence, the elements of the bitterest calamity. What so pure and ennobling as the passion of love in its virtuous form ?— what so frightful and degrading in its excesses and aberrations ? Improvidence and its inevitable effects—extreme and irremediable poverty—have been more fatal to connubial enjoyment than those comparatively rare

irregularities of passion which spring out of a distempered constitution, and betray a diseased imagination. The philosopher who lifts his voice against this calamitous improvidence, and who wishes to give their natural plenitude and endurance to the pure delights of virtuous passion, by exacting performance of the condition upon which alone nature has promised her indispensible sanction, is not the peevish and sullen enemy of enjoyment, but the steady and enlightened friend of humanity.

Nor is it less absurd to represent this important philosophical lesson as being favourable to the progress of despotism. We are taught indeed, by the theory of population, that society has other dangers to provide against than those which spring out of political institutions, and when we consider what temptations to jealous tyranny the vehemence of indiscriminate and groundless complaint presents—and reflect on the fatal and ignominious career which has been run by the masters of modern revolution, who first discovered the source of all human evils in the existence, and their remedy in the unsparing destruction of all established institutions, we ought to hail the doctrine which affords a manageable and efficient check upon their extravagant presumption, as a powerful instrument, not of despotism but of liberty. The just theory of population, which exacts of governments the arduous duty of extending the public resources, and exalting the national prosperity, instead of the cheap and vulgar function of adding indefinitely to the numbers of an unprovided, and of course, a profligate, population— which, instead of ministering to the crooked ambition of power, by the formidable aid of a needy and desperate gang, opposes to its projects the might and the wisdom of an independent, virtuous, and enlightened community ; which provides for the tranquillity of the state, by ensuring the comfort of the people, and for the perpetuity of genuine freedom, by averting those frightful commotions, of which the craft of demagogues and despots has in all ages known so well how to profit ; and finally, which addresses a perpetual and impressive remonstrance to the temerity of statesmen, who, amid the profound revolutions which their measures often produce, have not even a glance of the actual suffering which they create, and of that futurity of wo which they unconsciously decree; such a strain of philosophy, while it enlarges and exalts the duties of rulers, confirms the independence, and watches over the happiness of the governed, cannot be the ally of despotism, nor the enemy of man.

ART. IV.—*An Essay on the Principle of Population; or, a View of its past and present Effects on Human Happiness; with an Inquiry into our prospects respecting the future Removal or Mitigation of the Evils which it occasions.* By R. T. Malthus, A. M. late Fellow of Jesus College, Cambridge, and Professor of History and Political Economy in the East India College, Hertfordshire. The Fifth Edition, with important Additions.. Three Vols. 8vo. London. 1817.

THAT preposterous course which is a fatal error in morals, is indispensable in political science; mankind must act first, and reason afterwards. The axioms of political economy, like those of

natural

natural philosophy, can only result from experience and repeated observation: thus it happens that the progress of civilization, as it increases the variety of relations and combinations in which men are placed with respect to each other, and multiplies the transactions in which they are involved, has the collateral effect of introducing a new set of intellectual pursuits, and engaging mankind in the study of fresh sciences as it gradually advances. There is not a wider difference between the simple barter of wine or oxen for arms or slaves, and the bills of exchange which form the medium of modern commerce, than between the comparative knowledge of the principles by which national and individual transfers of property are regulated, as exhibited in the crude and contradictory ' Politics' of Aristotle, and in the scientific conclusions of the ' Wealth of Nations.' Aristotle was as well calculated as any man to build up a scientific system: but a sufficient series of experiments to found it upon, was wanting. Hence it was naturally to be expected that in the progress of civilization and political economy, the last subject studied and, explained should be the facts relating to PO-PULATION, because this branch of political science requires a collection of statistic details which can only be furnished by an advanced state of society: and because it is little likely to attract attention till men are generally placed in circumstances like those in which we find them in modern Europe. In ancient times, the density of population was limited by the facility, and still more by the habit of emigration, which, after all, while the distance is short, and climate similar, and artificial wants comparatively few, is a much milder process than expatriation from Europe to America, or from England to the shores of the Euxine. The universal habits of slavery, moreover, among the Greeks and Romans, and such a systematic demoralization as is betrayed by the enactment of a lex Julia, to say nothing of perpetual and murderous wars, would naturally tend to keep the subject out of view. During the middle ages, population had a regular preventive check in feudal habits, and a regular positive check in civil wars: and though famines were no less frequent than severe, it was quite evident that they did not originate in the redundancy of people, but in the want of channels for distributing produce, and in the total ignorance and neglect of agriculture. It was not, therefore, till the security of property and the tranquil state of things which followed the establishment of a settled government, made it the first desire of every man to sit down, if not under his own vine, at least by his own fire-side and in the circle of a family; it was not till avenues were gradually opened to industry and enterprise, and allowed that desire to be generally gratified; it was not till these prosperous circumstances gave an impulse to the power of population, that the inhabitants

of

of the various countries of Europe encroached rapidly upon the productive soil, and have made it at last a matter of speculation how far the territory itself may be able to support the numbers existing in it; and what proportion there is between the natural powers of the earth, and those of unrestrained population.

Unquestionably the details which we now possess from registers and statistical tables and other authentic sources, are of a nature to invite the curiosity and ensure the attention of all those who have a taste for researches into the history of their fellow creatures, even apart from all practical consequences. The first survey of the subject affords a striking problem. It presents us with a view of men essentially the same in their passions, constitutions, and physical powers, yet, in different countries, or in the same country at different times, varying in the rate in which they increase their numbers through every degree of a very extensive scale: in some cases requiring no more than twenty-five years, and in others perhaps no less than a thousand, to double them. There is no occasion to travel far in search of instances. Our own dominions exhibit the following variations.

In Canada, the population doubles	in	28	years.
In Ireland	in	34	
In England and Wales (calculating the whole of the last century)	in	100	
In Hindostan (perhaps)	in	1000	

Those who profess to see nothing remarkable in these variations, must have very different ideas from ours as to what is interesting in the history of the human race. Again, if we trace the subject back to the origin of the increase, we find in different countries a similar difference in the proportion which the number of annual marriages bears to the number of the existing population. Here, for the sake of wider illustration, we will extend our view beyond our own territories. In Russia, according to a table furnished by Mr. Tooke, it appears that among ninety-two persons one marriage is contracted, or of forty-six persons one marries annually: so that the proportion of marriages to the actual population is on the average as one to ninety-two. Whereas in most countries the proportion is considerably smaller: being

in Sweden	1	to	110*
in England	1	to	122†
in Norway	1	to	130*
in the Pays de Vaud	1	to	140*

---

* Malthus, vol. i. p. 410.
† Preliminary Observations on the Population Abstract, by Mr. Rickman, p. xxix.

It

It is further remarkable that the annual proportion of marriages is by no means uniform even in the different counties of our native land. According to the curious table, prefixed to the returns for 1811, it varies from one in a hundred and five, which is the highest, (with the exception of Middlesex,) to one in a hundred and fifty-three. For example,

in Yorkshire (East Riding) the marriages are as

	1	to	105	persons
in Warwickshire	1	to	116	
in Essex	1	to	128	
in Shropshire	1	to	143	
in Monmouthshire	1	to	153	

How are we to account for these striking variations? Confessedly we have no ground to assume either any material difference in the prolific power, or in the instincts on which the increase of the species depends. The American race is but a branch of the European stock, and, had it remained on its parent soil, would have partaken of the same gradual increase, doubling itself in a century at the quickest: but the same branch, when rooted in Transatlantic ground, doubles in twenty-five years. Take any given number: say 10,000: these persons remaining in France or England, would in a hundred years have increased to 20,000: but transplanted to America, in a hundred years they become 160,000. Nay, even in the same country the rate of increase is very different in different periods, and periods too with only a trifling interval between them. England, during the first half of the last century, only gained a million of inhabitants; increasing from 5,475,000 to 6,467,000: but during the last half, increased nearly three times as fast, having reached 9,163,000 at the census of 1801. At that period the rate of doubling was about eighty-three years; but the increase from 1801 to 1811 was in still greater proportion, and should it continue, would double the whole population in fifty-five years.

At this point, then, Mr. Malthus takes up the question. Why is it, that in America the numbers increase so fast, in Hindostan so slow? Why faster in Ireland than in England? Why is it, that in England the population increases at different rates in different periods? or that in those counties which either extensive marshes or crowded manufacturing towns render comparatively unhealthy, marriages are earlier and more general than in the more salubrious and agricultural districts? Are the natural inclinations colder in Shropshire than in Warwickshire, or in Monmouthshire than in either? or is it more reasonable to suppose that the natural inclinations are generally uniform, but that they are necessarily repressed in some situations by the difficulty of providing for a family, more than in the mining and manufacturing districts, where the average duration

of

of life is shorter, and the resources of labour more extensive ? Is it not that the power of increase in the human race is much greater than the power of adding to the supply of food, by which last, however, their increase must inevitably be regulated? Is it any thing but the impossibility of procuring a proportionate augmentation of subsistence which prevents mankind, in all healthy countries, from making an annual addition to their numbers as great as that which takes place in America or in some parts of the Russian territory?

So at least argues Mr. Malthus; and the returns of the annual marriages, which were not in existence at the publication of his Essay, afford a clear illustration of his original remark.

' It is evident that in every country where the resources are any way limited, the *preventive* and *positive* checks to population must vary inversely as each other; that is, in countries either naturally unhealthy or subject to a great mortality, from whatever cause it may arise, the preventive check will prevail very little. In those countries, on the contrary, which are naturally healthy, and where the preventive check is found to prevail with considerable force, the positive check will prevail very little, or the mortality be very small.'—p. 24.

Our readers will probably remember that we have not been hasty in adopting Mr. Malthus's conclusions; and that we have condemned without hesitation the unqualified severity and harshness with which they were originally accompanied and introduced to public notice. Whoever casts his eyes around him, and surveys the labour, the distress, the penury, and the ignorance in which a great part of the human race, even in the most favoured countries, are more or less immersed, must want all the finer feelings and most amiable charities of our nature, if he does not spontaneously give way to the benevolent desire of correcting so much vice and relieving so much misery. Under the influence of these feelings, even the chimerical visions of Mr. Owen have attracted attention; and for some time his violation of practical experience and defiance of common sense, appeared to find excuse, in consideration of the amiable sentiments to which they were sacrificed. Even when the rugged lessons of experience or the incontrovertible testimonies of evidence assure us of the utter hopelessness of realizing this amelioration to its desirable extent; still the hardest lesson to forget is that which was first imbibed in other schools than those of philosophy; and the hope of some effectual improvement in the condition of our species remains ' the last infirmity of noble minds.' Mr. Malthus himself, in the preface to his original edition, ' professes to have read some of the speculations on the future improvement of society in a temper very different from a wish to find them visionary; but he had not acquired

that

that command over his understanding which would enable him to
believe what he wishes, without evidence, or to refuse his assent
to what might be unpleasing when accompanied with evidence.'

Under circumstances thus confessedly disadvantageous, the author cannot have been surprized at the slow and reluctant assent
which his principles have obtained.   He has a prejudice to encounter at every step; and it must be owned that no pains were
originally employed to win an easy way, and make the reader part
readily with his prejudices.   Every succeeding edition has improved
in this respect; and in the present especially the author has equally
gratified our self-complacency and displayed his own candour, by
expunging those passages to which we had most pointedly objected,
as liable to misrepresent the subject, and inflict an unnecessary
violence on the feelings of the reader.*   The existing state of our
domestic economy certainly renders the inquiry peculiarly interesting at this moment; and we enter upon it with no slight advantage
after the discussions which this branch of political science (which

---

* The following quotations contain an account of the alterations and additions
which have been made since the last edition was published.

‘ On account of the nature of the subject, which it must be allowed is one of
permanent interest, as well as of the attention likely to be directed to it in future, I
am bound to correct those errors of my work, of which subsequent experience and
information may have convinced me, and to make such additions and alterations as appear calculated to improve it, and promote its utility.

‘ It would have been easy to have added many further historical illustrations of the
first part of the subject; but as I was unable to supply the want I once alluded to, of
accounts of sufficient accuracy to ascertain what part of the natural power of increase
each particular check destroys, it appears to me that the conclusion, which I had before
drawn from very ample evidence of the only kind that could be obtained, would hardly
receive much additional force by the accumulation of more, precisely of the same description.

‘ In the first two books, therefore, the only additions are a new chapter on France, and
one on England, chiefly in reference to facts which have occurred since the publication
of the last edition.

‘ In the third book, I have given an additional chapter on the Poor-Laws; and as it
appeared to me that the chapters on the Agricultural and Commercial Systems, and the
Effects of encreasing Wealth on the Poor, were not either so well arranged, or so immediately applicable to the main subject, as they ought to be; and as I further wished to
make some alterations in the chapter on Bounties upon Exportation, and add something
on the subject of Restrictions upon Importation, I have recast and rewritten the
chapters which stand the 8th, 9th, 10th, 11th, 12th, 13th, in the present edition; and
given a new title, and added two or three passages to the 14th, and last chapter of the
same book.

‘ In the fourth book I have added a new chapter to the one entitled *Effects of the
Knowledge of the principal Cause of Poverty on Civil Liberty*; and another to the chapter on *the different Plans of employing the Poor*; and I have made a considerable addition to the Appendix, in reply to some writers on the Principles of Population, whose
works have appeared since the last edition.

‘ These are the principal additions and alterations made in the present edition. They
consist in a considerable degree of the application of the general principles of the
Essay to the present state of things.

‘ For the accommodation of the purchasers of the former editions, these additions and
alterations will be published in a separate volume.'—Preface, pp. 12—14.

when

when Mr. Malthus first published his essay was almost an untried field of speculation) has recently undergone. At all events, respecting a book which has taken such firm hold of the public attention, and which, in the judgment of its partisans, is likely to effect a greater change in the current of public opinion than any which has appeared since the ' Wealth of Nations,' we owe a duty to the author and to our readers, which we shall endeavour impartially to perform.

The essay opens with an inquiry into the natural rate of the increase of mankind, compared with that of the subsistence necessary for their support. It appears from some well known examples, that population, where there is no difficulty in procuring a proportionate addition to the supply of food, doubles itself every twenty-five years, or proceeds in a geometrical ratio. Subsistence however, in countries once settled and limited, cannot possibly be accumulated at the same rate. If we can suppose that the produce of England in 1817 should by great exertions be doubled by the year 1842, that is, should be so far and so long able to support the probable increase of an unrestrained population; yet we cannot possibly imagine that it could be again doubled in twenty-five years more, and enabled to meet the demand of forty-four millions in 1867. The most sanguine speculator could only expect the produce to be increased in the same proportion as during the preceding period, or to proceed in the arithmetical ratio of 1, 2, 3; while population, as appears in America, has a natural tendency to increase in the geometrical ratio of 1, 2, 4, &c.

' Taking the whole earth, instead of this island, emigration would of course be excluded; and, supposing the present population equal to a thousand millions, the human species would increase as the numbers 1, 2, 4, 8, 16, 32, 64, 128, 256, and subsistence as 1, 2, 3, 4, 5, 6, 7, 8, 9. In two centuries the population would be to the means of subsistence as 256 to 9; in three centuries as 4096 to 13, and in two thousand years the difference would be almost incalculable.'—vol. i. p. 15.

After reading this prefatory statement, we naturally expect to learn, in the subsequent chapters, that a part, at least, of mankind are placed in some of these different relations as to their food and numbers; or at any rate, that these two opposite forces can only be brought to a tolerable equality by some process totally inconsistent with virtue or happiness. We forget that this is only an abstract view of the subject; that these different relations never can really exist, being uniformly checked at the first step of their hostile progress: and that we are in much more actual danger from every comet that traverses our system, than from the risk that population should ever be to the means of subsistence even as 4 to 3. For this reason we have always regretted the place which
these

these calculations hold in the head and front of the essay. Not because we demur to their justice as abstract truths; but because they seem to perplex the reasoning, by keeping out of sight the facts which it is the real object of the book to prove. The increase of population, no doubt, in favourable situations, is matter of historical notoriety, and may be ascertained on visible and undeniable evidence. But the degree of increase of which human subsistence is capable is necessarily in a great measure hypothetical. Here, therefore, is scope for argument and discussion; and it is for this purpose that the details which follow the author's leading statement are so practically valuable. But it must be observed, that according to the mode in which these details are introduced, they do not bear upon the original propositions, that subsistence increases according to one ratio, and population in another; but on a different set of propositions, which are enunciated in the second chapter, and which the various checks to population in different climates and stages of civilization are subsequently brought in to prove. The opening statements, therefore, are only made to be abandoned; and, if they were to be abandoned, had better not have been made, or at least not placed in so conspicuous a position.

It may be necessary, perhaps, to explain our objection more fully. The author's principle is this: that population has a natural tendency to increase much faster than food can be provided for it; and that the difference between these two ratios in the relative increase of subsistence and population has always occasioned a great deal of poverty and misery in the world. In order to establish his point, two separate courses of argument lay ready for his choice. First, to begin, as he has begun, with a statement of the geometrical and arithmetical ratio, taken as a probable assumption; and then to bring forward his statistical and historical details, in order to show the justice of that original proposition. For if there is this difference, or any such difference between the ratios in which population and subsistence naturally proceed, it follows that there must be in almost all countries a pressure of mankind against the existing supply of food. It must be obtained and increased with so much difficulty, that except in very particular situations, there must always remain some part of the people to whom the necessaries of life will be barely and scantily awarded. This would have given him occasion to appeal to the various records which we possess of the human race : and to prove, from history and experience, that notwithstanding the various drains on population occasioned in some countries by wars and outrages, in others by vicious customs, in others by epidemic disorders, and in others by unhealthy occupations, still there is a constant pressure against the available supply of subsistence; a pressure uniform in

its

its operation though variable in its degree. Other accounts satisfactorily show, that wherever the means of subsistence have been
suddenly increased, either by emigration, or by the addition of
some new territory, or by the effects of war and pestilence sweeping off a portion of the original inhabitants, this facility of supply
has immediately occasioned a start in the progress of population,
which has quickly either filled up the chasm or covered the vacant
surface. We possess, therefore, this further proof that the same
power of natural increase which keeps population fully up to the
level of subsistence, is constantly seeking opportunity to exert itself
still more; and, like a stream forcibly dammed up, will rush onward as soon as the sluices are opened; or, like a tree whose roots
are confined, is always pushing its fibres in every direction, and
searching for room to spread and expand them.

Such is, in fact, the general outline of the course of evidence
by which the leading principle of the book may be supported, and
the superiority of the power of population to the power of producing subsistence maintained. But those who are familiar with the
essay itself will be immediately aware that this is not the process of
reasoning which the author has actually pursued. Leaving altogether, as we observed, his original statement, he undertakes to prove
the following propositions:

' 1. Population is necessarily limited by the means of subsistence.
2. Population invariably increases where the means of subsistence increase. 3. The checks which repress the superior power of population, and keep its effects on a level with the means of subsistence, are
all resolvable into moral restraint, vice, and misery.'—p. 34.

Here we must remark, that these three propositions, considered
as a chain of argument, are thus far defective, that the *superior
power of population* is affirmed, not proved; which amounts to an
assumption of the very point in question. Should it be thought
that this superior power of population had been sufficiently
exhibited by the comparative ratios contained in the preceding
chapter, which is the opinion of the author himself;* still he must
allow that it ought to have been affirmed in a separate proposition,
in order to place the argument in a legitimate and logical form.

But although the arithmetical and geometrical ratios of subsistence and population respectively may satisfactorily and forcibly
illustrate the superior power of population to those who are disposed to admit their justice, still it must be remembered, that the
natural tendency to increase, and still more the comparative power
of augmenting subsistence, are only and can only be fixed hypo-
thetically. The population of America has increased geometrically

---

* See Note to Appendix, vol. iii. p. 344.

for

for the last century; granted; but America is still supported from her own soil; therefore in America subsistence has increased geometrically as well as population: has increased in the four periods of twenty-five years in the proportion of 1, 2, 4, 8.   In our own country, on the other hand, produce has been very far from increasing even arithmetically in the same periods of twenty-five years; instead of proceeding at the rate of 1, 2, 3, 4, it has proceeded as 1, $1\frac{1}{4}$, $1\frac{1}{2}$, $1\frac{3}{4}$, 2; and that barely; for our population, which in the course of the century has actually doubled, was not, at the end of it, independent of foreign supplies.

Without intending therefore to assert that Mr. Malthus's calculation is either too high in the one case or too low in the other, since he professes to consider the average state of the whole earth; the fact, we think, should always be kept in view, that the assumption of the comparative ratios is hypothetical, and necessarily must be so: and we may fairly object to its being propounded as a philosophical axiom no less indisputable than the principles of motion or gravitation, or any other of the ascertained and unerring laws of nature, that population increases in a geometrical, and subsistence in an arithmetical ratio.   As long as it is understood that this is a mere assumption for the sake of argument or illustration, all is well.   But when it is appealed to, as it commonly has been, and as we lately heard it at a public meeting, as a definite ordinance of the Creator; which is, to say the least of it, to place the laws of Providence under a very unprepossessing aspect; it is time to remember, that to prove this is neither the object nor the result of Mr. Malthus's essay.   Though the power of population may not be rated too high, speaking of an unlimited state, nor of production too low, speaking of a limited one; still, while the rate of population is taken from one state of society, and of subsistence from another, there will always remain a door of escape to a pertinacious adversary; who can only be chained down to the broad fact, that population has a tendency to increase beyond the means of subsistence.

The arrangement of which we complain has, without doubt, been injurious to the success and reception of the main principle of the Essay.   Many persons, for instance, have mistaken in this way the leading object of the work; and Mr. Malthus has found reason to complain of its being said that he had written a quarto volume to prove that population increased in a geometrical, and food in an arithmetical ratio. App. p. 344.   Others have caught hold of the belief, that such being the natural difference between the ratios of population and food—the details were introduced in order to show the necessity of misery to reconcile and bring them to a level. C'est la nécessité de misère qu'il s'agit de démontrer, says a French
antagonist

antagonist of Mr. Malthus; and then accuses him of uniformly arguing in a circle, and proving the necessity of misery by the existence of misery.   Mr. Grahame, another adversary, asserts in still rounder terms, that some philosophers, ' of whom Mr. Malthus is the leader, regard the vices and follies of human nature, and their various products, famine, disease and war, as *benevolent remedies* by which nature has enabled human beings to correct the disorders that would arise from that redundance of population which the unrestrained operation of her laws would create.'

' These are the opinions,' replies Mr. Malthus, ' imputed to me and the philosophers with whom I am associated. If the imputation were just, we have certainly on many accounts great reason to be ashamed of ourselves.   For what are we made to say ?   In the first place, we are stated to assert that *famine* is a benevolent remedy for *want of food*, as redundance of population admits of no other interpretation than that of a people ill supplied with the means of subsistence, and consequently the benevolent remedy of famine here noticed can only apply to the disorders arising from scarcity of food.

' Secondly, we are said to affirm that nature enables human beings by means of diseases to correct the disorders that would arise from a redundance of population;—that is, that mankind willingly and purposely create diseases, with a view to prevent those diseases which are the necessary consequence of a redundant population, and are not worse or more mortal than the means of prevention.

' And thirdly, it is imputed to us generally, that we consider the vices and follies of mankind as benevolent remedies for the disorders arising from a redundant population ; and it follows as a matter of course that these vices ought to be encouraged rather than reprobated.

' It would not be easy to compress in so small a compass a greater quantity of absurdity, inconsistency, and unfounded assertion.

' The first two imputations may perhaps be peculiar to Mr. Grahame ; and protection from them may be found in their gross absurdity and inconsistency.   With regard to the third, it must be allowed that it has not the merit of novelty. Although it is scarcely less absurd than the two others, and has been shown to be an opinion no where to be found in the Essay, nor legitimately to be inferred from any part of it, it has been continually repeated in various quarters for fourteen years, and now appears in the pages of Mr. Grahame. For the last time I will now notice it; and should it still continue to be brought forward, I think I may be fairly excused from paying the slightest further attention either to the imputation itself, or to those who advance it.

' If I had merely stated that the tendency of the human race to increase faster than the means of subsistence, was kept to a level with these means by some or other of the forms of vice and misery, and that these evils were absolutely unavoidable, and incapable of being diminished by any human efforts ; still I could not with any semblance of justice be accused of considering vice and misery as the remedies of these evils, instead of the very evils themselves. As well nearly might

I be open to Mr. Grahame's imputations of considering the famine and disease necessarily arising from a scarcity of food as a benevolent remedy for the evils which this scarcity occasions.

'But I have not so stated the proposition. I have not considered the evils of vice and misery arising from a redundant population as unavoidable, and incapable of being diminished. On the contrary, I have pointed out a mode by which these evils may be removed or mitigated by removing or mitigating their cause. I have endeavoured to show that this may be done consistently with human virtue and happiness. I have never considered any possible increase of population as an evil, except as far as it might increase the proportion of vice and misery. Vice and misery, and these alone, are the evils which it has been my great object to contend against. I have expressly proposed moral restraints as their rational and proper remedy; and whether the remedy be good or bad, adequate or inadequate, the proposal itself, and the stress which I have laid upon it, is an incontrovertible proof that I never can have considered vice and misery as themselves remedies.'—App. p. 389—392.

This answer is quite decisive. But still it might occur to Mr. Malthus that so great a misapprehension of his views could hardly have become so general, unless there had been something in the conduct and arrangement of his arguments which led to these erroneous conclusions, and counteracted the force of his frequent disclaimers. The explanation, we imagine, is to be found in the unaccommodating ratios of population and subsistence, and the commanding position assigned them in the outset of his book, while an equally formidable array of positive and preventive checks to population is drawn up on the other hand, with the apparent design of bringing them to a level. Whereas if the author had contented himself with beginning from the propositions which he really proves, his work would have had the same utility, and have exhibited the same practical truths, with the additional advantage of less outraging the feelings of his readers. Still the immense superiority of the power of unchecked population to that of production in a limited territory is so undeniable a fact, that it should by no means have been entirely omitted; and it might with great propriety have been brought forward as a corroboration of the general argument of the essay.

If, on the other hand, he had deemed it the most striking or philosophical mode of treating the subject to follow out his original statement, the different ratios of food and population, we think he would have pursued a clearer course of reason by adhering to it, instead of bringing forward a separate string of propositions: for as it is, an opponent may complain that he is required to assent to a different fact from that which is proved to his conviction; or he may find fault with the narrowness of the induction compared with the importance

portance of the conclusion, and appeal to exceptions which different ages and states of society cannot fail to furnish, or resort to some of the various shifts by which it is always possible to block up the avenues of a reluctant understanding. In short, the question is incapable of demonstrative proof, or of determination à priori; and the evidence, the practical evidence, that the power of population is infinitely greater than the power of production, must ultimately rest on the actual pressure of population against produce. It is only after pointing out the existence of great and undeniable checks to population, and still proving the close pressure against subsistence, that the superiority of the power of population can be satisfactorily and incontrovertibly established.

If we are right in these strictures upon the conduct of our author's argument, it may account for the known fact, that many intelligent persons have declared themselves dissatisfied with Mr. Malthus's reasoning, though they were unable to deny his conclusions. But whether we are right or wrong, it may be convenient at all events to place the subject in a somewhat different point of view: and accordingly we propose, without hesitation, the following axioms on the subject of population, as unanswerably proved in the Essay before us:—

1. ' Population is necessarily limited by the means of subsistence.' This requires only to be stated.

2. There are various ' checks which repress' the natural ' power of population, and keep its effects on a level with the means of subsistence; which are all resolvable into moral restraint, vice, and misery.'

3. Notwithstanding the effect of these checks, ' population always increases as the means of subsistence increase:' or, as it might be affirmed with perfect justice, always increases so as to press against the available supply.

Our readers will observe how far these propositions deviate from the author's own terms, which we stated in a preceding page; and that we consider the superiority of the natural power of population over the power of production, to be proved by the existence of the checks alluded to in the second of our propositions: in spite of which, the pressure of mankind against the existing produce is matter of universal experience. To recapitulate the evidence of these facts, collected by Mr. Malthus, would be to transcribe the first and second books of his work: it is taken from every region of the world, and every period of history, and every stage of society; and largely shews that mankind have uniformly increased and multiplied, in conformity with the command of their Creator; and also that, agreeably to the same Creator's denuncia-

tion,

tion, they have always been condemned to acquire their subsistence by painful and continual labour.

The practical conclusion resulting from the book is this: that redundancy is not only a much greater evil than deficiency of population, but much more to be apprehended, much more likely to happen; that legislators therefore begin in the wrong place when they employ any adventitious means to give direct encouragement to population; since they have only to increase subsistence, or the power of commanding it, and population will invariably follow; and in fact does always exist, to the full amount of the available supply of food. This is a question of no slight interest every where; but comes particularly home to our own country; where we have now in regular operation a principle allowed even by its advocates to be a forcing principle, and which, especially during the last twenty years, has been so exercised, as to become an actual bounty on population. If Mr. Malthus is right, such a bounty is not only unnecessary, but must lead to consequences injurious, if not fatal to national happiness. If on the other hand he is wrong, we may still persist in providing at the public expense a subsistence for all who may be born, even if there should be no demand on the part of the community for their labour. As the question is of such important and immediate interest, we will consider in their turn the various objections which may be thought to invalidate Mr. Malthus's conclusions.

I. The first and most obvious of these is taken from the present state of many countries which are known to have been formerly populous, and are now comparatively deserts; as Northern Africa, and Persia, and the immense territories which compose the Turkish empire. When we measure these vast districts on the map, and compare the square miles of fertile territory with the actual number of their inhabitants, the natural impression which the mind receives is that the pressure of population is a vain terror; or, as the French opponent of Mr. Malthus terms it, un sophisme très habilement soutenu.

Mankind however, it is very plain, cannot be supported by the *possible* abundance of their soil, but must depend upon its actual produce. It is sufficiently notorious that Egypt and Greece, and Syria and Anatolia, were formerly as much more populous, than in the state of degradation to which a wretched tyranny has now reduced them, as they were more distinguished in arts and comparative civilization. History points out to us as many cities in those districts, as we can now find villages; and there is little doubt but in those ages less actual distress was felt from insufficient supply than now, when families occupy the place of provinces.

Insecurity

Insecurity of property is the great bane of all these countries. Mankind seem upon the whole to be well enough inclined to industry, if they can only reckon upon reaping its fruits; but no one labours for labour's sake, or sows without a prospect of gathering the harvest. Throughout the whole of these districts, however, the peasant is uniformly subject to plunder of one sort or other; either the legalized exactions of tyranny, or to the devastation of barbarous incursions. Throughout Turkey the system of oppressing and pillaging all who may have collected the most trifling property begins from the throne, and systematically descends through all the ramifications of government. Where all offices are notoriously bought, and bought at a competition; where all are held during pleasure, the pleasure of an insecure and arbitrary despot; do we require the details of travellers to fill up the outlines of such a country, and throw in its darker shades? or is it sufficient to refer to the principles of our common nature, in order to paint the picture in its true colours?

Under circumstances of this nature, it is certainly not surprising that the inhabitants of these countries should be few, either in proportion to their extent, or their possible fertility: the wonder is greater that the people should reach, nay press rudely against the limits of their supply. This fact however is as undeniable as the wretchedness of their political situation, and is authenticated by the testimony of every traveller, Volney, Thornton, Clarke, Morier, &c. who furnish abundant materials to prove, that in spite of the little inducement there is either to live, or to propagate life in these countries, still they are inhabited fully up to the limits of the available subsistence. The want of regular government, and the various political evils under which they labour, can effectually extinguish virtue, and public spirit, and literature, and industry: but population still keeps equal pace with the measure of the supply; still treads so closely upon it, that any deficiency in the seasons, any unexpected drought, or epidemic among the cattle, reduces them to severe distress, and even to absolute famine.

The mistakes on this head are not to be set to the account of our author, but of those among his readers, who because he has represented the lowest classes in these countries as subject to seasons of penury and want, have understood him to mean that over-population is the *cause* of their misery. The cause of their misery is the government and the habits it generates; and while these remain, neither the addition nor subtraction of millions of people would make any permanent difference in their situation. The addition, indeed, would cause an immediate famine and mortality; and the subtraction immediate plenty. If half their number were

suddenly

suddenly exterminated, the remaining half would of course enjoy abundance for a single season: but that season over, the effect would only be to sink the ratio of industry in proportion to the decreased demand, till the numbers gradually reproduced occasioned the necessity of again cultivating the desolated lands.

The just inference from these and all other ill governed or barbarous countries, relates to the tendency of population considered as a law of our nature, and no way bears upon the effects of that law on human happiness. The condition of people so circumstanced would not be one jot the better, though the power of population were diminished to any conceivable extent : indeed it is sufficiently abated by vicious customs and wide-wasting plagues, and probably at the present time is absolutely retrograde. We wish this point to be borne in mind ; not only as being important to the question at issue, but as making part of a very general error with regard to the real conclusions deducible from Mr. Malthus's theory. The cause of the distress is moral and political vice ; and the distress itself is only brought in as evidence to attest the uniform law which raises population up to the supply of food even under most unfavourable circumstances of natural or civil discouragement.

II. The pressure of population against supply in countries far advanced in civilization is more generally acknowledged by all who have paid attention to the subject. Still it is very possible that those who have not looked into the details of political economy, or accustomed themselves to its language, may not recognize the existence of the pressure so confidently and familiarly assumed. We read of distant times and distant countries in which multitudes have died by famine. There the want of subsistence is a palpable fact. But since the improvements in the circulation and distribution of produce from one country to another introduced by commerce, and from one part of the same country to another, facilitated by internal communication, the misery of *famine* is exchanged for the milder operation of *scarcity*, which only shews itself in an enhancement of the money-price of corn. Besides, a great quantity of human food is wasted in manufactures, is employed in distilleries, or is prodigally consumed in various forms of luxury. How does this agree with the alleged fact, that population presses against the actual supply? This, no doubt, is a very superficial objection, and is answered by the first elements of political science. But as we see every day that many persons, even of those whom they concern, have been very partially imbued with these first elements, we are unwilling to pass it over altogether.

It is evident that the man whose assistance is necessary to any master or employer of workmen must be supported by that employer,

ployer, together with his family. For the precise purpose of obtaining this support, he consents to give his labour : and there are still many cases in which the recompense is actually made in the shape of provision. But one of the first and simplest operations of civilization, is to make all bargains through a common medium; and accordingly the return for labour, like other payments, is given in money. This money payment is very different in different countries, and in the same country at different times ; but whatever it is, the quantity of subsistence it will procure, and not the nominal amount of the payment, is the standard by which the labourer's return must be estimated. The only way therefore in which we can judge of the pressure of population, is by the rate of wages ; and the only way in which we can estimate the rate of wages, is by the quantity of support which it will procure to the labourer, according to the customary mode of living in the country.

For this reason, from the time when the weekly labour is recompensed in money, the pressure of population is less directly visible to the eye of the common observer. Its operation in itself becomes a more complex concern ; and it is moreover concealed from view by the quantity of machinery which is going on together. Its effect however is sufficiently discoverable in the diminished rate of wages, following the increased competition for employ. In countries like America, where there is plenty of fresh land ready to make an ample recompense to any capitalist who will take the pains of reclaiming it from the beasts of the forest, or the wandering savage of the plain, a labourer, in almost any department, may immediately meet with an employer. The competition there is among the masters, to find workmen ; not among the workmen to find employ : but in most of the old countries in Europe the tide is commonly setting the other way; and especially in the lowest and simplest operations of industry, the competition is on the side of the labourer. The labourer is therefore in a much greater degree dependent upon his employer, and his remuneration is seldom larger than the support of his family absolutely demands.

To understand in practice what has been thus far stated in theory, our readers have only to look around them, and see the mode in which a great part of their countrymen are at this moment living ; and then to answer, whether the human species in civilized countries does not increase up to the lowest quantity of support necessary to their preservation.

Beginning with the case of our peasants, the average wages in husbandry may be rated at 12s. per week: take the wife's earnings at two shillings, the total for the year will amount to £36:8s. With regard to the expenses, no one will place the consumption of a fa-

    mily

mily throughout at less than a half-peck loaf per week to each individual. It is not reckoned lower even by overseers. At 1s. the quartern loaf the expense will stand thus, for a family with three children.

Bread for five persons, at 10s. per week,	£26	0 per ann.
Soap and candles, at 8d. do. -	- 1	16
Rent - - - - - -	- 3	0
Clothing and furniture - -	- 3	0
Fuel, 2s. in winter, 1s. in summer -	- 3	4

                           Total -   £37 0

This calculation carries us at once beyond the earnings, though no allowance has been made for medicine, loss of time, or any other article of food than wheaten bread. Whatever *luxuries* are claimed, must be saved out of the necessaries of life, or by substituting a cheaper and less nutritious article for the favourite food of the country; and if there be four children instead of three, under the working age, the additional child brings an expense of £5 per annum, and of course diminishes the chance of the workman's earnings. In estimating the bread too at 1s., we have taken rather a favourable average. Experience of the last twenty years has proved to us that we must not expect a stationary price. In the present year (1817) the average price would be about 1s. 4d. thus adding nine pounds to the annual expenditure, and bringing us so far beyond the actual wages. Yet the poor must be supported in dear years as well as cheap; and the whole statement justifies us in asserting that our agricultural poor are brought by the competition of labourers to as low a rate of wages, both nominal and real, as will enable them to rear a family.

Whoever has travelled in a manufacturing district will not have found things wearing a brighter aspect, or venture to affirm that the population seem better fed, better clothed, or better lodged than nature requires in order to keep up their number. At times indeed there is more variation in their rate of wages than among the peasantry, owing to an unusual demand for some particular manufacture, or to some temporary speculation. But these demands are followed by a decline no less rapid, and the average wages of the year do not exceed a moderate pittance. These facts, gleaned from the very surface of our own country, are domestic proofs of a population reaching the average supply; and it is well known that the effect of the picture would not be altered for the better, if Scotland and Ireland were added to the view. But if we stop here, we shall stop, after all, short of the population. As a population cannot be supported without food, it can never, of course, materially exceed the average supply. Still the tendency

                                                  to

to increase is so strong, that in a civilized or fully peopled country
it never rests on this side, it always encroaches a little beyond it.
How is this possible? or if possible, how can it be proved?—Too
easily. We have seen that labour is the only claim to support
which the poorer classes can offer; to be without labour, therefore, is to be without support; and to multiply beyond the demand for labour, is to multiply beyond the available supply of
food. But it is matter of experience that in all the departments of
national industry there are always more claimants for employ than
can obtain it; and though the excess, for obvious reasons, is at
different periods very different in degree, the fact is undeniable,
that there are always more workmen, than can find employers in
manufactures; always more journeymen mechanics, than can be
supplied with work; always more agricultural labourers, than, taking
the year throughout, can be employed in useful husbandry. Every
individual of these superfluous labourers is evidence of a population exceeding the supply of food.

This argument cannot be set aside by urging that if there is an
excess of labourers in one department of manufacture, there is a
deficiency in another; or that if there is a want of work in one
part of the country, there is a want of workmen in another. We
must argue of these things as we practically find them; and it is
unnecessary to enter upon the question, whether if a central board
for labour could be established, as Mr. Colquhoun proposes, the
demand upon the whole would not, after a certain time, be just as
much above the supply of work that could be furnished, as it
is now. Neither is it any sufficient contradiction of the statement, to say that, after all, the number of unemployed workmen
is comparatively trifling. In the first place, we feel by too
sensible experience that this is not always true. But not to argue
on a general fact of our nature from accidental periods of distress,
we must remember that in England the law authorises the poor to
demand support, whether they can or cannot find employ : and accordingly many of them are set to sift gravel or level mole hills, or
something equally profitable, and receive perhaps ten shillings per
week for work which does not return a farthing to the employer.
In manufacturing towns also, the benevolent sympathy of the masters often keeps a larger number of hands on the list, than they
can employ with advantage to themselves; but the support of these
superfluous hands must in fairness be set down to the score of
charity, and not to an effectual demand for labour. Extensive
charities, public subscriptions, and speculative enterprise in this
country tend at all times to conceal from public observation the
competition of labourers; but we have no doubt that the testimony
of

of every parish in the kingdom, town and country taken together, would agree with the evidence actually laid before the Parliamentary Committees, and prove the population to be uniformly beyond the demand for labour, though it might be dangerous to assess the actual amount of the excess. Whether one in ten, or one in fifty labourers who are able and willing to work, are unable to provide a field for their industry, is not very material—it is evident that the redundance is on the side of the labourer: and somewhere between these two points, we imagine, the experience of different places and periods of time would justify us in fixing the degree of that redundance.

If this statement is correct, and a just result of what is continually passing before our eyes; then it becomes clear that there is no sufficient foundation for the opinion of an author whose principles we highly respect, and who argues that the collection of a larger part of the people into towns, and their engagement in unhealthy occupations in advanced states of society, so far increases the natural mortality and diminishes the average duration of life, as to equalize the acknowledged disproportion between the powers of population and production. Mr. Malthus, in his Appendix to the present edition, has considered this objection at some length. He admits the possibility of the case, which is provided for in the cautious terms in which his second proposition was enunciated; but he appeals to the state of the various countries in Europe, to shew that there is no appearance of any of them approaching that condition, when moral restraint may become a useless and unnecessary virtue; or when those who are disposed to marry, need employ no previous foresight as to their means of supporting a family.

‘ The question,’ he says, ‘ can only be determined by an appeal to experience. Mr. Weyland is always ready to refer to the state of this country; and, in fact, may be said almost to have built his system upon the peculiar policy of a single state. But the reference in this case will entirely contradict his theory. He has brought forward some elaborate calculations to shew the extreme difficulty with which the births of the country supply the demands of the towns and manufactories. In looking over them, the reader, without other informatiom, would be disposed to feel considerable alarm at the prospect of depopulation impending over the country; or at least he would be convinced that we were within a hair's breadth of that formidable point of *non-reproduction*, at which, according to Mr. Weyland, the population *naturally* comes to a full stop before the means of subsistence cease to be progressive.

‘ These calculations were certainly as applicable twenty years ago as they are now; and indeed they are chiefly founded on observations which were made at a greater distance of time than the period here noticed.

noticed. But what has happened since? In spite of the enlargement of all our towns; in spite of the most rapid increase of manufactories, and of the proportion of people employed in them; in spite of the most extraordinary and unusual demands for the army and navy; in short, in spite of a state of things which, according to Mr. Weyland's theory, ought to have brought us long since to the point of *non-reproduction*, the population of the country has advanced at a rate more rapid than was ever known at any period of its history. During the ten years from 1800 to 1811, as I have mentioned in a former part of this work, the population of this country (even after making an allowance for the presumed deficiency of the returns in the first enumeration) increased at a rate which would double its numbers in fifty-five years.

' This fact appears to me at once a full and complete refutation of the doctrine, that, as society advances, the increased indisposition to marriage and increased mortality in great towns and manufactories always overcome the principle of increase ; and that, in the language of Mr. Weyland, " population, so far from having an inconvenient tendency uniformly to press against the means of subsistence, becomes by degrees very slow in overtaking those means."

' With this acknowledged and glaring fact before him, and with the most striking evidences staring him in the face, that even, during this period of rapid increase, thousands both in the country and in towns were prevented from marrying so early as they would have done, if they had possessed sufficient means of supporting a family independently of parish relief, it is quite inconceivable how a man of sense could bewilder himself in such a maze of futile caculations, and come to a conclusion so diametrically opposite to experience.

' The fact already noticed, as it applies to the most advanced stage of society known in Europe, and proves incontrovertibly that the actual checks to population, even in the most improved countries, arise principally from an insufficiency of subsistence, and soon yield to increased resources, notwithstanding the increase of towns and manufactories, may I think fairly be considered as quite decisive of the question at issue.

' But in treating of so general and extensive a subject as the Principle of Population, it would surely not be just to take our examples and illustrations only from a single state. And in looking at the other countries Mr. Weyland's doctrine on population is, if possible, still more completely contradicted. Where, I would ask, are the great towns and manufactories in Switzerland, Norway, and Sweden, which are to act as *the graves of mankind*, and to prevent the possibility of a redundant population? In Sweden the proportion of the people living in the country is to those who live in town as thirteen to one ; in England this proportion is about two to one ; and yet England increases much faster than Sweden. How is this to be reconciled with the doctrine that the progress of civilization and improvement is always accompanied by a correspondent abatement in the natural tendency of population to increase? Norway, Sweden and Switzerland have not on the whole been ill-governed; but where are the necessary "anticipating alterations," which,

according

according to Mr. Weyland, arise in every society as the powers of the soil diminish, and " render so many persons unwilling to marry, and so many more, who do marry, incapable of reproducing their own numbers, and of replacing the deficiency in the remainder?" What is it that in these countries indisposes people to marry, but the absolute hopelessness of being able to support their families? What is it that renders many more who do marry incapable of reproducing their own numbers, but the diseases generated by excessive poverty—by an insufficient supply of the necessaries of life? Can any man of reflection look at these and many of the other countries of Europe, and then venture to state that there is no moral reason for repressing the inclination to early marriages; when it cannot be denied that the alternative of not repressing it must necessarily and unavoidably be premature mortality from excessive poverty? And is it possible to know that in few or none of the countries of Europe the wages of labour, determined in the common way by the supply and the demand, can support in health large families; and yet assert that population does not press against the means of subsistence, and that " the evils of a redundant population can never be necessarily felt by a country till it is actually peopled up to the full capacity of its resources?"—vol. iii. pp. 407—412.

The fact is, and Mr. Weyland as a sincere friend to humanity will rejoice at it notwithstanding its effect upon his argument, that the same progressive stage of civilization in which mankind are collected together in large towns, and subjected to the evils and diseases belonging to such a situation, brings also the antidote together with the malady; and by applying more general and more skilful attention to the means of prevention and cure, checks that premature mortality which unhealthy occupations and crowded streets would otherwise occasion. We have been at the pains to verify this observation; and it is a satisfactory result of the inquiry to find, that those closely-peopled seats of manufactories and trade which were once emphatically called the graves of mankind, and in which Mr. Weyland's argument would bury so large a proportion of his countrymen, are now comparatively the abodes of health and longevity; so humane, so successfully and indisputably humane have been the improvements in the management of prisons, and hospitals, and work-houses; the establishment of fever-wards, and the various rules for ventilating, and purifying, and fumigating crowded manufactories.

By a calculation which Mr. Weyland has taken from Price's Reversionary Payments, it appeared that the annual deaths even in the small town of Newbury were to the whole population as 1 in 28 or 29, at the time when that calculation was made. Whereas the register of that town for the last ten years shews that the average duration of life is now exactly double. The annual deaths, at the present period, are as 1 in 56 of the whole; the average number

for

for the last ten years amounting to 87, on a population which the last census states at 4900.

Thus it was formerly calculated that in Manchester, containing 84,000 souls, half the number born died under two years of age; in Northampton, containing 7000, under ten; and Mr. Weyland makes these calculations the hinges of his argument! We cannot put in so precise an answer to these particular cases; but common observation, and the judgment of the best-informed persons in those and similar situations concur in persuading us that matters are very different now; not to mention, that as the deaths in the whole of Lancashire are but as 1 in 48, and half the population of that county is contained in the two immense towns of Manchester and Liverpool, it is impossible to doubt the annual births must greatly exceed the annual deaths even in those unfavourable situations; and the population be progressive, instead of requiring continued supplies from the country to replace the domestic waste.

In fact, if this is true of Birmingham, no one will hesitate about Manchester. We have been favoured with an abstract of the baptisms and burials in Birmingham for thirteen years from the beginning of this century, out of which there have been only three, viz, 1801, 1802, and 1810, in which the former have not very considerably exceeded; and in the whole period the births have gained about one-seventh on the deaths, the baptisms averaging 2120 per annum, the burials 1979; or 1 in 43 of the whole population, taken at 85,753 in 1811. The register of the largest parish in the unhealthy city of Coventry gives nearly a similar result. So that the average duration of life in a town of 80,000 persons is fifteen years longer at the present time, than it was in a population of 4,000 fifty years ago. This increased healthiness of the community assists in accounting for the extraordinary increase of population within the last ten years, and in some degree for the pressure which has been lately experienced; as also for the flourishing state of Assurance Societies, and all other institutions which calculate upon the Swedish and other tables of fifty years date; and which ought no longer to be considered as authority for the general average of life in this country.

At all events it is very clear that we cannot depend on the mortality of towns, for ridding us of any superfluous population; and we own it is more gratifying to our minds to conclude that the advancement of civilization should counter-balance the unhealthiness which attends some of its occupations by the improvements of medical skill, than that there should be a constant and necessary waste of human life from premature mortality.

‘ If indeed such peculiar unhealthiness and mortality were the proper and natural check to the progress of population in the advanced stages
of

of society, we should justly have reason to apprehend that, by improving the healthiness of our towns and manufactories, as we have done in England during the last twenty years, we might really defeat the designs of Providence. And though I have too much respect for Mr. Weyland to suppose that he would deprecate all attempts to diminish the mortality of towns, and render manufactories less destructive to the health of the children employed in them; yet certainly his principles lead to this conclusion, since his theory has been completely destroyed by those laudable efforts which have made the mortality of England—a country abounding in towns and manufactories, less than the mortality of Sweden—a country in a state almost purely agricultural.'—vol. iii. p. 424.

The conclusion is, therefore, that the natural progress of civilization does not so far retard the natural progress of population, as to counteract its universal tendency to surpass the limits of subsistence : though it is no doubt true that where any such causes of comparative unhealthiness exist, population could never increase in its greatest possible or even its greatest known ratio.

In a country of limited resources, this comparative shortness of life has no other effect than to accelerate the period or increase the chance of marriage. We have before alluded to the different averages exhibited by the table of marriages in the different counties of England. In Warwickshire, 1 takes place annually among 116 persons; in Worcestershire, 1 among 132; in Dorsetshire, 1 in 135; in Monmouthshire, 1 in 153; in all England, 1 in 120; in Wales, 1 in 136. From which it would appear that Monmouthshire, notwithsanding its picturesque beauty, is the very worst place to be born in, and Warwickshire, notwithstanding the smoke of its collieries and steam engines, the very best; and so it is, for all who have learnt from circulating libraries that life without love is not worth the having; but if we proceed to the next column, it appears that the value of love is fairly placed in the scale against the value of life, and that the average expectation of life varies with tolerable exactness according to the average expectation of marriage: the annual burials being to the whole population in Warwickshire, 1 in 42; in Worcestershire, 1 in 52; in Dorsetshire, 1 in 57; in Monmouthshire, 1 in 64; in all England, 1 in 49; in Wales, 1 in 60. This proves, if any thing can prove, the great restraint which prudence imposes in this country upon the power of population; and yet notwithstanding both the prudential restraint and the unhealthiness of many districts, population has proceeded to a length and swelled to an amount which we now find inconvenient, and are obliged to meet by growing demands on public and private charity, and glad to remedy by extensive emigration.

III. The objection which next occurs affords a more plausible argument against the general position. This is the case of agricultural

tural countries, from which provisions of various kinds are regularly exported to supply the deficiency of those in a different state of civilization. The exportation of surplus produce conveys the idea that plenty is to be had at home for little or nothing : and there is no doubt but the country where labour is best rewarded in subsistence at least, if not in general comforts, is a country in this agricultural state, where a large family is a treasure, and where no apprehensions as to the difficulty of supporting one retard the progress of population.

Still, however, the general law asserts its power even here. Population pushes itself fully up to the means of subsistence, if by subsistence we speak of that which is available to their use ; though the productive power of the land being as yet commensurate with the activity of population, the one has not outstripped the other. The case therefore which was considered under the last head, of labourers without labour, rarely occurs ; but still those who look, even here, for gratuitous supply, will be bitterly disappointed. Those who from accident or misfortune cannot offer the return of labour for what they demand, or who from idleness will not, have much less chance of being maintained without than in a closely-peopled society like ours ; while the surplus returns of those who do labour, instead of feeding an idle population, are bartered for artificial luxuries, or for foreign manufactures of necessity, or ornament, or utility. This is even the best state of an exporting country. But in ill-regulated societies, exportation may habitually take place while the mass of the people, or the very labourers who produce the surplus provision, are reduced to a degree of poverty and privation comparatively unknown in the countries which are dependent on them, and receiving the annual supply. Ireland and Poland have long exported ; yet no one who knows the situation of their inhabitants will deny that there is more habitual distress, more squalid poverty endured there, than in their customers England and Holland. The actual supply of Ireland consists of the finest pork and beef ; but what does this avail the cotter, who is supported on milk and potatoes ? The actual supply of Poland consists of the finest wheat, to the growth of which the soil is more favourable than any in Europe ; but what does this benefit the peasant, whose ordinary subsistence is obtained from rye bread and an inferior kind of pulse ? It is true if the actual quantity of food in any given country could be equally divided amongst the members of it even in a year of the greatest want, and were consumed by them in the most frugal manner, there could seldom be an absolute scarcity, supposing the transaction to be extraordinary, and the division unexpected. But in the nature of things we know this is practically impossible ; and that must be taken as the supply of a country,

which

which its inhabitants in their several classes are able to command by the labour which in return they are able to offer.

It would therefore be an error to suppose that when we have found a country which, like Poland or America, or that part of Russia which borders on the Black Sea, regularly exports a quantity of human sustenance, we have found a country where mankind do not increase up to the supply. We have found a place, at least America and Russia are instances of it, where a man in possession of a certain capital may say, Here I will fix my standard, here my principal will find an easy employment, and here my labour will secure an ample support to any family which may be sent me. But we have not found a place where a man may say, here is a vacant space and a quantity of superfluous produce which will support me gratuitously at my ease. There is no superfluous food in the world; no where any thing to spare, or to be had without return.

This assertion, if necessary, might receive additional confirmation from inquiring what, after all, is the boasted export of these abundant countries, and what proportion it bears to their own population. The whole of the exports of corn from the United States to all parts of the world in 1805, amounted to

777,543 barrels of flour,
55,400 bushels of oats,
861,501 of Indian corn,
56,836 tierces of rice;

with an inconsiderable growth of rye, wheat, and barley;* all which would furnish, according to the average consumption of England, a year's subsistence to about 200,000 persons; i. e. would support an addition of one thirtieth to the domestic population, rated at that period at six millions. Poland, which has also been inconsiderately treated as an inexhaustible granary, could never supply, during the excessive demand of the late war, more than 500,000 quarters, and on an average not more than half that quantity, i. e. according to our average consumption, at the highest, food for 400,000 persons, at the lowest for 200,000, which probably bears about the same proportion to the Polish population as the exportation from the United States. Yet these are the countries which send abroad by far the greatest quantity of corn, taken in comparison with their population: and when we estimate the dependence of America upon foreign countries for many necessaries of civilized life, and most of its luxuries; when we remember that the extensive land proprietors in Poland depend altogether on their

---

* See Mr. Jacob's pamphlet on the ' Protection of British Agriculture,' p. 56, &c. If some theorists in political economy would consider these facts and calculations, we should hardly be harassed with their speculations for supporting a manufacturing population by foreign agriculture.

exports for the means of a most lavish profusion; when we consider the immense exertions to procure corn which continued from 1795 to 1812, and the enormous price, both actual and relative, which it bore, and that the demand, being in a great measure regular, must have materially increased the cultivation; when we take all these elements into the calculation, we shall be rather struck with the near approach of the inhabitants to the produce, than with the amount of the surplus. The exportation, when reduced to figures, rather tends to show the pressure, than to furnish an exception against it; when we reflect that if the whole of the exported produce had been retained at home, it would not have supported the existing population above ten days beyond the year, or maintained an addition of more than a thirtieth part to the whole. We are inclined to doubt whether all the human subsistence which is exported from all the countries of the world, and is not balanced by a return of equivalent imports, if it could be exactly computed, would be found to exceed what might suffice for a year's supply of a million of persons, i. e. for a thousandth part of the probable population of the world. If this calculation comes any where near the truth, it will powerfully demonstrate the strength of population, with which even the extent and fertility of America or the southern departments of the Russian territory can only just keep pace; and which even the slack demand for labour in Ireland and the wretched vassalage of Poland cannot effectually restrain.

IV. The next objection which we shall briefly notice is of a more delicate nature, and connected with our feelings of natural and revealed religion. Upon this point there is something which well deserves remark in the first reception experienced by our author. He who referred the greatest evils of human life to a strong natural principle, might have looked for popular applause and gratitude, while he seemed to take the blame off our own shoulders, and to throw it upon the constitution of things in which we have no active share; while he endeavoured to exonerate human laws or regulations, and to prove that the disease which preyed upon social happiness was more radical and inveterate than the wisest legislation could cure.

It might have been imagined that the discovery would be hailed as flattering our pride, and accepted as a satisfactory solution of many of those natural and civil evils, which, in spite of all our attempts to eradicate them, have always sprung up in every state of society, which are not only rankly luxuriant under bad administration, but have never been altogether extirpated even by the most careful culture.

On the contrary, the great majority of the public shut their eyes against the facts, and their ears against the conclusion; those who could not help acknowledging the force of both, took all possible pains to discard them from their minds, and to forget the assent which they could not entirely withhold; and those who were neither able to judge of premises nor inference, proclaimed by a general outcry their weakness and their fears, and started at the name of Malthus as the enemy of God and man. They preferred, it seems, that any imputation should lie against the institutions of society, rather than that they should be forced to give up the flattering prospect of a general amelioration in the condition of the human race. We have always thought this fact not a little remarkable; as furnishing a curious proof of the strong conviction inherent in mankind, that notwithstanding the distresses they see around them and the calamities they are subject to, they are still under the protecting dominion of a merciful as well as a powerful Creator; a conviction so deeply rooted that when they meet with a course of argument which appears to them (whether rightly or not) to end in a contrary conclusion, they at once infer the fallacy of the premises, and had rather mistrust the logic of their heads, than resign the consolatory feeling of their hearts.

Still it was soon found a much easier matter to disbelieve Mr. Malthus than to refute him. This ought earlier to have admonished his opponents, as it has at last taught them, to examine whether his premises, or their conclusions were really in the wrong; whether the fault were in his arguments, or in their impressions: whether, in short, the great features of the country, as he had represented them, were not correctly drawn, though the medium through which they were accidentally viewed had thrown a harsh and disagreeable tone of colouring over the picture: just as the state of the mind, in Crabbe's ingenious tale of the Lover's Journey, gives to the same objects the tint of a March east wind, or of a glowing autumnal evening. It is not difficult to trace a similar effect in the work before us, arising naturally from the leading principle in the author's view when he sat down to the composition. A visionary notion of theoretical perfectibility could only be met by a practical statement of the evils, moral and physical, which beset human nature. Society has no greater enemy than the man who would substitute theory for experience; and no sincerer friend than the man who appeals to experience to refute him. To the chimerical reformer of the political and moral world, Mr. Malthus justly answers, such hopes are illusory and such schemes impracticable, while mankind exist as they are; there is a principle inherent in their very constitution, which will uniformly bring them, as in all ages and countries it has already brought them, into a situation in which there will be labour, indigence, distress, and disease.

Here

Here we have at once a key to the peculiar turn which the ar⸳ gument takes, which is certainly, at first sight, not a little unprepossessing. The principle which the Essay undertakes to explain, is uniformly treated in the light of an EVIL. The very title-page announces ' an inquiry into our prospects respecting the future removal or mitigation of *the evil* which it occasions.' Speaking of moral restraint, the author says, ' if this restraint do not produce vice, it is undoubtedly the *least evil* that can arise from the principle of population.' He elsewhere argues that ' we must submit to the action of a great check to population in some form or other, as an inevitable law of nature; and the only inquiry that remains is, how it may take place with the *least possible prejudice* to the virtue and happiness of society.' Even that habitual prudence, which leads mankind, or ought to lead them, to consider the means of providing for a family before they incur the responsibility of supporting one, is uniformly entitled the ' *fear of misery.*'

It is well known what gave the argument this peculiar direction, and brought it into the notice of the world, with a more forbidding aspect than was likely to meet with a welcome reception. Had Mr. Godwin and his party followed another of the various mazes of error, and instead of attacking social institutions, directed their censures against the Creator of the world, who had interwoven with the constitution of mankind a principle which could not fail to render vice and misery universal; then we should have felt the advantage of the same enlightened understanding ready to meet the enemy on different grounds; shifting the line of his argument to encounter the opposite movements of his adversary, and prompt to take up another and an equally strong position. The merest sciolist in the book of nature, he might have argued, knows that he ought to search for good, and not evil, as the final object of any extensive principle in our constitution. The writer whom I oppose impeaches the wisdom of the Creator's measures because he is blind to His designs. Thales might as justly have blamed His arrangement, in revolving the larger round the smaller body, or Ptolemy have censured the want of a continent to balance Africa or Asia. Is it not evident how this pressure of population against the actual subsistence, is uniformly exciting the industry of mankind to render more subsistence available? how the necessities it occasions improve the human faculties by exercise, and invigorate virtue? how it thus furnishes the best opportunities of strengthening those powers which want of exertion uniformly impairs, and of exhibiting those virtues which most conspicuously adorn the moral nature of man? It is for the censurer of the providential arrangement of things to show how the same purposes might have been answered by other and better means. Above all, can we fail to observe that

this

this principle, imposed as it is by a Creator whom we see and feel to be benevolent, is a strong corroboration of the truth of that revelation which declares mankind to be placed here in a preparatory state? Have we not every reason from analogy to believe, that, if He had intended this for their final destination, He would have rendered perfection attainable; and that, as he has not placed perfection within their reach, he designs this world as a state of discipline?

That such would have been the general strain of our author's reasoning, had he been called upon by circumstances to refute one error instead of another, we never doubted, and the present edition confirms our previous conviction.

' It was my object,' says Mr. Malthus, ' in the two chapters on *Moral Restraint*, and its *Effects on Society*, to shew that the evils arising from the principle of population were exactly of the same nature as the evils arising from the excessive or irregular gratification of the human passions in general; and that from the existence of these evils we had no more reason to conclude that the principle of increase was too strong for the purpose intended by the Creator, than to infer, from the existence of the vices arising from the human passions, that these passions required diminution or extinction, instead of regulation and direction.

' If this view of the subject be allowed to be correct, it will naturally follow that, notwithstanding the acknowledged evils occasioned by the principle of population, the advantages derived from it under the present constitution of things may very greatly overbalance them.

' A slight sketch of the nature of these advantages, as far as the main object of the Essay would allow, was given in the two chapters to which I have alluded; but the subject has lately been pursued with considerable ability in the Work of Mr. Sumner on the Records of the Creation; and I am happy to refer to it as containing a masterly developement and completion of views, of which only an intimation could be given in the Essay.

' I fully agree with Mr. Sumner as to the beneficial effects which result from the principle of population, and feel entirely convinced that the natural tendency of the human race to increase faster than the possible increase of the means of subsistence could not be either destroyed or essentially diminished without diminishing that hope of rising and fear of falling in society, so necessary to the improvement of the human faculties and the advancement of human happiness. But with this conviction on my mind, I feel no wish to alter the view which I have given of the evils arising from the principle of population. These evils do not lose their name or nature because they are overbalanced by good: and to consider them in a different light on this account, and cease to call them evils, would be as irrational as the objecting to call the irregular indulgences of passion vicious, and to affirm that they lead to misery, because our passions are the main sources of human virtue and happiness.

' I have always considered the principle of population as a law peculiarly suited to a state of discipline and trial. Indeed I believe that,

in

in the whole range of the laws of nature with which we are acquainted, not one can be pointed out, which in so remarkable a manner tends to strengthen and confirm this scriptural view of the state of man on earth. And as each individual has the power of avoiding the evil consequence to himself and society resulting from the principle of population by the practice of a virtue clearly dictated to him by the light of nature, and sanctioned by revealed religion, it must be allowed that the ways of God to man with regard to this great law of nature are completely vindicated.

' I have, therefore, certainly felt surprise as well as regret that no inconsiderable part of the objections which have been made to the principles and conclusions of the Essay on Population has come from persons for whose moral and religious character I have so high a respect, that it would have been particularly gratifying to me to obtain their approbation and sanction. This effect has been attributed to some expressions used in the course of the work which have been thought too harsh, and not sufficiently indulgent to the weakness of human nature, and the feelings of Christian charity.

' It is probable, that having found the bow bent too much one way, I was induced to bend it too much the other, in order to make it straight. But I shall always be quite ready to blot out any part of the work which is considered by a competent tribunal as having a tendency to prevent the bow from becoming finally straight, and to impede the progress of truth. In deference to this tribunal I have already expunged the passages which have been most objected to, and I have made some few further corrections of the same kind in the present edition. By these alterations I hope and believe that the work has been improved without impairing its principles. But I still trust that whether it is read with or without these alterations, every reader of candour must acknowledge that the practical design uppermost in the mind of the writer, with whatever want of judgment it may have been executed, is to improve the condition and increase the happiness of the lower classes of society.'—vol. iii. pp. 424—428.

We introduce this passage, partly as furnishing the best reply to the objection under consideration, and partly to account for the different impression which the Essay itself formerly conveyed; but chiefly as an instructive example of that candour which always attends true philosophy. While the ignorant or bigoted writer is only rendered pertinacious by confutation, the philosophic reasoner gives its due weight to his adversary's argument, and is either more firmly settled in his own opinion by impotent attempts to subvert it, or ready to modify his statements where he sees occasion. Truth being his object, he would consent to gain his object even if he were obliged to forego the honours of victory; and, therefore, if the victory finally rest with him, he enjoys the splendour of conquest, and not the mere credit of obstinate resistance.

V. The last objection we shall notice relates to the value of

the

the whole subject, and of the conclusion to which it brings us. What after all is gained towards that important end, the regulation of private conduct, by these general views? How would it suit the gallantry of one sex, or the delicacy of the other, that public expediency should take place of individual attachment, or the ardour of love be graduated according to the current rate of population?

With respect to this, we know very well that men will marry, as they ought to marry, and as they always have married, on other considerations than those of philosophy or the general good. The high encomium passed upon Cato, *Urbi* pater est, *urbique* maritus, is not likely to be often claimed in our times, nor are we anxious that it should. Such qualities may be very grand, but they are very unamiable. There is little fear, however, lest men should begin to consult in these private matters any other rule than that which they have hitherto consulted, their own private interest. Can they support the probable expenses of the married state, in that sphere of life in which they were born and educated; or into which they may be contented-to descend, in order to gratify one passion at the expense of another? This is the only question they have to ask, and the answer to it will indicate their duty, and ought to direct their conduct. The wages of labour in every profession and vocation not only afford the only practicable rule of individual interest, but are, in fact, a general index of the proportion which the means of subsistence bear to the existing population.

But laying aside individual cases, we entirely concur with the author in the importance of general rules, and therefore in the practical value of that fact which he has added to our stock of universal truths, viz. the tendency of mankind to pass the limit of their subsistence. In all advanced societies mankind exist in a very artificial state, and laws, as we know, are enacted with the intent of directing the habits of the community into those channels which appear most beneficial in the view of the legislator. The question, then, is, what sort of laws are we to promulgate? are we to discourage celibacy? to accelerate the increase of population, and give a bounty on large families? Nor is this only an abstract question, such as Harrington or Sir Thomas More, or any other framer of an ideal commonwealth might have asked; but one that comes particularly home to our English interests. Our poor laws, as now administered, are neither more nor less than a standing bounty on increase, on redundant increase, by supporting at the public expense those fathers of families, who could not support themselves, even whilst single, by labour: and though formerly Mr. Malthus expressed a doubt whether they had really enlarged population so much as they had extended misery, while the redundant (i. e. the

unem-

unemployed) poor were crowded into workhouses or farmed out in manufactories, there can now be no question upon the subject, when public money is either added to the regular wages of labour, or supplied in its stead.

When the expediency of such a practice becomes matter of discussion, a general rule of reference is of the utmost importance ; and is furnished at once by the universal truth, that mankind have a tendency in all cases to multiply beyond the regular supply of food, or regular demand of labour. This determines the point, and shows that the impulse is to be first applied to labour, which will spontaneously increase population, and not to population, which may not so certainly obtain subsistence by finding labour : and even if it finally succeeds, there is an intermediate risk, and a certainty of distress and discontent.

The importance of having such a rule established may be best appreciated by reflecting on the consequences of wanting, or neglecting it. These were predicted by Mr. Malthus at a period when there was an extraordinary demand for men, and very little disposition to suppose the possibility of any evil arising out of the redundancy of population. But his remarks on the nature and effects of the poor laws have been in the most striking manner confirmed by the experience of the years 1815, 1816, and 1817.

‘ During these years, two points of the very highest importance have been established, so as no longer to admit of a doubt in the mind of any rational man.

‘ The first is, that the country does not in point of fact fulfil the promise which it makes to the poor in the poor-laws, to maintain and find in employment, by means of parish assessments, those who are unable to support themselves or their families, either from want of work or any other cause.

‘ And secondly, that with a very great increase of legal parish assessments, aided by the most liberal and praiseworthy contributions of voluntary charity, the country has been wholly unable to find adequate employment for the numerous labourers and artificers who were able as well as willing to work.

‘ It can no longer surely be contended that the poor-laws really perform what they promise, when it is known that many almost starving families have been found in London and other great towns, who are deterred from going on the parish by the crowded, unhealthy and horrible state of the workhouses into which they would be received, if indeed they could be received at all; when it is known that many parishes have been absolutely unable to raise the necessary assessments, the increase of which, according to the existing laws, have tended only to bring more and more persons upon the parish, and to make what was collected less and less effectual; and when it is known that there has been an almost universal cry from one end of the kingdom to the

other

other for voluntary charity to come in aid of the parochial assessments.'
—vol. ii. pp. 351, 352.

This evil, which we cannot help referring to the existing habit
of interference with the wages of labour, and with the ordinary
progress of population, can only be remedied by a return to the
natural course; and the easiest mode of accomplishing this object
is really the single question for Parliament to consider; the extent
as well as the cause of the evil itself being alike established by the
evidence which they have so laboriously collected. But we must
not digress into another wide and difficult field of discussion.

Secondly, it is no slight advantage to be provided with an incontrovertible answer to all sweeping reformers; and to know on
positive grounds that the face of civilized society must always remain uniform in its principal lineaments, and be distinguished by
the same features which it has hitherto borne; that our business
therefore is to lessen or remove its blemishes, and to prevent their
growing into deformities: but that we can no more organize a
community without poverty, and its consequence, severe labour,
than we can organize a body without natural infirmities, or add a
limb to the human frame. Some perhaps may think it a misfortune to know thus much—and certainly if ignorance in this case
would lead to bliss, it were folly to be wise; but it can only conduct to inevitable misery. In fact, the present year has shewn the
practical value of this advancement in our knowledge. The Spen-
ceans, it is true, who coolly talk of dividing the land among the
people and establishing an Agrarian Republic, are not of a sort to
be addressed by reason. But it is always satisfactory to have reason on the side of law; and to be prepared to prove, if any will
listen, that these new sons of the earth, these ΣΠΑΡΤΟΙ of modern sedition or modern ignorance, after having devoured all the
property of the country, would soon be reduced, like their predecessors of old, to the necessity of devouring one another. And
that their leaders, however ill-informed, have sense enough to discover the barrier which the Principle of Population opposes against
their schemes, is evident from the rancorous hostility with which
Evans, the Cadmus of the tribe, has attacked Mr. Malthus in
what he is pleased to entitle his ' Christian Policy.'

With this general view of the bearings of the subject upon our
internal economy, we shall close our remarks upon the important
addition to political science contained in Mr. Malthus's Essay.
Upon the book itself, which has already reached a fifth edition, it
would now be superfluous to pronounce an elaborate opinion.
The author, as we have often intimated, might have clothed his
principles in a more attractive garb, and have introduced them to the
public under a more favourable aspect: and we cannot help re-
gretting

gretting that the same masterly hand, which first pointed out why equality, and plenty, and community of goods were unattainable to beings constituted like mankind, had not also proceeded to show that they were no less undesirable ; that the same powerful guide, who first checked, in her untried course, the frail bark of universal happiness, sailing as she was ' with youth at the prow and pleasure at the helm,' and pointed out the unforeseen bank on which she could not fail to split, had not also taken the pains to prove that the course human nature was forced to pursue is also the best it could pursue, when the object and end of the voyage are added to the consideration.

Art. VI.—*Of Population. An Inquiry concerning the Power of Increase in the Numbers of Mankind, being an Answer to Mr. Malthus's Essay on that subject.* By William Godwin. London. 8vo. 1821. pp. 626.

ABOUT thirty years ago, Mr. Godwin published an Inquiry concerning Political Justice, with an intention, as he states in the preface of the present work, ' to collect whatever was best and most liberal in the science of politics, to condense it, to arrange it

more

more into a system, and to carry it somewhat farther, than had been done by any preceding writer.' The work bore the stamp of a mind accustomed to think deeply, and to feel strongly :—but it was a mind of such overweening confidence in its own powers, as rashly to pull down, in its imaginations, whatever had been held most venerable and valuable in society, in order to erect upon the ruins a visionary fabric of his own. To favour the reception of his sentiments, he employed all his ingenuity in exposing, or rather in exaggerating, the vices and follies which flow from the present system of society; and to depict the state of blessedness that would result from the adoption of his own,—that is, the virtue and happiness that would universally prevail, on the total abolition of religion, government, private property, marriage, and a few other inconvenient evils of a similar kind. We must do Mr. Godwin the justice, however, to observe, that he no where recommended the hasty or forcible overthrow of existing institutions. Reason alone was to be employed in securing the acquiescence of mankind in the removal of abuses, and their co-operation in the substitution of the meditated improvements. As the system was in itself so unreasonable, while reason only was to be engaged in its support, there seemed little danger of any mischievous effect from the book; but the author's skill in argumentation, joined to that fervour of manner, which, evincing conviction in the writer, so much aids it in the mind of the reader, contributed to procure it a considerable portion of attention, more especially as it appeared at a period when the signs of the times created a pretty general expectation of some political regeneration. Of those who fostered such expectations, the splenetic and the sanguine, the revolutionist and the reformer, were equally taken with a work, which dwelt with energy on the evils of present institutions, and with enthusiasm on the universal felicity of an ideal system. Contingent abuse was confounded with inherent evil; and the counterbalance of good, which the experience of all ages and nations had confirmed, held light in comparison with the happiness of that political millennium, where, indeed, no alloy of evil could be proved from experience; but where it seemed to be forgotten, that experience was equally wanting to corroborate the hope of good.

Mr. Malthus, however, left to others the defence of existing institutions, and the exposure of the gross errors and absurdities of Mr. Godwin's imaginary substitutes; and he undertook to prove, that, even admitting the whole of his premises, supposing him to have broken all the great bonds, which, for six thousand years, the closer they have been drawn have made society the stronger; and to have realized all that his imagination had suggested, yet there still existed in nature a principle against which Mr. Godwin *had*

provided,

provided, and *could* provide, no counter-action, and of which the operation would subvert the whole fabric of his system as soon as formed. For, suppose human nature to be so improved, that, instead of self-love, the love of mankind were the strongest incentive in the mind of each individual; and suppose *that* love so enlightened, that private judgment supersedes the necessity of all direction, and of all motives, derived from religion and law; suppose the whole earth to be cultivated as a garden, and the productions to be equally divided among its swarming inhabitants, all united, as one family, in mutual love; each labouring for the common physical support; and each exerting his mental energies for improving the intellectual powers, and increasing the moral excellence and enjoyments of all. Imagine all this to be realized, and in less than half a century, says Mr. Malthus, the whole fairy vision will vanish, and selfishness, vice and misery, take again triumphant possession of the world; and this from a law of nature, as simple as it is unchangeable; from the different rates at which population unobstructed, and fertility, however aided, tend to increase. For the tendency of population would be to double itself every twenty-five years; while the most sanguine speculator could not pretend to increase the powers of fertility, at every such period, by more than an amount equal to its first power; or, in other words, the increase of population is in a geometrical ratio, and of fertility in an arithmetical one. So that whilst population was tending to increase as 1, 2, 4, 8, 16, 32—fertility would only tend to be increased as 1, 2, 3, 4, 5, 6.

Mr. Godwin's happy population, therefore, who, with their united efforts of mind and body, might, in the first 25 years, have doubled the fertility of the earth, and in the second 25 made it three times more productive than at first, would, in the same period, have made their numbers four times greater than at first; and in the sixth period the population would become 32 times greater, whilst the products to support it would only be six times greater than at first, and so on,—the disparity between food and population continually increasing, as the number of assumed periods was augmented. It is, however, easy to perceive, that, if Mr. Malthus's principle be just, the series of periods must soon be cut short by starvation; and that, in the approach to that extreme, the importunate cravings of hunger would silence the delicate remonstrances of refined benevolence; that the strongest would seize the larger portion to himself; the weakest would perish; in a word, mankind would revert to a state of barbarism, from which ages would be required to bring them up to that point of civilization, where Mr. Godwin's theory had found them; and where, though, according to Mr. Malthus, the principle of population will not allow evil to
be

be banished, yet the reversion to barbarism, through the extremes of vice and misery, is checked by the control of religion and law; by the stimulus to individual exertion which the security of private property gives, and by ' the monopoly of marriage' fostering all the gentle feelings of conjugal, parental, and filial affections.

Mr. Godwin might, if he pleased, have urged in reply, that, admitting Mr. Malthus's principle of the different rates of increase in unchecked population, and in the assisted fertility of the earth, yet, in a state of such exalted virtue, as Mr. Godwin's theory supposes, we must not imagine, that individuals would allow the brute impulses of their nature to increase, for their own gratification, the number of beings beyond what the stock of public food could, without diminution of public comfort, supply. And he has not omitted to avail himself of this defence; but he has used it only as a collateral support; for he was perfectly conscious, that, if Mr. Malthus's principle were admitted, its immediate operation on the interest of actual society would throw into oblivion *his* speculations on remote and possible existences. He seems, indeed, to have experienced something of this. ' The Essay on Population had gotten possession of the public mind;' and the author of Political Justice waited, in vain, to see the errors of Mr. Malthus sunk by neglect, or demolished by the disciples of the Godwin school. Finding, however, that the book ' still held on its prosperous career,' Mr. Godwin determined (he says) ' to place himself in the breach,' and to attack, not only the collateral arguments, or the inferences, but, the ' main principle' of the Essay on Population. Thus, then, the parties are at issue.

Mr. Malthus founds his geometrical ratio on the experience of the North American colonies, which, for the last 150 years, are said to have doubled their population every twenty-five years. Mr. Godwin, with reason, objects to the vague manner in which so very material an assumption is supported; though indeed it was not easy to be much more precise : for had authorities been given, with the censuses, to bear out the conjectures and assertions of Price, Franklin, Styles, Pitkin, &c. still the assumption of a doubling, ' *by procreation only,*' every twenty-five years, could not have been satisfactorily proved; because all calculations must be much disturbed by the unknown quantity of immigration perpetually mixing itself with every part of the details. But, avoiding these details for the present, we wish to confine ourselves to the most general view of the question; to discuss the principle isself, not the degree in which it operates, or the rate at which it proceeds.

In the 4th chapter of the 2d book, Mr. Godwin gives some valuable tables of the population of Sweden, from which he makes

the

the following deduction. 'In Sweden there has been, for a certain period, a progressive increase of population; and we have great reason to believe, that this increase is chiefly, or solely, the effect of the principle of procreation. To judge from what has appeared in fifty-four years, from 1751 to 1805, we should say, that the human species, in some situations, and under some circumstances, might double itself in somewhat *more* than a hundred years.' *

Thus, then, it is agreed, that, in some situations, population tends to double itself in 100 years; and thus the principle of the geometrical ratio, in which population tends to increase, is at once admitted by Mr. Godwin, and established by the facts in his book; in which, however, we are told, that Mr. Malthus's 'theory is evidently founded upon nothing;' and that 'it is time, in reality, that some one should sweep away this house of cards;' which is thus performed.—Because the term geometrical ratio had been used, Mr. Godwin and his friend Mr. Booth (whom he employs to assist him in his mathematical disquisitions) have determined to hold the uses of it to the strict mathematical meaning. They employ a great deal of unnecessary labour to show, that if an equable progression from year to year be not proved, the doubling at equally distant periods cannot be called a geometrical ratio, as the law of the series remains unknown. They might, with equal truth and triumph, have demonstrated, that if a population of three millions in America became in twenty-five years, six millions minus an unit, and in fifty years twelve millions plus an unit, the population in the first period could not be said to have, to the population of the third period, the duplicate ratio of that which it has to the population of the second.

It is obvious that the term geometrical ratio could never have been intended to be employed in its rigidly mathematical sense. Hume, in speaking of a law, which made the violator of it, and those who had any intercourse with him, equally criminal, observes, 'by this severe, and even absurd law, crimes and guilt went on multiplying in a geometrical proportion.' He could not with more concise strength have expressed, that such a law gave to each transgression a tendency to increase the number of transgressors; in each of whom, from the social nature of man, was a like tendency to a similar increase. Yet if any mathematical critics had called on Hume to prove the law of the series, by which crime and guilt

---

* In somewhat *less* than 100 years, ought to have been the inference: for (without entering into the niceties of such a progression) if, in forty-four years, 1 became $1\frac{1}{2}$, that $1\frac{1}{2}$, in a second period of fifty-four years, would become $2\frac{1}{4}$; and, in 100 years, would be a small fraction *above* 2.

were multiplied, he might, if he had deigned a reply, have found it difficult to bring absolute proof of his geometrical proportion.

In considering the arithmetical ratio assigned as the rate of increase in the fertility of the earth, Messrs. Godwin and Booth choose to consider that expression, also, in a strictly mathematical sense. ' If (say they) the quantity of the food of man be increased, it is obvious it will not be by starts every twenty-five years, but that it will be increased through many intervening times.'—p. 248. What, however, is all this but captious trifling? If, as Mr. Malthus has asserted, population can be proved to have nearly doubled itself, in certain circumstances, every twenty-five years for 150 years together,—his business being only with the result at those periods, and not with the equable or unequable flow of the progression,—he may be well allowed to express and elucidate the rate of increase, as proceeding in a geometrical ratio; especially when contrasting it with the slow progress of the increase in the productiveness of the same spot of earth; in which experience having shown no tendency to exceed, at most, in any given periods, an increase at each period equal to its original quantity, its progress may well be expressed and elucidated, as being in an arithmetical ratio.

In order, however, that general readers may not suppose the case to involve any technically mathematical question, we will state what we conceive to be Mr. Malthus's principle in plain language. Population, in favourable circumstances, tends to increase; and whatever addition is made by that increase, has in itself a power and a perpetual stimulus to exert the power of still further increase. But if the fertility of any spot of earth be, by any favourable circumstances, increased, the addition made by that increase has no power or tendency in itself to produce a further increase of fertility. Thus, if population be doubled, the population so doubled has a tendency to double itself; but doubled fertility has no such tendency to double in itself. The doubled fertility cannot in itself be a cause of quadrupled fertility; the doubled population can be a cause of quadrupled population, and has besides, in itself, a strong stimulus to become so. The grand deductions from this principle are, that the natural tendency of population is to increase faster than the means for its support; and that therefore the efforts of nations, and the enactments of legislatures, should be directed to increase the productiveness of their soil, which has no natural tendency to increase itself; and that, having done this, we may safely rely on a proportionate increase of population, which *has* a natural power and stimulus for self-increase. Whereas legislators, by giving encouragement to population in the first instance, have added a stimulus where, from imprudence in individuals, there was already

already a proneness to excess; and thus augmented the misery and
vice, which are the necessary results of such improvidence.

When men were thus called upon to reverse the precepts of the
wisest in all ages and nations, we need not be surprized that much
prejudice, and even indignation, should be excited. And accordingly Mr. Malthus was assailed, with equal virulence, by the ignorant vulgar, and by those whose refined, but irritable, minds lead
them to contemplate with horror any wish to limit the number of
human beings by which they had accustomed themselves to estimate the quantity of human happiness : it was thwarting, they said,
' the first purpose of Nature to produce beings formed for enjoyment, and infringing the first command of Nature's God—to increase and multiply;' not staying to consider, that adding to population, without augmenting the means of subsistence, was producing
beings formed, indeed, for enjoyment, but therefore the more miserable, when destined only to suffer; and that the same Great Being,
who commanded us to increase and multiply, hath taught us, also,
that virtue consists in controlling the passions which He has given
us, so as to promote their ultimate purpose,—the production of
human happiness. We have been taught, too, by the same authority, (in the wisest petition, which frail man was ever instructed to
prefer,) to deprecate temptation : but to what greater temptation
can men be exposed than when their numbers exceed the means of
comfortable subsistence ? they must either live in physical misery,
or relieve themselves from its immediate pressure by vice, which is
only misery in another form. These, in their hideous combination, inflict the punishment which is provided by Nature for the
abuse of her powers; and by thinning, at length, the redundant
population, they check the universality of the evil.

Thus, then, it appears to us, that the general principles of Mr.
Malthus's book, and the general inference to be drawn from it,
continue unrefuted by his opponent. But there remains a very
important consideration, concerning the degree in which that principle operates; and, consequently, concerning the urgency of the
evil, and the strength of the remedy to be applied : for we are
by no means of Mr. Godwin's opinion, that, ' unless Mr. Malthus's
assumption be proved, of an inherent tendency in mankind to
double to the full amount of once in twenty-five years, the Essay on
Population is turned into waste paper.'—p. 141. For whilst an
inherent tendency to double is admitted in population, and no such
tendency is found in the fertility of the earth,—whether the period of doubling be twenty-five, fifty, or a hundred years, in the
most favourable circumstances, the difference in the mode of increase remains the same; though, doubtless, as we have observed,
the

the urgency of the remedy to be applied, as of the evil to be apprehended, may be less.

It has already been stated, that the proofs of a doubling in the
population of the United States, at periods of twenty-five years
for the last 150 years, and that from procreation only, as assumed
by Mr. Malthus, are far from being accurate, on account of the
unknown amount of immigration. Both parties however agree, on
the authority of the public censuses, that the population of the
United States has increased in twenty years, (viz. between 1790
and 1820,) from 3,929,326 to 7,239,903. This advance,
which would double the population in twenty-three years, Mr.
Malthus considers as admitting ' ample allowance for foreign
immigration.' Mr. Godwin, on the contrary, maintains, that
throughout the Union the population, so far as depends on procreation, is at a stand.'—p. 441. And, consequently, that the
increase is wholly by immigration ; and he supports this extravagant assertion by a most curious course of argument. ' To keep
up the population of a country, we must reckon upon four births to
a marriage. To double the population we must reckon upon
eight. Where there are four births to a marriage, the number of
births must double the number of procreants ; where there are eight
it must quadruple it.'—p. 440. But in the American census for
1810, the inhabitants ' under and above sixteen years of age are, as
nearly as possible, on an equality.' ' Hence it inevitably follows,
that throughout the Union the population, so far as depends on
procreation, is at a stand; and that there are not, on an average,
more than four births to every female capable of child-bearing.'—
p. 441. It will not be necessary to enter here on the dubious
assumptions of four births to a marriage, and of the proportion
which the child-bearing women hold to the total of a given population; on which assumptions Mr. Godwin's argument hinges :
for we may refer to undoubted facts, adduced by the author himself, to exhibit the fallacy of his reasoning.

In the Upsal Table, (*Godwin*, p. 159.) which is considered a
fair average for Sweden, the persons under fifteen are 507,176;
whilst those above that age are 1,402,005. Now, in order to
bring this state of the population into comparison with that
of America, we must calculate what may be presumed, from
these data, to be the number of persons under sixteen. And in this
we shall make ample allowance by assuming, according to the
Swedish tables, the annual number of births to be four per cent. of
the total population ; and by supposing half the born attain sixteen
years of age. This, in the present case of a population of
1,919,181, would give 38,383, as the number between fifteen and
sixteen, to be added to those under fifteen ; making the persons
under

under sixteen to be 545,559 ; and those above that age 1,373,622 : that is, the persons above sixteen are to those below somewhat more than two and a half to one.   And this state of the Swedish population Mr. Godwin frequently calls a nearly stationary one.   Now, at p. 441, the population of the United States is said to be 'at a stand,' because the persons under and above sixteen are equal in numbers.   So that when the numbers in the two classes are equal, and when they are in the proportion of two and a half to one, Mr. Godwin's inference is the same.

It might be expected that such a result, from facts of admitted authenticity, would have led the author to doubt his speculations on the number of child-bearing women in a given population, and the number of births to a marriage ; seeing that they conduct to so obvious a contradiction.   Indeed, when not under the immediate influence of these speculations, he seems to look at the subject in a right point of view, but through a magnifying medium.   'If (says he, p. 442.) it were true that the population of. the United States had been found to double itself for above a century and a half successively, in less than twenty-five years, and that this had been "repeatedly ascertained to be from procreation only," it is absolutely certain, that in that country the children would outnumber the grown persons two or three times over.   It would have been a spectacle, to persons from other parts of the world, of a most impressive nature.'   And, certainly, to any person (excepting Mr. Godwin) visiting Sweden, for example, and America, the contrast would be very impressive.   For it appears, by the above deductions from Mr. Godwin's own facts, that, in a Swedish population of one hundred persons, we should not meet with quite twenty-nine below sixteen ; whilst, in an American population of one hundred persons, we should find fifty below sixteen, that is, one-and-twenty per cent. more of children: and if this do not argue more frequent and more prolific marriages, what does?

But Mr. Godwin, compelled to admit a slow increase of population in Sweden, is determined to allow of no greater rate of increase in any country ; a determination which could only be justified by proving, that the Swedes were, of all mankind, the most favourably circumstanced for the increase of the species; and, accordingly, what he wants in proof he supplies in assertion.   'We learn (he says) from the example of Sweden, perhaps as nearly as possible, how fast the race of mankind, at least as society is at present constituted, can increase; and beyond what limits the pace and speed of multiplication cannot be carried.   Sweden is a country in every respect as favourable to the experiment as we could desire.   Almost all the women marry.   "The continual cry of the government," as Mr. Malthus expresses it, is for the increase

of

of its subjects. And the soil is so thinly peopled, that it would require many ages of the most favourable complexion for the inhabitants to become so multiplied, by the mere power of procreation, as to enable them to rear and to consume all the means of subsistence which the land might easily be made to produce.'— p. 188. This is an extraordinary specimen of bold assertion in the very face of notorious fact. Sweden is a country with a winter of nine months; encumbered with mountains not only uncultivated, but incapable of cultivation; studded with rocks, and bristled with forests; without a navigable river ; where support for a family is so difficult to be procured, that a government, ' craving for an increased population,' is obliged to prohibit unprovided males from marriage till the completion of their twenty-first year! and, above all, it is a country that has been agitated for centuries by revolutions, or settled only in aristocracy or despotism; the *soil* so thin, that it cannot furnish grain for even its scanty population; and the *people* so poor, that on a deficient harvest their imports little exceed the average imports of common years. With regard to the improvability of the soil, the *argumentum ad hominem* is fairly applicable. Mr. Godwin says, we have no proof of any higher power of increasing population than what the Swedish tables show ; therefore we have no right to presume any higher possible: if the people would increase in numbers, the soil is ready to increase in fertility. In like manner, Mr. Malthus may say, we have no proof of any higher fertility than what the history of centuries shows; therefore we have no right to presume any higher possible : if the fertility would increase, the people are ready to increase in numbers. The truth, however, is, that both soil and people in all countries, (particularly in old countries,) have greater powers of productiveness than either are enabled fully to exert. But, then, if we allow the existence of checks, to account for the non-increase of fertility, we must also admit the existence of checks, to account for the non-increase of population, both in the same country at different times, and in different countries at the same time.

That the whole increase of the population of the United States may be accounted for by immigration only, is further maintained (b. iv. c. v.) by arguments, that seem to prove only the desperate state of the disputant, who can have recourse to them. ' We are told that between the years 1630 and 1640, 21,200 British subjects were computed to have passed over to New England only.' The author then takes the tonnage of ships from 1663 to 1818, and adds, ' the simple deduction by the rule of three, from the two extremes of this statement, is, that if 142,000 tons yielded an emigration to America to the annual amount of 2000 persons,

3,072,409

3,072,409 tons in the year 1818, computing at the same rate, will yield an annual emigration of 43,000 persons from Great Britain only.'—p. 407. This, perhaps, is the first time that one of the best criteria of the wealth, industry, and employment, for a people at home, was taken as the measure of their disposition to seek their fortunes abroad. The author seems aware of his argument requiring some bolstering; and most clumsily he applies it: for his next resource is in the accounts from Niles's Baltimore Weekly Register, and from Cobbett's Weekly Register. We need not remark on the nature of such authorities in a question tending to elevate America, and depreciate England. ' In a letter of the latter, dated Long Island, in the State of New York, (he says,) I find the following assertion:—" Within the last twelve months upwards of 150,000 have landed from England to settle here."'—p. 414. We do not know the grounds of Mr. Cobbett's assertion; but if his inferences from those grounds be in the same style as Mr. Godwin's from Niles's Register, they are certainly not much to be depended upon. The inhabitants of the British isles, ' according to Mr. Niles, land on the shores of North America at the rate of 2 or 3000 per week.'—p. 416. Those who place more confidence in the authorities derived from this quarter than we are disposed to do, may, perhaps, consider this as the average result; if, however, they examine the details, they will find that the months specified are only August and September. What would have been the rate of arrivals in January and February? If Mr. Cobbett thus calculated from a week or a month the amount of a year, we might commend his skill in arithmetic, but would leave Mr. Godwin to applaud his candour. These statements too, such as they are, refer to 1817, 18, 19; whereas the question to be elucidated was the doubling of the North American population between 1790 and 1810. Mr. Godwin is aware of this, he says, but then, (he adds,) ' they will at least serve strikingly to illustrate the fact of the vast number of emigrants that may be conveyed across the Atlantic.' So that from the real point he diverts the reader's attention backward to 1630-40, and forward to 1817-19; backward to a period when intolerance and bigotry, despotism and faction, involved all who did not emigrate in the calamities of a civil war; and forward to a time of the most unexpected, as unexampled stagnation, or revulsion, in the whole circulating system of labour, manufacture, trade, commerce, and produce; just when that system had been excited, by long continued stimulus, into an activity at once feverish and plethoric! and this retrospect, and this anticipation, are adduced to furnish criteria for the rate of emigration between 1790 and 1810; when we were either at peace, or (after the first shock of war had been surmounted) engaged in enterprizes of

unpre-

unprecedented extent, warlike, and commercial; which called for, and amply remunerated, not only the arm of man, but the hand of woman, and even the fingers of infancy!

We are, however, ready to admit, that during this period the disturbed state of France, and of much of the continent of Europe, would tend, like a storm, to swell the tide of immigration into North America; though checked, at the same time, by the arbitrary nature of the governments increasing the difficulties of emigration from countries, a portion of which only could be considered as maritime. But this will not content Mr. Godwin. He insists on the North American increase being *wholly* owing to immigration; without which the population would be stationary. We have seen the strange course of argument employed to establish this proportion. And lest that should, to some fastidious reasoners, appear unsatisfactory, he engages further to prove, not only that the American increase is wholly owing to immigration, but that it *cannot* be at all from procreation.

Mr. Malthus, he says, ' pretends to enumerate certain causes, which keep down population to an immense extent in Europe, and which have no such operation (for here lies the pith of the question) in America. These causes, when narrowly looked into, crumble into nothing.'—p. 358. In the 3d and 4th chapters of Mr. Godwin's 3d book, we are presented with his own ' Rational Theory of the Checks on Population;' which seem in his estimate to resolve themselves into war, famine, pestilence, and bad government; and his exemplifications prove only so many details of Mr. Malthus's checks of vice and misery. Yet he says, ' I totally reject Mr. Malthus's vice and misery in their obscure details.'—p. 299. Now by 'obscure' details must be meant—not war, pestilence, famine, and bad government, which certainly do not their work in a corner,—but—what Mr. Malthus has called ' the pressure of population on the means of subsistence;' that is, not famine, but the fear of it; and hard fare in the mean time.. From the style of argument adopted by Messrs. Godwin and Booth, it might be supposed there was no such state as scarcity; that there was no degree between famine and abundance. ' It is impossible (say they) that any term in the progression of subsistence can be less than its corresponding term in that of population; else that corresponding term would cease to be. Experience never did, nor ever can, show different progressions in population, and in food, in favour of the former.'—p. 253. All this learned logomachy merely means, that people cannot live without food. That a population cannot exist without food sufficient for its production, is a truism; but it is equally certain, that it may perish from a want of food accruing after its production; and it is the

continual

continual tendency to this in old countries, (more or less, according to degrees of scarcity,) which Mr. Malthus calls the pressure of population on the means of subsistence, and which produces the vice and misery that he deprecates. These, then, are the ' obscure details' of vice and misery which Mr. Godwin ' totally rejects;' and which, yet, every man, not determined to shut out conviction, must observe ; and the question is, do not such checks to population exist in a much greater degree in old countries than in North America, where, Mr. Godwin informs us, ' land, by hundreds and thousands of acres, may be had for almost nothing,' and where ' the wages of labour are high ?'—p. 376. But all these advantages are only regarded as causes of the increase of population, by their being incentives to foreigners to immigrate ; they are not at all considered as motives to earlier marriage, and less frequent celibacy; as means of greater vigour in the parents, and robuster health in the children.

The conclusion, then, is this—Mr. Godwin has admitted Sweden to be a proof of inherent power in population, under certain favourable circumstances, to increase. North America has shown so much more rapid an increase, and enjoys all the favourable circumstances of Sweden in so much higher a degree, that we have a right to ascribe a considerable part of that more rapid increase to those more favourable circumstances; and thence to infer a greater inherent power of increase in population, than is evinced by the Swedish tables. This greater inherent power cannot be stated to be in the full proportion of the more rapid increase, on account of the uncertain increase by immigration. But though this greater inherent power cannot be expressed in numbers, it is obviously very considerable, and leaves Mr. Malthus's principle, of the tendency of population to increase faster than the means of subsistence, greatly corroborated.

But Mr. Booth controverts this inference in a manner, which is often seen in the loose compositions of Mr. Malthus's vulgar opponents ; but which we should not have expected in one so well versed in mathematics, which, in general, ' do remedy and cure many defects in the wit, and faculties intellectual.' ' As far,' says he, ' as animals constitute the food of man, its increase must be in the same sort of series, as that of human beings ; and if a geometrical ratio exist any where, it is surely in the vegetable produce of the soil,' p. 251 ; and again, p. 252, ' If America have doubled its inhabitants every twenty-five years, the prepared food must have increased in equal proportion; for all the inhabitants have plenty, and are able to export grain to foreign countries. In the only country, then, where Mr. Malthus has discovered any ratio of increase of human population, the same, if not a greater,

ratio has been observed in the increase of the means of subsistence.'
In the first of these passages fecundity is confounded with fertility;
and, in the second, the increased quantity of land brought into
cultivation is confounded with increased fertility in the original
tract. The fecundity of plants and animals, like that of the human
species, seems indeed unbounded by any thing but the power of
the earth to supply them : and unless the fertility of the soil be
augmented, the fecundity of all that live on it can only tend to
crowd the whole, and prevent any from coming to perfection. If
all the corn produced on an acre of wheat were sown on that acre,
the produce would be mere rank grass, where not a grain would
be ripened. And if all the stock of a field, with the young of this
year, were confined to the same unimproved field the next, the
whole would either die of hunger, or the old would be emaciated skeletons, and the young stunted dwarfs. It is idle, therefore, to talk of the fecundity of plants and animals, as a supply for
increasing population, unless there be provided an increased fertility, or increased extent of soil, proportioned to the demands on
that fecundity. And so far is North America from increasing (as
insinuated by the 2d passage above cited) in fertility of the same
cultivated tracts, that its power of supporting an increased population is, more than in any other country, owing to the increased
quantity of new lands brought into cultivation. For it is notorious,
that the excessive productiveness of the new lands is soon so reduced by cropping, that the cultivator, who has capital, very commonly, instead of employing it to recover his exhausted soil, applies
it in the purchase of newly cleared lands ; which he proceeds in
the same way to exhaust, and leaves them to the poorer capitalist,
who must content himself with the less productive, but more easily
cultivated farm. Indeed it is this practice, which swells the
apparent numbers of immigrants into the western states; of whom a
very large proportion are only transmigrants from other states of the
Union. The example of North America, therefore, instead of
proving, according to Mr. Booth, a similar ratio in the increase of
human population and of the means of subsistence, is one of the
most conspicuous examples of population outstripping fertility,
and casting off its swarms in search of new lands to be reclaimed
from the wilderness.

But Mr. Godwin has in reserve, an argument against population
increasing faster by procreation in America, than in Sweden ; viz.
that it is physically impossible : 'Throughout Europe,' he says,
'taking one country with another, the average falls short of four
births to a marriage;'—and ' in every instance where the evidence
has come to our hands, the fruitfulness of the human species
in the United States does in no way materially differ from what
occurs

occurs on the subject in many countries of Europe.' p. 425.
But, ' Mr. Malthus freely, and without hesitation, admits, that,
on this side of the globe, population is, and has long been, at a
stand,' p. 24, therefore, ' throughout the Union the population,
so far as depends on procreation, is at a stand.' p. 441.

The first observation to be made on this point is, that the
number of births is not the sole criterion of the progress of population: for, in two nations, where this proportion is the same,
the progress of population will differ according to the difference
in the ratio, which the number of marriages bears to the total
population in the respective nations; and, also, according to the
ratio, which the births bear to the deaths in each. Omitting, however, these considerations for the present, let us examine the question of the proportion of births to a marriage. The mode taken
to ascertain this proportion has been to divide the aggregate of the
births of a given number of years by the aggregate of marriages
in the same period; and the quotient has been assumed as indicating, in all circumstances of a people, the average number of births
yielded by a marriage. And this procedure is argued upon with
an unhesitating confidence, as if its legitimacy were universally
acknowledged; and no hint is ever given that its failure had been
ever suggested. The fallacy, however, has been pointed out, not
by some obscure writer, of whose existence Mr. Godwin might be
supposed to be ignorant; but by one, whose celebrity seems to
have given him no small annoyance; and in the very work, which
he is professing to examine, in form too so demonstrative, that he
ought in candour to have stated the argument, if he did not condescend to refute it.

' If the average proportion of annual marriages to annual births, in
any country, be as one to four, this will imply, that, out of four children
born, two of them live to marry, and the other two die in infancy, and
celibacy. This is a most important, and interesting piece of information, from which the most useful inferences are to be drawn; but it is
totally different from the number of births, which each individual marriage yields, in the course of its duration; so much so, that, on the
supposition, which has just been made, that half of the born lived to be
married, which is a very usual proportion, the annual marriages would
be to the annual births, as one to four, whether each individual marriage yielded four births, two births, or one hundred births. If the latter
number be taken, then, according to the present supposition, fifty would
live to be married, and out of every one hundred births there would
be twenty-five marriages; and the marriages would still be to the births
as one to four.'

' The only case, in which the proportion of annual births to annual
marriages is the same, as the proportion of births, which each individual
marriage yields, is when the births and deaths are exactly equal; and
the

the reason of their being the same, in this case, is, that, in order to make the births and deaths exactly equal, we must assume that each marriage yields exactly another marriage; and that whatever be the number of children born from each union, they all die in infancy, and celibacy, except one pair. Thus, if each marriage yielded five children, two of which, only, live to form a fresh union, the proportion of annual marriages to annual births will be as one to five; which is the same as the number of births yielded by each individual marriage, by hypothesis. But whenever each marriage yields either more, or less, than one marrying pair; that is, whenever the population is either increasing, or decreasing, then, the proportion of annual births to annual marriages can never be the same, as the proportion of births yielded by each individual marriage in the course of its duration. Hence, it follows, that, whenever we assume them to be the same, any increase of population is impossible.'—*Malthus*, book ii. ch. 4.

The principle, here briefly abstracted, is pursued in considerable detail, for which we can only refer to the able chapter just cited. But we shall add an illustration of the manner in which we conceive Mr. Godwin's mode of arguing may lead to fallacious results; and which may more familiarly elucidate the abstract principle maintained by his opponent.

The mode (as has been stated,) is to estimate the number of births yielded during each marriage, by comparing the aggregate of marriages, in any period, with the aggregate of births. But, towards the end of the period, many marriages must have been contracted, which would continue to produce children beyond the period; and yet the children, so to be produced, cannot be included in the number of children by which the fruitfulness of the marriages is to be computed. To this it will be replied, that there must, also, be a number of children towards the beginning of the period, from marriages contracted before the period; and yet these children are included in the number, by which the fruitfulness of the marriages of the period is to be estimated. It is clear, therefore, that the estimate can be true, only when the number of marriages, in any given number of years preceding the termination of the period, is exactly equal to the number of marriages in the same number of years preceding the commencement of the period. But if the number of marriages in the latter end of the period be greater, that is, if the population be increasing, the proportion of children (as relating to the number yielded during the whole of each marriage) will be reduced; and the actual progressive population will appear, according to Mr. Godwin's rule, to be retrograde.

Thus, then, it is proved there is no ground for confining the fruitfulness of American marriages within the limits of those of Europe; and therefore no physical impossibility in the North American women bringing more, on an average, than four births

L 2

to a marriage. On the contrary, it is shown, that the average number may be eight births to a marriage; and if, as in Europe, half the born live to be married, the annual births may still be to the annual marriages only as four to one. Having ascertained the *possibility,* we are next to inquire what is the *probability* of more prolific marriages in North American, than in Europe.

Mr. Godwin sneeringly observes, p. 30, 'The difference between the United States and the Old World does not, I presume, lie in the superior fecundity of their women.' But the sneer has its force from an equivocal phrase. The natural capability of each individual may be the same; but difference of circumstances may call these capabilities into action in very different proportions; and the fruitfulness of women, as a class, be, therefore, very different, whilst the capabilities of each individual of the class may be the same. In a given number of married women, America may not have fewer barren; but in a given number of women America may have fewer unmarried: and, in a given number of productive married women, those of America may not produce more in a given small number of years; but they may (from marrying earlier) produce for a greater number of years. We have already stated the superior incentives to early and frequent marriage, where food is cheap, and the wages of labour high; and we have shown, that the effect of such early and frequent marriages is proved by the number of children, or persons below fifteen, being equal to those above that age; while, in Sweden, they do not constitute a half. But we are often reminded, that the increase of population must depend on the increase of child bearing women: and where, it may be asked, is that class so likely to be increased, as where there is the largest proportion of children to grow into women? But Mr. Godwin is determined to keep down the American population to the rate of that of Europe; and, therefore, limits the child-bearing age to the period between twenty and forty-five. And, in Europe, perhaps this might be a fair average; but to limit America to the same, is contradicting the unanimous testimony of all writers on the subject. The author seems conscious of this, and talks of the unproductiveness of early marriages of the Persian women, (p. 191.) as if there were any analogy between the climate of Persia and of North America; or between the habits of the women in the two countries. And, again, admitting ' that where a country is in great distress, and the means of subsistence are difficult to be procured, marriage will often not take place at so early a period, as it might do in countries, which are placed in more favourable circumstances,' p. 428; yet he endeavours to obviate the force of his admission, by a most amusing consideration. ' The period of marriage,' says he, ' usually depends on the

the male,' and, 'whatever be the age of the bridegroom, he is almost sure to look out for a young bride ; and, then, unless he be indeed stricken in years, the chance of offspring is nearly the same, as if he had been himself as young as the woman he leads to the altar,' p. 429. That is, in Mr. Godwin's calculation of the probabilities of life, the bridegroom of fifty has nearly the same chance of living to give fruitfulness to his wife of twenty, during the whole of her child-bearing period, as a bridegroom of her own age would have. But this is not all : for, supposing the sexes to be equal in numbers, is it not evident, that, for every man, who waits till he is old to be married, there must a woman have remained unmarried to the same age? If all the present and rising generation of bridegrooms were to abstain from marriage till they were fifty, where would Mr. Godwin direct them ' to look out for a young bride?'

When Mr. Godwin admits, by way of argument, the superior productiveness of American marriages, he deduces from it consequences the most alarming to the feelings of humanity. The abstract of his argument (b. 1. ch. 6,) is this ; If population, when unchecked, doubles itself in twenty-five years, then, in a country where population is stationary, a number equal to the whole of that population must perish in twenty-five years, more than in a country, which doubles its inhabitants in that time. This argument appears in a variety of shapes throughout the volume ; but in no shape can it conceal the fallacious assumption, that as many, as early, and as prolific marriages will take place in a country, where labour is cheap, and provisions are dear, as in one, where labour is dear, and provisions are cheap. On the contrary, we know, that, where men feel the pressure of present difficulties, and foresee greater, they will not, universally, expose themselves to the extreme of evil ; but feel checked by the degrees of it, which the *tendency* to overpopulation produces. At the same time, it must be admitted, that great numbers do involve themselves in these extremes ; and that the consequent mortality, especially among the children of such improvident parents, is very great. And the prevention of this mortality, and of the vice and misery, which are the concomitants of it, is the object of Mr. Malthus's book ; which by no means considers an increasing population as, in itself, an evil ; but only so, where that increase is antecedent to a proportionate increase in the means of subsistence.

But Mr. Godwin has employed a whole book (Vth,) to show, that the means of subsistence are inexhaustible, and amply sufficient to maintain all the doubling of population, of which we have any evidence, ' for it is (as he facetiously observes) with a real, and not a possible, doubling, that we are concerned ; possible men

do

do not eat, though real men do.' p. 480. All this, and indeed much of the volume, is founded on the false ascription to Mr. Malthus of a wish to keep down population to its present level, even if all the possible means of subsistence were actually existing. Now all that Mr. Malthus says is—Do you produce the increase of subsistence, and population will increase itself; but do not encourage population on account of your ultimate possible means; for, remember, possible food cannot be eaten, though real food can. Yet Mr. Godwin, who cannot but know this to be his opponent's doctrine, can condescend to flatter popular prejudices, by joining in the vulgar clamour, and telling us, that Mr. Malthus ' would starve the present generation, that he may kill the next,' p. 505. and fain ' persuade us to hail war, famine, and pestilence as the true friends of the general weal; to look with a certain complacent approbation upon the gallows, and massacre; and almost to long for the decimation of our species, that the survivors might be more conveniently accomodated.' p. 586. In much the same style is nearly the whole of the author's 6th book; in which he discusses ' the moral and political maxims inculcated in the Essay on Population.' We shall not track him in all his misrepresentations, where the credit of Mr. Malthus only is concerned; but cursorily notice, merely as connected with his system, two subjects of the highest importance in the disquisitions of the politician, and the moralist,—the support of the poor,—and the exercise of charity.

In pressing the necessity of a gradual abolition of the poor laws, Mr. Malthus has distinctly stated, that it is a duty, as a preliminary measure, ' formally to disclaim the *right* of the poor to support.' The word *right* is susceptible of a variety of interpretations; and of this ambiguity Mr. Godwin has availed himself, p. 542, &c. The moral right is plainly the only one here meant: but again we must distinguish between moral rights in a state of nature, and in a civilized state. In a state of nature, every man has a moral right to his proportionate share of the spontaneous productions of the earth; and it would, then, be the duty of every man becoming possessed of any surplus, to give it to him who had less than his share. But so weak, in a state of nature, is the power of morality, that brute force is the sole arbiter of possession. When civil institutions are devised to control brute force, moral rights must be rendered compatible with those institutions. In this state of things, the rights of the poor become a political question; and subordinate, as those of every other class are, to the existence and general welfare of the whole. Mr. Godwin's aspirations, indeed, are after a state of society in which all property is to be equalized; and where the improvement of every individual in knowledge and virtue shall be

such,

such, that without civil institutions the well-being of the whole may be trusted to the uncontrolled actions of each. It would be idle, however, to discuss the rights of the poor, with reference to a state of society where no poor could exist. But certain it is, that if natural rights, with regard to property, were enforced in our present state of society, we should speedily return with the *rights* to the *state* of nature. But, it may be urged, it is not an equal share of property that is claimed as the right of the poor, but a portion adequate to their support. Admit a right to a portion, and who shall assign its limits, either as to the nature of the support, or the number to be supported? They who would limit either, admit the necessity of modifying the abstract claim, in order to render it compatible with the institutions of society. And yet support implies such a competence as will enable the poor to increase their numbers; and these additional numbers have a like claim to similar support, which will give the occasion of similar demands, till the whole property of the country be divided among the claimants. And this is, in fact, the *tendency* which is now felt in the rapidly increasing operation of the English poor-laws. We shall not enter on the various plans that have been proposed by Mr. Malthus and others, for the abolition or amendment of them; only wishing to clear away what may be considered as obstructions in legislating on this important subject, and to show the principle on which it stands.

In denying the *right* of the poor to support, Mr. Malthus has not failed to recognize the duty of the rich to assist them, in cases of unmerited or extreme distress. But, at the same time, he presses on the reader's attention, that this duty is not fulfilled by indiscriminate assistance. 'Those (says he) who are suffering in spite of the best-directed endeavours to avoid it, and from causes which they could not be expected to foresee, are the genuine objects of charity. Such objects ought to be relieved, according to our means, liberally and adequately; even though the worthless are starving. When, indeed, this first claim on our benevolence is satisfied, we may then turn our attention to the idle and improvident.' . . . . 'We are not, however, in any case to lose a present opportunity of doing good, from the mere supposition that we may possibly meet with a worthier object. In all doubtful cases it may safely be laid down as our duty, to follow the natural impulse of our benevolence.'—B. iv. ch. 9. Nor is this contrary to the doctrine, that the poor, who have by improvidence become such, should in general be 'left to the punishment of Nature,— the punishment of want.' But Mr. Godwin exclaims, with his usual suavity, 'What ignorant babble is this! When this kind benefactor saved this man and his family from perishing with

hunger,

hunger, he either did a right or a wrong; he did his duty, or the contrary: for every thing, in our treatment of our fellow-creatures, that is not duty, is of the nature of evil.'—p. 568. It is just this sweeping kind of conclusions, these uncompromising dogmas, and rules without exceptions, which have been the besetting sins of Mr. Godwin's life. Mr. Malthus, in the spirit of temperate philosophy, has observed, that 'the general principles on these subjects ought not to be pushed too far, though they should always be kept in view; and that many cases may occur, in which the good resulting from the relief of the present distress may more than overbalance the evil to be apprehended from the remote consequence.' —B. iv. c. 11. The exercise of compassionate beneficence is as much a moral duty as the exercise of justice. It is given us, like the prerogative of pardon in the Crown, to modify, in particular cases, the rigour of general law. And as the King is bound by his oath, so is every other man by his duty, and by the example of his Maker, to administer justice in mercy. And we do think, that all who advocate the doctrine of Mr. Malthus are particularly called upon to enforce the duties of a discriminating charity: for assuredly the tendency of that doctrine is to diminish our sympathy with the poor as a class; teaching us to consider them, in general, as improvident intruders. And, in the same proportion, its tendency is to furnish an apology to the selfishness of the wealthy.

These are the points to be guarded in the enunciation of Mr. Malthus's principles. But the important truth of those principles must not be suppressed, because the unfeeling and the vicious may occasionally pervert them to disguise from others, and perhaps from themselves, the selfishness of their hearts. Let such be loudly reminded, that when all claims shall be abolished for indiscriminate charity, and for that systematic supply which, by teaching the poor to reckon upon it, only increases the quantum of improvidence, and the number of the claimants; still enough will remain of unmerited distress, of failure in the best efforts of virtue, to take away all pretence for indulging in selfish monopoly and hard-hearted indifference.

Art. VI.—1. *An Essay on the Principle of Population.* By the Rev. T. R. Malthus, A.M., F.R.S. Sixth Edition. Murray.

2.—*Principles of Political Economy.* By John Stuart Mill. Parker.

3.—*The True Law of Population.* By Thomas Doubleday, Esq. G. Pierce, 310, Strand.

4.—*General Report of the Sanitary Condition of the Labouring Population, from the Poor-Law Commissioners.* 1842.

5.—*Reports of the Board of Health.* 1849.

6.—*Journal des Economistes.* Gillaumin, Paris, and Luxford, London.

WHAT is it limits production?

Upon this question hangs the solution of the most important problem of the day—the question of the rights of labour, and the means, if any exist, of meliorating the lot of the great mass of the people.

It has been amply proved by statistical writers, that an equal distribution of all the wealth now existing in the world, would, in the share that would fall to each, effect scarcely any appreciable improvement in the condition of the working classes. But why is not more wealth created? What is it hinders the production of the necessaries of life, in the abundance required for the comfortable subsistence of all?

Assuming *food* to be deficient—why is it not grown?

It has been calculated that the valley of the Mississippi would provide a sufficient supply of both corn and cotton to feed and clothe the whole population of Europe; and in Europe itself there are still vast tracts of waste land that might be rendered available for tillage, to say nothing of innumerable half-tilled and neglected farms admitting of a higher cultivation.

Granting that the town and country mansions of our nobility would not suffice to lodge, or suitably to accommodate the whole of our agricultural peasantry, we may still ask why, instead of mud cabins, garrets and cellars, every poor family in the United Kingdom cannot be provided with a substantial cottage, with sufficient accommodation, at least, to allow of a private room for every adult person? What are the materials?—principally clay, bricks, and chalk for the lime that is to hold them together—materials known to be inexhaustible.

Why do we ever hear of a general stagnation of manufacturing and agricultural operations?—of multitudes wanting bread and clothing, and yet ceasing to produce them? Why do we sometimes see industry paralysed in the midst of privations, instead of a redoubling of the energies of labour?

The mere statement of the case excites a suspicion that some hidden cause of social disorganization is at work, which has escaped the attention of political economists.

To detect it, if it be possible, is the object of the present inquiry.

Ratios of Population and Capital.

What is it limits production?

An answer has been given, supported by the weight of the highest intellectual authorities of the present century—one, therefore, which it is incumbent upon every thinking man to examine before requiring any other. The answer is, that the capital necessary to be employed in production cannot be made to keep pace with population, unless in exceptional cases;—that there is a natural tendency in population to press upon the means of subsistence; and therefore, that it is only by restraining the too rapid multiplication of the human species that a proper and healthful proportion between capital and numbers can be made to exist.

This doctrine, originally propounded by Mr. Malthus, is now accepted in nearly every university in which political economy is taught, as one of the fundamental truths of the science. M. Michel Chevalier, Professor of Political Economy to the College of France, seizes the opportunity of an inaugural address,* to pronounce a high eulogium upon Mr. Malthus as a philosophical observer, of extensive erudition, endowed with a rare spirit of analysis, and to whom the world has been indebted for having explained the "true or principal cause of the decay of nations,

---

* Delivered, February 28th, 1849, and reported at length in the ' Journal des Economistes' for March 15th, 1849,—page 350.

L 2

and of the social disorders by which great states are commonly afflicted."

In this country, Mr. John Stuart Mill, whose recent work on the principles of political economy has placed him in the first rank of living philosophical writers, tells us, in respect to the increase of population, that the discussions exhibited by Mr. Malthus' Essay have made the truth (although by no means universally admitted) so fully known, that it is unnecessary for him to dwell upon it; and then, after giving us several illustrations of the power of organized beings to increase in a geometrical ratio, he says—

" Twenty or thirty years ago, these propositions might still have required considerable enforcement and illustration; but the evidence of them is so ample and incontestable, that they have made their way against all kinds of opposition, and may now be regarded as axiomatic, although the extreme reluctance felt to admitting them, every now and then gives birth to some ephemeral theory, speedily forgotten, of a different law of increase in different circumstances, through a providential adaptation of the fecundity of the human species to the exigencies of society. The obstacle to a just understanding of the subject does not arise from these theories, but from too confused a notion of the causes which, at most times and places, keep the actual increase of mankind so far behind the capacity."

The consequences for good or evil of the currency thus given, among statesmen and legislators, to the opinions of Mr. Malthus, can hardly be overrated. For good, if the doctrine be true— since, if the tendency to increase be really a tendency to misery, it is well we should set about restraining that increase, and the sooner the better;—for evil, it must be feared, if the doctrine be an error—because an error on such a subject would establish a false, and therefore a mischievous relation between the sexes, divert the mind from every other remedy for human wretchedness; and this failing,—as fail it probably must, from the ignorance, if not perversity, of the masses,—would lead many persons to regard the cause of human improvement as altogether hopeless.

Assuming, in another place, the impossibility of production increasing, in old countries such as England, in the same ratio as population would increase, if unchecked by a deficiency of the means of subsistence, Mr. Mill observes that,

" The necessity of restraining population is not, as many persons believe, peculiar to a condition of great inequality of property. A greater number of people cannot, in any given state of civilization, be collectively so well provided for, as a smaller. The niggardliness of nature, not the injustice of society, is the cause of the penalty attached to over-population. An unjust distribution of wealth does not even aggravate the evil; but, at most, causes it to be somewhat earlier felt. It is in vain to say, that all mouths which the increase of mankind calls into existence bring with them hands. The new mouths require as much food as the old ones, and the hands do not produce as much."[*]

It may be well to note, before proceeding to the source of these doctrines, that the logical correctness of the argument, as here stated by Mr. Mill, is dependent upon the meaning of the phrase, "a given state of civilization." The argument implies, although it does not expressly assert, that, when population increases there is no corresponding increase of civilization; a position to which we may reasonably demur, as not only gratuitous, but opposed to a multitude of facts tending to quite an opposite conclusion. The civilization of Egypt, for example, in reference to the industrial arts, was evidently greater in ancient times, when it contained a population of ten millions, than it is at the present moment; and the present civilization of Great Britain, with its population of twenty millions, will, at least, bear a favourable comparison with its barbarous state at the time of the landing of Julius Cæsar.

It is further implied in the above extract, that all land producing food is already cultivated to nearly its utmost extent; although this is not a proposition which, plainly stated, would be seriously maintained by Mr. Mill nor any other writer. Upon lands ill-cultivated, it obviously does not follow that new hands must produce less than the old ones, the fact being that, in such cases, the crops are often doubled and quadrupled by a little additional capital and labour. On a model farm, it is quite true that additional labour would yield but a very slight additional return; but the world is not yet covered with model farms. If we take the contrary instance of undrained districts, which are much more numerous than model farms, no person would contend that the labour employed upon them would yield a less proportionate return after suitable drainage works had been executed than before. There are parts of Lincolnshire in which the drainage of the fens has increased the produce a hundredfold; and yet works of this description are wholly dependent upon the growth of population. A thin and scattered population may perish by the miasma of a marsh; a larger one cuts a canal through the marsh, and converts the marsh into a garden.

Indeed, as the division of labour and combination of effort are the mainsprings of wealth, and as there can be neither one nor

---

[*] ' Principles of Political Economy,' vol. i. p. 227.

the other without numbers, it appears almost self-evident that, up to a certain point, the increase of population must produce quite the opposite effect to that stated by Mr. Mill. The new hands must produce more, instead of less, than the old hands, by a greater division of labour and power of combination than was before practicable. With a stationary population, where there can be little further division of labour—progress in the mechanical arts commonly stops. Roads, bridges, canals, ships, factories, public buildings, public libraries, museums, are the privileges of densely-populated countries, not of small communities. In equal states of civilization, it is quite clear that a population of a million must always be enabled to command a greater share of the necessaries and comforts of life than one of a hundred thousand, provided only the soil does not become exhausted of food, or of the exchangeable products by which food might be commanded (customs' duties apart) from other countries—a state of things in which the argument of Mr. Mill would apply, but which has never yet been realized, unless in times of general dearth, by any country on the face of the globe.

Impressed with the necessity of restraining population, Mr. Mill, with perfect consistency, and if his premises be sound, with equal propriety, regards with the greatest favor those improvements of human institutions, which have most a tendency to promote this object; and in proposing as a remedy for the distress of Ireland the creation of a class of peasant proprietors, its great recommendation in his eyes is the check it would afford to improvident marriages. He thinks, that while a cottier tenant population is proverbially reckless, that it has been proved (and again we are referred to Mr. Malthus as the authority), that in countries where the occupier is the freeholder, a habit prevails of counting the number of acres required for a family, and of not bringing a greater number of children into the world than the land will maintain. Whether the fact be so or not is perhaps not very material to this inquiry, although belonging to it. If freehold tenures do not check the growth of population there are yet other means of restraining it: we have only to make up our minds on the subject whether or not this should be our foremost object, and the means could easily be found.

The doctrine is put forward under circumstances very similar to those which led to the appearance of the original Essay on Population, of Mr. Malthus, in 1798. The French Revolution had given birth to numerous speculations on the perfectibility of human society; and Mr. Malthus wrote to expose the common defect, as he considered it, under which they all laboured—of not providing against the indefinite multiplication of the human species; and to defend the rich, and the government of the day, from the charge of being the cause of the misery and poverty of the working classes. Half a century has elapsed, and another French Revolution has revived the old theories and the old objection; an objection which has not as yet been satisfactorily met.

Numerous replies were made to the essay of Mr. Malthus, and recently further replies have appeared from the pens of French socialist writers, but they are generally considered to have all more or less failed. It has been, of course, easy to raise a charge of inhumanity and impiety against the author; and unsparing advantage has been taken of a passage in his first edition (since expunged), in which the poor were told that nature had provided no room for them, and that they had no right to demand a seat at her table. Vituperation, however, is the weakest of weapons; the fact remains, that wretchedness exists in the world, and that men, of whose philanthropy as well as intelligence there cannot be a doubt, still attribute its existence to the too rapid influx of new comers. The doctrine is not, therefore, one to be lightly treated, or dismissed with a few passing remarks. Once then again let us return to this text-book of our most distinguished political economists, note carefully the positions therein laid down, and examine, step by step, the proof offered of their soundness.

And it will be prudent to begin by divesting our minds of all misconceptions respecting the real point at issue. The question is not of the fact that, *in some cases*, population increases faster than the means of subsistence; of this it would be idle to express a doubt; especially as it may be assumed that the human race was designed to spread. The question is, whether in such cases the deficiency of food is fairly attributable to the law of population, or to some neglect or abuse of the bounties of nature.

We cannot, for example, blame nature for the distress occasioned by a marauding excursion, during which the provisions of multitudes, stored up for a winter, may be destroyed in a day; nor for the waste of means occasioned by intemperate habits; nor for the temporary privations of a factory district, where mills may have been closed, to be re-opened the next month, upon a revival of trade; nor for the reaction of a speculative mania. Nor is nature in fault for that perversion of charity that often maintains a pauper population without productive employment; nor for the overgrowth of towns, when become the great centres of commerce and taxation; nor for a neglect of the science of colonization; nor, again, for improvident marriages.

It would betray a strange misconception of the subject to treat

Mr. Malthus as the author of the discovery that improvident marriages aggravate the evils of improvidence. The duty of insuring the means of support before marriage, and of making a provision for the helpless beings to be brought into the world, has been a theme for moralists from time immemorial, and properly so, although perhaps more has sometimes been made of it than is strictly warranted by the facts; for while the duty of parental forethought cannot be too much insisted upon, it must yet be allowed that marriage is more favourable to settled habits of industry than celibacy. It has been remarked of birds, that they pair first, and build their nests afterwards; and with human beings the instinct of attachment often calls forth, and probably was designed to call forth, energies, economy, and an amount of application, that otherwise would not have existed.* The question is not of isolated marriages, improvident or otherwise, but of the tendency of marriages generally to increase the severity of the struggle for bread, and place each successive generation in a worse position than the last.

To make the point at issue perfectly clear, let us imagine an educated, intelligent, and industrial population, in which no one shall enter the marriage state without having made every provision for the casualties of life that can reasonably be required of those who are to live by labour. Let us suppose every man and woman marrying to have a hundred pounds in the savings' bank, needful articles of furniture, and to be in good employment, with a fair prospect of its continuance. Let us suppose, further, of every such couple, that they have read the sanitary reports, studied the laws of health, and have become thereby enabled to protect themselves and their offspring from many of the ordinary chances of sickness. To what would such marriages lead? Obviously, one consequence of them would be, according to Mr. Malthus, that more children would be born and more reared, than would be

---

* The late Mr. J. Lackington, bookseller, who began life as a journeyman shoemaker, gives the following account of his marriage :—

"I renewed my correspondence with my old sweetheart, Nancy Smith. I informed her that my attachment to books, together with travelling from place to place, and also my total disregard for money, had prevented me from saving any; and that, while I remained in a single unsettled state, I was never likely to accumulate it."

When the expences of the wedding were paid, a single halfpenny was all he had left for the next week, without working for it. Afterwards, entering into the book trade, he established a business, which ultimately produced him an income of £4,000 per annum.

Benjamin Franklin confesses, in the autobiography of his own life, that he cured himself by marriage of "the irregularities and expenses," which had prevented his thriving in business before his union with Miss Read.

born and reared of an equal number of improvident marriages—
that population, therefore, would increase in a still more rapid
geometrical ratio than at present, and that the period would only
be postponed when marriages must be abstained from altogether
by the majority, or vice and misery again be allowed to act as
checks upon a further increase.

There is no middle course. The theory does not admit of the
slightest prospect of any permanent improvement of the condition of the mass of the people from the progress of temperance,
thrift, industry, intelligence, and skill, whatever that progress
may be, unless coupled with the condition of fewer marriages than
at present, or with some artificial means taken to reduce the
average number of births to a marriage.

In reference to the scheme of society advocated by Mr. Godwin,
founded upon industrial association and equal distribution, Mr.
Malthus reasons as follows:—

"Let us suppose all the causes of vice and misery in this island
removed. War and contention cease. Unwholesome trades and
manufactories do not exist. Crowds no longer collect together in
great and pestilent cities for purposes of court intrigue, of commerce,
and of vicious gratification. Simple, healthy, and rational amuse-
ments take place of drinking, gaming, and debauchery. The greater
part of the happy inhabitants of this terrestrial paradise live in hamlets
and farm-houses, scattered over the face of the country. All men are
equal. The spirit of benevolence, guided by impartial justice, divides
the produce of the country among all the members of the society,
according to their wants."

In such a happy community, in which there would be no
anxiety about the support of children, Mr. Malthus presumes
that there would be no young woman of twenty-three without a
family. Population would double itself in fifteen years—"certainly in twenty-five." Eleven millions of people would become
twenty-two; twenty-two millions would become forty-four; and
then,—

"The spirit of benevolence, cherished and invigorated by plenty,
is repressed by the chilling breath of want. The hateful passions
that had vanished re-appear. The mighty law of self-preservation
expels all the softer and more exalted emotions of the soul. The
temptations to evil are too strong for human nature to resist. The
corn is plucked before it is ripe, or secreted in unfair proportions;
and the whole black train of vices that belong to falsehood are immediately generated. Provisions no longer flow in for the support of a
mother with a large family. The children are sickly from insufficient
food. The rosy flush of health gives place to the pallid cheek and
hollow eye of misery. Benevolence, yet lingering in a few bosoms,

makes some faint expiring struggles, till at length self-love resumes his wonted empire, and lords it triumphant over the world." *

A practical application of this doctrine has been made by a section of the moral-force chartists, converts to the principle, by whom it is taught that no working man should allow himself to be the parent of more than three children ; and such a deduction is perfectly logical from the premises assumed.

Mr. Malthus opens his argument, chapter i., page 2,† with the following statement :—

" It is observed by Dr. Franklin, that there is no bound to the prolific nature of plants and animals, but what is made by their crowding and interfering with each other's means of subsistence. Were the face of the earth, he says, vacant of other plants, it might be gradually sowed and overstocked with one kind only—as, for instance, with fennel ; and, were it empty of other inhabitants, it might, in a few ages, be replenished from one nation only—as, for instance, with Englishmen."

Franklin would doubtless have reconsidered this observation, if he had been aware that it would be made the foundation of a treatise of philosophy ; but Mr. Malthus, without examining it, and, from its plausibility, suspecting no inaccuracy, proceeds at once to apply it. In fact, the entire reasoning of his work consists of illustrations of this position ; and subsequent economists, starting with the same assumption, have of course followed him in the same conclusions.

Mr. John Stuart Mill, repeating after Franklin and Mr. Malthus, remarks : " The power of multiplication inherent in organic life may be regarded as infinite."‡

The existence of any such inherent power has to be proved. What is known is, that in certain circumstances, plants and animals have multiplied to an extent beyond all calculation ; and, in other circumstances, have diminished and disappeared,§—so much so, that geologists tell us, that of the plants and animals belonging to the *Palæontological,* or most ancient strata of the earth, every single species has become extinct.

An increase for limited periods, in a geometrical ratio of progression, does not at all affect the conclusion, that races or spe-

* Vol. ii. page 27.
† The sixth edition—the last revised by the author, published in 1826. Subsequent quotations are all from the same edition.
‡ ' Principles of Political Economy,' vol. i. p. 187.
§ " Cuvier, from remains found chiefly in the neighbourhood of Paris, determined no less than ninety species of animals, not one of which is now represented by any living creature."—*Ansted's Geology,* vol. i. p. 40.

cies may be as finite and mortal as individuals. The evidence is altogether wanting that the principle of fecundity is even equal to the continuation of the same race or species, in an infinite series; and Franklin might have convinced himself, by a conversation with any country gardener or farmer, that there are many other causes than overcrowding, or an impoverishment of the soil, to affect the increase of the vegetable kingdom. Were it otherwise, we should of course never hear of a failure of the crops. A failure of the crops is a failure, more or less, of the principle of fecundity, the grain deficient being *the seed* on which the hopes of the next harvest depend. A botanist often misses some annual which he has been accustomed to meet with in his excursions, and perhaps may search a county without finding a single specimen of the same plant, the seed having failed the preceding year, from the season having been unfavourable at the time of flowering.

" The power of multiplication inherent in all organic life," instead of being infinite, is liable to periods of interruption and cessation, both in animal and vegetable organizations; the same cold rains, and nights of frost, which will sometimes destroy the seed in the ground, destroy the ova of the insect tribes, or at least prevent their vivification. When there are no turnips, there is no turnip-fly. Ascending higher in the scale of animated creation, the same rule may be observed. A wet summer is generally a bad breeding season for cattle, as was remarked in the summer of 1848, especially in the South of England; and among human beings the births in different years vary, with the varying effects upon the constitution of prevailing epidemics.

A little further examination will show us that, in strictness, there is absolutely no " inherent power of multiplication" in organic life, and that to speak of the " prolific nature of plants and animals," is to use a phrase scientifically incorrect. The germ of a plant, it is true, is essential to growth, but is only one of a thousand elements equally essential. Take away the influence of light, heat, numerous gases, water, mineral and decayed vegetable and animal substances, and the germ has no greater power of growth than a pebble.

It is nature, not the germ alone that is prolific, and nature is prolific only when she combines her powers for a prolific end. An important distinction; for on this subject, as on every other, the most fruitful source of error is rapid generalization.

Mr. Malthus proceeds to quote the opinion of various authors to the effect, that there is a capacity in population to double itself in somewhat less than thirteen years; and, as the population of the United States has for a century and a half actually doubled itself every twenty years, he deems it quite safe to assert, that population when unchecked goes on doubling itself every twenty-five years, or increases in a geometrical ratio; (the question in discussion). He next enters into some very simple calculations to show, that although the produce of any given quantity of land may go on doubling for a short time, it cannot do so for ever—a fact which is certainly incontrovertible.

Mr. Malthus then states, in form, the propositions intended to be demonstrated by his work. They are the following:—

"That population invariably increases where the means of subsistence increase, unless prevented by some very powerful and obvious checks.

"These checks, and the checks which repress the superior power of population, and keep its effects on a level with the means of subsistence, are all resolvable into moral restraint, vice and misery."

The conclusion, as before stated, is, that moral restraint—meaning thereby celibacy, or a restriction of the number of births to a marriage, are the only means by which vice and misery can be banished from the world.

The terms of the proposition appear extravagant, and countenance a morbid view of human affairs quite at variance with received opinions of divine wisdom and benevolence, and which, therefore, it is hard to believe can be philosophical. The question naturally arises, *why* this surplus fecundity if our first duty be to restrain it ? And the kind of apology for it, offered by Mr. Malthus, does not supply a reasonable answer. He says—

"The desire of the means of subsistence would be comparatively confined in its effects, and would fail of producing that general activity so necessary to the improvement of the human faculties, were it not for the strong and universal effort of population to increase with greater rapidity than its supplies. If these two tendencies were exactly balanced, I do not see what motive there would be, sufficiently strong to overcome the acknowledged indolence of man, and make him proceed in the cultivation of the soil."*

The motive which overcomes "the acknowledged indolence of man," is the law of labour:—"If a man will not work, neither shall he eat," a law quite independent of the principle of population; for, if there were only half a dozen families left in the world, this law would continue to operate, and with even greater rigour than at present. Mr. Malthus reasons as if the inhabitants of a country thinly-populated were in some way supplied with food and raiment gratis, and that the necessity of exertion to procure them, only arises with the increase of numbers. The

---

* Vol. ii. page 267.

very opposite of this statement we know would be more consistent with the fact. The first settlers of a new colony have always been mere slaves as compared with the condition in which they have generally left their descendants. Take, for example, the history of the United States, and contrast the privations of those who laboured at the first clearings of the forest, with the present state of the American people.* But it will be unnecessary to dwell upon this, because, as will presently be seen, some of the most forcible, although exaggerated instances of misery, selected by the author himself, are taken from thinly populated countries.

There is another obvious mistake in this paragraph, for the principle assumed that the returns of labour diminish relatively with the increase of population, has a tendency rather to discourage industry than to promote it. Industry is fed on hope, and dies when hope fails. Tell a man that, work as he may, he will only grow poorer and poorer, and he will be apt to take to a life of plunder, or to sink into apathy and despair.

The objection to the morbid terms of the proposition, as irreconcileable with our ideas of divine goodness, is not one of feeling, which might be dismissed as a weakness, but one of some weight as an argument; for if, in the works of nature there be any evidence of design stronger than another, it may be found in that of the sexual functions. Some may doubt this, but there is a limit of doubt at which all argument must cease, as putting an end to reasoning, since reasoning consists of nothing but deductions; and we have arrived at that limit if we cannot deduce, from a consideration of the female organization, the fact that women were designed to be mothers, and that in the apparatus provided for suckling, the means of subsistence for their offspring were not overlooked.

Another striking evidence of design may be remarked in the varying fecundity of different animals.

If the law of population were merely some blind geometric principle, having no adaptation to the means of subsistence, we might expect to see the ratio of increase of living creatures very much alike—insects and elephants, for example, doubling their numbers in about the same time. But we find, on the contrary, that the fecundity of animals of different species diminishes in the inverse ratio of their size, and with their longevity. Twenty-four hours are sufficient, in a hop-garden, to cover the leaves of the

---

* Of the pilgrim fathers, 101 souls in number, who landed from the *May-flower*, on Plymouth Beach, Massachusets, December 22nd, 1620, one half perished from the severity of the first winter and inefficient means of shelter. *Lyall's Second Visit to the United States*, vol. i. page 114.

plants with a population of Aphides greater than that of Europe; but in the first thunder-storm the whole disappear. An elephant lives for upwards of a century, but takes from twenty to thirty years to attain its full growth; the female produces but one at a birth, and the period of gestation is from twenty-two to twenty-three months.

The population of hares and rabbits, says Mr. Mill, would in a few years, were it not for their liability to be eaten, overstock the earth; but his attention does not appear to have been called to the fact, that the fecundity of the larger animals that feed on hares and rabbits is much more slowly developed; and the rule that the powers of procreation of birds and beasts of prey are only in a distant proportion to the fecundity of the creatures that serve them for food,* is so universal, that it is alone sufficient to raise a strong presumption that, in the case of no species has the law of population a tendency to outstrip its supplies.

It is true that rats and wolves, and perhaps all carnivorous animals, will devour each other when in a state of starvation; but the instances of their being driven to such an extremity are rare. No creature depends for its supplies upon the slaughter of its own species; rats in a barn clear it of mice, but live together themselves in tolerable harmony; and wolves hunt together in packs.

Man was not formed to prey upon man, although cannibals eat their enemies, and shipwrecked mariners on a raft in the midst of the ocean, without provisions, will cast lots which shall die first to prolong the lives of the rest. To found an argument upon such cases is to confound the incidence of a general law with the law itself; a distinction which it is always material to observe, for without it we cannot avoid a confusion of ideas, and a false interpretation of all observed phenomena. We should smile at a Hindoo who were to assert that it was a law of European

---

* " We see that all the smaller creatures which serve us for food are particularly fruitful, and that they increase in a much greater proportion than others. Of the birds it is extremely remarkable, that, lest they should fall short of a certain number of eggs, they are endowed with the power of laying others in the place of those that are taken away; but that, when their number is complete, they invariably stop. Here is an operation, like many others, much beyond the reach of our faculties to comprehend. How the mere privation of part should cause a fresh production, is not, indeed, easy to understand. The organization of an offspring should, in this case, almost seem a voluntary act of the female; but in what manner it is done, we are not only ignorant at present, but shall most probably ever remain so. *Noxious animals* in general multiply slowly; and whenever we find an unusual increase of such, we generally discover that something has been given by Providence for the purpose of destroying and counterbalancing them."—*Bingley's Animal Biography*.

civilization that locomotive engines, like the car of Juggernaut, should crush their passengers. It is an incidence in the use of locomotives that they should sometimes occasion a loss of life; but the law or principle by which they are directed is, that they should not crush their passengers, but carry them.

The rule of nature is to anticipate and prevent the evils, both of starvation and lingering disease, by the more merciful process of a sudden death; and this, without limiting the fecundity of animals more than would otherwise be necessary, the law of prey accomplishes—a law that provides for the support of myriads of creatures that could otherwise have no existence.

It is most worthy of observation that every creature, although surrounded by enemies, is provided with the means of escaping from them, while in the full enjoyment of its natural powers. When those powers fail, the means of escape also fail, and instead of dying in misery, death overtakes it in a moment; not through invisible agency, but impersonated in the form of some larger and stronger animal, to which the life extinguished may be said to be transferred.*

The commonly received opinion, therefore, that nature is not an improvident mother, is not a mere vulgar prejudice; and as it cannot be said of the inferior animals, that the process employed by nature for limiting their numbers is misery alone,† the presumption is a strong hope, that such a proposition cannot be affirmed, with truth, of men.

Misery alone, for the postulates of Mr. Malthus, may be condensed without any violation of their sense. He means by vice, the misery to which it tends. He admits moral restraint to imply a state of privation; and he would hardly deny the facts brought to light by physiological writers, that enforced celibacy

---

* The cruelty of a cat in sometimes relaxing her hold of a mouse, and torturing it with vain hopes of escape, has been noticed, but this is incidental only to her domestic state, in which she is generally overfed. There is no playfulness in hunger. The rapidity of death by the law of prey, may be remarked in the familar instance of the terrier dog employed for the destruction of rats. A single bite is fatal, and death instantaneous.

† It is mentioned by Dr. Carpenter, as an instance of a kind, although seemingly cruel providence in this respect, that when the first cold nights of autumn indicate the approach of winter, wasps immediately proceed to kill the larvæ left in their nests, which there is then no longer a possibility of rearing, and eject their bodies from their cells.

This remarkable instinct might by some be adduced, as an argument for infanticide, or for that theory of "painless extinction" which has not been without its formal advocates; and the justification would be complete if we had no opposite examples for imitation in animals with greater resources than wasps, and if the case could be fairly made out that we had reached the limit of our own.

is a cause of impaired health, especially as affecting the organization of females.   Without health there can be no enjoyment of
life, and thus, practically, it is misery alone, according to the
doctrine assumed, that prevents the over-population of the world.

We have to notice, besides, in the terms of the propositions,
a want of that precision which is necessary to a clear conception
and a practical application of every sound principle.   The one
idea which pervades the work, and the one doctrine which Mr.
Malthus laboured to expound, was the proposition that population has a tendency to increase faster than the supply of food; a
tendency counteracted, as he supposed, by a struggle for the
means of subsistence and an increased mortality thence resulting.
But while this was his object, he, at the same time, uses the
terms vice and misery, as generalities embracing every cause of
mortality excepting old age.   He enumerates under these heads:

" All unwholesome occupations, severe labour, and exposure to the
seasons ; extreme poverty ; bad nursing of children ; great towns ;
excesses of all kinds ; the whole train of common diseases and epidemics, war and famine."

This is materially altering the ground of the whole controversy.   The only question which, practically, society is in the
least degree interested in discussing, is whether population
should be restrained artificially or not ?—and the answer of course
must be in the affirmative, if it can be proved that, without such
artificial restraints, multitudes would only be born to the misery
occasioned by increasing want.   We ask, then, for the evidence
of this increasing want, and find, mixed up with it, " excesses
of all kinds," and diseases of all kinds, as if even the mortality
occasioned by intemperate habits were a proof of deficiency, and
the whole catalogue of ills that flesh is heir to, including the
rich man's gout, and the death of a fox-hunter by a fall from his
horse, were to be traced to the law of population.   Such a mode
of sustaining the argument almost reduces it to a statement that
the world would soon be too full if all who were born lived for
ever: an axiom which may be conceded.   But all who are born,
were born to die, and to die at various ages; without which death
would approach with a painful certainty of the precise period of
our demise, which has been benevolently concealed; and it is
not at all clear, that if the earth were a thousand-fold more productive than it is, and poverty were absolutely banished from
the world, there would not be as many casualties of life as at
present, partly from natural causes, and partly from the increased
habits of indolence and dissipation which would then prevail.

The unfortunate effect of this vagueness of definition upon the
public at large has been to produce an impression, strengthened

by what is considered philosophical testimony, that the excessive mortality of unhealthy districts, especially when inhabited by the working classes, is always to be traced to destitution; and that, on the whole, such mortality is not to be regretted, because the sole means of checking the evil of a redundant population. This is a double error, which has been fully exposed in the late sanitary reports of the Poor Law Commission; and the following observations of Mr. Chadwick deserve our attention:—

" How erroneous the inferences are in their unrestrained generality, which assume that the poverty or the privation which is sometimes the consequence, is always the cause, of disease, will have been seen from such evidence as that adduced from Glasgow and Spitalfields, proving that the greater proportion of those attacked by disease are in full work at the time; and the evidence from the fever hospitals, that the greatest proportion of the patients are received in high bodily condition. If wages be taken as the test of the means of subsistence, it may be asked, how are such facts to be reconciled as these, that, at a time when wages in Manchester were 10s. per head weekly on all employed in the manufactories, including children or young persons in the average, so that if three or four members of a family were employed, the wages of a family would be 30s. or 40s. weekly, the average chances of life to all of the labouring classes were only seventeen years; whilst in the whole of Rutlandshire, where the wages were certainly not one-half that amount, we find the mean chances of life to every individual of the lowest class were thirty-seven years: or, to take another instance, that of Leeds, where, according to Mr. Baker's report, the wages of the families of the worst-conditioned workers were upwards of £1 1s. per week, and the chances of life amongst the whole labouring population of the borough were only nineteen years; whilst in the county of Wilts, where the labourer's family would not receive much more than half that amount of wages in money, and, perhaps, not two-thirds of money's worth in money and produce together, we find the average chances of life to the labouring classes thirty-two years."

In a report of the Board of Health for July, 1849, it is noticed that in the small village of Nordelf, in Norfolk, there had occurred fifty cases of cholera, out of a population of only 150 souls;* and many similar cases might be cited. But admitting, as every one must, that a certain amount of disease is occasioned by over-

---

* It was remarked of the cholera in Paris, during the year 1832, that it " more especially attacked those whose professions commanded competent means, *and, above all, those employed in the open air.*" If it had been occasioned by over-crowding alone, women, from their indoor occupations, would have suffered greatly more than men; but the proportions of deaths was only 9,232 females to 9,170 males.—*Journal des Economistes.* March, 1849.

crowding, and some over-crowding by destitution, it is yet evident that over-crowding may often be traced not to the want of common necessaries, but the temptation of superior comforts. Rich bankers crowd together in Lombard-street for the sake of greater wealth; and, by so doing, raising the rents of the neighbourhood, merchants and brokers seeking the same convenient centre for their operations, are compelled to crowd together in counting-houses, on separate floors of the same building. A poor man employed by them takes lodgings in a back court from the same motive. He might get cheaper and more healthy lodgings for his family at a distance, but at a distance he would earn less; and, perhaps, which is often the case, he prefers the convenience of having his home near his occupation, to the long walk morning and evening, which would save his pocket and improve his health. In other districts, the rich crowd into the neighbourhood of a Royal Court, and, attracted by their expenditure, the working classes crowd after them into the same precincts. Ambition, habit, and bad structural arrangements are answerable for the misery thence arising—not the law of population.

Habit and ignorance have a much greater share in occasioning the dirt, diseases and wretchedness of large sections of the population, than has been generally understood by philosophers and philanthropists. The Scottish highlander gives up the best room in his cabin to a cow, the Irish cottier to a pig; they sleep surrounded with filth, and, whether the potato-crop has failed or been abundant, makes no difference in this respect to their condition. Poverty is not the cause of the dung-heap before their doors, but indifference to cleanliness; an indifference which they carry with them as emigrants, and retain in the United States when their wages have been quadrupled. Upon this subject the sanitary reports have rendered invaluable service to the public in removing prevalent misconceptions by plain statements of fact. They abound with instances of disease and wretchedness, occasioned not by poverty, but a total disregard of the laws of health; and this not merely in towns, but in rural villages and situations naturally salubrious: and they trace the effect of causes of mortality, by which the rich are, relatively to their numbers, as frequently the victims as the poor.

The fallacy of supposing that fever, cholera, and other diseases among the poor, are the especial remedies of Providence for a redundant population, has been shown by Mr. Chadwick. The sanitary reports establish the fact, that an unusual mortality is generally followed by an unusual number of births, and that the result is a larger and feebler, and consequently, a less productive population than before, consisting principally of children, who, where the causes of disease are permanent, as in marshy and un-drained districts, seldom attain an advanced age, but in their turn are prematurely cut off. Thus, in the lower districts of Man-chester, Mr. Chadwick states the deaths to be in 1 in 28, and the births at 1 in 26; while in Rutlandshire, where the deaths are 1 in 52, the births are only 1 in 33 of the population.

These figures perfectly agree with the proportions given by Mr. Malthus himself, who tells us, that when the deaths are but 1 in 45, the proportion of births will be generally 1 in 36; and that when the deaths rise to 1 in 32, births will increase to 1 in 26; and on this subject he gives an explanation which is doubt-less sound, as applicable to one class of cases; but, as usual, he commits the mistake of supposing that there can be no other causes in operation to account for similar results. He says, that when the head of a family dies, room is made for a younger man, who thereupon enters into a marriage, which otherwise he would have been compelled to defer; and that deaths among the poor lead to an increased demand for the labour of the survivors, and a consequent improvement of their position favourable to early marriages. Thus, in Prussia, after a plague in 1709 and 1710 which destroyed a third of the population, the marriages rose in 1711, according to the tables of Sussmilch, from the average of •6,082 to 12,028, and the births from 26,896 to 32,522.* An extreme case, partly to be accounted for from the average given not including the two plague years, of which there are no returns, but during which it is reasonable to conclude there were fewer marriages than usual.

Mr. Malthus did not, however, remark the inconsistency into which he had been led by these figures. He had first told us that war and pestilence were among the most effectual positive checks of population; and he then reasons to show that they have just the opposite tendency, operating as a stimulus to early marriages, to which he frequently refers as more prolific than later marriages. † A distinction was required which he failed to make, through his besetting sin of rapid generalization. Wars and pestilence are checks to population, when unusually severe. A war of extermination, of course, destroys a population altogether. But in ordinary cases, where the greater part of the inhabitants of a country are still left, the immediate effects are—first, a general

---

* Table iv. page 500.

† An opinion which appears to be unfounded; unless by later marriages are meant marriages contracted beyond the age of thirty.

deterioration of the condition of the population; and next, a rapid increase of its numbers.* The same remark applies to vice and misery; they seldom exterminate, but tend at once to premature deaths, and a premature development of the prolific faculties; perhaps, also, for reasons which we shall subsequently assign, to a positive increase, in some cases, of the powers of fecundity. Vice and misery are not, therefore, checks to population, even upon Mr. Malthus's own showing; but causes which act and re-act upon each other, tending to the perpetuation of evils for which another cure must be sought.

How then are the propositions of Mr. Malthus supported ? Extraordinary as it may seem, the solitary argument upon which he and his followers rely for their hypothesis is the fact that population sometimes doubles itself every twenty years, as in the case before mentioned, of the United States. Many thousand instances might of course be adduced in which population has not so doubled itself; but these are all got rid of by the assumption, that in some way or other, vice and misery,— bad passions, and bad institutions,—have been the sole operative check. To prove this, Mr. Malthus proceeds to adduce a multitude of cases in which vice and misery have undoubtedly contributed to thin the numbers of mankind; and, after adding a few statistical tables, closes his first volume, imagining the demonstration complete; and proceeds to apply it in the second.

The kind of syllogism on which the demonstration rests, may be stated as follows :—

" *Major*—Population has been known to double itself every twenty years.

" *Minor*—Vice and misery are checks to population.

" *Conclusion*—Population would always double itself every twenty years, but for vice and misery."

---

* The destruction of life occasioned by war has always been a subject of great exaggeration. At the battle of Waterloo, the actual loss in killed (excluding the wounded and missing), on the side of the Allies, appears from Captain Siborne's narrative, to have been as follows :—

British	..	..	..	..	..	1334
German regiments		..	..	..	..	1007
Dutch and Belgians		..	..	..	..	246
Prussian troops	..	..	..	..	..	1203
						3790

Supposing the loss on the French side to have been double this number, we have still a total of only 11,370. The deaths by cholera in Paris, during the one month of April, 1832, were 12,733.

The fallacy of this *non sequitur* may be illustrated by another :—

" *Major*—The length of human life is three-score years and ten.

" *Minor*—Some who have not lived for seventy years have died of cholera.

" *Conclusion*—All die of cholera who do not live to three-score years and ten."

If Mr. Malthus had been a grazier instead of a clergyman, he might, perhaps, have been led by his experience in the breeding of cattle, to suspect the existence of many other causes than the supply of food, or than vice and misery, to account for the expansion at one time, and decrease at another, of population. He would have discovered, for example, that a continued attempt to breed cattle from the same stock produces a degeneracy, which ultimately ends in sterility, and that the intermixture of herds fed on different pastures is from time to time necessary, even to maintain the stock in an average condition. He would have discovered, also, that an abundance of food has often the very opposite effect to that which his theory would ascribe to it. The tendency of a too luxuriant pasture, or of high-stall feeding, not being to make cattle multiply faster, but to make them fat, and leave off breeding; and these facts would have probably led him to reflect that a hardy emigrant population, such as that with which the United States has been peopled, brought together from all parts of the world, might very possibly show a tendency to increase faster, from the twofold operation of more births and fewer deaths, than a settled population of old families, the latter living, for the most part, in a higher style of comfort, and inter-marrying within closer degrees of affinity.

For ourselves, we have only to look around in the circle of our own acquaintance, to perceive the operation of causes in the limitation of human fecundity, which, however obscure, are at least quite distinct from vice and misery. There are few of us who have not known instances of women who have been the mothers of twenty children; and of others who, although married for the same term of years, and living in similar circumstances of life, have only borne three, five, or two, or perhaps have been altogether childless; and as these differences are clearly not occasioned by deficiency of means (for, on the whole, large families of children are more numerous among the poor than among the rich), the question naturally occurs, whether it be not possible that, in equal states of civilization, and with equal supplies of food, the average of births, as well as deaths, of a whole population might not be very different at one time from that of

another, and from causes not included in the category of Mr.
Malthus, but which might possibly be traced by investigation.

We are entitled also to inquire, whether the proportion of
male to female births has corresponded in all ages of the world;
for a very slight diminution of the number of female births
would obviously affect, very materially, the ratio of general
increase, and *vice versâ*. This question cannot be answered in
the affirmative, for the proportions are known to vary in different
countries at the present time, and especially where there is a
crossing of races. It is a mystery which no one yet has been
able to penetrate, why the offspring of one couple should sometimes be all girls, and that of another all boys: there must, however, be a cause for the difference, and some inquiry is certainly
called for into the general result, not merely as affecting our own
day and generation, but other times and circumstances than the
present.

The work is not one of investigation in reference to any of
these topics. Mr. Malthus notices an assertion of Bruce, that in
countries where polygamy prevails, the proportion of girls born
to boys is as three to one, but passes it over with an expression
of incredulity, without examination, and assumes a geometrical
principle of doubling equally for all varieties of the human race—
Indian, Negro, Asiatic, or European; for all climates capable of
sustaining human life—frigid, temperate or torrid; for all states
of human society—that of the hunter, the shepherd, and the
agriculturist; and he assumes it for all time; the thought never
apparently having crossed his mind that races, like plants, may
wear out when not renewed from another soil; and any diminution of the power of fecundity being treated throughout his work
as requiring a miraculous interposition.

Reserving for the present a further consideration of this part
of our subject, it will be useful now to accompany Mr. Malthus
some distance in his melancholy tour through the world, and to
look a little into the kind of facts he has collected to prove that
population everywhere shows, and has always manifested, a tendency to press upon the means of subsistence, and that vice and
misery, in the absence of moral restraint, are the only effective
agents for its repression.

Redundant Populations.

The evidence stated under this head commences with the third chapter; and the first case quoted is the following:—

"The wretched inhabitants of Terra del Fuego have been placed by the general consent of voyagers at the bottom of the scale of human beings. Of their domestic habits and manners, however, we have few accounts. Their barren country, and the miserable state in which they live, have prevented any intercourse with them that might give such information; but we cannot be at a loss to conceive the checks to population among a race of savages, whose very appearance indicates them to be half-starved, and who, shivering with cold, and covered with filth and vermin, live in one of the most inhospitable climates in the world, without having sagacity enough to provide themselves with such conveniences as might mitigate its severities, and render life in some measure more comfortable."—Vol. i. chap. 3, page 25.

The land called Terra del Fuego is the largest of a group of islands, forming the extreme southerly point of South America; separated from the continent by the Straits of Magellan. From the anxiety of mariners to keep at a safe distance from a dangerous coast, in doubling Cape Horn, these islands have been but little visited; and the supposition that the whole of the country corresponded with the barren rocks first seen, and most exposed to the tempestuous winds of the South Atlantic, was a very natural conclusion on the part of our early navigators. It is unfortunate, however, for the credit of a philosophical work, that this conclusion, cited as the first fact to which the author deemed it important to direct the attention of his readers, should now be discovered to have been premature, and altogether unwarranted. The land is not barren; the climate is not inhospitable, although boisterous, and with more than a usual prevalence of rain. The natives have always fire with them for cooking, and are not generally found "shivering with cold." They consist of different tribes, some of whom wear a rude clothing of skins, while others go entirely naked, and this apparently, like most of the South Sea Islanders, from choice rather than necessity. Their occupation is that of sailors, constantly engaged in boating, whence arise broad chests and length of arm; but from a want of development of the muscles of the leg, a shortness of stature. These peculiarities, in the case of the Fuegians, were, at first, attributed to malformation proceeding from want of food; a deficiency which we now know, from the ample accounts furnished by the American exploring expedition in 1839, to have no existence. Captain Wilkes recommends Orange Harbour, Terra del Fuego, for the ample supplies of wood and water to be there obtained. He speaks of "dense forests of beech, birch, willow, and winter bark," of "an abundance of fish," the principal food of the natives, and of "great quantities of wild fowl, geese, ducks, and the usual sea-birds, to be seen at all times in the harbour." Lieutenant Johnson, of the same expedition, visiting a neighbouring port in Deception Island, found penguins in countless numbers "covering some hundreds of acres on the hill side," and a small white pigeon, sufficiently tame to be taken by hand.*

---

* "While lying in a snug cove off Wollaston's Island (one of the same group), we were here visited by a canoe with six natives—two old women, two young men, and two children. The two women were paddling, and the fire was burning in the usual place. They approached the vessel singing their rude song, ' Hey meh leh,' and continued it until they came alongside. The expression of the younger ones was extremely prepossessing, evincing much intelligence and good humour. I have seldom seen so happy a group. They were extremely lively and cheerful, and anything but miserable, if we could have avoided contrasting their condition with our own. The colour of the young men was a pale, and of the old a dark, copper colour. Their heads were covered with ashes; but their exterior left a pleasing impression. Contentment was pictured in their countenances and actions, and produced a moral effect that will long be remembered."—*Capt. Wilkes' Narrative of the United States Exploring Expedition.* Vol i. p. 142.

Mr. Malthus proceeds to state, that the natives of Van Dieman's Land are almost as low in genius and resources as the Fuegians, but that

" Some late accounts have represented the islands of Andaman in the East, as inhabited by a race of savages still lower in wretchedness even than these. Everything that voyagers have related of savage life is said to fall short of the barbarism of this people. Their whole time is spent in search of food; and as their woods yield them few or no supplies of animals, and but little vegetable diet, their principal occupation is that of climbing the rocks, or roving along the margin of the sea in search of a precarious meal of fish, which, during the tempestuous season, they often seek in vain. Their stature seldom exceeds five feet; their bellies are protuberant, with high shoulders, large heads, and limbs disproportionately slender; their countenances exhibit the extreme of wretchedness—a horrid mixture of famine and ferocity; and their attenuated and diseased figures plainly indicate the want of wholesome nourishment. Some of these unhappy beings have been found on the shores in the last stage of famine."

The authorities* quoted for the above, describe the natives as having the appearance of a degenerate race of negroes, with woolly hair, flat noses, thick lips, in complexion sooty black, and speaking a language having no affinity with any of the languages of the opposite coasts of Siam and Hindostan. From these circumstances it was conjectured by Mr. Symes, that the original stock had been settled upon the island by the accidental shipwreck of an Arab slave-ship; and the case is therefore an exceptional one, upon which no valid argument can be built. But the negro denizens of these islands are not their only inhabitants: Lieut. Alexander, landing in a boat on the " Little Andaman," found himself surrounded by a crowd of " strong, able-bodied men, far from a puny race, and many of them very lusty."† They were armed with bows and arrows, spears made of hard wood, and shields of bark, and evinced " surprising dexterity in shooting and spearing the fish which abound in their bays and creeks." No doubt, in the Andamans, as elsewhere, the tempestuous season is not the best for fishing; but we read besides of " pigeons, crows, parroquets, kingfishers, curlews, fish-hawks, and fowls, seen in the woods," and that " the caves contain the edible birds' nests prized by the Chinese as one of the rarest luxuries of the table." The extent of the Andaman Islands is 170 miles in length by about 40 miles in breadth; and as the entire population is supposed not to exceed 2,500 souls, this is, perhaps, as doubtful an illustration as could well have

---

* ' Symes's Embassy to Asia,' and the ' Asiatic Journal.'
† ' Alexander's Travels from India to England.'

been selected of the results of a pressure upon the means of subsistence. The emaciated appearance observed among some of the negro natives, had been probably occasioned by the tropical fevers incidental to the climate, which has been found too sickly for a settlement of Europeans.

The next case cited by Mr. Malthus, is that of the natives of New South Wales, of whom he copies from the accounts of them first published, some particulars of diet, revolting to English tastes ;* and, in addition (which is not a little curious), presses into his service their very ingenuity in the climbing of tall trees for wild honey, as an evidence of extreme physical degradation.

" They are compelled to climb the tallest trees after honey, and the smaller animals, such as the flying squirrel, and the opossum. When the stems are of great height, and without branches, which is generally the case in thick forests, this is a process of great labour, and is effected by cutting a notch with their stone hatchets for each foot successively, while their left arm embraces the tree. Trees were observed notched in this manner to the height of eighty feet, before the first branches where the hungry savage could hope to meet with any reward for so much toil."

The proper pendant to such a picture would be the misery of English schoolboys, spending their half holidays in bird's-nesting, or in filling their stomachs with nuts and blackberries. The following requires more serious comment :—

" The prelude to love in this country is violence, and of the most brutal nature. The savage selects his intended wife from the women of a different tribe, generally one at enmity with his own. He steals upon her in the absence of her protectors, and having first stupified her with blows of a club, or wooden sword, on the head, back and shoulders, every one of which is followed by a stream of blood, he drags her through the woods by one arm, regardless of the stones and broken pieces of trees that may lie in his route, and anxious only to convey his prize in safety to his own party. The woman thus treated becomes his wife ; is incorporated in the tribe to which he belongs, and but seldoms quits him for another. The outrage is not resented

---

* The late Governor of Australia, Captain Grey, has fully exposed the misconceptions of former travellers on this subject. He has shown that some of the very articles of food referred to as evidence of the destitution to which the natives of Australia are sometimes driven, as certain roots, gums, and grubs, are sought, not to satisfy the necessities of hunger, but as dainties, in the same way as an Englishman, after a dinner of roast beef, might order shrimps and oysters; the principal difference being, that the natives of Australia dislike oysters, although they will eat every other kind of shell fish. Mr. Grey enumerates among their articles of food, six sorts of kangaroo, three kinds of turtle, with emus, wild turkeys, and birds of every kind.

by the relations of the female, who only retaliate by a similar outrage when it is in their power."

It is impossible not to admire the faith of philosophers in any statements submitted to them, however extravagant, or self-contradictory, that may appear to support a favourite hypothesis. Mr. Malthus would hardly have denied, that throughout the animated creation the sexual passion is accompanied with more or less of the instinct of mutual attachment between male and female; and yet, upon the testimony of a solitary traveller,* writing under the influence of jaundiced views occasioned by the failure of a first settlement, he proceeds at once to place the instincts of human beings in the uncivilized state, below the level of either the birds of the air or the beasts of the field. The savage, he says, in New South Wales, does not woo his mistress, but knocks her down with his club. In striking her he is careful, not that the blows shall be gentle, but that blood shall flow from each of them; and although anxious to convey away his prize in safety, he does not at all mind the risk of killing his intended bride, by dragging her bleeding body against the stones, or broken pieces of trees, by which his path may be obstructed.

The sober truth, which, divested of all exaggeration and high colouring, may be found in the above statement, has been reduced to its proper limits by later travellers, and rendered intelligible; but, instead of supporting the argument of Malthus, militates against it. The natives of Australia have a custom (one of the earliest and most universal customs of the human race) of betrothing their female children almost as soon as they are born; out of which often, and necessarily, arise ill-assorted unions, intrigue, and consequent scenes of cruelty and violence. A young woman finds herself claimed as the property of a man she detests. She resists; endeavours to escape; is struck, bound, and carried off by force; and if the case be one in which the legal rights of the claimant are recognised by the relatives, they do not interfere.† They do interfere where no such legal rights exist; and the stealing of a wife is a crime punishable with death. A crime, however, frequently committed, and with reason; for polygamy being allowed, and women being, besides, valuable as domestic servants, the female portion of the popula-

---

* The authority quoted by Mr. Malthus is ' Collins's Account of New South Wales.'

† A case of this kind is related by Layard. An Arab claimed his betrothed. The girl fled. The mother was induced to take the part of her daughter, and was killed by the Arab, in revenge—or, rather, according to his own notions on the subject—as a just punishment for the violation of her word. (See *Nineveh and its Remains*, vol. i. p. 359.)

tion is very unequally distributed, and the majority of the young men would have to go without wives if they did not sometimes contrive to steal them from the harem of an old chief. This practice, under such circumstances, instead of being a *check* to population, as which it is adduced, must obviously have a contrary tendency. The rape of the Sabines laid the foundation of the Roman empire.

The present population of New South Wales—and that of the Australian colonies generally—would probably be now quoted by Mr. Malthus, were he living, as an example of a rapid multiplication of the human species (independent of emigration), in a country of boundless resources; but this would not at all help his case of aborigines brutalized by want. To admit the existence of these resources, and to assume greater helplessness and less sagacity in respect to them, on the part of the aborigines, than in the sheep and cattle that have run wild and multiplied in the woods, is to push an argument to the extremest verge of improbability.

Thus far it can hardly be said, by the warmest disciples of Mr. Malthus, that his instances of the pressure of population on subsistence, from natural causes, have been very happily selected; and it would not be difficult to show that he has been equally unfortunate in most of the evidence that follows to the same effect.

The explanation, in part, is, that during the last century, at the close of which the 'Essay on the Principle of Population' appeared, the true condition of any of the aboriginal populations of newly discovered countries, or of old countries at a great distance, was very imperfectly understood. A tribe of nations without clothing, and painting or otherwise disfiguring their bodies* to terrify their enemies, were simply *savages,* not human beings, whom it was very difficult to persuade our first settlers, especially in the penal colonies, that they had not as much right to shoot, as they had to fire at a monkey in the woods. At that time, Clarkson and Wilberforce had not convinced the British public that the coloured man was not intended by nature as a slave to the white; and although philosophers did not hold the opinion that he was so intended, they shared in many of the prejudices of the public as to the extreme physical and moral degradation of other races; prejudices which subsequent experience has greatly tended to dissipate.

---

* A relic of this custom nearer home, is found in the practice of English sailors, who, in the heat of a naval engagement, will strip to the skin, and are then seen with their bodies often covered with marks burnt in with gunpowder.

Perhaps the strongest case of this kind is the opinion entertained by Mr. Malthus of the Chinese; and it must not be passed without notice, because the practice of infanticide in China was, by many of his disciples, the argument most relied upon in support of his hypothesis.

The accounts at one time credited of the redundant population of China were certainly alarming, as ominous of a disastrous future for the rest of mankind. It was commonly understood that every rood of ground throughout that vast empire had been long ago cultivated to the extreme limit of its capabilities; that there was scarcely to be found a city containing less than a million of inhabitants; that the towns were insufficient for the population; that multitudes lived in floating houses on the water, not for the convenience of the carrying or fishing trades, but because of the little elbow-room left on land; and that the exposure of children was of every-day occurrence, and a sight so familiar, as to have entirely destroyed there the maternal instincts which prevail in other parts of the world.

Although Mr. Malthus did not yield to the full extravagance of these impressions, it will be seen at a glance that his judgment was affected by them. He expresses little hesitation in adopting, as sufficiently accurate for his argument, the Chinese census of a population of 333 millions, drawn up by a government which has always sought to blind foreigners to the real weakness of its resources;* and quoting from the inaccurate, and now obsolete Letters of the Jesuits, edited by Duhalde, in 1735, and from Sir George Staunton's account of the brief and abortive embassy of Lord Macartney to Pekin, in 1793, fills a chapter with loose statements, to the effect that " the whole surface of the empire is, with trifling exceptions, dedicated to the production of food for man alone;" that there are no commons or lands suffered to lie waste by the neglect, or the caprice, or for the sport of great proprietors; that the consequence of the encouragements given to marriage among the poor, is " to press them down to the most abject state of poverty;" that " a Chinese will pass whole days in digging the earth, sometimes up to his knees in water, and in the evening is happy to eat a little spoonful of rice, and to drink the insipid water in which it was boiled, as all that they have in general;"

---

* During the war with China, in 1842, it was a common stratagem of the Chinese, with a view of imposing upon the English force, to parade a garrison in different uniforms, so as to magnify it into an army; and to construct mock fortresses with matting, armed with guns, appearing at a distance of heavy calibre, but which, on a near examination, proved to be earthern jars.—(See the *Narrative of the Expedition to China, of Commander J. Elliott Bingham.*)

that the practice of infanticide is so sanctioned by custom, as even to operate as an inducement to marriage; for, says Malthus, " contemplating this extreme resource beforehand, less fear is entertained of entering into the married state:" and on the next page, he repeats from Duhalde, that " the shocking sight of the exposures of infants in the great cities, such as Pekin and Canton, is very common."*

Since the expulsion of the Jesuits, whose scheme of Christianizing China was founded upon the rearing, as catechists, of as many children as they could support, we have heard less and less of the exposure of Chinese infants; and the practice now appears of such rare occurrence that there are good reasons for doubting whether, throughout the whole of China, there could be found as many deserted children as are annually abandoned in England to the care of the parish; and if we were to include with the latter recently reported cases of the poisoning of children by their parents, for the sake of the fees to be obtained from a burial club, the comparison of England with China would perhaps not be to the advantage of this country. It is remarked by Sir John Davis, that " the Chinese are, in general, peculiarly fond of their children," and that the instances at Canton of the bodies of infants being seen floating, "are not frequent, and may reasonably, in some cases, be attributed to accident, where multitudes are brought up from their birth in small boats."† Canton, as the principal seaport of China, and from its connexion with the smuggling trade of the coast, is supposed to contain a more licentious and vagrant population than any other Chinese town; so that, if the cases there of infanticide were numerous, they would not establish a general rule; but another crime which was brought to light in that city, and for which six men and three women were apprehended and punished in 1820—that of kidnapping children for sale in distant provinces, is quite irreconcileable with the idea of infanticide on a large scale. If it be worth while to steal children, from the commercial value of their prospective labour, and to steal them at an age sufficiently tender to render detection difficult, they can hardly be the burden which would make it policy

---

* Vol. i. chapter 12, page 213.

† " There never was a more absurd blunder than to charge to infanticide those instances in which the infants are found floating with a hollow gourd about their persons, as if the gourd were part of the system of exposure! Why, the very object of attaching these gourds to the children living in boats, is to save them from the risk of being drowned, and to float them until they can be pulled out of the water; although that children should sometimes be found drowned, in spite of this precaution, is possible enough."—*Davis's Chinese*, p. 121.

to drown them.* In all parts of the world infanticide has prevailent to some extent, but by Chinese writers it is mentioned only to be reprobated; and it seems probable that the practice has been chiefly confined to seasons of great dearth, or a time of some other unusual national calamity—as when, at the capture of Chin-keang-foo, by Sir Hugh Gough, many of the unfortunate inhabitants, unable to escape, killed their wives and children, and then destroyed themselves, to avoid, as they supposed, a more cruel fate at the hands of the enemy—whole families thus perishing together.†

Of the state of the Chinese agricultural population the following account has recently been given by Mr. Fortune, a gentleman who, while engaged in making the extensive botanical collections with which his name is now associated, has had better opportunities than most men of comparing the condition of the peasantry of different countries.

" The farms are small, each consisting of from one to four or five acres; indeed, every cottager has his own little tea-garden, the produce of which supplies the wants of his family, and the surplus brings him in a few dollars, which are spent on the other necessaries of life.

---

* Hume, writing on the slave trade, puts it as cheaper to steal a lad from Ireland and Scotland than to rear one in London; but he would have questioned the economy of stealing a lad in London to sell him in Scotland or Ireland. Canton is the most flourishing commercial town in China, and virtually its second metropolis.

† The Rev. George Smith, late missionary in China, made minute inquiries on the subject, but was unable to obtain any decisive evidence of the custom of infanticide in Canton, Changhai, Ningpo, and other parts of China that he visited; but he tells us (see his ' Narrative of a Visit to the Consular Cities') that he found it to prevail extensively in the province of Fokeen, the inhabitants of which he terms the Irish of China. He there met with a man who confessed that, having had a family of eight girls, he had suffocated five of them soon after birth, by placing them in a tub of water. Mr. Smith states, however, that the practice is wholly confined to the infanticide of female children, and on the ground that daughters are burdensome, while the son, when grown up, is compelled by law to assist in the support of his parents. The villagers were generally reluctant to admit that they had themselves destroyed, in any case, their female children; and as they added that it was esteemed good luck when sons and daughters came alternately in a family, the testimony is not conclusive as to the extent of infanticide even in the particular district mentioned. Mr. Sirr observes:—

" It appears contrary to reason and common sense to suppose that infanticide is generally practised, or of daily and hourly occurrence, when we take into calculation the amount of the female population of the Celestial Empire, and the numerous handmaidens belonging to each man, in addition to his wife—the poor having one or more concubines, in proportion to their means."—*China and the Chinese,* vol. ii. page 57.

The explanation may be in the possible fact, that polygamy really produces a great excess of female births, as stated by Bruce; a subject of some interest, upon which nothing certain is known.

The same system is practised in everything relating to Chinese agriculture. The cotton, silk, and rice farms are generally all small, and managed upon the same plan. There are few sights more pleasing than a Chinese family in the interior, engaged in gathering the tea leaves; or, indeed, in any of their other agricultural pursuits. There is the old man, it may be the grandfather, or even the great-grandfather, patriarch-like, directing his descendants, many of whom are in their youth and prime, while others are in their childhood, in the labours of the field. He stands in the midst of them, bowed down with age; but, to the honour of the Chinese as a nation, he is always looked up to by all with pride and affection, and his old age and grey hairs are honoured, revered, and loved. When, after the labours of the day are over, they return to their humble and happy homes, their fare consists chiefly of rice, fish, and vegetables, which they enjoy with great zest, and are happy and contented. I really believe there is no country in the world where the agricultural population are better off than they are in the north of China. Labour with them is pleasure, for its fruits are eaten by themselves, and the rod of the oppressor is unfelt and unknown."—*Fortune's Wanderings in China*, p. 201.

That multitudes of the Chinese are overtaken by great distress on the failure of a rice harvest, may be readily admitted, if only upon the evidence of the improvident habits engendered by the practice of opium-eating in the south, and spirit-drinking in the northern provinces; causes quite adequate to the effect: but that extreme distress is not the habitual state of the Chinese, is evident from a multitude of facts at variance with such a conclusion, which appears incidentally in the accounts of all recent voyagers to this part of the world. Sir John Davis speaks of the superior physical character of the Chinese, in comparison with many other Asiatics, and remarks that—

" A finer-shaped and more powerful race of men exist nowhere than the coolies or porters of Canton. The weights which they carry with ease, on a bamboo between two of them, would break down most other Asiatics; and the freedom of their dress gives a development to their limbs that renders many of the Chinese models for a statuary. As sailors, they have been found always much stronger and more efficient than Lascars on board of English ships, though the obstacles which exist to their entering into foreign service prevent their being frequently engaged."[*]

This statement, doubtless, does not apply to the whole population; but it has been corroborated, in respect to classes, in every published narrative of officers employed in the war with China, concluded by the treaty of Nankin in 1842. The Chinese soldiers were over-matched in the science, discipline, and destructive weapons of the troops

---

[*] 'Davis's Chinese,' p. 121.

employed against them, but not in strength of limb. Instances were not wanting of Chinese of "herculean" form and "gigantic" stature; and the appearance of belonging to a race emaciated by bad living was certainly more on the side of the English officers than the mandarins.*

The supposed general scarcity of food in China is also inconsistent with the fact, that rice with the Chinese is seldom an article of foreign importation. We grow opium for them in our East India possessions, not rice; and no English merchant would dream of a rice cargo for Canton as an outfit. The stories told of the straits to which they are driven, compelling them to eat vermin, birds' nests, or anything that will support life, are, again, answered by the fact that they are sufficiently choice in their food to despise potatoes, introduced by the Portuguese at Macao half a century ago, and to refuse milk, butter, and cheese as articles of food; a peculiarity of taste in which they form a remarkable exception to all other nations of the world. Edible birds' nests are only seen at the tables of the rich, and the fault may be with us and not with the Chinese, if we think a fatted dog may be less wholesome as food than the more uncleanly animal—a fatted pig. But the following evidence will dissipate any notions that may yet linger among us of scarcity in a Chinese town in an average season :—

"It is sometimes a difficult matter to get through the streets for the immense quantities of fish, pork, fruit, and vegetables which crowd the stands in front of the shops. Besides the more common kinds of vegetables, the shepherd's purse and a kind of trefoil or clover are extensively used amongst the natives here ; and really these things, when properly cooked, more particularly the latter, are not bad. Dining rooms, tea houses, and bakers' shops, are met with at every step, from the poor man who carries his kitchen or bakehouse upon his back, and beats upon a piece of bamboo to apprise the neighbourhood of his presence, and whose whole establishment is not worth a dollar, to the most extensive tavern or tea-garden crowded with hundreds of customers. For a few cash (1,000 or 1,200=one dollar) a Chinese can dine in a sumptuous manner upon his rice, fish, vegetables, and tea ; and I fully believe, that in no country in the world

* "On the 20th, Captain Eyres, waiting on the admiral, found him entertaining at breakfast a party of mandarins from Mia-Tau, the chief of whom was a huge mountain of flesh—say *thirty-five stone*—whose great boast was that a sheep only furnished him with three days' supply of food; and to judge from the justice they all did to the substantial breakfast before them, it could easily be believed. By his countrymen he must be thought much of; fatness with them being a sure sign of wealth and wisdom; for, they argue, ' a thin man must be a poor devil, or he would have wisdom to eat more.' "—*Ibid.* page 258.

is there less real misery and want than in China. The very beggars seem a kind of jolly crew, and are kindly treated by the inhabitants."—*Fortune's Wanderings in China,* page 120.

The absence of sheep and cattle, in certain districts, is now explained by the fact that rice-fields were not exactly the place to look for them ;* and so far from its being true that there is little or no uncultivated land in China, the appropriation of waste lands for the benefit of the poor was the subject of a memorial of the Canton Government in 1833, which obtained the sanction of the Emperor.† "Wild and wooded tracts"—"extensive alluvial flats, exhibiting a dreary waste"—and "unreclaimed marshes," are more frequently met with in the approach to the capital from the Gulf of Pecheley, than that garden cultivation described by travellers, which is chiefly confined to the vicinity of great towns.

Mr. Fortune observes, speaking of the most fertile mountain districts of Central China, that,

"It would be ridiculous to assert, as some have done, that the whole, or even the greater part, is under cultivation. On the contrary, by far the greater part lies in a state of nature, and has never been disturbed by the hand of man. I am anxious to state this fact in express terms, in order to set those right who have been led to believe that every inch of land in the empire, however bleak and barren, is under cultivation, having given way to Chinese industry and skill! I myself, before I visited China, was under the same impression ; but the first glance at the rugged mountainous shores soon convinced me of my error. Unfortunately, our opinions of a distant unknown country are apt to go to extremes—either fancying it entirely barren, or else a paradise of fertility."—*Fortune's Wanderings in China,* page 294.

With regard to populousness, the evidence is tolerably conclusive that there is no part of China so densely inhabited as the county of Middlesex, or the department of the Seine ; but the streets of Canton being so narrow as to admit of only three or four foot-passengers abreast, are often impassable; and this crowding of the population makes it appear greater than it is. The walls of Pekin enclose many void spaces destitute of habitations, with fields and gardens devoted to the growth of vegetables. One-fifth only of the area of Nanking, the ancient

---

* " On passing the Keisan Islands we observed that they were well stocked with horned cattle. The main land assumed a bold mountainous character, the sides of which were well cultivated, and on them cattle and sheep appeared to be much more numerous than we had before seen."—*Narrative of the Expedition to China. By Commander J. Elliott Bingham.* Vol. i. p. 209.

† ' Davis's Chinese,' p. 343.

capital of China, is covered with houses; and these for the most part houses of but one story.*

The only lofty edifices seen in China are public buildings. Private dwelling-houses, even of the better class, consist of a suite of rooms on the ground floor, with at most a single floor above. A fact which, while it would seem to indicate a degree of internal security in past times far greater than existed in Europe during the middle ages, when men built castles instead of houses, and first learnt to construct them as *towers* for observation and defence, would also lead us to the conclusion that were private houses in Europe built as in China, the area of London or Paris would necessarily greatly exceed that of any town in China of which the actual extent has yet been ascertained.

Instead of a population so redundant as to have exhausted the utmost resources of the soil, it is now certain that in former ages many parts of China were far more densely inhabited than at the present moment. It abounds in monuments of high antiquity, of a character to which the present Chinese are unequal. The great wall of China, 25 feet thick at the base, 20 feet high, and extending a length of many hundred miles along its northern frontier, was erected 200 years before Christ; and the population and wealth of the country must then have been immense, or a work of such magnitude and labour could not have been undertaken and completed. Its pagodas faced with porcelain, and pagodas of cast-iron, belong wholly to the past; and numerous ancient towns in ruins, or but partially occupied, like Nanking, tell of a period of by-gone splendour.

---

* "The appearance of Nanking, from the summit of the Porcelain Tower, was somewhat disappointing,—fully four-fifths of the space enclosed by the ramparts revealing to us only a tract of cultivated land, instead of the teeming mass of buildings which we had been led to expect."—*The Chinese War. By Lieutenant John Ouchterlony*, p. 476.

Decay of Ancient Populations.

Signs of decay in China arrest our attention the more when we take into consideration the historical evidence, which it will not be necessary here to adduce, of a civilization as ancient, and of as high an order, as that of the early Egyptian and Assyrian monarchies. There is not the slightest reason to doubt that upwards of 500 years before the Christian era the Chinese were a great and powerful nation, trading with other nations in silk and porcelain ;* the law of non-intervention with foreigners not having at that time been passed—a law which was only adopted as part of the fundamental policy of the empire about the time the great wall was built. Among existing nations the Chinese empire is unquestionably the oldest, and the one which has suffered the least of any from the desolating effects of wars. It has never aimed at conquests, and its struggles with the Tartars, who would appear, physiologically, to belong to the same race, have been more like our own with the Picts and Scots, in the time of the Romans, than contentions with a foreign enemy. The laws and customs of the country, moreover, favour marriage. It is held

---

* " Bottles of Chinese porcelain, with Chinese characters upon them, were found by Rosellini in a tomb at Thebes, which had not been opened since the days of the Pharaohs. Similar discoveries of bottles, identical in shape and appearance with those manufactured in China to this day, were made in the Egyptian tombs by Lord Prudhoe and Mr. Wilkinson."—*Davis's Chinese,* p. 288.

to be an obligation on the child to maintain its parent in age, and families club together for this object, eating at a common table, and forming something like socialist communities, bound together by ties of relationship. The most sacred of all religious duties is held to be that of offering sacrificial rites at the tomb of a man's ancestors; and every man desires offspring, by whom the same sacrificial rites may be performed for him. Such institutions would not justify us in assuming more of moral restraint or vice and misery in the case of the Chinese than for any other people; and according to the theory, therefore, of Mr. Malthus, we ought long ago to have seen not only China overflowing, but the habitable globe overrun with countless swarms of Chinese Huns and Vandals.* This has not happened. The Chinese are neither warriors nor emigrants. When tempted abroad by the inducements of high profits or wages, they have gone not as settlers, but generally only to make money and return.

It is, of course, easy to assume the slaughter of any imaginable number of millions on the last conquest of China by the Tartars, and a corresponding increase since that time; but such assumptions, without proof, and in the absence of all authentic data on the subject, are entitled to no consideration.

The tendency of ancient populations to decay, has, in a multitude of instances, been too strongly marked to have escaped the observation of Mr. Malthus. Let us look at his mode of accounting for it in one of the most familiar and decided cases of the kind.

The continent of America contained, even within the memory of living travellers, a numerous Indian population, that has now comparatively disappeared. The Indians of North America were supposed to have amounted to about sixteen millions at the period of our first settlements, and are now estimated at only two millions.† In the south, after the conquests of the first Spanish and Portuguese adventurers, the natives were taken under the protection of the Roman Catholic Church; and the Society of Jesuits undertook the task of teaching them Christianity, and the arts of civilization. The well-meant efforts of this ·society,

---

* From the description given by historians of the Huns, they would appear to have belonged to the Tartar tribes of Asia, some of which were probably the progenitors of the Chinese, but the Chinese themselves have kept behind their wall from the time it was built, about the year 200 B. C. to the present moment; and 1400 years have elapsed since the death of Attila, a sufficient period to revive the hosts that threatened the Western Empire if there were a constant and permanent tendency in population to geometric increase.

† Catlin's 'North American Indians,' vol. i, p. 6,

although on the largest scale, have failed, to the extent even of not preserving the existence of the race the society was to instruct. M. Horace Say, in his *Histoire de Brésil,* remarks upon the general abandonment and universal decay of the Indian villages, or *aldéas,* established by the Jesuits, on land declared inalienable by the state, and upon the tendency of the race to extinction; while, at the same time, he speaks of the higher qualities of the negro slave population of the same country, and notices its rapid increase.

Among the facts mentioned by other writers is the comparative sterility of the women, of which Mr. Malthus adopts the following explanation:—

" The causes that Charleroix assigns of the sterility of the American women are, the suckling their children for several years, during which time they do not cohabit with their husbands; the excessive labour to which they are always condemned, in whatever situation they may be; and the custom established in many places of permitting the young women to prostitute themselves before marriage. Added to this, he says, the extreme misery to which these people are sometimes reduced, takes from them all desire of having children. Among some of the ruder tribes it is a maxim not to weaken themselves with rearing more than two of their offspring. When twins are born, one of them is commonly abandoned, as the mother cannot rear them both; and when the mother dies during the period of suckling her child, no chance of preserving its life remains, and, as in New Holland, it is buried in the same grave with the breast that nourished it."

Upon this we may observe that the custom of mothers suckling their own children is not a new one, and that there is no reason to suppose that it tends to produce sterility now more than in former times, when tribes of shepherds and hunters grew into powerful nations. The same remark applies to libertinage. It would hardly be asserted by any one that in the earliest and rudest stages of society the laws of chastity were better observed than they have been since, when some notions of family obligations and rights of property had begun to prevail, nor could we be justified in the conclusion that a female unused to a life of labour, even when that labour may fairly be termed excessive, becomes necessarily unfitted for child-bearing. We see, on the contrary, in the case of many of our own female peasantry, constantly employed in field occupation, or in carrying loads to and from market, that the muscular power thereby acquired enables them to bring their children into the world with far less suffering than females of the upper classes, and that the most hard-worked women are often mothers of the largest families. It is of course true enough that miscarriages may be occasioned by over exertion, but the slightest exercise is over exertion to those who have been brought up in the lap of luxury, and it is among females of this class, and not among the poor, that miscarriages are the most frequent. There is no evidence that the labour of Indian women is now more intolerable than it was when the tribes to which they belong were sufficiently numerous to spread over the whole of the American continent.

It seems remarkable that Mr. Malthus should have noticed the fact of the comparative unfruitfulness of Indian women in the cases mentioned, without being struck with its importance, and with the weakness of the reasoning quoted respecting it; but once having assumed a permanent law of geometric increase, he was not to be drawn from it by any demand upon his credulity, however large. He could imagine no cause in operation to reduce the common average of births short of a miracle, but he could believe that, in Indian communities mothers are monsters, killing their children as a matter of course, when inconveniently numerous, and destitute of compassion for the orphan child they might sometimes nurse and protect, leaving it in every case to be exposed and abandoned.*

The popular theory of the decrease of the aboriginal American population attributes it to the introduction among them of European vices and diseases, especially those arising from the intemperate use of spirituous liquors. This has doubtless been one cause, while a natural tendency of the race to extinction, by an exhaustion of its physical powers, may have been another. They have clearly, however, not decreased from any pressure of population upon the means of subsistence. Food and employment have always been found for them when they could be induced to adopt habits of settled industry; and if their hunting-grounds have been encroached upon, they have, on the other hand, been very generally taught to breed pigs, and grow potatoes—which we are told by some are the bane of Ireland, from the encouragement they afford to population. The American Indians have had abundant opportunities of profiting by the arts introduced among them; and where they have not done so, but have turned them to

---

* "From the enslaved and degraded condition in which the women are held in the Indian country, the world would naturally think that theirs must be a community formed of incongruous and unharmonizing materials, and consequently destitute of the fine reciprocal feelings and attachments which flow from the domestic relations in the civilized world; yet it would be untrue, and doing injustice to the Indians to say that they were the least behind us in conjugal, in filial, and in paternal affection."—*Catlin's North American Indians,* vol. i. p. 120.

purposes of self-destruction, the fault lies in the inveteracy of old predatory habits, or habits of indolence and self-indulgence, and not in the inadequacy of human resources as compared with human fecundity.

The decay of ancient populations may be observed in the present comparatively desolate state of Asia Minor, and the adjacent countries of Egypt, Arabia, and Persia. There are satisfactory reasons for believing that the large fertile plains watered by the Nile, the Euphrates, and the Tigris, once contained a population approaching, if not fully equal, to that of the whole of Europe at the present moment. In the centre of these plains was situated the capital of Assyria—Nineveh, that "exceeding great city of three days' journey," the site of which has now been discovered by Mr. Layard, together with the sculptured remains of a civilization far higher than we have been accustomed to think could have existed, unless in Egypt, at the remote period of 1,500 or 2,000 years before Christ. Of the once densely-peopled district in which the ruins of Nineveh were found buried, Mr. Layard says—

" From the walls of the castle of Tel Afer I had an uninterrupted view over a vast plain, stretching westwards towards the Euphrates, and losing itself in the hazy distance. The ruins of ancient towns and villages rose on all sides; and, as the sun went down, I counted above one hundred mounds, throwing their dark and lengthening shadows across the plain. These were the remains of Assyrian civilization and prosperity. Centuries have elapsed since a settled population dwelt in this district of Mesopotamia; now, not even the tent of the Bedouin could be seen. The whole was a barren deserted waste."*

Here is an instance of one of the most powerful nations that existed in ancient times having so completely disappeared, that not a single living trace of the people who formed it can now be found. It is not known whence they came, to what race they belonged, nor whether there are yet, in other parts of Asia, any of their descendants left.

The case of Egypt is very similar. Egypt has been called the cradle of civilization. It abounds in monuments of a date so remote that, even in the time of Augustus, they were brought to Rome and set up as curiosities of antiquity, just as, in modern times, we have imported into Europe from the same motive the black stone of Rosetta and the column of Luxor. But where are the descendants of the people who erected them, built the pyramids, excavated the rock temples of the Nile, the tombs discovered by Belzoni, and whose cities were for many centuries

---

* Layard's ' Nineveh and its Remains,' vol. i. p. 315.

the capitals of the world? They are the insignificant occupiers of a handful of scattered villages in Nubia—a now ignorant and barbarous race—all but unknown and forgotten.*

The ready answer that these countries have been desolated by wars and misgovernment, would apply if there had been no wars and misgovernment in ancient times, when these countries were populous; but we are referring to a period when wars were more frequent, and despotism more absolute and capricious than they have been for the last thousand years. Ancient Egypt was incessantly conquering or being conquered; and we can hardly look at a single piece of sculpture among the ruins of Nineveh, without tracing upon it the records of a battle. The modern Turks it is true are cruel masters; but how is it that the Turks do not supply the place of the ancient populations, with equal numbers? Where are the Musselmen hosts that successfully resisted the crusaders, and subsequently attempted in their turn the conquest of Europe, laying siege to Vienna as late as the year 1683? The Turks are themselves decaying as a people; in a few years they will cease to have any footing in Europe, and in as many centuries will probably sink back into their primitive condition of a few pastoral and predatory tribes of Asia.

The decay of the ancient population of Greece is also a case to be noted, because the authority of Solon, Plato and Aristotle

---

* The reasons for believing the Nubians, or certain tribes of them that are met with on the cataracts of the Nile, to be the descendants of the ancient Egyptians are, that their features, stature, and complexions correspond with those of the figures depicted on the tombs. They also wear their hair in the same peculiar manner as the ancient Egyptians, retain in use the ancient Egyptian lyre, the wooden pillow, and other articles, of which the forms are of the same antiquity. Their complexion is chocolate or bronze, deepening in colour towards the south so that Herodotus was hardly in error in describing them as black, although they are not so dark as the negro, from whom they differ also in the configuration of the head. There is no evidence that the ancient Egyptians where white men, although this opinion is still maintained by some writers, and is flattering to European prejudices. The difference between the native Egyptian and the Caucasian is well marked on the monu-ments, especially in the celebrated tableau, copied by Rossellini from the tomb of Osirteren, supposed to have reference to Greek or Jewish captives, and by some to Joseph and his brethren. It is in Nubia also in which the most ancient monumental remains chiefly abound; and in the elaborate and splendid work of Gau, Nubia is shown to have been the cradle of Egyptian architecture. The Nubians resident in Egypt are estimated at only 5,000. The Copts, so called by the Greeks probably from Coptus, a town in Egypt, which may have given rise to a sect, are the next of the oldest indigenous population of Egypt; but among them there have been frequent intermarriages with the Turks and Arabs. They profess the Christian religion, and their numbers are supposed to be about 150,000. The greater part of the present population of Egypt consists of Arabs, or Fellahs, of whom Mr. Lane thinks there may be about 1,750,000. The Turks and Franks make up a total of about 2,000,000.

is quoted by Mr. Malthus, in favour of the necessity of artificial restrictions to limit the growing numbers of mankind,—doubtless, in the time of these philosophers on the increase where their own sphere of observation extended. A few centuries later, however, Plutarch, writing about the year A. D. 90, laments the depopulation of Greece in a passage quoted by Hume in his 'Essay on the Populousness of Ancient Nations,' as follows :—

" The author, endeavouring to account for the silence of many of the oracles, says that it may be ascribed to *the present desolation of the world,* proceeding from former wars and factions ; which common calamity, he adds, has fallen heavier upon Greece than on any other country ; insomuch that the whole could scarcely at present furnish three thousand warriors ; a number which in the time of the Median war, was supplied by the single city of Megara. The gods, therefore, who assist works of dignity and importance, have suppressed many of their oracles, and deign not to use so many interpreters of their will to *so diminutive a people.*"

Of the fact itself here described, that Greece had become depopulated to a great extent, there cannot be a doubt, but the causes assigned for it are so inadequate to the effect, that Hume confesses that he did not know what to make of the passage. In the time of Plutarch the intestine wars and factions of the ancient Grecian states had long ceased ; these states had all become merged in the Roman Empire, and the people had been left at liberty to cultivate the arts of peace, subject only to a moderate taxation, for a period of two hundred and fifty years. Plutarch appears to have referred to " former wars and factions," without much reflection, as the first reason that occurred to him ; and he had doubtless not been led to inquire whether there might not be causes, coincident with prosperity, of a decrease of population, more powerful than war with its attendant calamities.

The following is another extract from the same Essay, showing that a tendency towards depopulation in Italy, as well as in Greece, had commenced as early as the year 130 B.C., twenty years after the close of the last Punic war, when Rome was victorious over all her enemies, mistress of Egypt, Greece, Macedonia and Asia Minor, and of the whole wealth of the then civilized world.

" The laws, or as some writers call them, the seditions of the Gracchi, were occasioned by their observing the increase of slaves all over Italy, and *the diminution of free citizens.* Appian ascribes the increase to the propagation of the slaves ; Plutarch to the purchasing of barbarians, who were chained and imprisoned, βαρβαρικα δεσμωlκρια. It is to be presumed that both causes concurred."

The fact of a diminution in the number of the free citizens, amongst whom the plunder of the world was distributed in the shape of money, land, and corn, is confirmed by Polybius and Diodorus Siculus, who give data for the conclusion that the free population of Italy was greater between the first and second Punic wars than in the days of the Triumvirate; and by Tacitus, who mentions the total decay, in the time of Augustus, of the families of the old patricians:* but no better evidence of it can be needed than the laws passed by Augustus and Trajan for the express encouragement of marriage.

Hume confesses his perplexity at the consideration of a result so opposite from that which he should have inferred from the influx of wealth, and resorts to infanticide as an explanation; forgetting that, if the custom of exposing children in Italy prevailed when the country was rich, it must have prevailed to a greater extent when the country was poor: and Mr. Malthus, also forgetting this influx of wealth, endeavours to persuade himself that the majority of Roman citizens had become paupers from the competition of slave labour, overlooking the statement that the class most decaying was that of the patricians—the owners of the slaves; and that, although in the time of Augustus there were 200,000 pensioners who received gratuitous supplies of corn, such grants were equivalent to the poor-laws of England, which he condemns on the ground that they have a tendency not to restrain, but "to increase population, without increasing the food for its support."†

There is another remarkable instance of the tendency to decay which may sometimes be observed in populations in periods of political calm and physical well-being—(although the rule cannot of course be regarded as an invariable one)—in the history of our own country, from the accession of Henry the Seventh to the reign of Elizabeth.

Sir Frederick M. Eden says, "from 1488, and for a century and a half after this period, depopulation continued to be the theme of the legislature." In the fourth year of Henry the Seventh, an Act was passed (c. 19) to remedy the decay and consequent pulling down of houses and towns, in which mention is made of places in which there had been 200 persons that had been reduced to "two or three heardsmen." ‡ In the same year

---

* "Jisdem diebus in numerum Patriciorum adscivit Cæsar vetustissimum quemque e Senatu, aut quibus clari parentes fuerant. Paucis jam reliquis familiarum quas Romulus Majorum, et Lucius Brutus Minorum Gentium, ad pellaverat; exhaustis etiam quas Dictator Cæsar Lege Cassia, et Princeps Augustus Lege Sænia, sublegere."—*Annal.* lib. xi. cap. xxv.

† Vol. ii. chap. vi. p. 81.

‡ This Act is given at length in Mr. Doubleday's 'Essay on the True Principle of Population,' in which work several of the facts here mentioned are stated at greater length.

(1489) another Act was passed, in which allusion is made to "a great decay of people in the Isle of Wight." The preamble of an Act passed in 1511, the third year of the following reign (c. 8, Henry VIII.), states that "*many* and the most part of *cities, boroughs,* and *towns corporate* had fallen to decay."

This was at a time when England was at peace abroad and at home. The civil wars had been terminated by the battle of Barnet, in 1471; and the battle of Bosworth Field, in 1485, which seated Henry the Seventh upon the throne, had been the only sanguinary contest that had occurred since. Chief Justice Sir John Fortescue, writing in 1640, describes, in his 'De Laudibus Legum Angliæ,' the people at this period as in a state of great ease and comfort, living principally upon animal food, "drinking no water," wearing fine woollen cloth, and having "great store of all hustlements *(hostilimentis)* and implements of household."

This, too, was a period of general progress; the era of the discovery of printing; the eve of the Reformation; the time when the pointed and florid style of Gothic architecture had been carried to a degree of perfection in ornamental decoration which has never been surpassed, nor, indeed, equalled by later builders. Half a century had elapsed of peace and security, and we hear not of a great increase of population, but of the "decay of cities, boroughs, and towns corporate."*

Another case of a tendency towards depopulation is supplied by Mr. Malthus himself, in his chapter on Switzerland. He says:—

"About thirty-five or forty years ago, a great and sudden alarm appears to have prevailed in Switzerland respecting the depopulation of the country; and the transactions of the Economical Society of Berne, which had been established some years before, were crowded (1766) with papers deploring the decay of industry, arts, agriculture, and manufactures, and the imminent danger of a total want of people. The greater part of those writers considered the depopulation of the country as a fact so obvious as not to require proof. They employed themselves, therefore, chiefly in proposing remedies; and, amongst others, the importation of medicines, the establishment of foundling hospitals, the portioning of young virgins, the prevention of emigration, and the encouragement of foreign settlers."†

---

* In 1485, and again in 1506, 1517, 1528, and 1551, England and the Continent were visited with an epidemic called "the sweating sickness," which often proved fatal to those attacked in twenty-four hours, and carried off many thousands. In the absence of registration returns, we cannot tell to what extent the mortality this occasioned led to "the decay of cities, boroughs, and towns corporate," and the precise extent is not material to this inquiry; it is important only to note that the epidemic of that period could not, in England at least, have originated in a pressure of population upon the means of subsistence.

† Vol. ii. p. 337.

M. Muret, however, minister of Vevay, had published some statistical tables showing a gradual diminution of births from 1550 to 1760, which gives Mr. Malthus an opportunity of proving that a diminution of births is quite compatible with an increase of population, when the proportion of annual deaths diminishes in a greater ratio;—a fact quite indubitable in reference to short periods. But, on the other hand, it is evident that if births were to continue to diminish every year through many centuries, the inhabitants of a country would ultimately become extinct, even if every individual lived to the age of a hundred; and the ingenuity of the reply does not affect the evidence that a positive decay of population had been observed and had become a subject of general comment. The fact itself is also confirmed, incidentally, by another statement of Mr. Malthus in the same chapter.

" In the town of Berne, from the year 1583 to 1654, the sovereign council had admitted into the Bourgeoisie 487 families, of which 379 became extinct in the space of two centuries ; and in 1783, only 108 of them remained. During the hundred years from 1684 to 1784, 207 Bernoise families became extinct. From 1624 to 1712, the Bourgeoisie was given to 80 families. In 1623, the sovereign council united the members of 112 different families, of which 58 only remain."*

This extinction of families Mr. Malthus attributes solely to the influence of the preventive check. He finds that in 1796, the number of single persons in Berne (including widows and widowers) was greater than the married, and infers therefore that the old families wore out, because their children had grown too poor to marry. It is unnecessary to point out the rashness of a conclusion dependent upon such narrow and imperfect data.

Returning to our own country, it may be observed, that the interference of the crown has been repeatedly required to counteract the tendency towards extinction of our own aristocracy. Mr. Doubleday, remarking of the peers and baronets of Great Britain that they are a class of men possessing large estates, and privileges of the most enviable nature, with every motive for transmitting them in lineal succession that can be inspired by love of power and family pride, asks what has been the result of the efforts made to perpetuate the two orders, both among themselves and with the assistance of royal creations?—

" This it has been :—that the peerage of England instead of being old, is recent; and the baronetage, though comparatively of modern origin, equally so. In short, that few, if any of the Norman nobility,

---

* Vol. ii, page 352.

and almost as few of the original baronets' families of King James the First, exist at this moment; and that but for perpetual creations, both orders must have been all but extinct. The following table shows that the great majority of the House of Peers has been created since the year 1760; that is to say, within eighty years of the present time, and since the commencement of the reign of George the Third, whose accession was in the October of that year; a period within the memory of many now living.

Number of Peers in 1837.	*Number created since* 1760.
Dukes 21	5 Dukes.
Marquesses 19	18 Marquesses.
Earls 108	58 Earls.
Viscounts 17	13 Viscounts.
Barons 185	153 Barons.
350	247
Scottish Peers ... 16 ⎱	25
Irish „ ... 28 ⎰	
394	272 Total created since 1760.

" Thus it appears, that within the memory of man 272 of the 394 peers of Parliament in 1837, have been created.

" The decay of the order of baronets has been perhaps still more rapid and extraordinary. The order itself was commenced only in 1611, by King James the First, as a means of raising money, principally for the Irish war of that period. It was suggested as a cheap mode of raising supplies by the celebrated Lord Bacon—one whose name was in the original baronetage, and is one of the few of those originally created whose descendants remain. The sum paid for the honour was very large, and it is therefore certain that the earlier baronets were all wealthy men, and of great estate. The results are as follows:—

" Since the creation, in 1611, of the order of baronets, 753 baronetcies have become extinct. The number of *extinct* baronets are more *in toto* than the *existing* baronets, up to the year 1819, when the baronets were 635 only.

" Of the original number 139 baronets had been raised to the peerage between 1611 and 1819; but supposing all these peerages to be now existing (which is not the case), this would only make the whole present number (including those made peers) 774; that is to say, the living baronets and baronet peers would, in that case, only exceed the extinct baronets by twenty-one.

" Thus it is evident, that but for perpetual new creations we should hardly have a baronet existing. Of James the First's creation in A.D. 1611, only *thirteen families* now remain; a decay .certainly extraordinary, and not to be accounted for upon the ordinary ideas of mortality, and power of increase amongst mankind."*

* 'True Law of Population,' by T. Doubleday, Esq., page 32.

It may be said that numerous collateral branches of the same families may be living, notwithstanding the extinction of the direct line,—an objection, if it be one, which must be allowed. The case is sufficiently striking as it stands, without any attempt at exaggeration; but a still stronger one is that of the decay of the nobles of Venice, where not one son alone, but all the sons are ennobled by birth. Addison, noticing this circumstance, has the following observation :—

"Amelot reckoned in his time 2,500 nobles that had voices in the council; but at present I am told there are not at most 1,500, notwithstanding the addition of many new families since that time. It is very strange that with this advantage they are not able to keep up their numbers, considering that the nobility spreads equally through all the brothers, and that so very few are destroyed by the wars of the republic."

Similar remarks have been made of the decay of the French nobility, which was fast dying out of itself, before the revolution of 1789 came to accelerate the process of destruction.

Several instances from humbler, but still wealthy, or at least comfortable classes of society, are given by Mr. Doubleday, tending to the same conclusion, that an ample provision of the means of subsistence does not necessarily act as a stimulus to population, but often seems to have a directly contrary tendency ; as if ease and abundance were the real check of population, and a certain amount of poverty and privation were essential to any considerable increase. Thus he mentions the case of the free burgesses of the wealthy corporation of Newcastle-upon-Tyne, a body in 1710 of about 1800, possessing estates and endowments, and exclusive privileges, amply sufficient to protect every individual among them from want, and shows that although all the sons of every citizen were free by birth, their numbers would have diminished had they not been recruited from without ; and that even with the aid of contested elections, when freemen by purchase were admitted for the sake of votes, the entire body of burgesses remained nearly stationary for upwards of a century. This, too, while the poorer corporation of Berwick-upon-Tweed doubled the number of its free citizens during the same period.*

The examples of the Corporation of Durham, and Richmond in Yorkshire, are adduced, to the same effect ; but we need not go so far north for corroborative evidence of the same class of facts. In the Corporation of London, all the children of a citizen, whether male or female, enjoy the right of freedom by inherit-

---

* 1737—Number of Burgesses 583
  1837—   „   „   1,116

ance, and as many of the exclusive privileges of this body have not yet been done away, women still exercise in the city various avocations in their own name (such, for instance, as the trade of a town carman*), from which the rest of the inhabitants of the metropolis, non-freemen, are excluded. Until recently, the freedom of the Corporation of London was essential to a share in the administration of revenues amounting to upwards of a million per annum,† and is still indispensable to a large portion of them. We may reasonably conclude that it was an object of some importance to the ancient citizens of London to keep the patronage connected with such large funds in their own hands, or to leave it in the hands of their own posterity. This object, however, has been so entirely defeated, that if we now inquire into the origin of the present holders of the good things in the gift of the London Corporation and the trading companies, we find they are nearly all north countrymen, who have elbowed their way into the city from Scotland or the provinces, and that the descendants of such men as Sir William Walworth and Sir Thomas Gresham are nowhere to be found.

During the forty years from 1794 to 1833, the admissions by patrimony to the freedom of the Corporation of London were only 7,794 out of a total of 40,221 admitted—a third of the number having been strangers who purchased their freedom, and one-half sons of strangers obtaining their freedom by apprenticeship.‡

This decay of the wealthy and comfortable classes is quite irreconcileable with the hypothesis that vice and misery, or moral restraint, are the only preventive checks to a geometric increase of population; but the opinion of Mr. Mill has been adverted to, and may here be examined,—founded upon the statement of Mr. Malthus respecting Switzerland and Norway,—that moral

---

* Non-freemen's carts are subject to a toll on passing through the city, and a non-freeman's cart is not allowed to ply for hire.

† Trust Estates—for the relief of the poor, cure of the sick, education, religion, and general purposes, including the five city hospitals...　... £360,000
Local rates (1842)　...　...　...　...　...　...　230,000
Coal and metage duties—Street and market tolls　...　...　...　200,000
Freedom and livery fines, fees, and other charges for corporate and trading privileges　...　...　...　...　...　...　...　...　50,000
Port of London and conservancy of the river ...　..　...　...　60,000

　　　　　　　　　　　　　　　　　　　　　　　　　　　　　£900,000

The above is exclusive of the income of the trading companies, which is supposed to amount to at least £250,000 per annum.

‡ Second report of the Municipal Inquiry Commissioners for 1837, page 65.

restraint comes largely into operation, and tends to produce a stationary population in countries of small landed proprietors.

Of the facts cited on this subject, a more probable explanation has been supplied by M. Passy, who says that the disposition of a peasant proprietor in France is not to sub-divide his little estate, but to enlarge it, and that his children commonly settle at a distance, and sell their interest in the property to one of the family. This may account for a small ratio of births in a particular district, without assuming for peasant proprietors a greater command over the passions than is commonly to be found in the world, and of which moral command certainly no evidence whatever is offered by Mr. Malthus. The Swiss have long been a migratory population. Swiss guards, Swiss valets, Swiss governesses and Swiss nursery-maids abound in every state in Europe, and we cannot follow them in their wanderings to determine the true value of their supposed virtue or self-denial, and compare it with that of any other class.

Neither emigration, however, nor "moral restraint," will fully and satisfactorily account for the decay of the families of Bernese citizens mentioned by Mr. Malthus, nor for the present stationary character of the population of Geneva, noticed by other writers. Both causes may have been combined; but enough has, probably, been stated to excite a reasonable suspicion that other causes, more influential, may have contributed to produce this result.

The case of Norway is equally inconclusive, and need not detain us a moment. Mr. Malthus finds a mountainous and somewhat barren pastoral country, thinly peopled, and at the time of his visit (1799) an apparently large proportion of single men and women; upon which he hastens to the conclusion that the comparatively slow rate of increase of its population has been owing to the preventive check of moral restraint, or obstacles thrown in the way of early marriages. The figures, however, that he adduces from statistical tables, instead of supporting this supposition, deprive it of any weight. On comparing them with the English registration returns, of which he could not avail himself, as they had not then been commenced, it appears that the proportion of marriages to the population is, after all, less than in the most pauperized of our own agricultural counties, and the proportion of births to deaths only about the same.

	Proportion of yearly marriages.	Proportion of yearly births.	Proportion of yearly deaths.
Norway*	1 to 130	1 to 35	1 to 49
Wiltshire†	1 to 154	1 to 34	1 to 49

The expenditure in relief to the poor for the year ending March 25, 1844, was, in Wiltshire, 10*s.* 6*d.* per head of the whole population; that of Buckinghamshire, the next most pauperized district, 9*s.* 9*d.* per head; in Lancashire, 3*s.* 11*d.* It should teach us caution in this class of investigations, when we see the opposing principles (as they were described by Mr. Malthus) of the preventive check of moral restraint, and the stimulating effect of poor-laws, both coincident, as in this instance, with a like result.

We may conclude our references to this celebrated Essay with a passage from the chapter on Epidemics. Dr. Short having given a table of 399 plagues, or wasting sicknesses, since the Christian era, Mr. Malthus remarks that a return of these visitations may be anticipated at periodical intervals of about four years and a half; and then observes, that—

" How far these ' terrible correctives to the redundance of mankind ' have been occasioned by the too rapid increase of population, is a point which it would be very difficult to determine with any degree of precision. The causes of most of our diseases appear to us to be so mysterious, and are really so various, that it would be rashness to lay too much stress upon any single one; but it will not perhaps be too much to say, that among these causes we ought certainly to rank crowded houses and insufficient or unwholesome food, which are the natural consequences of an increase of population faster than the accommodations of a country with respect to habitation and food will allow." ‡

Mr. Malthus here practically abandons the high ground of his original propositions, and takes refuge in a modest assumption, which is of course unassailable. No one can doubt the fact, that crowded lodging-houses and unwholesome food aggravate the evils of epidemics; but our starting-point was the position that the only preventive checks to population (moral restraint excepted)

---

* As stated by Mr. Malthus, vol. i. pages 261 and 274.
† Average of the three years, from 1839 to 1841. *See the Fifth Annual Report of the Registrar General, page* 53.
‡ Vol. i., page 522.

were vice and misery. Unless, therefore, it were proved that all epidemics, as well as all crowded lodging-houses, and every murrain that may seize the sheep in the field or the cattle in the shed, arise in some way out of the tendency of population to outstrip its supplies, the necessity of *restraining* population, as insisted upon, cannot clearly be maintained, and the whole case breaks down.

Here, then, let us leave it.

The original assertion was, that population was only kept on a level with the means of existence by moral restraint, or vice and misery. The answer is, that these causes are not adequate to the effect; that vice and misery tend even to opposite results; and that nature employs other and more powerful agencies for the object in view; that the ratio of fecundity is variable with circumstances, and not fixed; and that there are numerous causes of mortality totally unconnected with any deficiency of the necessaries of life.

It may be useful to conclude with a brief summary of the principal laws, which seem to govern the ratio of increase, as far as they have yet been ascertained.

Laws of Population.

The principle of life, throughout the vegetable and animal kingdoms, is dependent upon two sets of organs, called by Dr. Carpenter *the germ preparing, and the germ nourishing* organs.* In the vegetable kingdom the germ of a future plant is contained in the *pollen* produced by the *stamen* of the flower, and is made to penetrate into the ovule, or seed bed of the *pistil,* where it finds the food that is to nourish it, until sufficiently matured to burst its cell, and appear as a green shoot in the light and air.

In animals the process is analogous, and we need not illustrate it further than by the hatching of a chicken. The germ of the future chicken is conveyed to the egg by the act of impregnation. The egg is the storehouse of food by which the embryo is to be supported for twenty-one days, and out of which it has to form, by assimilation, sinews, bones, and feathers. When these are completed it breaks its shell and appears as a living bird.

We notice this to remark that during the first period of our existence, the ratios of increase of population and food are necessarily, and incontestably, equal;—Nature herself supplying the provision required, up to the moment of birth.

During the second period, that of suckling (confining our attention to the class *Mammalia*), the same care and foresight of nature are strikingly manifested. In the cow a milk-producing apparatus is provided by anticipation for the support of a calf. Months and years elapse before it is necessary that the apparatus

---

* 'Animal Physiology,' page 552.

should act, but, when the calf is dropped—the next minute there is the milk.

Over the third period, and beginning with the second, we see the providence of Nature for the support and defence of the young, while yet feeble, in the instinct of parental attachment; an instinct which so entirely changes the nature of some animals, that even the wolf ceases to be savage, and the sheep timid, when their young are concerned. A wolf is said to make an excellent mother, weaning her young by changing their food by degrees, and teaching them to hunt; and I have myself seen a ewe, when alarmed for the safety of her lamb, give chase to a dog half as big again as herself, and the dog run from his unexpected antagonist and escape by leaping over a style.

In the next period, when the powers of the animal are fully developed, and when it has to depend for food upon its own exertions, we find it endowed with the sagacity which teaches it where its food is to be obtained, and, as a part of its organization, with the precise weapons, or implements, best adapted for securing it. —Man, himself, gifted with still higher faculties, and enabled to convert every stick or stone into a tool for the same end.

In the last period, when the powers of life fail, and the means of obtaining food fail with them, we see the process of decay mercifully quickened by the law of prey—lingering disease, and the prolonged misery of starvation rendered nearly impossible among wild animals; and Nature, still intent upon the same object of supplying *food*, converting death itself into the elements of life; carrion rendered the fit sustenance of certain species of beasts, birds, and insects—the rotting fibre that of other species; and the entire vegetable kingdom employed in reproducing, and in greater abundance than before, from the dead animal substances which are the best manure of plants—the materials destined ultimately to form the flesh and blood of new living organizations.

Finally, in the law of *a diminishing ratio of fecundity*, from the largest and longest-lived animals downwards to the insect tribes, we see a special adaptation of the prolific faculties to the quantity of food upon which each species is to live, and without which every species would speedily be destroyed.

A stronger case than this of design—of design to prevent the very class of evils supposed by Mr. Malthus to be inevitable, from the principle of population, without artificial restrictions, has never been established by the laws of induction. Is it possible to believe, after considering it, that Nature has committed a blunder in the case of man, and one sufficient to disturb the whole balance of creation?—That there is a tendency in population so to press upon the means of subsistence, that the time may arrive when all other creatures than man shall have been devoured, and the human species left alone on the earth, to prey upon itself?—That such a time would have already arrived, but for the vices which promote self-destruction; and that the progress of society is to depend upon our putting Nature right—by partially or wholly *extinguishing* (not regulating merely) the passions she has given us?

It remains only that we should endeavour to trace the causes of those varying ratios of increase which the social history of mankind has exhibited, and which were erroneously supposed by Mr. Malthus to have been solely connected with an abundance or deficiency of the means of subsistence.

To begin with man in his lowest physical and moral condition, the state in which we find him in uncivilized communities, and in the back streets and courts of crowded towns, we may observe that this is precisely the state in which he appears the most prolific; for wherever, from the combined effects of intemperance, dirt, bad ventilation and drainage, the mortality is greatest, there also the ratio of births to the population is the highest; a fact noticed before in preceding quotations from the sanitary reports, and which may be again remarked in the following examples :—

*England.**	*Marriages.*	*Births.*	*Deaths.*
Hampshire	1 in 134	1 in 36	1 in 53
Lancashire	1 in 112	1 in 27	1 in 36
France.†	*Marriages.*	*Births.*	*Deaths.*
Mountain parishes of the department de L'Ain ..	1 in 179	1 in 34	1 in 38
Marshy districts of the same department ..	1 in 107	1 in 26	1 in 20

It has been further noticed by Mr. Chadwick, upon the authority of Humboldt, and Sir F. d'Ivernois, that the fecundity of an inferior class of the Mexican population, described as half clothed, idle, and stained with leprosy, from the effects of bad diet and bad lodging, is greater than that of any other known population in Christendom ; the proportion of births to deaths having been as under, in the province of Guanaxuato, in 1845 and 1846.‡

Births	Deaths
1 in 16	1 in 19

Registration returns do not convey with accuracy an idea of the relative fecundity of different districts, because a large proportion of illegitimate births escape registration, from the desire

---

* Fifth Annual Report of the Registrar-General. 1843.
† From the tables of M. Rossi, quoted in the Secretary's Report for 1842.—Page 180.
‡ ' Sanitary Report, for 1842,' page 181.

of the parents for concealment; and because the returns of marriages do not give the age of marriage, nor separate, except in isolated cases, the marriages of spinsters and bachelors from those of widows and widowers; a distinction of much importance, as in districts where the mortality is excessive, the number of widows and widowers re-married greatly exceeds the average. The broad fact, however, is now fully established, that in such districts births follow each other with greater rapidity than in the case of couples married at the same age in districts where the mortality is less;—arising, in part, at least, from the cause assigned by Dr. Griffin, * that among women who nurse their own children, an interval of about two years usually occurs between the birth of one child and that of the next, but that when a child dies early on the breast the interval is shorter. In Lancashire 17 per cent. of all the children born die under one year of age: in Wiltshire only 11 per cent. †

This explanation is sufficient in itself to dispose of one of the difficulties felt by Mr. Malthus, who could only account for an excess of births coincident with an excess of deaths, on the supposition of the superior fecundity of early marriages over those contracted at a riper age; a supposition which has since been proved to be without adequate foundation. In reference to late marriages, the statement of Dr. Griffin must be qualified by another from Dr. Granville, showing that the interval of two years between separate births applies only to young women, and that when marriages have been postponed to a later age, the births succeed faster, whether the children live or not,—as if there were an effort of Nature to make up for lost time,—as in the case of the rapid growth of vegetation after a long protracted winter. According to a table prepared by Dr. Granville, assisted by Mr. Finlayson, the average offspring of females married from 16 to 20 is a child in two years. Married at the ages of from 20 to 32, somewhat more than a child every two years. Married from 33 to 36, two births in three years; and from 37 to 39, a child every year.‡

The tendency to early unions, which is found to be almost invariably coincident with a great mortality, must sometimes arise from the cause assigned by Mr. Malthus—the stimulus of improved means to the survivors, to which may be added some amount of

---

* 'On the Sanitary Condition of the town of Limerick.'

† 'Second Report of the Health of Towns Commission,' page 453.

‡ The table was based upon the particulars of 876 cases attended by Dr. Granville, as Physician to the Benevolent Lying-in Institution, and Westminster Dispensary, and is given at length in *Doubleday's* '*True Law of Population*,' p. 140.

imprudence traceable to the loss of parental guidance; but there must be other and more permanent causes of this tendency in populations such as the lower classes of Ireland and Mexico, where early unions have been so much the habit of the people that no increased demand for labour has ever made any perceptible difference in the number.

The more permanent cause may be, and probably is, *a precocity consequent upon an inferior amount of vital energy;* a cause corresponding with the law which we have remarked before to prevail universally throughout the vegetable and animal kingdoms,—that the powers destined to attain the greatest longevity shall be the most slowly developed.

In the tropics, where a girl becomes a mother as soon as she has attained her teens, she is an old and wrinkled woman at forty; and the term of life seldom extends beyond the ages of fifty-five and sixty. Horticulturists are aware that the trees which the most rapidly produce their fruit are those placed in the most unfavourable circumstances for growth, or the growth of which is checked by lopping and pruning. Upon this head the following observations by Mr. Doubleday are both interesting and instructive :—

" It is a fact, admitted by all gardeners as well as botanists, that if a tree, plant, or flower, be placed in a mould either naturally or artificially made too rich for it, a plethoric state is produced, and fruitfulness ceases. In trees, the effect of strong manures and over-rich soils is, that they run to superfluous wood, blossom irregularly, and chiefly at the extremities of the outer branches, and almost, or entirely, cease to bear fruit.

" With flowering shrubs and flowers, the effect is, first, that the flower becomes double, and loses its power of producing seed ; next, it ceases almost even to flower. If the application of the stimulus of manure is carried still further, flowers and plants become diseased in the extreme, and speedily die ; thus, by this wise provision of Providence, the transmission of disease (the certain consequence of the highly plethoric state, whether in plants, animals, or in mankind) is guarded against, and the species shielded from danger on the side of plenty. In order to remedy this state when accidentally produced, gardeners and florists are accustomed, by various devices, to produce the opposite, or deplethoric state ; this, they peculiarly denominate ' giving a check.' In other words, they put the species in danger in order to produce a corresponding determined effort of nature to ensure its perpetuation—and the end is invariably attained. Thus, in order to make fruit trees bear plentifully, gardeners delay, or impede, the rising of the sap, by cutting rings in the bark round the tree. This, to the tree, is the production of a state of depletion, and the abundance of fruit is the effort of nature to counteract the danger. The fig, when grown in this climate, is particularly liable to drop its fruit when half matured. This, gardeners now find, can be prevented by pruning the tree so severely as to give it a check ; or, if grown in a pot, by cutting a few inches from its roots all round, so as to produce the same effect. The result is, that the tree retains, and carefully matures, its fruit.

"In like manner, when a gardener wishes to save seed from a gourd or cucumber, he does not give the plant an *extra* quantity of manure or warmth. He does just the contrary: he subjects it to some *hardship*, and takes the fruit that is *least* fine looking, foreknowing that it will be filled with seed, whilst the finest fruit are nearly destitute. Upon the same principle, it is a known fact, that after severe and long winters, the harvests are correspondingly rapid and abundant. Vines bear most luxuriantly after being severely tried by frost ; and grass springs in the same extraordinary manner. After the long and trying winter of 1836-7, when the snow lay upon the ground in the northern counties until June, the spring of grass was so wonderful as to cause several minute experiments by various persons. The result was, that in a single night of twelve hours the blade of grass was ascertained frequently to have advanced full three-quarters of an inch ; and wheat and other grain progressed in a similar manner.

"Aware of this beautiful law of preservation, the florist, when he wishes to ensure the luxuriant flowering of a green-house or hot-house shrub or plant, exposes it for a time to the cold. The danger caused by the temperature, too low for the nature of the species of plant, is followed invariably by an effort of nature for its safety, and it flowers luxuriantly ; and, if a seed-bearing plant, bears seed accordingly.

"There is another curious modification of this law exhibited by the vegetable creation, and this is, that immediately before the death, or the sudden cessation of fruitfulness of a tree or shrub, it is observed to bear abundantly. This is remarkably the case with the pear and apple, when the roots touch the harsh cold blue clay, or any other soil inimical to the health of the tree. It is a last effort to preserve and perpetuate the species, and is the effect of that state of *depletion* through which the tree passes to sterility and death." *

The experience of the grazier, the farmer, and the breeder of horses, corresponds with the observations of the horticulturist. Animals are the most prolific when they are kept in a low physical state, and not allowed to get into what is termed "high condition."

" Fecundity is totally checked by the plethoric state, when induced, and increased and rendered doubly certain by the de-plethoric or lean state; while a moderate prolificness is the effect of the state between the two.

" The rabbit and the swine are extraordinary for their prolificness, yet every schoolboy knows that the *doe*, or female rabbit, and every

---

* 'True Law of Population,' page 12.

farmer and breeder knows that the *sow*, will not conceive if fat to a certain height of fatness, and that the number of the progeny is generally in the ratio of the leanness of the animal. All cattle-breeders know the same law to be especially true in the cases of the mare, the cow, and the ewe, with which leanness is indispensable to conception; and upon their knowledge of this truth they invariably act. In the *mare* this is sometimes evinced in an extraordinary degree. A friend of the author, who, being of the medical profession, is peculiarly observant of all cases of this nature, has assured him that he has known a highly bred blood mare, which for a length of time appeared to be incurably barren, rendered fertile, and ultimately the dam of a numerous progeny, by being put literally to the plough and cart, fed sparingly, and worked down to a state of extreme leanness and temporary exhaustion by this unusual employment.

"In the sheep this principle of increase or decrease is most nicely developed. It is invariably found that if over-fed, sterility is the consequence. On the other hand, when the animal is in a state of leanness, a produce of one, two, or three lambs takes place. Upon their knowledge of this fact, the breeders of sheep are accustomed to act. In order to afford the best chance of a perfect animal, it is believed that a produce of one lamb at a birth is desirable; and this the breeders of sheep contrive to secure by apportioning the food of the ewe to such a nicety that, avoiding sterility on the one hand, and a double or triple birth on the other, a single lamb is almost invariably the result.

" The conflicts that take place among all wild animals at the time of rutting are no doubt intended for the same end—to lower their condition to the prolific point.

Upon birds a state of plethora produces the same effects. This is well-known to be the case with domestic poultry, of which the French fable of *Une femme et sa poule* is an amusing evidence. The good dame, desirous of an increased supply of eggs, crams the poor pullet with double rations of grain. The hen, as well she may, becomes enormously fat, but not another egg will she lay." *

Mr. Doubleday adduces a corresponding class of facts in the case of human beings. He notices a statement made by a writer in the ' Cyclopædia of Medicine,' that it had been his lot to witness in the lying-in hospital of Dublin, " *the birth of numberless infants, whose unfortunate parents had not for years partaken of a wholesome meal,*" and compares it with the often opposite result of good living, as in the following instance given by Dr. Coombe, in his work on Digestion and Dietetics:—

" A young woman of a healthy constitution, brought up in all the simplicity of country habits, passed at once, on her marriage, to a less active mode of life, and to a much more elegant table. In a short

---

* Doubleday, on the ' True Law of Population,' p. 16.

time she began to complain of irritability, lassitude, various spasmodic sensations, and habitual constipation. Hypochondria was soon added to the other symptoms. *Her hope of becoming a mother being always deceived,* an additional glass of wine, bark, and other tonics were ordered. The evil increased. The patient became melancholy, and believed that she was swallowing pins. In the course of the year she became so emaciated and yellow, that her mother, who had not seen her for eleven months, could hardly recognize her. *After an eighteen months' course of purgatives, and two courses of Marienbad water, she entirely recovered."*

This it may be said is a case of disease, but it belongs to a class of cases extremely common among the middle and higher ranks of society; and the important fact to be noticed, by those who may be inclined to pursue this investigation, is, that all the diseases arising out of luxurious habits tend towards depopulation, while many of those engendered by poverty, and especially spare diet, act in an opposite direction, although enfeebling the constitution and shortening the term of life.* Hence the remark of the Health of Towns Commissioners, that among the poor—"singular and incredible as it may appear—the scourges of disease and pestilence are not merely powerless to restrain, but actually give an impulse to population."

" Where the condition of human beings is scarcely above that of animals, — where appetite and instinct occupy the places of higher feelings, — where the barest means of support encourage the most improvident and early marriages, — we must not expect to find a diminishing, nor even a stationary population. For the early unions there are followed by early offspring ; and although more than half that offspring may be swept away by disease during infancy, yet nearly a third of it will grow up in spite of all the surrounding evils, to follow in the steps of their parents, and in their turn, to continue a race, ignorant, miserable, and immoral as themselves."†

Mr. Doubleday adds a great number of facts to show that in countries where the diet of the people is what is considered of an impoverishing kind—as fish, potatoes, rice, yams, and other vegetables—the ratio of increase is more rapid than in pastoral countries, or wherever the diet is principally animal food. He quotes the opinion of Magendie that a full diet of animal food and wheaten bread, with wine and sugar in combination, liquid

---

* The effects of insolvency may be added to this class of cases. Numerous instances have occurred of rich men remaining childless while in prosperous circumstances, and after passing through the Bankruptcy Courts becoming the fathers of large families.

† Report of Dr. Lyon Playfair on the state of large towns in Lancashire, vol i. p. 444.

or solid, is apt to be accompanied with a development of *acid,* of which the gout is the most painful symptom, and concludes, that as in vegetable manures, the principal stimulus of growth of plants has been traced to *alkali,* that a somewhat *alkalescent* state of body, which can be induced only by a lower diet, is essential to animal fecundity. In this there is doubtless some truth, but *alkali* stimulates without perfecting the growth of a plant. When burnt ashes have been spread on a corn field, without other manure, there will often be abundance of straw but no grain,—perhaps another indication of the general law already noticed, of slow development for the more perfect organizations. It is not that a generous diet, when not indulged in to excess, and not taken without active exercise, is unfavourable to fecundity, but that a lower diet tends to precocity.

On the subject, however, of the precise effects of differences of diet in stimulating or retarding the prolific faculties, further data require to be collected. Mr. Doubleday speaks of the rice-eating populations of Hindostan and China, but in both countries there are classes consuming a large proportion of animal food—the Mahometans in the one country, and the Mandarins in the other. The results in each case should be stated. Even the information which might be obtained at home upon this head is at present defective, and but a feeble and an uncertain light is thrown upon it by our registration returns. In Manchester, for example, there is a class of highly-paid factory operatives, consumers of more animal food than perhaps any other operatives in Europe; and in the same town there is another class, partly Irish, or of Celtic extraction, whose food is wholly composed of potatoes, oatmeal, and the herring. Separate returns for each should be obtained, where possible.

The opposite tendencies of a plethoric state, and a state of depletion, are what Mr. Doubleday calls the *true* law of population. But here he commits a similar error of rapid generalization to that which produced the theory of Mr. Malthus. The world does not turn upon a single pivot;—nearly every effect is the result of combined causes. The causes that affect population are many and various. Diet is one of them, and an important one doubtless; but there are other influences perhaps even more important. The qualities of the air we breathe, changes of climate, physical habits, and mental occupations, are all powerful agencies of life and death, and therefore governing, directly or indirectly, the ratios of increase and decrease of population.

Hereafter, when we may be enabled to form a more accurate estimate of the separate influence of these than can now be even attempted, it may possibly be found that the cultivation of the intellectual faculties is alone sufficient to produce a slower ratio of increase than is compatible with the mere animalism of ignorance. Nor can this be regarded as an improbable conjecture, for putting aside the fact that literary men and literary women have rarely been the parents of large families, which may sometimes have arisen from health impaired by a too sedentary life, it is certain that the tendency of mental pursuits is to moderate the intensity of the passions, and that, in all cases, those organs which are most frequently brought into exercise take something from the rest. It is said that the brain of a full-grown negro does not weigh so much as the brain of an English educated lad, but that his powers, mental and corporeal, are earlier developed. Reverse the state of the two brains, by education in the one case, and neglect in the other, and probably in a few generations the ratio of development in each would also be reversed.

But there are yet other causes of variations in fecundity, and perhaps more powerful than any of those that have yet been mentioned;—causes connected with *the question of races.*

It is not necessary here to go into the inquiry of whether there were originally several pairs of human beings, or whether the whole family of mankind have descended from a single pair (supposed by some to have been black), and that time and climate, and other circumstances, have occasioned the differences which exist. Differences there are in either case—differences of colour, stature, features, conformation of skull, weight of brain, length of heel, shape of the nail, &c.; and to these, when strongly marked, we give the name of characteristics of race.

Now it is a familiar fact in natural history, that *hybrids,* a race produced by the union of distinct species of plants or animals, are sterile, or speedily become so. Dr. Carpenter states that hybrid plants have never been continued without intermixture beyond the fourth or fifth generation, and among animals so nearly allied as the horse and the ass, the dog and the fox, the pheasant and the domestic hen, where a cross is attempted, the offspring is invariably barren.* An anatomical professor, whose lectures have recently been reported in the *Medical Times* (Dr. Knox), asserts the same results of attempted amalgamations between different races of men. He says that the offspring of the white man and the negro, or of the copper-coloured Indian and the European, cannot be continued beyond the third or fourth generation by the intermarriages of their descendants; and he carries this so far as to assert that all attempts at a permanent

* 'Vegetable Physiology,' page 279.

amalgamation of Celtic and Saxon populations, or Sarmatian and Sclavonian, will prove fruitless, and that in the end these four will be the only national distinctions recognised in Europe.

Very little evidence has been collected by Dr. Knox to support his positions; and his arguments are much more suggestive than conclusive, but it can scarcely be doubted that they contain some element of truth. He says,—

" When mulattoes intermarry, they seem to die out in two or three generations; whether as being in direct violation of that specific law, as yet so little understood by us, which determines the species of all things,—*the law of specialization*, or hereditary descent,—or that having come within the tide of *the law of deformation*,—that is, the law of viability,—forms and structures are produced by the marriage of mulattoes, which are not viable.

" The deaths, for example, of very young children, whose structures present so many varieties, even of the present races, are extremely numerous; one reason of which, with others, no doubt, may be that their structure, being within the *law of variety*, may have rendered them *non-viable*, or unequal to resist the bad effects of external influences. In a mulatto I examined, the nerves of all the limbs were a good third less than in a person of any pure race, fair or dark."*

On the other hand, there is the case of the population of Pitcairn's Island, in which greater prolificness would seem to have been induced by the crossing of races, than would otherwise have existed;—although this part of the history of that singular colony has not been generally noticed. The settlers consisted of fifteen males, of whom six were Otaheitans; and of twelve Otaheitan females : and it is a curious fact, that the six Otaheitan males, although they lived with their wives for two years before the quarrel arose in which they were killed, left no children; while the marriages of the Europeans with the Otaheitan women were all fruitful, and those of the second generation more fruitful than the first; not, however, so much as to have exceeded the

---

* ' Medical Times,' June 24, 1848.

In a subsequent lecture reported in the same publication, September 29, 1848, Dr. Knox gives the following table of the comparative mortality of different races in *Algeria*, as illustrative of the incapacity of some races to extend themselves in certain quarters of the globe, and of the superior adaptation of others.

1845.

Jews	36·1	died in every 1,000
Mahometans	40·8	„ „ „ „
Europeans	45·5	„ „ „ „

The mortality of European children born in Algeria is four times greater than in England, taking the period from birth to fifteen.

common average of about four births to a marriage.* Half a century hence, it will be an interesting point, for those who may follow us, to learn whether this fruitfulness has continued, and what have been the rates of mortality—upon which at present nothing can be said, the latest accounts from Pitcairn's Island still leaving it with a comparatively youthful population.†

The following observations from the ' Quarterly Review,' by a writer evidently well-qualified to speak by experience of the results of cross-breeding in cattle, bear upon this part of our subject:—

"Our lamented friend, Mr. Edge, of Strelly, having shaped in his imagination a breed of cattle formed on his own model—great size, symmetry, and a propensity to fatten, spared no expense to realize his vision. Aided by a most correct eye, and with no prejudices, personal or local, he selected at any cost, and from any quarter in which he found them, the animals, both male and female, which he thought likely to answer his expectations. Nor was he disappointed in the qualities of their offspring. But after some years, when he seemed to have attained, or to be on the point of, perfection, he came to a dead lock: his females, though much solicited, refused to give

---

* The first settlers of Pitcairn's Island (January 23, 1790) consisted of—

	Males.	Females.
White	9	0
Coloured	6	12

In 1793, the six coloured men and six of the whites were killed in the quarrels which arose among the settlers for mastery, and chiefly about the women. Subsequently, the number of the original settlers was further reduced by deaths. In 1825, the population of the island was as follows:—

	Males.	Females.
Original settlers	1	5
Children of the white settlers (the men of colour having left none)	10	10
Their grandchildren	22	15
	33	30
Recent settlers	2	0
Child of one of them	1	0
	36	30

Among the children there were but two natural deaths and three deaths by accident out of sixty-two births during thirty-five years.—*Beechy's Voyage to the Pacific*, vol. i., p. 136.

† Some have quoted the case of Pitcairn's Island as an illustration of the power of population to triple itself in thirty years, reckoning from the death of the six coloured men; but this is a mistake, as the island does not at present contain the usual proportion of the aged, without which the comparison is valueless.

The same remark will apply to much that has been said of the tendency of the population of the United States to double itself every twenty-five years. As a new community, and one constantly receiving accessions by emigration, from the ranks of the young and enterprizing, it possesses a more youthful population than other countries, and the ratio of births greatly exceed the deaths, partly because the deaths of the aged have yet to be registered.

him produce. On this ground, and on this only, we believe, he broke up his herd and discontinued the pursuit. Lord Spencer, an enthusiastic advocate of short-horns, admitted, in more than one public speech, that in his herd fecundity had diminished to an inconvenient degree, and was only maintained by a degree of care and attention which could hardly be extended to the general breeding stock of a kingdom. We know the ready answer,—the females are too fat. But that is not the whole question. We lately inspected a herd of Herefords, the property of a distinguished and (we speak on the authority of his farming accounts) very successful agriculturist. The breeding cows and heifers living solely on crushed gorse were considerably above the point of marketable beef in fatness. We have no doubt they would be bad milkers. The bulls were loaded with fat; but there was no deficiency of calves; the drafts on account of barrenness were very few. The expression of the owner was—'I have no trouble on that score.' Twins were by no means unknown in the herd. Since short horns have been very generally introduced into the Midland counties, barrenness has been a very great trouble to the cheese-making farmer." *

With respect to the Herefords here mentioned, it cannot be admitted, notwithstanding the eulogy of them by the owner, that fat had not impaired their qualities as breeders, if it had injured them as milkers. A falling off in milk shows in itself a tendency to sterility; for the cow that could not support its own calf after birth would, from the same cause, certainly be incapable of producing one. The principal fact, however, here shown is, that in certain circumstances, cross-breeding tends to sterility.† Under other circumstances, again, we have the testimony of the same writer that cross-breeding is the only means of *preventing* sterility.

" When Bakewell died he left on his farm a good flock of sheep— perhaps, for his purposes, the best in the kingdom. His successor imagined that a breed had been created which could perpetuate itself and

---

* 'Quarterly Review' for March, 1849, p. 397.

† " We inherited a long-legged sow, hog-backed, bristly-maned, flat-sided, slouch-eared, rather a ferocious looking animal. Twice a year she was followed down the lane by an almost interminable series of little grunters—reduplications of mamma—sixteen, eighteen, we believe even twenty at a litter. But how could these satisfy the eye of a critic? So we began afresh; and a few years of judicious selection and crossing gave us animals of almost perfect symmetry. The litters, however, from far in the teens, dwindled to six, four,— and at length our favourite sow produced one. Nor was this all. The roaded bacon, three inches thick, for which, when trimmed with beans, we have seen gastronomers of undoubted authority desert farther-fetched dainties, was replaced on our table by six inches of rather flabby fat, unredeemed by lean. So when we could not even save our bacon we gave up the pursuit; and we are inclined to think that our experience was a sort of epitome of hog-breeding." —'Quarterly Review,' for March, 1849.—p. 408.

its merits; but under that system, and in his hands, the flock came to a melancholy end—size, constitution, fertility, flesh, wool—all gone; nothing but a little tallow left. The successor of this gentleman was a Derbyshire man, and he brought with him on the farm a good flock of sheep. They had in them a good deal of Bakewellian blood; but when their owner saw them dwindle, he had recourse to a large, roughish race, from the limestone district of his native country, a big-headed, big-boned, big-muscled animal—

'Omnia magna,
Pes etiam.'

Under such management, this flock, of which we have now lost sight, for a long time retained its celebrity."

This brings us to the principle, at which we have before glanced, of *close affinities*, and which is perhaps more intimately connected with the cause of stationary and decaying populations than any other. If, in respect to species, there are certain lines of demarcation which Nature will not allow to be passed, so also there are certain lines of affinity which she will not suffer to be approached; and it is this latter principle which is the foundation of the laws forbidding the crime of incest.

From the universality of the laws or customs which interdict the marriages of near relations—(for even among the natives of Australia the principle is recognised, and carried by superstition to such an extreme that they will not marry persons of the same *name*, although belonging to a different tribe*),—we may reasonably conjecture that the physical deterioration produced by such marriages, or by what a grazier would technically call the "breeding in and in," had been observed at a period preceding the dawn of the earliest civilization of which any record exists; and we may here assume the fact of such deterioration without troubling ourselves unnecessarily with the proof.

But in what consists the essence of the law by which the marriage of brothers and sisters is properly prohibited? It is not in the mere fact that they are brothers and sisters, but in the tendency to the exhaustion of a species produced by the union of like with like. Following out, then, this idea, it will be seen that the intermarriages of an aristocracy, the intermarriages of the inhabitants of towns, and even of villages, where there is little movement of the population, and no influx of strangers, must tend more and more to a similar result. Partaking constantly of food grown on the same soil; breathing the same air; clothed and lodged in the same manner; pursuing similar occupations; they must day by day become more and more physically alike in constitution, and consequently more and more incapable

---

* Grey's 'Narrative of Travels in Western Australia.'

of reproducing some one or other of the many elements of health and strength which each may have parted with in the wear and tear of life.

We may trace in the vegetable world the operation of the same law. One of the first lessons that a young farmer learns is the necessity of a rotation of crops; he must not sow wheat after wheat, year after year, on the same soil, even if he doubles every time the quantity of his manure, and, what is equally important, he must not sow frequently upon the same soil seed of his own growth;—it will thrive elsewhere, but not where it grew. Sown and re-sown frequently on the same soil, the produce will be less and less; probably from an imperfect impregnation at the time of flowering.*

The law of a rotation of crops is not peculiar to cultivation, but is followed by nature in the plain and the forest, when untouched by the hand of man.

---

* " It is well known that of two parcels of wheat, for instance, as much alike in quality as possible, the one which had been grown on a soil differing much from that on which it is to be sown, will yield a better produce than the other that grew in the same or a similar soil and climate. The farmers of Scotland, accordingly, find that wheat from the south, even though it be not, as it usually is, better than their own, is a very advantageous change; and oats and other grain, brought from a clayey to a sandy soil, other things being equal, are more productive than such as grow on the sandy soil."—*Encyclopedia Brit.* Art. Agriculture.

" Evelyn, in his letter to Sir John Aubrey, states that beech-trees grew in place of oaks which had been cut down by his grandfather, and that birch succeeded beech which his brother had extirpated. In the ' Memoirs of the Philadelphia Society for promoting Agriculture,' vol. i., there are several papers on this subject. In the third volume, Mr. Isaac Wayre, son of the American general the late A. Wayre, gives some interesting details respecting the appearance of timber trees of a kind different from those which formerly covered the ground in his vicinity, and which had been cut down by the American army, when encamped there in the autumn and winter of the year 1777, and spring of the following year. One of the writers refers to the relation of Mr. Hearne (' Journey to the Northern Ocean,' p. 452), for the fact of strawberries growing up wild near Churchill River, and in the interior parts of the country, particularly in such places as have been formerly set on fire; and for that of hips and raspberry-bushes shooting up in great numbers in burnt places, where nothing of the kind had ever been seen before. Cartwright is also quoted in proof of the same point. He observes, ' that if, through carelessness, the old spruce woods are burnt, or destroyed by lightning, Indian tea first comes up, currants follow, and after them birch.' (' Journal of Transactions at Labrador,' vol. iii. p. 225.) Nine years after the publication of this last work, M'Kenzie stated, that ' land covered with spruce-pine and white birch, when laid waste by fire, produced nothing but poplars.' Recently we have additional testimony on this subject. In the ' Manual on the Culture of Silk,' prepared in consequence of a resolution of the House of Representatives of the American Congress, and published in the Session of 1828, it is stated (p. 38) that ' in Tennessee, when a native forest is cut down, if the land be enclosed, a growth of red mulberry trees soon takes place.' "—*Correspondent of Loudon's Gardener's Magazine, for August,* 1829.

A tendency to increase can exist only with a power to spread; when the power to spread ceases there begins a tendency to decay.

This principle supplies an important link in the chain of causation, which was necessary to account for the whole of the phenomena to which our attention has been directed; and we may trace it in new as well as in old countries, when we compare a migratory population with one that is settled. Thus, while in many parts of the United States the average proportion of births to marriages is as 5 to 1, the average in the city of Philadelphia is stated by Mr. Balfour, for the year 1818, as somewhat less than 3 to 1, which is about the same as the proportion given by M. Mallet in the case of the now stationary population of Geneva, where the result of marriages is only about 2¾ births to each marriage, although in the 17th century they produced an average of five children and more.

It is a great relief to be now enabled to dismiss entirely from the mind a theory which has served only to cloud the vision of moral philosophers, and which has too long weighed like a nightmare on the hopes of philanthropists. We have not, thank God! to put our trust in the vice and misery of our fellow-creatures as the only means of retaining our own position in a crowded world; nor to undertake, in order to escape from this dilemma, the impossible achievement of placing the passions of mankind in a procrustean marriage-bed, accurately adjusted to the production of the precise number of human beings for whom we may be of opinion room might possibly be made in creation without a very troublesome effort. Any scheme of the kind acted upon by the educated classes (as it is said to be by some portion of them in Paris) being necessarily confined to those classes and not extending to the lower, must always have the effect of adding to the disproportion, already too great, between the ignorant and the intelligent, the feebler races and the stronger, and may, therefore, be condemned as a contrivance by which a few only could possibly benefit, and calculated to aggravate the evils sought to be remedied in respect to the interests of society at large.

It remains only to suggest some of the objects of inquiry connected with the question we have discussed, which would yet repay the labours of statistical collectors and philosophical observers.

One of them is the relative proportions in the births and deaths, and deaths at different ages, shown in the several cases of progressive, decaying, and stationary populations. Captain Grey, the late governor of Western Australia, remarked a very decided paucity of female births among the native tribes. Humboldt mentions an equally decided excess of female births among certain Creole populations of South America. The effect, also, as we have before noticed, of polygamy in the East, upon the proportions of the sexes, has yet to be examined.

Another subject for further inquiry, and one of the highest interest, as calculated, perhaps, to open the most cheering views of man's future destiny, is the effect upon civilization of that entire decay of classes and races among nations which we have noticed, and their renovation from other sources.

Looking at the inveteracy of error when interwoven with our earliest habits of thought and most cherished associations, and the strength of old institutions, however inimical to public interests, when identified with the civil polity of a state and made the road to wealth and power, it may be doubted whether any considerable progress could have been made by mankind in true knowledge and civilization, from the earliest times to the present, but for the tendency in populations to receive an influx of new elements, and for the old elements to wear out. If the priests of Egypt could have retained their relative position in succeeding ages, millions of men would now, in the nineteenth century, have been employed in embalming crocodiles. If the slaves of the Pharaohs had not multiplied faster than their task-masters, there would have been no kingdom of Judea. If there had been no decay of Roman patricians, and of Roman citizens of the original stock that subdued the world, or if "the barbarians" of their time had not increased in a greater proportion, there would have been still a temple of Diana on the site of St. Paul's, and a temple of Apollo where there is now Westminster Abbey. If the Norman barons and their retainers could have held their own in England as a separate race, the mass of Englishmen would still have been "serfs and villains."

In the up-hill work of reformers of all ages and nations, the heaviest and most discouraging obstacle they have had to encounter has always been the determined hostility of a dominant class, composed often of men of the highest intellectual powers, and, as private individuals, of great moral worth, but all equally (or with but few noble exceptions) dreading the innovations that might lessen the privileges of their order ; and while in their hearts despising superstition and reprobating abuse, in their public capacity countenancing both. The interests of this class have been the altar on which the blood of the world's martyrs has been shed, and often in vain ; but a higher power takes up the quarrel. The proudest aristocracies are the first to disappear. "Old families," said Sir Thomas Brown, "do not last out three oaks." Royal families follow the same rule, although sometimes prolonged by the new blood of foreign alliances. And vain are feudal customs and laws of primogeniture to secure the earth to a given line of descendants. Nature laughs at entails : she has her own process of "fine and recovery" for every estate tied up, and in a few generations they are the inheritance of strangers. New men then take the precedence, and new ideas are advanced.

Lastly : While collecting the facts that may further explain the various changes, decay, and renewals of races, we should seek also for data that may throw some light upon the question of *a progression of races.* The fact of a progression in the history of all created organizations has now been clearly established by physiological and geological investigations. The precise order of that progression is an object of inquiry that may worthily occupy the noblest faculties of the mind. We know that the soil on which the oak grows was first prepared for it by the humble *lichen.* We know that man is one of the latest inhabitants of the earth. Who or what was his immediate progenitor ? Who or what will be his successor ?

Such an inquiry is not to be confounded with the notion of resolving the work of creation into the gradual transmutation of distinct species. There are sufficient grounds for assuming that the original types of all existing species were as distinct as the species themselves, and we can hardly conceive of a state of being, however superior to the present, in which there will not be as numerous and as distinct varieties of organizations, adapted to the numerous varieties of circumstances, as any that now exist. Gradations it is probable will always be preserved, but they may advance together. Whither we are tending we know not, but it is clearly ONWARD. The earth is visibly becoming peopled with races gifted with a more commanding intelligence than that of the mass of its former inhabitants. Every step in science induces the reflection that the problems of moral and physical evil with which we are yet perplexed are dependent for their solution upon a knowledge of "the before and after," which may one day be attained ;—that with that knowledge our difficulties will vanish, and the end of all that is partial and incidental, as well as universal be found,—good.

W. E. HICKSON.

Newcastle, January 1st, 1837.

TO THE RIGHT HON. LORD BROUGHAM AND VAUX.

My Lord,

I shall not affect to deny that in thus addressing your Lordship, I do so with mixed motives ; and that one of these is the hope that your name appended to my composition may possibly obtain for it attention from some who would not be likely to notice it, either on account of that of its author, or from any idea of its possibly containing any thing on such a subject deserving the slightest attention.

For any further apology to your Lordship, I do not know that I am fairly your debtor. Your Lordship is a public man, and to that public you have declared your readiness to "champion to the utterance" the most extreme doctrines of that system now known as that of " Malthus." You have thrown down your gage to defend the Malthusian doctrines of population against all opponents, and therefore cannot complain of an attack, from what quarter soever it may come.

If, then, humble as I am, I venture forth against your Lordship " with a sling and with a stone," the attempt may be ridiculous, but cannot be impertinent.

Be it so, my Lord. I happen to be one who would think more meanly of himself if he feared to stand by his opinions against any odds, than if he were defeated in the encounter after a manner the most obnoxious to that self-love which he possesses in common with the rest of mankind.

In this attempt to impugn the doctrine of Malthus, permit me *first*, my Lord, to say that it is any thing but my intention to mince or mystify the matter. I shall at all events meet the question boldly, fairly, and openly. I shall give a distinct and unhesitating denial to the system. I shall assert that his pretended law of population does not exist; and that his asseverations regarding it are contrary to evidence, and as false as falsehood can possibly be—in short, altogether false. I shall next *show* that these assertions are totally at variance with truth, and founded in a total ignorance on the part of Mr Malthus of what the nature of the law which regulates the amount

of population really is. At the same time I shall endeavour to point out, and to illustrate that law as clearly as I can, and to prove that it applies generally not only to all mankind of all nations, but to the animal creation, and also, with certain modifications, to the vegetable world. I shall strive to show the great probability of its pervading *all* animated and vegetable nature, universally; and that it affords one of the most beautiful illustrations of the deep wisdom and all-pervading beneficence of the Creator that has yet been discovered. Lastly, I shall deduce that, being what I have described it, it is in the most complete opposition possible to the astounding and cruel practical conclusions drawn from the opinions of Malthus, and now attempted to be brought into active operation in this country, to the deep shame and everlasting disgrace of its rulers. This I am now to attempt to do : and this your Lordship will, at least, acknowledge is no bush-fighting.

The doctrine of Malthus rests then, my Lord, upon two sweeping and emphatic assertions. If these two assertions *are* true, and can be *proved* to be so, the rest of his theory, being plain deductions from them, follows of course. What are the two grand assertions of Malthus ? They are these. I. That the natural tendency of population, if unchecked by other causes, is to increase, in a geometrical ratio, of 1, 2, 4, 8, 16, 32, &c. &c. II. That food can only at most be made to increase in an arithmetical ratio of 1, 2, 3, 4, 5, 6, &c. From these two assertions, if granted, he deduces à third ; *viz.* that population must *always* tend to be in advance of its own resources; and that the people of every country must *always* press too heavily upon the means of subsistence, unless this tendency to increase be checked. The natural checks he declares to be misery and vice—the artificial checks, moral and prudential restraint, and fear of too much offspring. Building upon these general assertions a superstructure of asserted facts, he goes on to state, that if it were possible to afford an unlimited supply of efficient food to mankind, they would double their numbers in each twenty-five or thirty years, and that it is the *impossibility alone* of obtaining sustenance that prevents this:—and these assertions he attempts to prove by a reference to the different states of population in different countries—the general view attempted to be given being, that there is some constant increase of people in all countries, but the greatest in new countries where food is supposed to be more plentiful—the increase, in all cases, arising out of an extension of the means of obtaining food. This, my lord, I take to be a fair statement of the general theory of the celebrated —I had almost said *too-celebrated,* Malthus. If it be not so, I can only say that I have not designedly misrepresented it; and that I am quite willing to amend any error that shall be pointed out.

Now I would first observe, my Lord, of this theory, that with the exception of the assertion of the geometrical ratio of increase in one case, and the arithmetical ratio of increase in the other—it was not originated by Malthus, but was broached many years before. In fact, the whole of the doctrine of the tendency of a people to increase more rapidly than their food can be made to increase, unless moral or natural checks interpose, is to be found in the work of " Wallace on the Prospects of Mankind." That it should be suffered to sleep unheeded in the book of Wallace, as a mere fantastical speculation under the guise of philosophy, to be so eagerly adopted when resuscitated by Malthus, may, perhaps, seem unaccountable to your Lordship. To me, I must confess, it does not seem so; but with my way of accounting for it, it would be irrelevant to the immediate matter in hand to trouble your Lordship at present.

I now address myself immediately to the point at issue. Unless I have much misrepresented him, the theory of Malthus rests entirely upon the truth or falsehood of the two ratios of increase of numbers and of food, respectively—and I meet your Lordship upon the first. The second may, for aught I know to the contrary, be true, but the first is false. I deny its truth, and assert, in direct opposition to Malthus, that there is not any such constant tendency to increase amongst mankind. I affirm that this tendency only exists under certain definable

circumstances, and never pervades the entire of any people. I affirm, further, that under certain known circumstances, the *opposite* tendencies exist; that is to say, the tendency to decrease, and the tendency to remain stationary, in numbers. And I lastly affirm that all these different tendencies may and do exist in society at one and the same time—increase going on amidst one portion of a people, decrease amongst another, and another portion neither increasing nor decreasing; and that it is upon the proper balance of these that the welfare of society depends. I can here readily imagine your Lordship to recoil from these assertions, if you should deign to look at this paper at all, as being amongst the most strange, and apparently most at variance with truth and common sense that ever met your notice. I can easily imagine this. But, at the same time, I must respectfully beg of your Lordship not to suffer an apparent improbability at the outset to divert your attention altogether from any *new view* of a matter so deeply important, little recommended as that view may seem to be either by the manner or the matter of its author.

I have affirmed that these different tendencies of increase and decrease, and the mean betwixt these two, may and do exist at one and the same time amongst a people. I have asserted that these tendencies exist because of the different circumstances in which different portions of a population are placed. I am now to show, *first,* what *are* these circumstances; and then *how* and *why* these circumstances produce such opposite tendencies. I shall proceed to do this, and in doing it I shall have to crave your Lordship's attention, whilst I point out what *is* the *real law* which regulates the population of all countries— a very different law from that of Malthus. The law to which I allude is one which is more or less admitted by all physiologists, naturalists, and medical persons, to be a law of nature, and of the existence of which the proofs are innumerable and undoubted; and it is only because this law *generally* pervades nature, animate and inanimate, that we have this general admission from scientific men, totally differing in the objects of their pursuits and studies, and have it corroborated by men not scientific but practical—engaged practically in the same pursuits.

This law is, that when a species, whether animal or vegetable, is put in danger, nature invariably provides an extraordinary effort for its perpetuation ; and that when, on the contrary, the means of perpetuation are profuse, the powers of perpetuation are diminished. In short, that what I may call the " Plethoric State," is *unfavourable* to increase ; the " Deplethoric State" (or opposite state), *favourable*, in the same ratio, and according to the intensity of the different states, the mean being, of course, between the two.

In attempting to bring before your Lordship some of the most striking *proofs* of the *existence* of this GENERAL LAW, I shall begin with the vegetable creation, and go up to human nature through the world of inferior animals. I shall cite as evidence the experience of the gardener and farmer, as well as of the botanist and natural historian ; and confirm the experience of the physician by the details of statistics and the actual history of the world as it now is.

First then, as to the vegetable world ; the existence of this general law of increase or decrease is admitted by all men, scientific or practical, engaged in horticultural pursuits. All gardeners as well as botanists know, that if a tree, plant, or flower, be placed in mould *too rich* for it, the " plethoric state" is immediately produced, and it ceases to be fruitful. If a tree, it runs to superfluous wood, blossoms irregularly, and is destitute of fruit. If a flowering shrub, or flowering plant, it becomes double, and loses its power of producing seed—and next ceases, or nearly ceases, even to flower. In order to remedy this, gardeners and florists are accustomed to produce the opposite, or " deplethoric state," by artificial means. This they denominate " giving a check." In short, they put " the species" *in danger*, in order to produce a correspondingly determined effort of nature to ensure perpetuation, and their end is attained. Thus, to make trees bear, gardeners *delay* and impede the flow of the sap, by *cutting rings* in the bark round the tree. This to the tree is a process of " depletion," and the abundance of fruit is the effort of nature to counteract the danger. The fig,

when grown in this climate, is peculiarly liable to drop its fruit when about half mature. This, gardeners now find, can be prevented by pruning the tree so *severely* as to " give it a check ;" or if it be grown in a pot, by cutting a few inches from its roots all round, so as to produce the same effect. The invariable result is, that the tree retains and matures its fruit. In like manner, when a gardener wishes to save seed from a cucumber, he does not give the plant an *extra* quantity of manure or warmth, but the contrary. He takes the fruit *least* fine looking, and subjects it to some hardship, foreknowing that it will turn out to be *filled with seed*, whilst finer grown fruit are nearly destitute. Upon the same principle the florist, to insure the luxuriant flowering of a plant, exposes it for a time to the cold. The danger caused by a temperature lower than that natural to it, is followed by nature's usual effort to ensure the continuation of the species, and it vegetates and flowers profusely and luxuriantly ; and, if a seed-bearing plant, seeds accordingly. After the same great law of nature, vines and other fruiting trees and shrubs are observed to bear most abundantly after severe winters, and many trees, especially apples and pears, always fruit abundantly as soon as they touch the blue clay or any soil injurious to them ; such profusion of fruit being preparatory to the death of the tree, and the effect of the state of " depletion," through which it passes *to* death.

Such is the most wise and beneficent dispensation of the Deity throughout the vegetable world, by which fruitfulness increases in the ratio of danger, and *vice versa ;* the effort to perpetuate being according to the risk of non-perpetuation, and an absurd superfluity, or profusion of nourishment, on the other hand, being invariably productive of sterility, irregular vegetation, and disease. Such being the law apparently regulating the comparative degrees of fruitfulness throughout the vegetable kingdom, we now come to animal life, and here the direct evidence of practical men, the experience of the farmer, the breeder, and the horse-dealer, abundantly bear out the analogy, in this particular, between vegetable and animal productiveness. What does the farmer, the grazier, or the breeder, if he wishes to obtain a breed from some particular mare, sow, or heifer? Does he *fatten* the animal in order to secure its fecundity? He does *precisely the contrary*. He keeps it lean. He keeps it in that state in which nature, keeps all animals engaged in search and travel for food, and exposed to perpetual interruptions during their time of feeding. He does this because he knows that to "fatten" the animal; to bring it into the "plethoric state" by means of plenty of food and leisure, would inevitably be to destroy the chances of its fruitfulness. This is a piece of knowledge which *is* acted upon every day, which *has been* acted upon through hundreds of years; and as to the certainty of which, no person engaged in the pursuits of grazing or agriculture, hesitates for a moment. With the prolific rabbit every schoolboy knows this to be the case. He knows that in the domestic state they must be *stinted in food*, and kept clean, to make them breed. That the same law holds good with domestic fowls, the little French fable of "*Une Femme et sa Poule*," sufficiently proves. The dame (who is a sort of *Malthusian* in her way), thinks to get a double supply of eggs by giving her hen double rations of barley! What is the consequence? The poor pullet becomes like the Lord Hamlet, "fat and scant of breath"— "*fortgrassé*," and not an egg from that time forward will she lay! *Why*, my lord—*why* will we persist in shutting our eyes to homely *facts*, and opening them, at full stretch, to boldly asserted and merely plausible *theories?*

I now come to the home point of my argument. I have now arrived at the time when I must show—if I can show—that the analogies upon which I have already touched, and in some degree enlarged, are most fully borne out in the *human world;* and that even a cursory examination as to the phenomena of population, will show that the same laws which regulate the march of vegetable and animal productiveness, govern also the peopling of the world by beings made of the same clay with your Lordship and myself. To do this I have not a paucity, but a superabundance of materials. I am embarrassed only by the variety of the facts as to which I am to treat. I am to go back to the vague traditional lore of former ages,

and to more modern but still bygone notions of a time nearer to our own; and then to show them how these old fantastic notions or prejudices singularly agree with the truth, when developed, being, in point of fact, built upon that truth, and all along supported by it. To this I now proceed; and first, my Lord, let me beg your Lordship's attention to the ancient but widely diffused notions of the superior fecundity of those people who were known by the title of "*Icthyophagi*," or Fish-eaters. These people were universally believed in ancient times to be more prolific than the rest of mankind, Aristotle, amongst others, bearing witness as to the fact. From this universal belief arose the fable of the origin of Venus from the sea. Strange mixture of truth the most important, with imagination the most fantastical! That any people living exclusively upon the low and meagre diet of fish must be unnaturally prolific, the experience of modern times will sufficiently prove. The fecundity, however, is, not because the sustenance is "*fish*," but because the sustenance is *poor*. This I shall, in the proper place, make apparent, by a comparison between the prolificness of people, such as the inhabitants of the Highlands and Western Islands of Scotland, who subsist upon a low diet, chiefly of fish and vegetables, and that of the natives of more favoured countries, whose fare is richer, more plentiful, and more solid—and whose labour and exposure are less. This general notion of a thin and meagre diet being favourable to fruitfulness, is borne out by the recorded opinions of medical writers upon this subject down to the present day. Dr Cheyne and others, in their Dietetic Treatises, insist upon it, and instances are enumerated, by medical writers of all ages, of persons, who, being childless during their prosperity, became parents of families after being subjected to privations and the scanty table and hard bed of misfortune. The extraordinary tendencies to propagation, evinced by all persons convalescent, after enfeebling diseases, pestilences, fevers, &c., is known to all medical men, elucidating the same law. These considerations, however, are *general*, and as general narrations of facts, given by writers ancient and modern, without any reference to the peculiar point now in dispute, I alone refer to them. Let us proceed to try the evidence of facts more specific, and under our own immediate notice, and within our own immediate knowledge. And here, my Lord, I shall come home to your Lordship, and refer you to the history of that House in which your Lordship sits, and of which you are one of the principal ornaments. In that House, what description of spectacle do we behold? We behold a collection of men, selected originally on account of their power and wealth, invested with enviable privileges and irresponsible power, and inheriting these privileges and that power because they belonged to their forefathers. Such men have every inducement that human nature can devise to transmit their valuable possessions to their posterity, and to have lineal successors to whom to transmit them. Yet what has been the event? Have they increased in numbers, as, according to the Malthusian theory, they must have done? No such thing! It is notorious that, but for perpetual "creations," they would have gone on decreasing in number. That nearly half of the present House of Peers have been made Peers during the last half century; and that, had they been left to their own powers of adding to their numbers, since the accession of the Tudors to the throne, they could hardly have reckoned past a score or two. Why is the principle of increase dead, then, here, where of all conceivable places it ought to live; and why is it living in the instance which I am about to quote, where of all places it ought to have died?

A few years ago, was, by a mere chance, discovered upon a small and barren island, named "Pitcairn's Island," a little colony founded by four or five of the mutineers who ran away with his Majesty's ship Bounty, when under the command of Captain Bligh, on what was called "the Breadfruit-Tree Expedition." This mutiny took place not quite fifty years ago; and after some vicissitudes, it should seem that John Adams, the patriarch of this colony, with four other Englishmen, and an equal number of male native Otaheitans, with a corresponding number of females, took refuge in this little Island of Pitcairn. Here, from accident and the effects of ungoverned

passions, their population was soon diminished. One man fell from a cliff and was killed—the others quarrelled as to the possession of the females, and in a few months Adams and his three companions, with seven women in all, and with the children then existing, not amounting to twenty individuals, were the inhabitants of the island. It was a spot by no means abounding in articles of sustenance. *Animal food* there was none, save such as could be derived from a few rabbits and rats. The birds were principally sea fowl; and upon their eggs, and upon the fish, with which the coast abounded, the colonists for the most part subsisted—obtaining a precarious livelihood with much toil and some danger—and ekeing out these scanty supplies with the fruits which the woods afforded. Grain they had none, nor, as it should seem, any variety of esculent vegetables.— When discovered, Adams and his descendants had been upon the island forty years and upwards; and during this period the numbers of this singular colony amounted to one hundred and eighty persons of all ages. Here the theory of Malthus had taken its full swing in practice. Not content with *doubling* their numbers in each *twenty-five years*, this prolific community had at least *oc-tupled* itself in *forty years*; but is there any man to believe that this was in consequence of the truth of this theory? If so, then such believer must hold, that out of their rabbits and their rats, these colonists contrived to obtain more and better dinners than the House of Lords could do from their estates, if comparative plenty or scarcity of victuals be the cause of high or low states of population; for, whilst the one went on decreasing, the other went on increasing at this fearful rate! This, my Lord, it is impossible to believe; but upon the principle I have laid down, how easily is the whole accounted for?— These colonists thus rapidly increased, not because they had abundance to sustain life, but for the opposite reason, because their fare was meagre and scanty, and obtained only through incessant exercise and exposure of all kinds. Thus they "increased and multiplied," whilst the manors of the luxurious lords were passing into alien hands for want of heirs, and the second estate was literally eating itself off the face of the earth. It may be said that these islanders were removed from contact with many contagious diseases. True—but were they more so than the children of the English peers, surrounded with their wide and lofty park walls, and secured by every means man can devise from the vicissitudes of heat and cold, the stroke of the sun, or the chill of the damp evening sea-breeze? Not so ; deprived of medicine or medical assistance in case of disease or accidents, their exposure to casualties must have been great, and I defy you or any one, my Lord, to account for the different situations of these two bodies of persons, with any show of probability, on grounds other than those I have adduced.

Similar consequences are observed to take place in the black population of the Southern United American States. The numbers of the slaves increase, whilst the emancipated Negroes or freed-blacks decrease in numbers. The first are worked and moderately fed. The second, destitute of taste for the most ordinary luxuries, are enabled by a little labour to indulge themselves to the uttermost in the vulgar sensualities of our nature ; and the *consequence* is remarked by Americans to be as I have described it.

Still these are extreme and insulated instances. Let us take larger bodies, with the circumstances of whose lives we are familiar, and see whether the theory of Malthus explains the phenomena better than I can do, or so well. Look, my Lord, at the " Society of Friends," or " Quakers," as they were at first derisively called. This sect is probably the most opulent in proportion to its numbers of all the bodies of Dissenters. It keeps its own poor in so admirable a manner, that a destitute, or even apparently poor Quaker, is not to be seen—the members of this body almost universally marry, and yet not having been aided by accessions to their numbers by means of conversion to any extent, it is believed that the body has decreased during the last century. I cannot find that they have the means of a correct knowledge of their numbers at any stated periods, but this is their impression. Some may deny the decrease, but no one argues for any sensible increase. This might puzzle

Malthus, but I will take another body as an instance of the slowness of increase where men are properly fed. Of this body your Lordship has, I believe, some knowledge—I mean the body of the freemen or free burgesses of the town from which I now address your Lordship—Newcastle-upon-Tyne. Here I have better *data* on which to proceed. The freemen of Newcastle, I need hardly tell your Lordship, have had, up to the commencement of the last half century, an almost entire and complete monopoly of the trade of this flourishing town. No non-freeman was, before that time, allowed to open a shop within the liberties of the town and county of Newcastle. Of many of the employments they enjoyed also a monopoly— the corporate offices were filled by them alone. The election of members of Parliament being also vested in them, they exclusively had the enjoyment of almost all the local Government official situations, as well as of those under the corporation. They possessed property, both separately, as companies or guildries, and conjointly —they tenanted hospitals exclusively, and were in every possible way a *favoured caste,* enjoying all " the good things" of one of the richest corporations in England or any where else. Hence, without gross imprudence, no free burgess needed to be poor—all might be, and many were, prosperous and wealthy. There were *two* ways of obtaining the freedom of the town —*inheritance* and *servitude*—but as *all* the sons of a freeman were free by birth, they had ample means (according to Mr Malthus) for increasing their numbers. Strange to say, with all these aids, and with the extrinsic aid of the perpetual addition of freemen by servitude, they do not seem to have done so materially, at all events not during the last hundred-and-twenty years. The means I have of shewing this is by a reference to the books of the stewards of the companies, which give the *poll on all the contested elections* from the year 1710 inclusive. The extracts I have obtained through the kindness of my excellent friend their worthy secretary, and his are the calculations of the numbers actually voting. Before, however, going into these results, I shall show, from the same source, the probable proportion of the additions to the body by persons acquiring freedom by servitude.

The following table shows the numbers claiming freedom on each ground for five years.

	Birth.	Servitude.
1832,	43 claimed.	83 claimed.
1833,	40	57
1834,	47	63
1835,	86	88
1836,	31	59
Totals,	247	350

Great total, 597 claimants.

Of these my friend remarks, " 311 persons only were *admitted*. I do not know the proportion of the parties admitted by birth or servitude, but conclude they are in the same ratio as the claimants." Thus, then, it should seem that the additions by servitude have *more than kept pace* with those by birth. The chief cause of non-admission is the inability or unwillingness of many to pay *the Fees*, which amount to about *Eight Pounds*—a heavy sum for a young man in narrow circumstances. This obstacle, however, generally disappears before contested elections, when those, whose claims are valid, become mysteriously possessed of the needful for " taking up their freedom," as it is called ! The *servitude*, however, must be a *bonâ fide* apprenticeship of *seven* years ; and the omission of the father to take up freedom bars the son, though the grandfather may have been free.

I shall now give the particulars of the polls at all the contested elections, from that of the year 1710, down to the passing of the Reform Bill in 1832. From these returns your Lordship will see that the number of votes given in the election of 1722 is nearly equal to the numbers polled in the other subsequent great contests which occurred in 1741, in 1774, in 1777, and in 1780.

Numbers of votes polled at the contested Elections for Newcastle-upon-Tyne, calculated from the books of the Stewards of the Incorporated Companies, by John Brown, Esq., Secretary to the Stewards :—

A.D.		Votes.	
1710.	Sir William Blackett,	1177	Two days only.
	Mr Wrightsen, . .	886	1700 voters probably.
	Mr W. Carr, . .	609	
1715.	Sir William Blackett,	639	
	Mr Wrightsen, . .	550	No time given.
	Mr Clavering, . .	263	
1722.	Mr W. Carr, . .	1234	
	Sir William Blackett,	1158	Probably 2000 voters.
	Mr Wrightsen, . .	831	
1727.	Sir William Blackett,	1202	Three days.
	Mr N. Fenwick, . .	1189	Probably 2000 voters.
	Mr Carr, . . .	620	
1734.	Mr Walter Blackett, .	1354	Eight days.
	N. Fenwick, . . .	1083	1795 voters.
	Mr W. Carr, . .	716	
1741.	Sir Walter Blackett, .	1453	A great contest. Six days.
	Mr N. Fenwick, . .	1231	2391 voters.
	Matthew Ridley, . .	1131	
	William Carr, . .	683	
1774.	Sir Walter Blackett, .	1432	A great contest.
	Sir Matthew Ridley	1411	2162 voters.
	Captain Phipps, . .	795	
	Mr Delaval, . . .	677	
1777.	Sir John Trevelyan, .	1163	2231 voters.
	A. R. Stoney Bowes, .	1068	
1780.	Sir Matthew Ridley, .	1408	
	A. R. S. Bowes, . .	1135	2245 voters.
	Mr Delaval, . . .	1085	

| 1820. The Hon. Mr Scott, Sir Matthew Ridley, Mr Ellison, | } | A single day. 800 only voted.* |

From all this it is evident, that though it is certain that the population of Newcastle-upon-Tyne has been steadily increasing, and from causes capable of being easily pointed out, the freemen or free burgesses, despite the aid of those acquiring freedom by apprenticeship, have not materially added to that increase. Yet, according to the notions of Malthus, this particular set of men, favourably situated as they have been as to worldly circumstances, ought to have been active agents in this increase. What, then, has here checked the " geometrical ratio ?" " Vice, misery, or moral restraint ?" Nothing of the kind. I can answer for it, that none of these have existed in any *extraordinary* degree for many years amongst the freemen of Newcastle.

I shall now, my Lord, attempt to show, by some more extended enquiries, how far these ideas of mine are borne out by national statistics, by a comparison of the known states of the population of countries or parts of countries, with those of other countries or parts of countries, comparing at the same time the modes of living in all and each. I shall endeavour to show this—And first, I would refer your Lordship generally to the state of the Highlands of Scotland, and to that of Ireland, and compare these states with that of Belgium.

The food of the Scotch Highlanders is, your Lordship knows, mostly oatmeal, fish, and potatoes, and other esculent vegetables. The food of the Irish (abundant as that country is in cattle) is, as we all know, much the same. In these countries, families of sixteen, eighteen, or twenty children, are quite common ; and amongst the poor, unhappily the great mass of the people, eight, ten, or even a dozen children are universally to be met with. What the real *average family* amongst these classes, in these countries, actually is, I do not know ; but I should calculate it at not less than *six living children* to each family. Contrast this with the rich pastoral country of the Netherlands, where flesh meat, and rich cheese, and milk, constitute the food of the inha-

bitants to a great extent. In these countries a family of half the number of a Highland or Irish family would be, and is looked at as a prodigy, and the father and mother would probably be presented to King Leopold as most meritoriously adding to the number of his lieges—without a thought of Malthus. This, however, is a *general* comparison, and I shall now go more methodically to work, and show how the calculated populations of various countries rise or fall according to the nature and quantity of their food.

The most striking and curious exemplification of the effects of the different modes of living upon population, is to be found, perhaps, in the statistics of the Russian empire, including, as it does, various races of people, living in climates the most different, upon soils the most opposite in quality, and all under one government, though foreign to each other in habits, modes of life, and language. The great area of the Russian empire, that is to say, all its Asiatic, and a large part of its European dominions, is inhabited by people the most truly pastoral of any existing in the world. Their wealth is cattle—their exports the tallow, hides, and horns—their food the flesh. A small portion of the Russian empire is, however, of a totally different character. The kingdom of Poland, and the provinces bordering upon it, are essentially corn countries, and hence the food of the people is totally different from that of the population of the rest of the immense empire of the Czars. Throughout the immense pastoral provinces, where the *cattle are killed for the sake of the tallow and hides,* the flesh, salted or frozen, is of course the food of the people, being so plentiful as to be almost valueless. This is apparent in the fact, that even in the capital, in St Petersburg itself, beef may always be had at a price *hardly amounting to an English penny per lb.*, and the very choicest meat at three halfpence, English, per lb., though the cattle are driven from a great distance for the supply of the capital; and frozen game and salt meats of all descriptions are plentiful and cheap in the extreme.

* In 1832, the number of freemen resident within seven miles of Newcastle, was 1619 only. (*Mr Brown's note.*)

It is also to be observed, that there exist no political or other checks to the increase of the Russian population. The serfs being a valuable part of the estate, the Russian landlord, so far from wishing to clear his lands, counts up his boors, as he does his cattle, by the head, wishing both to increase; and the conscriptions for the armies are far more burthensome in his eyes, when directed towards the two, than the four-legged stock on his estate. Bearing all these circumstances in mind, let us look at the facts as detailed in " M. Hassel's tables of the population of Russia," as reprinted by Malte Brun, taking first the great divisions. In giving these I must premise, that the *Russian square mile* of M. Hassel is equal to *twenty English square miles,* or rather more than *two English square leagues.*

Name of Divisions.		Square miles in it.	Population.	No. of people to a square mile.
RUSSIAN EMPIRE, (divided into)	.	367,494	59,263,700	161
European Asia,	.	72,861	44,118,600	606
Kingdom of Poland,	.	2,293	3,541,900	1,544
Asiatic Russia,	.	268,339	11,663,200	43⅝
American Russia,	.	24,000	50,000	2¼

Here then we see that in the kingdom of Poland, where corn is a great proportion of the food of the people, rather than animal food, but at the same time with abundance of it, the numbers on a Russian square mile are 1544 individuals, or nearly *ten times* the average of all the rest of the empire! If we take more minute divisions, the same results show themselves. In the Duchy of Courland, for instance, and in Western Russia, the results are as follows. These countries border upon Poland, and are for the most part similar as to the other circumstances.

Division.		Square miles in it, (fractions omitted).	Population.	Persons to a square mile.
Courland, . .	.	509	581,300	1,142
WESTERN RUSSIA, (including)	.	7,537	8,488,900	1,125
Government of Wilna,	.	1,081	1,357,400	1,255
—————— of Grodno,	.	326	868,100	1,619
—————— of Bialystock,		158	224,600	1,422
—————— of Witepsk,	.	668	934,900	1,398
—————— of Mohilew,	.	918	985,400	1,073
—————— of Minsk,	.	1,832	1,160,100	633
—————— of Volhynia,	.	1,394	1,496,300	1,072
—————— of Podolia,	.	948	1,462,190	1,542

I have been thus particular, in order to show that this population is spread equally over these countries, and not arising from masses collected in a few large cities or towns.

If we contrast with these tables some of the lesser divisions of Eastern or Asiatic Russia, the difference will be found to be, even under the most favourable circumstances, very striking. Let us instance the two kingdoms of Kasan and Astrakhan. These contain some of the finest pastoral provinces of Russia. The quantities of tallow produced by them are very large, and of remarkably fine quality, though less skilfully dealt with than in other districts.

Names of Divisions.		Square miles.	Population.	Persons to each mile.
KINGDOM OF KASAN, . (including)	.	11,521	5,746,250	498
Government of Kasan,	.	1,123	1,028,150	915
—————— of Viatka,	.	2,221	1,293,800	582
—————— of Perm,	.	5,996	1,269,900	212
—————— of Simbrisk,	.	1,402	1,119,400	798
—————— of Pinsa,	.	777	1,035,000	1,331

Names of Divisions.	Square miles.	Population.	Persons to each mile.
KINGDOM OF ASTRAKHAN, (including)	13,823	2,598,700	118
Government of Astrakhan,	3,899	222,700	57
—————— of Sawtow,	4,297	1,333,500	310
—————— of Orenburgh,	5,626	1,043,500	185

These tables, published under sanction of the Russian Government, are, past doubt, substantially correct. The contrasts they present are surely extraordinary ; and what is there in the theory of Malthus to account for these discrepancies, unless vice, misery, and moral restraint can be shown to exist where animal food is to be had nearly gratis, and where population is encouraged both by the owners of the soil, and the government of the country !

Such results, one would imagine, might have led M. Malte Brun, and others conversant with such details, to have doubted of the soundness of the notion, that mere populousness was a sign of the prosperity of nations. Theories, however, are spectacles through which men unhappily look at facts, as the following extract from M. Malte Brun's description of France (for to France I now turn) will evince. Thus speaks Malte Brun of Southern France :—

" We have had occasion to observe the mild climate, the romantic sites, and the remains of Roman power in the twenty-eight departments that form the southern region of France. The inhabitants, it has been seen, are favoured by nature ; the different productions are admirably suited for their country ; with the exception of the mountains, the soil is every-where fruitful. But if the *population* be compared with the surface, it will be found that the result accords ill with the natural advantages of the same vast region which makes up more than a third part of the kingdom. The extent is equal to 9000 square leagues ; the population to 8,404,000 individuals ; thus the number of inhabitants to every square league does not amount to nine hundred and thirty-four, a result below the mean number in the other divisions of the same country. Such facts are not without their value ; (*très veritable, M. Malte Brun !*) if the best and most fruitful part of France is comparatively poor and ill-peopled, it proves how much the munificence of nature may be surpassed by the industry and resources of man. Government, too, may derive an important lesson from the same fact ; it may thus be taught to appreciate the elements of its wealth and power. Thirteen departments make up the western region ; the population relatively to the surface is greater than the last, for 5,428,000 inhabitants are scattered over a surface of 4200 square leagues ; consequently, the average number to every square league exceeds 1290. Still the advantages of education are little known in the western region ; in that point it is almost on a level with the preceding. How much, then, might the population and wealth be increased, if ignorance no longer formed a barrier to the expansion of industry ?"—*Malte Brun, Geography,* vol. viii. p. 273.

Let us *analyze* this passage, strange and self-contradictory as it is. The southern departments of France, it seems, are eminently fruitful. But then the people are only 934 to the square league—much below the mean number of other divisions. *Therefore,* says he, these districts are comparatively *poor* and ill-peopled, and places them below the other better peopled regions with 1290 to the square league, admitting, at the same time, that, in point of *education and science, they are on a par !* He, in the same breath, *blames the Government* for this disparity. Now, is not this monstrous, my Lord ? Here we have a region stigmatized as " poor," because it divides *greater natural wealth* amongst *fewer inhabitants* than another region. At the same time, we have this other region held forth as comparatively *better,* because it has more people, though these people are admitted to have no more scientific skill than their rivals to do away with the effects of the natural sterility of their soil, and augment their means of living comfortably nearer to their numerical extent. How, too, was a Government to help this ? If the really poor country—I mean the populous one—were to be helped, Government *might* do this, either by giving them money and provisions, or enabling them to emigrate. But how is it to help the *really rich district?* If, in despite of the absence of Malthus's check of "*misery*," they will not produce more children—if, according to Malte Brun, they will not produce *this unerring evidence* of "industry"—how, in the name of all that is rational, can "Government" help that? The truth here is, that the po-

verty has produced the population; and, in proof of this, I shall cite as evidence the poorest province of all France—the province which all travellers agree in describing as being the *likest to Ireland*—Bretagne or Brittany. It is as follows:—

BRETAGNE, OR BRITTANY,
including—

1.	Department of Finisterre,	1376 Population to the square league.
2.	— Cotè du Nord,	1470
3.	— Le Mortchan,	1157
4.	— Isle de Vilaine,	1661
5.	— Bas de Loire,	1405

5)7069

1414 Average to the square league.

And yet this is confessedly the poorest and most squalid, the least comfortable and most ragged, of the French departments : so true is it that want and numbers always go on *increasing together*, and *vice versa*.

Let us now look at India, and we shall find precisely the same results. In the immense territory of Indostan, it is well known that the principal food of the inhabitants is rice. The Braminical religion forbids the use of animal food, and this religion is predominant over the greater portion of this vast region. The consequence of this mode of life is, that the numbers of the people so press upon their means of subsistence, that famines frequently occur, and the population is actually thinned, for a brief space, by death from hunger; soon, however, to be replenished by fresh myriads.

M. Malte Brun states the area of Indostan, including both the British and native territories, at *one million two hundred and eighty thousand square miles English*. This broad expanse is crossed by chains of immense mountains quite uninhabitable, and much of the more level parts of the country is yet forest, swamp, and jungle, the domain of the elephant, the tiger, the buffalo, and the rhinoceros; and yet the population is estimated as high as *one hundred and thirty-four* millions of human beings, being, in round numbers, about *eleven hundred to the British square league for the whole*, which is far beyond that of the most fertile departments of the beautiful country of France, and probably, if the space they in fact occupy could be accurately estimated, far beyond that of any *European*

country, not excepting even poor and miserable Ireland, which is the most populous of all. In China, similar causes are known to have produced similar consequences; and frightful scenes of child-murder and child-abandonment are believed to be of constant occurrence throughout the Celestial empire. The exact population can only be guessed at, and the guesses are various. Allerstein, in 1743, estimated the Chinese people at one hundred and ninety-eight millions, which Malte Brun reduces to one hundred and fifty millions, but which Macartney, in 1795, made to amount to three hundred and thirty millions. Taking the medium of *two hundred millions*, the result to the square mile is enormous, the area of China being only one million two hundred and ninety-seven thousand nine hundred and ninety-nine square miles, or, in round numbers, one hundred and forty-five thousand square leagues— whilst Macartney's estimate would give two thousand seven hundred persons to every square league of this immense empire; which, however, over-peopled as it is known to be, is hardly credible. But what a contrast here with beef-crammed, gross, swinish Russia!

It is lamentable to think, my Lord, that next to these Eastern countries, one of the most populous in the world is poor and squalid Ireland. The entire area of Ireland is 31,875 square English miles. The population is now eight millions, at least; but if the rate of increase from 1821 to 1831 be taken, probably nearer eight millions and a-half, or, in round numbers, *two thousand five hundred persons* to each square league; and this in a country from which much of the wheat, and nearly all the live-stock are exported, and where it is known that, out of twenty million acres, only fourteen millions are cultivated, or in any way productive of food for the inhabitants. In countries where pasturage and tillage are both pursued, and the food of the inhabitants is of average goodness, the population is always moderate. In highly fertile Italy, for instance, there are *sixteen millions* of persons upon *ten thousand French square leagues*, which are its area, being 1600 to the league—and the rate of increase is trifling—the *average* of births to a marriage being *three only*. In the Netherlands, which is beyond question the most fertile and most and best cultivated tract in Europe —where there are no mountains, and hardly an impediment to tillage ; in short, where every rood of land is productive, and where pasturage and tillage are equally pursued, we have similar results, a stationary and not immoderate population, living well, and their numbers only in accordance with their food. In this beautiful country, which is like one great garden, there is not one person for each hectare of land (two and a-half acres English), despite the influx of persons thither since the end of the war in 1815, and yet these lands are nearly all in the highest state of productiveness (a population below that of half-cultivated, half-starved Ireland) ; whilst *here*, instead of families of a dozen children being seen, the *average produce of a marriage is only four children ;* and the population remains nearly stationary, the proportion of deaths to births being of course very high. The increase of population in the United States has been much harped upon by Mr Malthus and others. Of this I have only to say, that, of all countries, it is the least likely for obtaining true results ; the *immigration* there of persons, fleeing from the wretchedness of Europe, being so great and constant as to baffle calculation.

Here, my Lord, I conclude, not from want of matter, but from a fear of tedious repetition. The facts I have adduced, however, are enough for me.

I conclude from them the following **axioms**, as to the truth of which I am confident :

1st, That where a people are amply and sufficiently supplied with solid food, their tendency is upon the whole not to increase.

2d, That in all societies so supplied, the great bulk of the population are stationary as to number, and that any increase at one end amongst the poorest is counteracted by a diminution at the other end amongst the luxurious.

3d, That this law generally pervades nature, inasmuch as the inferior animals, and all vegetable productions, cease to be productive if their food or soil be naturally or artificially too abundant or too rich.

4th, That, on the other hand, if the species be endangered, by want of sufficient sustenance, or by other enfeebling causes, the tendency to increase is immediately augmented, and that this general law pervades the vegetable as well as animal kingdom.

5th, That these laws clearly account for the great differences as to increase of population in different countries, and that no other theory has accounted, nor can account, for these differences.

Such, my Lord, are the effects which the foregoing considerations have produced upon my mind. That they should produce a similar impression upon your Lordship's, it would be arrogant in me to hope. If, however, this paper should meet the eye of your Lordship, and have cogency enough to induce you to pause and reconsider this question, or deem it worthy of a reconsideration, I shall be amply repaid by the feeling that I have not, at all events, written in vain. Nor do I altogether despair of this ; because I, like your Lordship, was at one time wholly subdued by the at once confident and plausible assertions of Malthus, to which, at that period, I had absolutely nothing to oppose, but which, I am now convinced, are altogether futile, and founded on a total ignorance of physiology and existing facts.

With every deference for your Lordship, and a deep respect for your Lordship's great and varied acquirements and talents,

I have the honour to remain,
My Lord,
Your Lordship's most obedient
and humble servant,
THOMAS DOUBLEDAY.

ART. IV.—A THEORY OF POPULATION, DEDUCED FROM THE GENERAL LAW OF ANIMAL FERTILITY.

1. *Principles of Physiology, General and Comparative.* By William B. Carpenter, M.D., F.R.S., F.G.S. Third Edition. London. John Churchill.

2. *Outlines of Comparative Physiology, &c.* By Louis Agassiz and A. A. Gould. London. H. G. Bohn.

3. *On Parthenogenesis; or, the Successive Production of Pro-creating Individuals from a Single Ovum.* By Richard Owen, F.R.S., &c. London. John Van Voorst.

4. *On the Alternation of Generations.* By Joh. Japetus Sm. Steenstrup. Translated by George Busk. London. Printed for the Ray Society.

5. *The True Law of Population shown to be connected with the Food of the People.* By Thomas Doubleday, Esq. Second Edition. London. George Peirce.

6. *The Cyclopædia of Anatomy and Physiology.* Edited by Robert B. Todd, M.D., F.R.S. Longman and Co.

" IN a very recent publication," says Dr. Whately, " I have seen mention made of a person who discovered the falsity of a certain doctrine (which, by the way, is nevertheless a true one, that of Malthus) *instinctively.* This kind of instinct, *i. e.,* the habit of forming opinions at the suggestion rather of feeling than of reason, is very common." * There can be little doubt that this remark refers to a passage in the preface to Double-day's " True Law of Population," wherein the writer says :—

" Happening many years ago, in the presence of a late relative, long since deceased, remarkable both for the sagacity and extended benevolence of his general views on philosophical subjects, to draw some of those startling, though not illogical, conclusions which seemed to flow from theories then recently broached as to this subject, and much in vogue at the time, the reply was this :—' Depend upon it, my dear nephew, that you and I may safely decline to yield an implicit assent, though we may not, on the instant, be able to refute them, to views from which consequences, such as you have drawn, legitimately flow. Though I may not live to see it, nor you, a time will come when this mystery will be unveiled, and when a perhaps now mysterious, but, beyond doubt, a beneficent law will be discovered, regulating this matter, in accordance with all the rest that we see of God's moral government of the world.' "

On comparing these extracts we cannot compliment Dr.

---

* Introductory Lectures on Political Economy, 3rd edit., p. 163.

Whately, either upon the fairness of his stricture or the depth of his insight. To apply the term instinctive to the conclusion thus drawn, indicates a misunderstanding of the mental process leading to it. Not a feeling but a broad generalisation is the basis on which such a conclusion rests. He who arrives at it in the manner above implied does so by comparing, in a more or less conscious way, the alleged truth with other truths, and discovering that it is not congruous with them. By daily-accumulating experience he becomes impressed with the inherent tendency of things towards good—sees going on universally a patient self-rectification. He finds that the *vis medicatrix naturæ*—or rather the process which we describe by that expression—is not limited to the cure of wounds and diseases, but pervades creation. From the lowly fungus which, under varying circumstances, assumes varying forms of organization, up to the tree that grows obliquely, if it cannot otherwise get to the light—from the highest human faculty which increases or dwindles according to the demands made on it, down to the polype that changes its skin into stomach and its stomach into skin when turned inside out—he everywhere sees at work an essential beneficence. Equally in the attainment of fitness for a new climate, or skill in a new occupation—in the diminution of a suppressed desire, and in the growing pleasure that attends the performance of a duty—in the gradual evanescence of grief, and in the callousness that follows long-continued privations— he perceives this remedial action. Whether he contemplates the acquirement, by each race, of a liking for the mode of life circumstances dictate—whether he regards the process by which different nations are slowly forced to produce those commodities only, that it is best for the world they should produce—or whether he looks at the repeated re-establishment, amongst a turbulent people, of the form of government best fitted for them —he is alike struck with the self-sufficingness of things. And when, after recognising this throughout the whole organic world, he finds that it extends to the inorganic also—when he reads that though Newton feared for the stability of the solar system, yet Laplace found that all planetary perturbations are self-neutralizing—when he thus sees that perfection exists even where so high an intelligence failed to perceive it—he is still more convinced that in all cases we shall discover harmony and completeness when we know how to look for them. Hence, if any one propounds to him a theory implying in nature an ineradicable defect, he hesitates to receive it. That the human constitution should include some condition which must ever continue to entail either physical or moral pain, is at variance with all that a wide experience teaches him. And finding the alleged fact conflict with universal facts, he concludes that it is probably untrue. He concludes this, not instinctively, but rationally, and his argument corresponds completely with the logical form—as in all other cases I have observed a certain sequence of phenomena, I infer that there will be the same sequence in this case also. Moreover, such a belief is not only a rational, but the truly religious one. Faith in the essential beneficence of things is the highest kind of faith. And considering his position, a little more of this faith would have been by no means unbecoming in the Archbishop of Dublin.

But however right the point of view from which Mr. Doubleday, influenced by his relative, has studied the population question, it does not follow that he has solved it. We are of opinion that he has not done so. There is one fact which seems to us at once fatal to his hypothesis; namely, that it does not fulfil the very condition which it purports to fulfil: it does not disclose a self-adjusting law. The theory which Mr. Doubleday seeks to establish is, that throughout both the animal and vegetable kingdoms—

" Over feeding checks increase; whilst, on the other hand, a limited or deficient nutriment stimulates and adds to it." (P. 17.)

Or, as he elsewhere says,—

" Be the range of the natural power to increase in any species what it may, the *plethoric* state invariably checks it, and the *deplethoric* state invariably develops it; and this happens in the exact ratio of the intensity and completeness of each state, until each state be carried so far as to bring about the actual death of the animal or plant itself." (P. 20.)

In this arrangement Mr. Doubleday sees a guarantee for the maintenance of species. He argues that the plethoric state of the individuals constituting any race of organisms presupposes conditions so favourable to life that the race can be in no danger; and that rapidity of multiplication becomes needless. Conversely he argues that a deplethoric state implies unfavourable conditions—implies, consequently, unusual mortality; that is, —implies a necessity for increased fertility to prevent the race from dying out. And hence, applying the law to mankind, he infers that there is a state of body intermediate between the plethoric and the deplethoric, under which the rate of increase will not be greater than needful; and that a sufficient supply of good food to all, is the chief condition to the attainment of such a state.

Now, without denying that there is some such law of variation as this which Mr. Doubleday points out, we hold that it cannot alone constitute the law of population, because, as already hinted, it does not really disclose a self-rectifying arrangement. We shall quickly see this on applying it to the human race as now existing. Mr. Doubleday will admit, or rather, will assert, that on the average mankind are at present in the deplethoric state; he will argue that the undue rate of increase commonly complained of results from this; and he will infer that to produce a comparatively plethoric state in all is the only remedy. But how, under the alleged law, can a comparatively plethoric state ever be attained to? If the present production of necessaries of life is insufficient for the normal nutrition of the race, and if the resulting deplethoric state involves that the next generation will greatly exceed the present in numbers, then, for anything that appears to the contrary, the next generation will be in a more deplethoric state still. Unless Mr. Doubleday can show that the means of subsistence will increase *more* rapidly than the unduly fertile people, he cannot prove the existence of any remedial process. Nay, indeed, he must show that his law *involves*, under such circumstances, a greater increase of food than of people. Now he neither does nor can show this; and thus the alleged law lacks that very property of self-adjustment, which he rightly regards as the test of the real law.

Mr. Doubleday has given us, not the whole truth, but only a small fraction of it. He might, *à priori*, have inferred this, had he taken a wider view of the phenomena. For just the same necessity that demands variations in the fertility of each race to balance variations in its mortality, *still more imperatively demands variations in the fertilities of different races to balance variations in their mortalities;* and whoever has duly familiarised himself with the simplicity and universality of natural agencies, can scarcely doubt that *these minor variations of fertility observable in the same species, and these great variations of fertility which distinguish different species, are determined by the same cause.* Had Mr. Doubleday recognised this probability, he would have seen that no such special cause as that he assigns, was likely to be the true one; but that some more general cause must be looked for: and he would further have seen, that such more general cause was not to be discovered without inquiring more deeply into organic phenomena than he has done.

Some clear idea of the nature of Life itself, must, indeed, form a needful preliminary. We may be sure that a search for the influences determining the maintenance and multiplication of living organisms, cannot be successfully carried out unless we understand what is the peculiar property of a living organism —what is the widest generalization of the phenomena that indicate life. By way of preparation, therefore, for the Theory of

Population presently to be developed, we propose devoting a brief space to this prior question.

And here we are at once met by the difficulty, that the widest, and it would appear also, the best definition of Life, is one that includes both the organic and inorganic. Startling though the assertion will be to most, it nevertheless seems true that, as Coleridge or rather Schelling points out, the characteristic which, manifested in a high degree, we call Life, is a characteristic manifested, only in a lower degree, by so-called inanimate objects. And hard as it is to believe this, yet the discoveries of chemists, who find that the alleged distinction between organic and inorganic compounds does not hold good, and the discoveries of physiologists, who are rapidly narrowing the once broad boundary line between the two divisions, day after day serve to confirm it. Hence, in seeking for a definition that shall distinguish organic existence from inorganic existence, we must not expect to find one that will be rigidly true in all cases. For if there be not such a line of demarcation in nature, no ingenuity of ours can establish one. All we can hope for is, some expression that shall conveniently classify the two, and shall be generally, though not universally, applicable.

Employing the term, then, in its usual sense, as applicable only to organisms, Life may be defined as—*the co-ordination of actions*. The growth of a crystal, which is the highest inorganic process we are acquainted with, involves but one action—that of accretion. The growth of a cell, which is the lowest organic process, involves two actions—accretion and disintegration—repair and waste—assimilation and oxidation. Wholly deprive a cell of oxygen, and it becomes inert—ceases to manifest vital phenomena; or, as we say, dies. Give it no matter to assimilate, and it wastes away and disappears, from continued oxidation. Evidently, then, it is in the balance of these two actions that the life consists. It is not in the assimilation alone; for the crystal assimilates: neither is it in the oxidation alone; for oxidation is common to inorganic matter: but it is in the joint maintenance of these—the *co-ordination* of them. So long as the two go on together, life continues: suspend either of them, and the result is—death.

The attribute which thus distinguishes the lowest organic from the highest inorganic bodies, similarly distinguishes the higher organisms from the lower ones. It is in the greater complexity of the co-ordination—that is, in the greater number and variety of the co-ordinated actions—that every advance in the scale of being essentially consists. And whether we regard the numerous vital processes carried on in a creature of complex structure as so many additional processes, or whether, more philosophically, we regard them as subdivisions of the two fundamental ones—oxidation and accretion—the co-ordination of them is still the life. Thus turning to what is physiologically classified as the *vegetative system*, we see that stomach, lungs, heart, liver, skin, and the rest, must work in concert. If one of them does too much or too little—that is, if the co-ordination be imperfect—the life is disturbed; and if one of them ceases to act—that is, if the co-ordination be destroyed—the life is destroyed. So likewise is it with the *animal system*, which indirectly assists in co-ordinating the actions of the viscera by supplying food and oxygen. Its component parts, the limbs, senses, and instruments of attack or defence must perform their several offices in proper sequence; and further, must conjointly minister to the periodic demands of the viscera, that these r ₍y in turn supply blood. How completely the several attributes of animal life come within the definition, we shall best see on going through them *seriatim*.

Thus *Strength* results from the co-ordination of actions; for it is produced by the simultaneous contraction of many muscles and many fibres of each muscle; and the strength is great in proportion to the number of these acting together, that is—in proportion to the co-ordination. *Swiftness* also, depending partly on strength, but requiring also the rapid alternation of movements, equally comes under the expression; seeing that, other things equal, the more quickly sequent actions can be made to follow each other, the more completely are they co-ordinated. So, too, is it with *Agility* ; the power of a chamois to spring with safety from crag to crag implies accurate co-ordination in the movements of many different muscles, and a due subordination of them all to the perceptions. The definition similarly includes *Instinct*, which consists in the uniform succession of certain actions or series of actions after certain sensations or groups of sensations; and that which surprises us in instinct is the accuracy with which these compound actions respond to these compound sensations; that is—the completeness of their co-ordination. Thus, likewise, is it with *Intelligence*, even in its highest manifestations. That which we call. rationality is the power to combine, or co-ordinate a great number and a great variety of complex actions for the achievement of a desired result. The husbandman has in the course of years, by drainage and manuring, to bring his ground into a fertile state; in the autumn he must plough, harrow, and sow, for his next year's crop; must subsequently hoe and weed, keep out cattle, and scare away birds; when harvest comes, must adapt the mode and time of getting in his produce to the weather and the labour market; he must afterwards decide when, and where, and how to sell to the best advantage; and must do all this that he may get food and clothing for his family. By properly co-ordinating these various processes (each of which involves many others)—by choosing right modes, right times, right quantities, right qualities, and performing his acts in right order, he attains his end. But if he have done too little of this, or too much of that; or have done one thing when he should have done another—if his proceedings have been badly co-ordinated—that is, if he have lacked intelligence—he fails.

We find, then, that *the co-ordination of actions* is a definition of Life, which includes alike its highest and its lowest manifestations; and not only so, but expresses likewise the degree of Life, seeing that the Life is high in proportion as the co-ordination is great. Proceeding upwards, from the simplest organic cell in which there are but two interdependent actions, on through the group in which many such cells are acting in concert, on through the higher group in which some of these cells assume mainly the respiratory and others the assimilative function—proceeding still to organisms in which these two functions are subdivided into many others, and in which some cells begin to act together as contractile fibres; next to organisms in which the visceral division of labour is carried yet further, and in which many contractile fibres act together as muscles—ascending again to creatures that combine the movements of several limbs and many bones and muscles in one action; and further, to creatures in which complex impressions are followed by the complex acts we term instinctive—and arriving finally at man, in whom not only are the separate acts complex, but who achieves his ends by combining together an immense number and variety of acts often extending through years—we see that the progress is uniformly towards greater co-ordination of actions. Moreover, this co-ordination of actions unconsciously constitutes the essence of our common notion of life ; for we shall find, on inquiry, that when we infer the death of an animal, which does not move on being touched, we infer it because we miss the usual co-ordination of a sensation and a motion : and we shall also find, that the test by which we habitually rank creatures high or low in the scale of vitality is the degree of co-ordination their actions exhibit.

Further evidence that this is the true definition of life may be found in the fact, that the latest and most philosophical classification in zoology is based upon the structure of the co-ordinating apparatus, or what we commonly term the nervous system. Hunter aptly defined the function of the nerves as *internuncial.* That the separate parts of an organism may act in concert, a constant intercommunication must be kept up.

This intercommunication is maintained by the nerves; and there are no actions—visceral, muscular, perceptive, or other—but what are directed and adjusted by them. When, therefore, we find that the modern division of the animal kingdom into *Acrita, Nematoneura, Homogangliata, Heterogangliata,* and *Vertebrata,* is a division expressive of the several forms of the internuncial or co-ordinating apparatus; and when, still more significantly, we find that these several classes rank *according to the degree in which the co-ordinating apparatus is developed,* and this, even up to man, in whom the development of it is the greatest; we have strong confirmation of the doctrine that Life and the co-ordination of actions are iden-tical*.

There remains but to notice the objection which possibly may be raised, that the co-ordination of actions is not life, but the ability to maintain life. Lack of space forbids going into this at length. It must suffice to say, that life and the ability to maintain life will be found the same. We per-petually expend the vitality we have that we may continue our vitality. Our power to breathe a minute hence depends upon our breathing now. We must digest during this week that we may have strength to digest next. That we may get more food, we must use the force which the food we have eaten gives us. Everywhere vigorous life is the strength, activity, and sagacity whereby life is maintained; and equally in descending the scale of being, or in watching the decline of an invalid, we see that the ebbing away of life is the ebbing away of the ability to preserve life.

Ending here this preliminary dissertation, let us now proceed to our special subject.

§ 1. On contemplating its general circumstances, we perceive that any race of organisms is subject to two sets of conflicting influences. On the one hand by natural death, by enemies, by lack of food, by atmospheric changes, &c., it is constantly being destroyed. On the other hand, partly by the strength, swiftness, and sagacity of its members, and partly by their fertility, it is constantly being maintained. These conflicting sets of influences may be conveniently generalized as—the forces destructive of race, and the forces preservative of race.

§ 2. Whilst any race continues to exist, the forces destructive

---

* It may be needful to remark, that by the proposed expression it is in-tended to define—not Life in its essence ; but, Life as manifested to us—not Life as a *noumenon ;* but, Life as a *phenomenon.* The ultimate mystery is as great as ever ; seeing that there remains unsolved the question—What *determines* the co-ordination of actions ?

of it and the forces preservative of it must perpetually tend towards equilibrium. If the forces destructive of it decrease, the race must gradually become more numerous, until, either from lack of food or from increase of enemies, the destroying forces again balance the preserving forces. If, reversely, the forces destructive of it increase, then the race must diminish, until, either from its food becoming relatively more abundant, or from its enemies dying of hunger, the destroying forces sink to the level of the preserving forces. Should the destroying forces be of a kind that cannot be thus met (as great change of climate), the race, by becoming extinct, is removed out of the category. Hence this is necessarily the *law of maintenance* of all races; seeing that when they cease to conform to it they cease to be.

Now the forces preservative of race are two—ability in each member of the race to preserve itself, and ability to produce other members—power to maintain individual life, and power to propagate the species. These must vary inversely. When, from lowness of organization, the ability to contend with external dangers is small, there must be great fertility to compensate for the consequent mortality; otherwise the race must die out. When, on the contrary, high endowments give much capacity of self-preservation, there needs a correspondingly low degree of fertility. Given the dangers to be met as a constant quantity; then, as the ability of any species to meet them must be a constant quantity too, and as this is made up of the two factors—power to maintain individual life and power to multiply—these cannot do other than vary inversely.

§ 3. To show that observed phenomena harmonise with this *à priori* principle seems scarcely needful. But, though axiomatic in its character, and therefore incapable of being rendered more certain, yet illustrations of the conformity to it which nature everywhere exhibits, will facilitate the general apprehension of it.

In the vegetable kingdom we find that the species consisting of simple cells, exhibit the highest reproductive power. The yeast fungus, which in a few hours propagates itself throughout a large mass of wort, offers a familiar example of the extreme rapidity with which these lowly organisms multiply. In the *Protococcus nivalis*, a microscopic plant which in the course of a night reddens many square miles of snow, we have a like example; as also in the minute *Algæ*, which colour the waters of stagnant pools. The sudden appearance of green films on damp decaying surfaces, the spread of mould over stale food, and the rapid destruction of crops by mildew, afford further instances. If we ascend a step to plants of appreciable size, we still find that in proportion as the organization is low the fertility is great. Thus of the common puff-ball, which is little more than a mere aggregation of cells, Fries says, "in a single individual of *Reticularia maxima,* I have counted (calculated?) 10,000,000 sporules." From this point upwards, increase of bulk and greater complexity of structure are still accompanied by diminished reproductive power; instance the *Macrocystis pyrifera,* a gigantic sea-weed, which sometimes attains a length of 1500 feet, of which Carpenter remarks, "This development of the nutritive surface takes place at the expense of the fructifying apparatus, which is here quite subordinate."* And when we arrive at the highly-organized exogenous trees, we find that not only are they many years before beginning to bear with any abundance, but that even then they produce, at the outside, but a few thousand seeds in a twelvemonth. During its centuries of existence, an oak does not develop as many acorns as a fungus does spores in a single night.

Still more clearly is this truth illustrated throughout the animal kingdom. Though not so great as the fertility of the Protophyta, which, as Prof. Henslow says, in some cases passes comprehension, the fertility of the Protozoa is yet almost beyond belief. In the polygastric animalcules spontaneous fission takes place so rapidly that "it has been calculated by Prof. Ehrenberg that no fewer than 268 millions might be produced in a month from a single *Paramecium;*"† and even this astonishing rate of increase is far exceeded in another species, one individual of which, "only to be perceived by means of a high magnifying power, is calculated to generate 170 billions in four days."‡ Amongst the larger organisms exhibiting this lowest mode of reproduction under a modified form—that of gemmation—we see that, though not nearly so rapid as in the Infusoria, the rate of multiplication is still extremely high. This fact is well illustrated by the polypes; and in the apparent suddenness with which whole districts are blighted by the Aphis (multiplying by internal gemmation), we have a familiar instance of the startling results which the parthenogenetic process can achieve. Where reproduction becomes occasional instead of continuous, as it does amongst higher creatures, the fertility equally bears an inverse ratio to the development. "The queen ant of the African *Termites* lays 80,000 eggs in twenty-four hours; and the common hair worm (*Gordius*) as many as 8,000,000 in less than one day."§ Amongst the *Vertebrata* the lowest are still the most prolific. "It has been calculated," says Carpenter, "that above a million of eggs are produced at once by a single cod-

---

* Prin. of Phys., 2nd edit. p. 77.   † Ibid., 3rd edit. p. 249.
‡ Ibid., p. 124.   § Agassiz and Gould, p. 274.

fish."* In the strong and sagacious shark comparatively few are found. Still less fertile are the higher reptiles. And amongst the Mammalia, beginning with small Rodents, which quickly reach maturity, produce large litters, and several litters in the year; advancing step by step to the higher mammals, some of which are long in attaining the reproductive age, others of which produce but one litter in a year, others but one young one at a time, others who unite these peculiarities; and ending with the elephant and man, the least prolific of all, we find that throughout this class, as throughout the rest, ability to multiply decreases as ability to maintain individual life increases.

§ 4. The *à priori* principle thus exemplified has an obverse of a like axiomatic character. We have seen that for the continuance of any race of organisms it is needful that the power of self-preservation and the power of reproduction should vary inversely. We shall now see that, quite irrespective of such an end to be subserved, these powers could not do otherwise than vary inversely. In the nature of things species can subsist only by conforming to this law; and equally in the nature of things they cannot help conforming to it.

Reproduction, under all its forms, may be described as the separation of portions of a parent plant or animal for the purpose of forming other plants or animals. Whether it be by spontaneous fission, by gemmation, or by gemmules; whether the detached products be bulbels, spores or seeds, ovisacs, ova or spermatozoa; or however the process of multiplication be modified, it essentially consists in the throwing off of parts of adult organisms for the purpose of making new organisms. On the other hand, self-preservation is fundamentally a maintenance of the organism in undiminished bulk. Amongst the lowest forms of life, aggregation of tissue is the only mode in which the self-preserving power is shown. Even in the highest, sustaining the body in its integrity is that in which self-preservation most truly consists—is the end which the widest intelligence is indirectly made to subserve. Whilst, on the one side, it cannot be denied that the increase of tissue constituting growth is self-preservation both in essence and in result; neither can it, on the other side, be denied that a diminution of tissue, either from injury, disease, or old age, is in both essence and result the reverse.

Hence the maintenance of the individual and the propagation of the race, being respectively aggregative and separative, *necessarily* vary inversely. Every generative product is a deduction from the parental life; and, as already pointed out, to diminish life is to diminish the ability to preserve life. The portion

---

* Prin. of Phys., 3rd edit. p. 964.

thrown off is organised matter; vital force has been expended in the organisation of it, and in the assimilation of its component elements; which vital force, had no such portion been made and thrown off, *would have been available for the preservation of the parent.*

Neither of these forces, therefore, can increase, save at the expense of the other. The one draws in and incorporates new material; the other throws off material previously incorporated. The one adds to; the other takes from. Using a convenient expression for describing the facts (though one that must not be construed into an hypothesis), we may say that the force which builds up and repairs the individual is an attractive force, whilst that which throws off germs is a repulsive force. But whatever may turn out to be the true nature of the two processes, it is clear that they are mutually destructive; or, stating the proposition in its briefest form—Individuation and Reproduction are antagonistic.

Again, illustrating the abstract by reference to the concrete, let us now trace throughout the organic world the various phases of this antagonism.

§ 5. All the lowest animal and vegetable forms—*Protozoa* and *Protophyta*—consist essentially of a single cell containing fluid, and having usually a solid nucleus. This is true of the Infusoria, the simplest Entozoa, and the microscopic Algæ and Fungi. The organisms so constituted uniformly multiply by spontaneous fission. The nucleus, originally spherical, becomes elongated, then constricted across its smallest diameter, and ultimately separates, when " its divisions," says Prof. Owen, describing the process in the Infusoria, " seem to repel each other to positions equidistant from each other, and from the pole or end of the body to which they are nearest. The influence of these distinct centres of assimilation is to divert the flow of the plasmatic fluid from a common course through the body of the polygastrian to two special courses about those centres. So much of the primary developmental process is renewed, as leads to the insulation of the sphere of the influence of each assimilative centre from that of the other by the progressive formation of a double party wall of integument, attended by progressive separation of one party wall from the other, and by concomitant constriction of the body of the polygastrian, until the vibratile action of the superficial cilia of each separating moiety severs the narrowed neck of union, and they become two distinct individuals." * Similar in its general view is Dr. Carpenter's description of the multiplication of vegetable cells, which he says

---

* Parthenogenesis, p. 8.

divide, "in virtue, it may be surmised, of a sort of mutual repulsion between the two halves of the endochrome (coloured cell-contents) which leads to their spontaneous separation." * Under a modified form of this process the cell-contents, instead of undergoing bisection, divide into numerous parts, each of which ultimately becomes a separate individual. In some of the Algæ "a whole brood of young cells may thus be at once generated in the cavity of the parent-cell, which subsequently bursts and sets them free." † The *Achlya prolifera* multiplies after this fashion. Amongst the Fungi, too, the same mode of increase is exemplified by the *Protococcus nivalis.* And "it would appear that certain Infusoria, especially the *Kolpodinæ,* propagate by the breaking-up of their own mass into reproductive particles." ‡

Now in this fissiparous mode of multiplication, which "is amazingly productive, and indeed surpasses in fertility any other with which we are acquainted," § we see most clearly the antagonism between individuation and reproduction. We see that the reproductive process involves destruction of the individual; for in becoming two the parent fungus or polygastrian must be held to lose its own proper existence; and when it breaks up into a numerous progeny, does so still more completely. Moreover, this rapid mode of multiplication not only destroys the individuals in whom it takes place, but also involves that their individualities, whilst they continue, shall be of the lowest kind. For assume a protozoon to be growing by imbibition at a given rate, and it follows that the oftener it divides the smaller must be the size it attains to; that is, the smaller the development of its individuality. And a further manifestation of the same truth is seen in the fact that the more frequent the spontaneous fission the shorter the existence of each individual. So that alike by preventing anything beyond a microscopic bulk being attained, by preventing the continuance of this in its integrity beyond a few hours, and by being fatal when it occurs, this most active mode of reproduction shows the extremest antagonism to individual life.

§ 6. Whether or not we regard reproduction as resulting from a repulsive force (and, as seen above, both Owen and Carpenter lean to some such view), and whether or not we consider the formation of the individual as due to the reverse of this—an attractive force—we cannot, on studying the phenomena, help

---

* Prin. of Phys., p. 92.   † Ibid., p. 93.
‡ Ibid., p. 917.
§ A General Outline of the Animal Kingdom. By Prof. T. R. Jones, F.G.S., p. 61.

admitting that two opposite activities thus generalized are at work; we cannot help admitting that the aggregative and separative tendencies do in each case determine the respective developments of the individual and the race. On ascending one degree in the scale of organic life, we shall find this truth clearly exemplified.

For if these single-celled organisms which multiply so rapidly be supposed to lose some of their separative tendency, what must be the result? They now not only divide frequently, but the divided portions fly apart. How, then, will a diminution of this separative tendency first show itself? May we not expect that it will show itself in the divided portions *not* flying apart, but remaining near each other, and forming a group? This we find in nature to be the first step in advance. The lowest compound organisms are "*simple aggregations of vesicles without any definite arrangement, sometimes united, but capable of existing separately.*"* In these cases, " every component cell of the aggregate mass that springs from a single germ, being capable of existing independently of the rest, may be regarded as a distinct individual."† The several stages of this aggregation are very clearly seen in both the animal and vegetable kingdoms. In the *Hæmatococcus binalis,* the plant producing the reddish slime seen on damp surfaces, not only does each of the cells retain its original sphericity, but each is separated from its neighbour by a wide interval filled with mucus; so that it is only as being diffused through a mass of mucus common to them all, that these cells can be held to constitute one individual. We find, too, that "the component cells, even in the highest Algæ, are generally separated from each other by a large quantity of mucilaginous intercellular substance."‡ And, again, the tissue of the simpler Lichens, "in consequence of the very slight adhesion of its component cells, is said to be pulverulent."§ Similarly the Protozoa, by their feeble union, constitute the organisms next above them. Amongst the Polygastrica there are many cases "in which the individuals produced by fission or gemmation do not become completely detached from each other."‖ The *Ophrydium,* for instance, "exists under the form of a motionless jelly-like mass ... made up of millions of distinct and similar individuals imbedded in a gelatinous connecting substance;"¶ and again, the *Uvella,* or "grape monad," consists of a cluster "which strongly resembles a transparent mulberry rolling itself across the field of view by the ciliary

---

* Carpenter.
‡ Ibid., p. 203.
‖ Ibid., p. 249.

† Prin. of Phys., p. 873.
§ Ibid., p. 209.
¶ Ibid., p. 249.

action of its component individuals."* The parenchyma of the Sponge, too, is made up of cells " each of which has the character of a distinct animalcule, having a certain power of spontaneous motion, obtaining and assimilating its own food, and altogether living *by* and *for* itself;" and so small is the cohesion of these individual cells, that the tissue they constitute " drains away when the mass is removed from the water, like white of egg." †

Of course in proportion as the aggregative tendency leading to the formation of these groups of monads is strong, we may expect that, other things equal, the groups will be large. Proceeding upwards from the yeast fungus, whose cells hold together in groups of four, five, and six ‡, there must be found in each species of these composite organisms a size of group determined by the strength of the aggregative tendency in that species. Hence we may expect that, when this limit is passed, the group no longer remains united, but divides. Such we find to be the fact. These groups of cells undergo the same process that the cells themselves do. They increase up to a certain point, and then multiply either by simple spontaneous fission or by that modification of it called gemmation. The *Volvox globator*, which is made up of a number of monads associated together in the form of a hollow sphere, develops within itself a number of smaller spheres similarly constituted; and after these, swimming freely in its interior, have reached a certain size, the parent group of animalcules bursts and sets the interior groups free. And here we may observe how this compound individuality of the Volvox is destroyed in the act of reproduction as the simple individuality of the monad is. Again, in the higher forms of grouped cells, where something like organisation begins to show itself, the aggregations are not only larger, but the separative process, now carried on by the method of gemmation, no longer wholly destroys the individual. And in fact, this gemmation may be regarded as the form which spontaneous fission must assume in ceasing to be fatal; seeing that gemmation essentially consists in the separation, not into halves, but into a larger part and a smaller part; the larger part continuing to represent the original individual. Thus in the common *Hydra* or fresh-water polype, " little bud-like processes are developed from the external surface, which are soon observed to resemble the parent in character, possessing a digestive sac, mouth, and tentacula; for a long time, however, their cavity is connected with that of the parent; but at last the communication

---

* Prin. of Phys., p. 250. † Ibid., p. 256.
‡ Ibid., p. 212.

is cut off, and the young polype quits its attachment, and goes in quest of its own maintenance." *

§ 7. Progress from these forms of organisation to still higher forms is similarly characterized by increase of the aggregative tendency or diminution of the separative, and similarly exhibits the necessary antagonism between the development of the individual and the increase of the race. That process of grouping which constitutes the first step towards the production of complex organisms, we shall now find repeated in the formation of series of groups. Just as a diminution of the separative tendency is shown in the aggregation of divided monads, so is a further diminution of it shown in the aggregation of the divided groups of monads. The first instance that occurs is afforded by the compound polypes. "Some of the simpler forms of the composite *Hydroida*," says Carpenter, "may be likened to a *Hydra*, whose gemmæ, instead of becoming detached, remain permanently connected with the parent; and as these in their turn may develop gemmæ from their own bodies, a structure of more or less arborescent character may be produced."† A similar species of combination is observable amongst the *Bryozoa*, and the compound *Tunicata*. Every degree of union may be found amongst these associated organisms; from the one extreme in which the individuals can exist as well apart as together, to the other extreme in which the individuals are lost in the general mass. Whilst each *Bryozoon* is tolerably independent of its neighbour, "in the compound *Hydroida*, the lives of the polypes are subordinate to that of the polypdom." ‡ Of the *Salpidæ* and *Pyrosomidæ*, Carpenter says:—"Although closely attached to one another, these associated animals are capable of being separated by a smart shock applied to the sides of the vessel in which they are swimming. * * * In other species, however, the separate animals are imbedded in a gelatinous mass," and in one kind "there is an absolute union between the vascular systems of the different individuals." §

In the same manner that with a given aggregative tendency there is a limit to the size of groups, so is there a similarly-determined limit to the size of series of groups; and that spontaneous fission which we have seen in cells and groups of cells we here find repeated. In the lower *Annelida*, for example, "after the number of segments in the body has been greatly multiplied by gemmation, a separation of those of the posterior portion begins to take place; a constriction forms itself about the beginning of the posterior third of the body, in front of

* Prin. of Phys., p. 266.   † Ibid., p. 267.
‡ Ibid., p. 276.   § Ibid., 2nd edit. p. 115.

which the alimentary canal undergoes a dilatation, whilst on the segment behind it a proboscis and eyes are developed, so as to form the head of the young animal which is to be budded off; and in due time, by the narrowing of the constriction, a complete separation is effected."* Not unfrequently in the *Nais* this process is repeated in the young one before it becomes independent of the parent. The higher *Annelida* are distinguished by the greater number of segments held in continuity; an obvious result of comparatively infrequent fission. In the class *Myriapoda*, which stands next above, "there is no known instance of multiplication by fission."† Yet even here the law may be traced both in the number and structure of the segments. The length of the body is still increased after birth " by gemmation from (or partial fission of) the penultimate segment." The lower members of the class are distinguished from the higher by the greater extent to which this gemmation is carried. Moreover, the growing aggregative tendency is seen in the fact, that each segment of the Julus " is formed by the coalescence of two original segments,"‡ whilst in the *Scolopendridæ*, which are the highest of this class, " the head, according to Mr. Newport, is composed of eight segments, which are often consolidated into one piece;"§ both of which, phenomena may be understood as arrests of that process of fission, which, if allowed to go a little further, would have produced distinct segments; and, if allowed to go further still, would have separated these segments into groups.

§ 8. Remarking, first, how gradually this mode of multiplication disappears—how there are some creatures that spontaneously divide or not according to circumstances; others that divide when in danger (the several parts being capable of growing into complete individuals); others which, though not self-dividing, can live on in each half if artificially divided; and others in which only one of the divided halves can live—how, again, in the Crustaceans the power is limited to the reproduction of lost limbs; how there are certain reptiles that can re-supply a lost tail, but only imperfectly; and how amongst the higher *Vertebrata* the ability to repair small injuries is all that remains— remarking thus much, let us now, by way of preparation for what is to follow, consider the significance of the foregoing facts taken in connection with the definition of Life awhile since given.

This spontaneous fission, which we have seen to be, in all cases, more or less destructive of individual life, is simply a

---

* Prin. of Phys., p. 954.　　　† Ibid., p. 958.
‡ Ibid., p. 688.　　　　　　　§ Ibid., p. 958.

cessation in the co-ordination of actions. From the single cell, the halves of whose nucleus, instead of continuing to act together, begin to repel each other, fly apart, establish distinct centres of assimilation, and finally cause the cell to divide; up to the Annelidan, whose string of segments separates, after reaching a certain length; we everywhere see the phenomenon to be fundamentally this. The tendency to separate is the tendency not to act together, probably arising from inability to act together any longer; and the process of separation is the process of ceasing to act together. How truly non-co-ordination is the essence of the matter will be seen on observing that fission takes place more or less rapidly, according as the co-ordinating apparatus is less or more developed. Thus, " the capability of spontaneous division is one of the most distinctive attributes of the acrite type of structure;"* the acrite type of structure being that in which the neurine or nervous matter is supposed to be diffused through the tissues in a molecular state, and in which, therefore, there exists no distinct nervous or co-ordinating system. From this point upwards the gradual disappearance of spontaneous fission is clearly related to the gradual appearance of nerves and ganglia—a fact well exemplified by the several grades of *Annelida* and *Myriapoda*. And when we remember that in the embryotic development of these classes, the nervous system does not make its appearance until after the rest of the organism has made great progress, we may even suspect that that coalescence of segments characteristic of the *Myriapoda*, exhibits the co-ordinating power of the rapidly-growing nervous system overtaking and arresting the separative tendency; and doing this most where it (the nervous system) is most developed, namely, in the head.

And here let us remark, in passing, how, from this point of view, we still more clearly discern the antagonism of individuation and reproduction. We before saw that the propagation of the race is at the expense of the individual: in the above facts we may contemplate the obverse of this—may see that the formation of the individual is at the expense of the race. This combination of parts that are tending to separate and become distinct beings—this union of many incipient minor individualities into one large individuality—is an arrest of reproduction—a diminution in the number produced. Either these units may part and lead independent lives, or they may remain together and have their actions co-ordinated. Either they may, by their diffusion, form a small, simple, and prolific race, or, by their

---

* A General Outline of the Animal Kingdom. By Professor T. R. Jones, p. 61.

aggregation, a large, complex, and infertile one. But manifestly the aggregation involves the infertility; and the fertility involves the smallness.

§ 9. The ability to multiply by spontaneous fission, and the ability to maintain individual life, are opposed in yet another mode. It is not in respect of size only, but still more in respect of structure, that the antagonism exists.

Higher organisms are distinguished from lower ones partly by bulk, and partly by complexity. This complexity essentially consists in the mutual dependence of numerous different organs, each subserving the lives of the rest, and each living by the help of the rest. Instead of being made up of many like parts, performing like functions, as the Crinoid, the Star-fish, or the Millipede, a vertebrate animal is made up of many unlike parts, performing unlike functions. From that initial form of a compound organism, in which a number of minor individuals are simply grouped together, we may, more or less distinctly, trace not only the increasing closeness of their union, and the gradual disappearance of their individualities in that of the mass, but the gradual assumption by them of special duties. And this "physiological division of labour," as it has been termed, has the same effect as the division of labour amongst men. As the preservation of a number of persons is better secured when, uniting into a society, they severally undertake different kinds of work, than when they are separate and each performs for himself every kind of work; so the preservation of a congeries of parts, which, combining into one organism, respectively assume nutrition, respiration, circulation, locomotion, as separate functions, is better secured than when those parts are independent, and each fulfils for itself all these functions.

But the condition under which this increased ability to maintain life becomes possible is, that the parts shall cease to separate. If they are perpetually separating, it is clear that they cannot assume mutually subservient duties. And it is further clear that the more the tendency to separate diminishes, that is, the larger the groups that remain connected, *the more minutely and perfectly can that subdivision of functions which we call organization be carried out.*

Thus we see that in its most active form the ability to multiply is antagonistic to the ability to maintain individual life, not only as preventing increase of bulk, but also as preventing organization—not only as preventing homogeneous co-ordination, but as preventing heterogeneous co-ordination.

§ 10. To establish the unbroken continuity of this law of fertility, it will be needful, before tracing its results amongst the higher animals, to explain in what manner spontaneous fission is now understood, and what the cessation of it essentially means. Originally naturalists supposed that creatures which multiply by self-division, under any of its several forms, continue so to multiply perpetually. In many cases, however, it has latterly been shown that they do not do this; and it is now becoming a received opinion that they do not, and cannot, do this, in any case. A fertilised germ appears here, as amongst higher organisms, to be the point of departure; and that constant formation of new tissue implied in the production of a great number of individuals by fission, seems gradually to exhaust the germinal capacity in the same way that the constant formation of new tissue, during the development of a single mammal, exhausts it. The phenomena classified by Steenstrup as "Alternate Generation," and since generalised by Professor Owen in his work "On Parthenogenesis," illustrate this. The egg of a *Medusa* (jelly-fish) develops into a polypoid animal called the *Strobila*. This *Strobila* lives as the polype does, and, like it, multiplies rapidly by gemmation. After a great number of individuals have been thus produced, and when, as we must suppose, the germinal capacity is approaching exhaustion, each *Strobila* begins to exhibit a series of constrictions, giving it some resemblance to a rouleau of coin or a pile of saucers. These constrictions deepen; the segments gradually develop tentacula; the terminal segment finally separates itself, and swims away in the form of a young *Medusa;* the other segments, in succession, do the same; and from the eggs which these *Medusæ* produce, other like series of polypoid animals, multiplying by gemmation, originate. In the compound Polypes, in the *Tunicata*, in the *Trematoda*, and in the Aphis, we have repeated, under various modifications, the same phenomenon.

Understanding, then, this lowest and most rapid mode of multiplication to consist essentially in the production of a great number of individuals from a single germ—perceiving, further, that diminished activity of this mode of multiplication consists essentially in the aggregation of the germ-product into larger masses—and seeing, lastly, that the disappearance of this mode of multiplication consists essentially in the aggregation of the germ-product into *one* mass—we shall be in a position to comprehend, amongst the higher animals, that new aspect of the law, under which increased individuation still involves diminished reproduction. Progressing from those lowest forms of life in which a single ovum originates countless organisms, through the successive stages in which the number of organisms so originated becomes smaller and smaller; and finally arriving at a stage in which one ovum produces but one organism; we have now, in our further ascent, to observe the modified mode in which this same necessary antagonism between the ability to multiply, and the ability to preserve individual life, is exhibited.

§ 11. Throughout both the animal and vegetable kingdoms, generation is effected " by the union of the contents of a ' sperm-cell' with those of a ' germ-cell;' the latter being that from within which the embryo is evolved, whilst the former supplies some material or influence necessary to its evolution."* Amongst the lowest vegetable organisms, as in the *Desmideæ*, the *Diatomaceæ*, and other families of the inferior *Algæ*, these cells do not appreciably differ; and the application to them of the terms " sperm-cell" and " germ-cell" is hypothetical. From this point upwards, however, distinctions become visible. As we advance to higher and higher types of structure, marked differences arise in the character of these cells, in the organs evolving them, and in the position of these organs, which are finally located in separate sexes. Doubtless a separation in the *functions* of " sperm-cell" and " germ-cell" has simultaneously arisen. That change from homogeneity of function to heterogeneity of function which essentially constitutes progress in organization may be assumed to take place here also; and, indeed, it is probable that the distinction gradually established between these cells, in origin and appearance, is merely significant of, and consequent upon, the distinction that has arisen between them in constitution and office. Let us now inquire in what this distinction consists.

If the foundation of every new organism be laid by the combination of two elements, we may reasonably suspect that these two elements are typical of some two fundamental divisions of which the new organism is to consist. As nothing in nature is without meaning and purpose, we may be sure that the universality of this binary origin, signifies the universality of a binary structure. The simplest and broadest division of which an organism is capable must be that signified. What, then, must this division be?

The proposed definition of organic life supplies an answer. If organic life be the co-ordination of actions, then an organism may be primarily divided into parts whose actions are co-ordinated, and parts which co-ordinate them—organs which are made to work in concert, and the apparatus which makes them so work—or, in other words, the assimilative, vascular, excretory, and muscular systems on the one hand, and the nervous system on the other. The justness of this classification will become further apparent, when it is remembered that by the nervous

---

* Prin. of Phys., p. 907.

system alone is the individuality established. By it all parts are made one in purpose, instead of separate; by it the organism is rendered a conscious whole—is enabled to recognise its own extent and limits; and by it are all injuries notified, repairs directed, and the general conservation secured. The more the nervous system is developed, the more reciprocally subservient do the components of the body become—the less can they bear separating. And that which thus individuates many parts into one whole, must be considered as more broadly distinguished from the parts individuated, than any of these parts from each other. Further evidence in support of this position may be drawn from the fact, that as we ascend in the scale of animal life, that is, as the co-ordination of actions becomes greater, we find the co-ordinating or nervous system becoming more and more definitely separated from the rest; and in the vertebrate or highest type of structure we find the division above insisted on distinctly marked. The co-ordinating parts and the parts co-ordinated are placed on opposite sides of the vertebral column. With the exception of a few ganglia, the whole of the nervous masses are contained within the neural arches of the vertebræ; whilst all the viscera and limbs are contained within, or appended to, the hæmal arches—the terms neural and hæmal having, indeed, been chosen to express this fundamental division.

If, then, there be truth in the assumption that the two elements, which, by their union, give origin to a new organism, typify the two essential constituents of such new organism, we must infer that the sperm-cell and germ-cell respectively consist of co-ordinating matter and matter to be co-ordinated—neurine and nutriment. That apparent identity of sperm-cell and germ-cell seen in the lowest forms of life may thus be understood as significant of the fact that no extended co-ordination of actions exists in the generative product—each cell being a separate individual; and the dissimilarity seen in higher organic types as expressive of, and consequent upon, the increasing degree of co-ordination exhibited*.

That the sperm-cell and germ-cell are thus contrasted in nature and function may further be suspected on considering the distinctive characteristics of the sexes. Of the two elements they respectively contribute to the formation of a fertile germ, it may be reasonably supposed that each furnishes that which it possesses in greatest abundance and can best spare. Well, in

---

* Should it be objected that in the higher plants the sperm-cell and germ-cell differ, though no distinct co-ordinating system exists, it is replied that there *is* co-ordination of actions, though of a feeble kind, and that there must be some agency by which this is carried on.

the greater size of the nervous centres in the male, as well as in the fact that during famines men succumb sooner than women, we see that in the male the co-ordinating system is relatively predominant. From the same evidence, as well as from the greater abundance of the cellular and adipose tissues in women, we may infer that the nutritive system predominates in the female *. Here, then, is additional support for the hypothesis that the sperm-cell, which is supplied by the male, contains co-ordinating matter, and the germ-cell, which is supplied by the female, contains matter to be co-ordinated.

The same inference may, again, be drawn from a general view of the maternal function. For if, as we see, it is the office of the mother to afford milk to the infant, and during a previous period to afford blood to the fœtus, it becomes probable that during a yet earlier stage it is still the function to supply nutriment, though in another form. Indeed, when, ascending gradually the scale of animal life, we perceive that this supplying of milk, and before that of blood, is simply a continuation of the previous process, we may be sure that, with Nature's usual consistency, this process is essentially one from the beginning.

Quite in harmony with this hypothesis concerning the respective natures of the sperm-cell and germ-cell is a remark of Carpenter's on the same point :—

" Looking," he says, " to the very equal mode in which the characters of the two parents are mingled in *hybrid* offspring, and to the certainty that the *material* conditions which determine the development of the germ are almost exclusively female, it would seem probable that the *dynamical* conditions are, in great part, furnished by the male." †

§ 12. Could nothing but the foregoing indirect evidence be adduced in proof of the proposition that the spermatozoon is essentially a neural element, and the ovum essentially a hæmal element, we should scarcely claim for it anything more than plausibility. On finding, however, that this indirect evidence is merely introductory to evidence of a quite direct nature, its significance will become apparent. Adding to their weight taken separately the force of their mutual confirmation, these two series of proofs will be seen to give the hypothesis a high degree of probability. The direct evidence now to be considered is of several kinds.

---

* It is a significant fact that amongst the diœcious invertebrata, where the nutritive system greatly exceeds the other systems in development, the female is commonly the largest, and often greatly so. In some of the Rotifera the male has no nutritive system at all. See *Prin. of Phys.*, p. 954.

† Prin. of Phys., p. 908.

On referring to the description of the process of multiplication in monads, quoted some pages back (§ 5), from Professor Owen, the reader will perceive that it is by the pellucid nucleus that the growth and reproduction of these single-celled creatures are regulated. The nucleus controls the circulation of the plasmatic fluid; the fission of the nucleus is the first step towards the formation of another cell; each half of the divided nucleus establishes round itself an independent current; and, apparently, it is by the repulsion of the nuclei that the separation into two individuals is finally effected. All which facts, when generalised, imply that the nucleus is the governing or *co-ordinating* part. Now, Professor Owen subsequently points out that the matter of the sperm-cell performs in the fertilised germ-cell just this same function which the nucleus performs in a single-celled animal. We find the absorption by a germ-cell of the contents of a sperm-cell " followed by the appearance of a pellucid nucleus in the centre of the opaque and altered germ-cell; we further see its successive fissions governed by the preliminary division of the pellucid centre;" and, led by these and other facts, Professor Owen thinks that " one cannot reasonably suppose that the nature and properties of the nucleus of the impregnated germ-cell and that of the monad can be different."* And hence he further infers that " the nucleus of the monad is of a nature similar to, if not identical with," the matter of the spermatozoon. But we have seen that in the monad the nucleus is the co-ordinating part; and hence to say that the sperm-cell is, in nature, identical with it, is to say that the sperm-cell consists of co-ordinating matter.

Chemical analysis affords further evidence, though, from the imperfect data at present obtained, less conclusive evidence than could be wished. Partly from the white and gray nervous substances having been analysed together instead of separately, and partly from the difficulty of isolating the efficient contents of the sperm-cells, a satisfactory comparison cannot be made. Nevertheless, possessing in common, as they do, one element, by which they are specially characterised, the analysis, as far as it goes, supports our argument. The table on the following page, made up from data given in the *Cyclopædia of Anatomy and Physiology, Art.* NERVOUS SYSTEM, gives the proportion of this element in the brain in different conditions, and shows how important is its presence.

This connection between the quantity of phosphorus present and the degree of mental power exhibited, is sufficiently significant; and the fact that in the same individual the varying

---

* Parthenogenesis, pp. 66, 67.

	In Infants.	In Youth.	In Adults.	In Old Men.	In Idiots.
Solid constituents in a hundred parts of brain	17·21	25·74	27·49	26·15	29·07
Of these solid constituents the phosphorus amounts to . . .	0·8	1·65	1·80	1·00	0·85
Which gives a percentage of phosphorus in the solid constituents of	4·65	6·41	6·54	3·82	2·92

degrees of cerebral activity are indicated by the varying quantities of alkaline phosphates excreted by the kidneys*, still more clearly shows the essentialness of phosphorus as a constituent of nervous matter. Respecting the constitution of sperm-cells chemists do not altogether agree. One thing, however, is certain—that they contain unoxidized phosphorus; and also a fatty acid, that is not improbably similar to the fatty acid contained in neurine †. In fact, there would seem to be present the constituents of that oleophosphoric acid which forms so distinctive an element of the brain. That a large quantity of binoxide of protein is also present, may be ascribed to the fact that a great part of the sperm-cell consists merely of the protective membrane and its locomotive appendage; the really efficient portion being but the central contents ‡.

Evidence of a more conclusive nature—evidence, too, which will show in what direction our argument tends—is seen in the marked antagonism of the nervous and generative systems. Thus, the fact that intense mental application, involving great waste of the nervous tissues, and a corresponding consumption of nervous matter for their repair, is accompanied by a cessation in the production of sperm-cells, gives strong support to the hypothesis that the sperm-cells consist essentially of neurine. And this becomes yet clearer on finding that the converse fact is true—that undue production of sperm-cells involves cerebral inactivity. The first result of a morbid excess in this direction is headache, which may be taken to indicate

---

* Lectures on Animal Chemistry. By Dr. Bence Jones. *Medical Times*, Sept. 13th, 1851. See also *Prin. of Phys.*, p. 171.

† Cyclopædia of Anatomy and Physiology, vol. iv. p. 506.

‡ From a remark of Drs. Wagner and Leuckart this chemical evidence seems to have already suggested the idea that the sperm-cell becomes "metamorphosed into the central parts of the nervous system." But though they reject this assumption, and though the experiments of Mr. Newport clearly render it untenable, yet none of the facts latterly brought to light conflict with the hypothesis that the sperm-cell contains unorganized co-ordinating matter.

that the brain is out of repair; this is followed by stupidity; should the disorder continue, imbecility supervenes, ending occasionally in insanity.

That the sperm-cell is co-ordinating matter, and the germ-cell matter to be co-ordinated, is, therefore, an hypothesis not only having much *à priori* probability, but one supported by numerous facts.

§ 13. This hypothesis alike explains, and is confirmed by, the truth, that throughout the vertebrate tribes the degree of fertility varies inversely as the development of the nervous system.

The necessary antagonism of Individuation and Reproduction does indeed show itself amongst the higher animals, in some degree in the manner hitherto traced; namely, as determining the total bulk. Though the parts now thrown off, being no longer segments or gemmæ, are not obvious diminutions of the parent, yet they must be really such. Under the form of internal fission, the separative tendency is as much opposed to the aggregative tendency as ever; and, *other things equal,* the greater or less development of the individual depends upon the less or greater production of new individuals or germs of new individuals. As in groups of cells, and series of groups of cells, we saw that there was in each species a limit, passing which, the germ product would not remain together; so in each species of higher animal there is a limit, passing which, the process of cell-multiplication results in the throwing off of cells, instead of resulting in the formation of more tissue. Hence, taking an average view, we see why the smaller animals so soon arrive at a reproductive age, and produce large and frequent broods; and why, conversely, increased size is accompanied by retarded and diminished fertility.

But, as above implied, it is not so much to the bulk of the body as a whole, as to the bulk of the nervous system, that fertility stands related amongst the higher animals. Probably, indeed, it stands thus related in all cases; the difference simply arising from the fact, that whereas in the lower organisms, where the nervous system is not concentrated, its bulk varies as the bulk of the body, in the higher organisms it does not do so. Be this as it may, however, we see clearly that, amongst the vertebrata, the bodily development is not the determining circumstance. In a fish, a reptile, a bird, and a mammal of the same weight, there is nothing like equality of fecundity. Cattle and horses, arriving as they do so soon at a reproductive age, are much more prolific than the human race, at the same time that they are much larger. And whilst, again, the difference in size between the elephant and man is far greater, their respective powers of multiplication are less unlike. Looking in these cases at the nervous systems, however, we find no such discrepancy.

On learning that the average ratio of the brain to the body is—in fishes, 1 to 5668; in reptiles, 1 to 1321; in birds, 1 to 212; and in mammals, 1 to 186 *; their different degrees of fecundity are accounted for. Though an ox will outweigh half-a-dozen men, yet its brain and spinal cord are far less than those of one man; and though in bodily development the elephant so immensely exceeds the human being, yet the elephant's cerebro-spinal system is only thrice the size attained by that of civilized men †. Unfortunately, it is impossible to trace throughout the animal kingdom this inverse relationship between the nervous and reproductive systems with any accuracy. Partly from the fact that, in each case, the degree of fertility depends on three variable elements—the age at which reproduction begins, the number produced at a birth, and the frequency of the births; partly from the fact that, in respect to most animals, these data are not satisfactorily attainable, and that, when they are attainable, they are vitiated by the influence of domesticity; and partly from the fact that no precise measurement of the respective nervous systems has been made, we are unable to draw any but general and somewhat vague comparisons. These, however, as far as they go, are in our favour. Ascending from beings of the acrite nerveless type, which are the most prolific of all, through the various invertebrate subkingdoms, amongst which spontaneous fission disappears as the nervous system becomes developed; passing again to the least nervous and most fertile of the vertebrate series—Fishes, of which, too, the comparatively large-brained cartilaginous kinds multiply much less rapidly than the others; progressing through the more highly endowed and less prolific Reptiles to the Mammalia, amongst which the Rodents, with their unconvoluted brains, are noted for their fecundity; and ending with man and the elephant, the least fertile and largest-brained of all—there seems to be throughout a constant relationship between these attributes.

And indeed, on turning back to our *à priori* principle, no other relationship appears possible. We found it to be the neces-

---

* Quain's Elements of Anatomy, p. 672.

† The maximum weight of the horse's brain is 1 lb. 7 oz.; the human brain weighs 3 lbs., and occasionally as much as 4 lbs.; the brain of a whale, 75 feet long, weighed 5 lbs. 5 oz.; and the elephant's brain reaches from 8 lbs. to 10 lbs. Of the whale's fertility we know nothing; but the elephant's quite agrees with the hypothesis. The elephant does not attain its full size until it is thirty years old, from which we may infer that it arrives at a reproductive age later than man does; its period of gestation is two years, and it produces one at a birth. Evidently, therefore, it is much less prolific than man. See Müller's *Physiology* (Baly's translation), p. 815, and Quain's *Elements of Anatomy*, p. 671.

sary law of maintenance of races, that the ability to maintain individual life and the ability to multiply vary inversely. But the ability to maintain individual life *is in all cases measured by the development of the nervous system.* If it be in good visceral organization that the power of self-preservation is shown, this implies some corresponding nervous apparatus to secure sufficient food. If it be in strength, there must be a provision of nerves and nervous centres answering to the number and size of the muscles. If it be in swiftness and agility, a proportionate development of the cerebellum is presupposed. If it be in intelligence, this varies with the size of the cerebrum. As in all cases co-ordination of actions constitutes the life, or, what is the same thing, the ability to maintain life; and as throughout the animal kingdom this co-ordination, under all its forms, is effected by nervous agents of some kind or other; and as each of these nervous agents performs but one function; it follows that in proportion to the number of the actions co-ordinated must be the number of nervous agents. Hence the nervous system becomes the universal measure of the degree of co-ordination of actions; that is, of the life, or ability to maintain life. And if the nervous system varies directly as the ability to maintain life, it *must* vary inversely as the ability to multiply *.

And here, assuming the constitution of the sperm-cell above inferred to be the true one, we see how the obverse *à priori* principle is fulfilled. Where, as amongst the lowest organisms, bulk is expressive of life, the antagonism of individuation and reproduction was broadly exhibited in the fact that the making of two or more new individuals was the *un*making of the original individual. And now, amongst the higher organisms, where bulk is no longer the measure of life, we see that this antagonism is between the neural elements thrown off, and that internal neural mass whose bulk *is* the measure of life. The production of co-ordinating cells must be at the expense of the co-ordinating apparatus; and the aggregation of the co-ordinating apparatus

---

* That the size of the nervous system is the measure of the ability to maintain life, is a proposition that must, however, be taken with some qualifications. The ratio between the amounts of gray and white matter present in each case is probably a circumstance of moment. Moreover, the temperature of the blood may have a modifying influence; seeing that small nervous centres exposed to rapid oxidation will be equivalent to larger ones more slowly oxidized. Indeed, we see amongst mankind, that though, in the main, size of brain determines mental power, yet temperament exercises some control. There is reason to think, too, that certain kinds of nervous action involve greater consumption of nervous tissue than others; and this will somewhat complicate the comparisons. Nevertheless, these admissions do not affect the generalization as a whole, but merely prepare us to meet with minor irregularities.

must be at the expense of co-ordinating cells. How the antagonism affects the female economy is not so clear. Possibly the provision required to be made for supplying nervous as well as other nutriment to the embryo, involves an arrest in the development of the nervous system; and if so, probably this arrest takes place early in proportion as the number of the coming offspring makes the required provision great: or rather, to put the facts in their right sequence, an early arrest renders the production of a numerous offspring possible.

§ 14. The law which we have thus traced throughout the animal kingdom, and which must alike determine the different fertilities of different species, and the variations of fertility in the same species, we have now to consider in its application to mankind.

From the fact that the human race is in a state of transition, we may suspect that the existing ratio between its ability to multiply, and its ability to maintain life, is not a constant ratio. From the fact that its fertility is at present in excess of what is needful, we may infer that any change in the ratio will probably be towards a diminution of fertility. And from the fact that, on the whole, civilization increases the ability to maintain life, we may perceive that there is at work some influence by which such diminution is necessitated. Before inquiring for this influence, let us consider what directions an increase of ability to maintain life may take—what scope there is for an increase. In some further development of the co-ordinating system, that is, in some greater co-ordination of actions, the increase must of course consist. But there are several kinds of co-ordination; and it will be well to ask of what kind or kinds increase is most requisite, and therefore most likely. For, doubtless, in conformity with the general law of adaptation, increase will take place only where it is demanded.

Will it be in strength? Probably not. Though from prehistoric remains, we may gather that the race has become more bulky, yet the cause of this change seems now diminishing. Mechanical appliances are fast supplanting muscular force, and will most likely continue to do so until they leave to be done by manual labour only as much as is needful for the healthy maintenance of the body at its then attained size.

Will it be in swiftness or agility? Probably not. In the savage these form important elements of the ability to maintain life; but in the civilized man they subserve that end in quite a minor degree, and there seems no circumstance likely to necessitate an increase of them.

Will it be in mechanical skill, that is, in the better co-ordination of complex movements? Most likely in some degree. Awkwardness is continually entailing injuries and loss of life. Moreover, the complicated tools developed by civilization are constantly requiring greater delicacy of manipulation. Already the cerebellum, which is the nervous centre directing compound motions, is larger in man than in any other creature except the elephant; and the daily-increasing variety and complexity of the processes he has to perform, and the appliances he has to use, may be expected to cause a further growth of it.

Will it be in intelligence? Largely, no doubt. There is ample room for progress in this direction, and ample demand for it. Our lives are universally shortened by our ignorance. In attaining complete knowledge of our own nature, and of the nature of surrounding things—in ascertaining the conditions of existence to which we must conform, and in discovering means of conforming to them under all variations of seasons and circumstances—we have abundant scope for intellectual culture and urgent need for intellectual development.

Will it be in morality, that is, in greater power of self-regulation? Largely also; perhaps most largely. Normal conduct, or in other words, conduct conducive to the maintenance of perfect and long-continued life, is usually come short of more from defect of will than of knowledge. To the due co-ordination of those complex actions which constitute human life in its civilized form, there goes not only the prerequisite—recognition of the proper course; but the further prerequisite—a due impulse to pursue that course. And on calling to mind our daily failures to fulfil often-repeated resolutions, we shall perceive that lack of the needful desire, rather than lack of the needful insight, is the chief cause of faulty action. A further endowment of those feelings which civilization is developing in us—sentiments responding to the requirements of the social state—emotive faculties that find their gratifications in the duties devolving on us—must be acquired before the crimes, excesses, diseases, improvidences, dishonesties, and cruelties, that now so greatly diminish the duration of life, can cease.

But whether greater co-ordination of actions take place in any or in all of these directions, and in whatever degree or proportions, it is clear that, if it take place at all, it must be at the expense of fertility. Regarded from the abstract point of view, increased ability to maintain life in this case, as in all others, necessarily involves decreased ability to multiply. Or, regarded in the concrete, that further development of the co-ordinating system, which any advance presupposes, implies further decrease in the production of co-ordinating cells.

§ 15. That an enlargement of the nervous centres is going on in mankind, is an ascertained fact. Not alone from a general

survey of human progress—not alone from the greater power of
self-preservation shown by civilized races, are we left to infer
such enlargement; it is proved by actual measurement. The
mean capacities of the crania in the leading divisions of the
species have been found to be—

> In the Australian . . . 75 cubic inches.
> „ African . , , . 82   „
> „ Malayan . . . 86   „
> „ Englishman . . . 96*   „

showing an increase in the course of the advance from the savage
state to our present phase of civilization, amounting to nearly 30
per cent. on the original size. That this increase will be continuous, might be reasonably assumed ; and to infer a future
decrease of fertility would be tolerably safe, were no further
evidence forthcoming. But it may be shown why a greater development of the nervous system *must* take place, and why,
consequently, there *must* be a diminution of the present excess
of fertility; and further, it may be shown that the sole agency
needed to work out this change is—*the excess of fertility itself.*

For, as we all know, this excess of fertility entails a constant
pressure of population upon the means of subsistence; and, as
long as it exists, must continue to do this. Looking only at the
present and the immediate future, it is unquestionably true, that,
if unchecked, the rate of increase of people would exceed the
rate of increase of food. It is clear that the wants of their redundant numbers constitute the only stimulus mankind have to
a greater production of the necessaries of life ; for, were not the
demand beyond the supply, there would be no motive to increase
the supply. Moreover, this excess of demand over supply, and
this pressure of population, of which it is the index, cannot be
eluded. Though by the emigration that takes place when the
pressure arrives at a certain intensity, a partial and temporary relief may be obtained, yet, as by this process all habitable
countries must gradually become peopled, it follows, that in
the end the pressure, whatever it may then be, must be borne
in full.

But this inevitable redundancy of numbers—this constant increase of people beyond the means of subsistence—involving as
it does an increasing stimulus to better the modes of producing
food and other necessaries—involves also an increasing demand
for skill, intelligence, and self-control—involves, therefore, a constant exercise of these, that is—involves a gradual growth of
them. Every improvement is at once the product of a higher
form of humanity, and demands that higher form of humanity

---

* Lecture by Prof. Owen, before the Zoological Society, Nov. 11th, 1851.

to carry it into practice. The application of science to the arts is simply the bringing to bear greater intelligence for satisfying our wants; and implies continued increase of that intelligence. To get more produce from the acre, the farmer must study chemistry—must adopt new mechanical appliances —and must, by the multiplication of tools and processes, cultivate both his own powers and the powers of his labourers. To meet the requirements of the market, the manufacturer is perpetually improving his old machines, and inventing new ones ; and by the premium of high wages incites artizans to acquire greater skill. The daily-widening ramifications of commerce entail upon the merchant a need for more knowledge and more complex calculations; whilst the lessening profits of the ship-owner force him to employ greater science in building, to get captains of higher intelligence, and better crews. In all cases, increase of numbers is the efficient cause. Were it not for the competition this entails, more thought would not daily be brought to bear upon the business of life; greater activity of mind would not be called for; and development of mental power would not take place. Difficulty in getting a living is alike the incentive to a higher education of children, and to a more intense and long-continued application in adults. In the mother it induces foresight, economy, and skilful housekeeping; in the father, laborious days and constant self-denial. Nothing but necessity could make men submit to this discipline, and nothing but this discipline could produce a continued progression. The contrast between a Pacific Islander, all whose wants are supplied by Nature, and an Englishman, who, generation after generation, has had to bring to the satisfaction of his wants ever-increasing knowledge and skill, illustrates at once the need for, and the effects of, such discipline. And this being admitted, it cannot be denied that a further continuance of such discipline, possibly under a yet more intense form, must produce a further progress in the same direction—a further enlargement of the nervous centres, and a further decline of fertility.

And here it must be remarked, that the effect of pressure of population, in increasing the ability to maintain life, and decreasing the ability to multiply, is not a uniform effect, but an average one. In this case, as in many others, Nature secures each step in advance by a succession of trials, which are perpetually repeated, and cannot fail to be repeated, until success is achieved. All mankind in turn subject themselves more or less to the discipline described ; they either may or may not advance under it; but, in the nature of things, only those who *do* advance under it eventually survive. For, necessarily, families and races

whom this increasing difficulty of getting a living which excess of fertility entails, does not stimulate to improvements in
production—that is, to greater mental activity—are on the high
road to extinction; and must ultimately be supplanted by those
whom the pressure does so stimulate. This truth we have
recently seen exemplified in Ireland. And here, indeed, without further illustration, it will be seen that premature death,
under all its forms, and from all its causes, cannot fail to
work in the same direction. For as those prematurely carried
off must, in the average of cases, be those in whom the
power of self-preservation is the least, it unavoidably follows,
that those left behind to continue the race are those in whom
the power of self-preservation is the greatest—are the select of
their generation. So that, whether the dangers to existence be
of the kind produced by excess of fertility, or of any other
kind, it is clear, that by the ceaseless exercise of the faculties
needed to contend with them, and by the death of all men
who fail to contend with them successfully, there is ensured
a constant progress towards a higher degree of skill, intelligence, and self-regulation—a better co-ordination of actions—
a more complete life.

§ 16. There now remains but to inquire towards what limit
this progress tends. Evidently, so long as the fertility of the
race is more than sufficient to balance the diminution by deaths,
population must continue to increase: so long as population
continues to increase, there must be pressure on the means of
subsistence: and so long as there is pressure on the means of
subsistence, further mental development must go on, and further
diminution of fertility must result. Hence, the change can
never cease until the rate of multiplication is just equal to the
rate of mortality; that is—can never cease until, on the average,
each pair brings to maturity but two children. Probably this
involves that each pair will rarely produce more than two offspring; seeing that with the greatly-increased ability to preserve
life, which the hypothesis presupposes, the amount of infant and
juvenile mortality must become very small. Be this as it may,
however, it is manifest that, in the end, pressure of population
and its accompanying evils will entirely disappear; and will
leave a state of things which will require from each individual
no more than a normal and pleasurable activity. That this
last inference is a legitimate corollary will become obvious on a
little consideration. For, a cessation in the decrease of fertility
implies a cessation in the development of the nervous system;
and this implies that the nervous system has become fully equal
to all that is demanded of it—has not to do more than is
natural to it. But that exercise of faculties which does not ex-

ceed what is natural constitutes gratification. Consequently, in the end, the obtainment of subsistence will require just that kind and that amount of action needful to perfect health and happiness.

Thus do we see how simple are the means by which the greatest and most complex results are worked out. From the point of view now reached, it becomes plain that the necessary antagonism of individuation and reproduction not only fulfils with precision the *à priori* law of maintenance of race, from the monad up to man, but ensures the final attainment of the highest form of this maintenance—a form in which the amount of life shall be the greatest possible, and the births and deaths the fewest possible. In the nature of things, the antagonism could not fail to work out the results we see it working out. The gradual diminution and ultimate disappearance of the original excess of fertility could take place only through the process of civilization; and, at the same time, the excess of fertility has itself rendered the process of civilization inevitable. From the beginning, pressure of population has been the proximate cause of progress. It produced the original diffusion of the race. It compelled men to abandon predatory habits and take to agriculture. It led to the clearing of the earth's surface. It forced men into the social state; made social organization inevitable; and has developed the social sentiments. It has stimulated to progressive improvements in production, and to increased skill and intelligence. It is daily pressing us into closer contact and more mutually-dependent relationships. And after having caused, as it ultimately must, the due peopling of the globe, and the bringing of all its habitable parts into the highest state of culture—after having brought all processes for the satisfaction of human wants to the greatest perfection—after having, at the same time, developed the intellect into complete competency for its work, and the feelings into complete fitness for social life—after having done all this, we see that the pressure of population, as it gradually finishes its work, must gradually bring itself to an end.

ON POPULATION.

MR MALTHUS was one of those writers to whom the world stands indebted for calling its attention to a great and neglected truth; and, like all writers who perform this essential service to mankind, he presented the truth he had taken under his especial charge in a position of greater prominence than it was found deserving to retain. This is excusable, for it is almost unavoidable; the task of re-instating any one verity in its due position, was perhaps never yet performed, without advancing it for a time into exaggerated relief and a disproportionate importance. The modest, cautious, limited statement, must follow afterwards, as the result of a bold uncompromising advocacy.

The statement, however, which Mr Malthus himself put forth, is not, by any means, so far from moderation, or that subdued tone of enquiry which succeeds to the excitement of novelty, as those would judge who have taken their impression of the " Essay on Population," not from perusal of the work itself, but from opinions and loose expressions afloat upon the surface of society, or from that panic on the subject of population which it certainly spread, at one time, amongst no small portion of our fellow-countrymen. Amongst those a vague idea prevailed, that this over-population was some new evil with which the world, in these later days, was threatened; and that, to avert it, certain strange, unheard-of, and intolerable restraints were to be laid on the future generations of mankind. The world was coming to an end by reason of its own too great fecundity— stifling itself in its own crowded and prolific progeny; and society was to be disorganized, and resolved into a corrupted mass, by the starving and endless swarms of a too-teeming race.

This alarm, which has certainly no foundation in the " Essay on Population," was combated and allayed by an argument which has quite as little bearing on the line of reasoning adopted in that work. The quantity of waste land in every part of the globe was measured, or guessed at; the further capabilities of the soil, as yet imperfectly cultivated, ingeniously calculated; and thus a result so comforting was obtained, and the evil day was postponed to such a remote, and almost incalculable period, that men held themselves justified in laying aside all alarm whatsoever. And justified they certainly were in thus recovering from their own panic; meanwhile, Mr Malthus had neither been read nor answered.

It is no new law—it is no remote result, which the " Essay on Population" expounds and anticipates; but a law operating incessantly on human society, and which as incessantly is felt in beneficial or disastrous results, according to the circumstances in which any social community is placed. Casting out of our calculation every thing except the two items of food and population, and looking at men simply as cultivators of the soil multiplying their numbers at a given rate of increase, it is impossible to deny that population has a tendency to outstrip the means of subsistence. A race of beings, amongst whom the births more than supply the room of those whom old age and disease carry off, must increase in a geometrical ratio; at every succeeding generation it starts with greater numbers, and with the same fecundity. The amount of food, on the contrary, attainable from a given territory, can increase only in an arithmetical ratio; the land itself cannot be doubled, nor does each successive application of the capital, or the industry of the farmer, yield a greater return than the preceding one. This, as an abstract proposition, is undeniable; and the law here indicated is, and always has been, in perpetual operation. Along the whole line of human progress, there is a *tendency* in the population of every nation or community to increase beyond the means of subsistence which its own territory can supply.

This law Mr Malthus pointed out

The " Principles of Population, and their Connexion with Human Happiness. By Archibald Alison, F.R.S.E., Advocate, Sheriff of Lanarkshire, and author of ' History of Europe' during the French Revolution."

as highly deserving, which it unquestionably is, of the consideration of all who take an interest in examining the constitution, or speculating on the progress of human society. But now the question occurs, how far is this law, or this tendency, counteracted and reduced to a safe and beneficial action by other laws and other tendencies of the human being? Looking back through the annals of history,—what proportion of the evils which mankind have suffered has been produced by the operation of this law of increase? Looking round on our own actual position, how far does this law of our nature call upon us for any change in our dealings with the poor, and in that legislative relief we bestow upon their wants, or for any modification in our moral opinions upon the subject of early and imprudent marriages? Looking forward to the future, does the recognition of this ineradicable tendency operate to dash and perplex our hopeful reasoning on the progressive amelioration of society?

In answering these questions, Mr Malthus, as might be anticipated in one who wrote with something of the zeal and passion of a discoverer, has assigned a too great prominency, and a too absolute and unrestricted operation to his law of population. This, we think, he has done both in his historical survey, and in the application of his doctrine to our own times, and to matters of practical importance.

When, for instance, Mr Malthus ascribes the great irruption of the northern barbarians to a deficiency of supply, he is giving an economic character to events which are directly traceable to warlike passions. These Germans who, because we have accounts given us of their frequent and systematic emigrations, he describes as having been driven from their native land by want of food, had a law amongst themselves which forbade the same soil to be cultivated two successive years by the same person, for fear the people should grow less warlike. Such is the reason of this law which we learn from Cæsar; Mr Malthus wishes to engraft this further reason—that they might thereby be better prepared to submit to that periodical emigration rendered necessary by the pressure of their numbers upon their agricultural produce. The

conjecture is not happy. The inhabitants are first supposed to emigrate because of the scarcity of provisions, and then, in order to facilitate an emigration thus called for, to enact a law most palpably adverse to every improvement in agriculture—a law which could not possibly have been devised amongst a free people who had any regard for agriculture. For it can need no science of political economy to demonstrate, that to take away from a man his improved soil at the end of the year, must deprive him of all inducement to labour at improvement; neither would a free people who had ever laboured to improve their soil submit to so great a violence to all the natural feelings of property. No doubt these Germans were often, in fact, straitened for food; but as they preferred to obtain it by ravaging other lands rather than cultivating their own, such distress can have no place whatever in an argument relating to the proportion between produce and population. We may find described in the Essay itself the sort of rude uncultured home which these hunger-driven barbarians left behind them. " Julian had conquered as soon as he had penetrated into Germany; and, in the midst of that mighty hive which had sent out such swarms of people as to keep the Roman world in perpetual dread, principal obstacle to his progress were almost impassable roads, and vast unpeopled forests."—P. 71, Qu. Ed.

There is indeed a fallacy, or rather an irrelevancy, to be detected in many of the historical illustrations which Mr Malthus has supplied. If these illustrations are regarded merely as proofs that men have, in sundry times and places, been afflicted by hunger, and that their numbers have been kept down by various correctives, more or less painful, they are somewhat redundant, and scarce necessary; they become valuable only for the collateral information they may occasionally afford; for such a general proposition as this, admits not, unhappily, of a moment's doubt. But the law which Mr Malthus undertakes to establish is, that there is a *different ratio* in the increase of food and the multiplication of the human race, whereby such hunger is occasioned; and if his historical examples are intended to illustrate the operation of this law, they are, many of them, quite inapplicable. He has insisted, with good right, that, in order to show the agency of this law, it is not incumbent on him to point to an instance where the whole territory has been industriously cultivated—it is not necessary for a people to have attained the utmost limit of agricultural prosperity, before they are made aware that their numbers are increasing at a faster *rate* than agricultural prosperity can possibly advance ; but it is equally clear that, if the different ratio of progress be the subject of illustration, agriculture ought to be shown, in the instances brought forward, to be making *some progress*. If a rude people are quite stationary in the degree of skill and industry with which they cultivate the soil, it is true that their numbers may bear, with most painful pressure, upon the means of subsistence ; but they cannot be pointed out as a proof of the different ratio between the increase of food and population. Such a people has not even advanced so far as to put itself under the disadvantage of these different ratios. In the position they occupy, their indolence and ignorance are the operating causes which entail on them a scarcity of supply. Had these ratios been both of the same description, both geometrical, or both arithmetical, the same distress must have occurred. If every addition of the farmer's skill and industry—if every successive dose of capital, to use an expression of our political economists, which was applied to the land, met with a greater and greater remuneration ; yet if men made no addition to their industry, and had not a single dose of capital to apply, and continued to increase, no matter how slowly, the same scarcity of provisions must ultimately be felt. This stationary condition of agriculture is observable in most of the illustrations taken from savage life. The arithmetical ratio in the produce of the soil cannot be detected, and therefore cannot be compared with the geometrical ratio in the multiplication of the species. To show the conjoint operation of the two, examples should be taken where there was progress, as well in the agricultural industry, skill, and capital of a nation, as in its numbers. Confined to such legitimate examples, we should probably find that, in a community industrious, and therefore

prosperous, there were invariably so many counteracting influences to a diseased increase of the population, that the abstract proposition which forms the basis of Mr Malthus' essay, and which, at first, appears as alarming as it is incontrovertible, may be admitted, without any concern for the stability of society, or the happiness of mankind.

" If the proportion," says this writer, arguing at the time against the notion that the redundancy of numbers is merely an evil of some remote indefinite period—" if the proportion between the natural increase of population and food, which was stated in the beginning of this essay, and which has received considerable confirmation from the poverty that has been found to prevail in every stage and department of human society, be in any degree near the truth, it will appear, on the contrary, that the period when the number of men surpass their means of subsistence has long since arrived, and that this necessary oscillation, this constantly subsisting cause of periodical misery, has existed ever since we have had any histories of mankind—does exist at present, and will for ever continue to exist, unless some decided change take place in the physical constitution of our nature." —P. 357. Now, the antagonist proposition to this statement we conceive to be this, that if, along the whole line of human progress, there is a tendency or power in the population to exceed the means of subsistence ; there is also, along the same line, and running ever before it, a perpetual and generally *sufficient* counteracting influence in the wants, habits, and institutions of civilized life.

But the practical application which Mr Malthus made of his theory, to determine the measures which should be adopted for the relief of the poor, and the amelioration of life amongst the lowest rank of society, will generally be thought of far more importance than the accurate elucidation of the theory itself. Here we think he was grievously and perilously wrong. He proceeded upon these two grounds, both clearly erroneous :—1. That distress of the poor must necessarily arise from the want of food for the whole community, and therefore a legal provision for their wants must act as a bounty on over-population ;

whereas that distress may, and in our manufacturing country does, more frequently arise from the periodical inability of the poor to obtain that employment which is to entitle them to a share in the *distribution* of the products of the soil. To such extent, therefore, as the necessities of the poor arise from this latter source, to such degree also must a poor-law be regarded, not as a bounty on population, but as a redress of evils occasioned by other bounties on population; as a relief to destitution occasioned by the changeful caprices of fashion, or the fluctuating prosperity of commerce. But the second ill-chosen ground is even still less tenable; for he proceeded on the principle—2. That to withhold relief from the destitute poor would check the growth of population amongst that portion of mankind, while a systematic charity would as inevitably promote it. This view of the subject is contradicted by experience, and opposed by juster and more profound reflection upon human nature. It is wretchedness that is so prolific— it is despondency that breeds so fast amongst us. Relinquish all national charity—resign all steady effort to uphold that class which is most exposed to adversity, and least wise to guard against it—let them sink, and you will open the door to a redundancy of the most frightful description—to a population, the result of mere sensuality and despair—to the offspring of men having all the recklessness of savages or wild beasts, and who yet live and multiply within the fold of civilization.

We have taken this rapid survey of the celebrated "Essay on Population," chiefly as a fitting introduction to our notice of an admirable work which has lately recalled us to this subject—the work of Mr Alison on the "Principles of Population." We have thus obtained for ourselves a station from which to observe the course taken by the later writer, and put ourselves in such a position, that, in passing our own strictures, or, what will more frequently be the case, in expressing our own assent and admiration, we shall run the less risk of being misunderstood. The work of Mr Alison contains many bold views, put forth in free and eloquent language; it is full of well selected information, rich in historical example—a work which all will read who are interested in the

topic it discusses; and which no one, let his reading elsewhere be what it may, will peruse without obtaining from it some valuable material for the completion of his own views. It is not a book, however, which can be trusted to, or adopted, as the sole expositor of its subject. Perhaps there is no such work in existence on this or any other speculative theme; it is something more, however, than the absence of an unattainable perfection that we point at. Mr Alison is not always logical, not always consistent with himself: he needs watching; and the reader must sometimes stay himself upon principles he has obtained elsewhere, if he would avoid being carried off by the impetuous stream of this author's eloquence.

Mr Alison commences his investigation by pointing out " the relation established by nature between the produce of human labour and the wants of the human species, in the essential article of subsistence." The labour of one man's hands produces *much more* than is necessary to maintain himself. On this fundamental relation the prosperity of the social body depends; for it is this excess which gives support to all those classes of society who are engaged in arts, and commerce, and intellectual pursuits. In newly peopled countries, where an unappropriated soil extends around the infant community, this fertility of the earth is manifestly superior to any demands that an increasing population can make upon it. But when limits have been drawn round an occupied territory, then it matters not what the proportion may be between the number of agriculturists and of other classes of men: the question to be resolved is, how will the produce of the whole soil answer the demands of the growing population? There is no controversy between Mr Alison and Mr Malthus, or between any two rational men, that the time *might* come, when, under such circumstances, the land might be cultivated to its utmost, and yet the community continue to increase. " But if it is meant," says Mr Alison, (and such undoubtedly *is* the meaning of Mr Malthus,) " that long *before* this ultimate limit has been attained, population has a tendency to increase faster than subsistence can be provided for it, then a little reflection must be sufficient to show that it is not only erroneous, but diametrically the reverse of the truth."

To this absolute contradiction of the abstract principle laid down in Mr Malthus's work, we cannot subscribe—we can hardly understand it; and the arguments by which it is supported seem to us irrelevant. It is in vain that Mr Alison gives us an instance, and a very striking and encouraging one, from statistical tables, of an increase of population in Great Britain almost equal to its increase in lately colonized countries, accompanied by a corresponding increase of food.* It would be manifestly absurd, as a general proposition, to say that the pressure of population does not intervene till agriculture has reached its perfection, and become stationary. To indicate the exact point when that pressure intervenes which legitimately arises from the prolific vigour of the race, is impracticable; but as this inconvenience is, from its nature, one of *gradual* approach, it must make itself felt long before the last grain, or the last potato, has been extorted from the soil. There may exist a large quantity of waste land within a nation's territory, and yet the pressure be felt. This cannot always be brought into cultivation without much dressing or manure, the supply of which is not unlimited. The reclaiming of waste lands may be an expensive process; and then, if the starving poor man cannot undertake it, and if his wealthier neighbour has no inducement to lay out his capital in the enterprize, the land itself, so far as the immediate provision of that country is concerned, might as well not be in existence. Neither would it be logical to say that this tendency does not exist, and does not manifest itself, because it *might* or *ought* to have been counteracted by the institutions of civilized life. It is one thing to say we are safe, because, in general, a certain tendency has a sufficient counterpoise, and another thing to deny the existence, or operation, of that tendency.

Mr Alison proceeds to support this direct denial of the Maltbusian tenet,

---

* "The population of Great Britain, including the army and navy, in 1801, was 10,942,000 souls, and in 1831 it was 16,539,000, and it is at present (1840) nearly 20,000,000. This is probably the greatest authentic instance of the increase of an old state on record in the world. It is almost as great as the celebrated augmentation of the American states, if the addition of the settlers from Europe, and that of the black slaves, be deducted from the increase of the latter state; for the total free population of America was—

In 1820	. .	9,637,000
1828	. .	11,348,000

1,711,000 or 17 four-tenths per cent.

The increase therefore in eight years was, of free people 1,711,000, or 17 four-tenths per cent. This rate would give an increase yearly of 177,000, or in ten years about 22 per cent. In thirty years it would be about 66 per cent, an increase not greater than 52 per cent in great Britain, if the immense annual emigration of Europeans to America be taken into consideration.

"Here then is an instance which has practically occurred, of the increase of an old and opulent state, with a circumscribed territory, by no means very fertile even in the very best places, and extremely barren in others. And what has been its condition in regard to subsistence during the latter period, and especially for the last five-and-twenty years, during which stringent corn-laws, except in years of scarcity, have prevented the importation of foreign grain? During that time almost the whole of its subsistence has been derived from its own soil, of only moderate fertility; and so far has the fact been from any deficiency having been experienced in the means of subsistence, that the greatest distress has existed, especially during the latter period of the progress, from the redundance and low price of agricultural produce. Further, the consumption of food during that period has enormously increased in proportion to the number of the people: luxurious habits, and costly living, have descended to an unparalleled degree in the ranks of society: a vast proportion of the land of the state has been directed to the raising of butcher-meat, the feeding of horses, and the use of breweries and distilieries; and yet, so far from there having been any difficulty in feeding the people with what remained, the only distress amongst the cultivators has arisen from the general redundancy of their supply in the market."—P. 43.

on the ground (p. 57) that nations,
as they advance, raise a greater *surplus produce*, in proportion to their
numbers, than they do in their early
stages. But this is beside the question. As a nation advances in its
career, it is found that, owing to improved modes of culture, and the excited industry of man, there are fewer
agricultural labourers employed in
proportion to the number fed by the
agricultural produce. Thus we learn,
that "in Poland twenty agriculturists
are required to produce a surplus for
one manufacturer, and in America
twelve are required for the same purpose ; in France, only two cultivators
are needed to support one manufacturer, while in Great Britain one agriculturist is able to maintain, in ordinary years, above *three* manufacturers," p. 61. But this sort of *surplus produce* is not the species of abundance we are at present concerned with.
The question is—no matter how large
or how small the proportion of agricultural labourers—whether amongst
the whole population to be fed by the
whole produce, there is not felt an increasing difficulty in obtaining a subsistence ? Such an increasing difficulty
will perhaps be thought to be indicated by the very circumstance that
the agricultural labourer is tasked to
so much greater exertion, in order to
obtain his share in the harvest he is
raising. In every species of simple
labour, how much more *work* is required from the Englishman than from
the native of less populous countries ?
Nor is Mr Alison more successful
in another argument which is levelled
against this *tendency*, although, like
the preceding, it is stated with such an
air of confidence as almost to surprise
the reader into involuntary acquiescence. As capital in populous states
continues to increase, and as capital is
the creature of this surplus produce of
the economist, he gathers, (p. 62,)
that population cannot have pressed
upon the means of subsistence. Between this conclusion and his premises, there appears but slender connexion. The industry of man, generation after generation, accumulates
wealth, or capital, in the shape of
houses or furniture, machinery, or the
valuable metals ; but if one class of
society enjoy this accumulation, does
it follow that another class, that which

exerts this very industry, may not be
straining every nerve in a cheerless
competition for a miserable pittance—
may not be growing more impoverished as they work the harder, till employment itself seems on the point of
forsaking them ? Is the enjoyment of
the capitalist any test of what passes
in the hovel of the artisan ?
But although there exists this tendency in the population to press upon
the means of subsistence, there exist
also, we believe, in every industrious
and prosperous community, such moral
restraints, arising out of the habits of
civilized life, as are sufficient, if aided
by general education and good government, to control this tendency, and
keep the expansive force of population,
energetic as it may be, to its true office
and character—that of the necessary
mainspring of all the activity and enterprise of life. As these moral restraints act with more certainty, with
greater power and uniformity, in the
advanced stages of society, the evil of
over-population may be regarded as
one belonging to a less perfect state
of civilization, not as one which increases in magnitude, and grows more
terrible as a civilized nation proceeds
upon its career. If we may not hope
altogether to leave it behind us, it, at
all events, no longer stands in our
path as the great impediment to our
future progress. This view of the
question, Mr Alison has most ably and
triumphantly displayed. The expli-
cation of these moral restraints—their
illustration in historical and contemporary examples ; and, above all, the
argument drawn from their nature to
uphold our national charities for the
relief of the poor—constitute the great
and distinguishing excellence of his
work. It is not to be supposed that
Mr Malthus lost sight entirely of this
important view of his subject—it forms
one distinct section of his book. The
difference between him and Mr Alison
lies in the different degree of prominence and efficacy accorded to these
moral restraints, and the very different
measures suggested for increasing their
efficacy amongst the poor. The following quotation, in which he developes this argument, is long ; but it
will be read with untiring interest.
We have abridged it as much as possible, by omitting whole paragraphs ;
but as the continuity of the sense was

preserved, we have not thought it necessary always to indicate these omissions.

" It has already been shown that in the first ages of the world, and in an infant state of society at any period, the want which is most severely felt, is that of man to carry on the numerous undertakings which are every where required—to clear forests, drain marshes, cultivate plains, construct roads, and build cities. The difficulty which becomes most pressing in its advanced periods, is *employment* to engage, and subsistence to feed, the multitudes who are continually brought into the world. The disproportion between the number of mankind and the extent of nature, seems prodigious in the infancy of the world; but as their numbers increase, the relation changes. Human labour appears, and is found by experience to be commensurate to the greatest undertakings; the species seems capable of an unlimited increase, until at length the proportion turns the other way; the apprehensions of men take a different direction, and the earth, notwithstanding its extent, is thought to be inadequate to the possible multiplication of the species.

" Nothing can be more obvious, therefore, than that the interest of mankind requires that the principles of population, unrestrained in the first stages of the world, to secure the existence and extension of the species, should be gradually limited as civilization and wealth advance, and subjected to the control of principles dependent on the circumstances in which society is placed in its later stages.

" Such a check is provided in the *artificial wants* and *habits of foresight*, which the progress of society developes. Strong as the principle of population is, experience proves that these restraining principles, when they are suffered to develope themselves, are still stronger. Their influence over the human mind in ages of civilization and refinement, becomes unbounded. They increase with the extension of wealth and the diffusion of useful knowledge; they derive their best support from the precepts and practice of Christianity; they expand with the growth of civil liberty; they flourish in the midst of public felicity. The nearer a state approaches to the termination assigned by nature to its increase—the more that a restraint upon the multiplication of its inhabitants is required—the more powerful do these causes of retardation become. Long before society arrives at the limit where an increase of its numbers is impossible, the progress of population is checked in the order of nature, by the habits which that very state engenders, without privation or suffering having been imposed on any of its members. The moving power in this mighty change is the efforts of individuals for their own welfare: the agents by which it acts, are the desires and wishes which spring up in the breasts of all classes by the progressive objects which, as society advances, are brought to bear on their minds; the foundation on which they rest is public happiness.

" *The developement and cultivation of reason* is the first cause of the voluntary restraints which men impose upon the increase of their numbers. The habit of early marriages, indispensable to the progress of the race in the first ages of the world, gradually becomes unnecessary, and at last burdensome. Where civilization has taken a lasting root, the individual finds himself protected by the society in which he is placed. The necessity for an early marriage to form a little circle round himself, is less strongly felt. The burden of an offspring increases with the increase in the wants and desires of civilized life, and with the multiplication of those who are seeking a livelihood around him. Imprudent marriages are every where seen to be the sources of much suffering, and frequently to involve the parents in irretrievable ruin.

" It is in this view that the instruction of mankind becomes so important an element in the formation of public happiness. Education unfolds the rational faculties of the mind, and fits men to contend with their active propensities; it enables them to survey the world in which they are placed, and to regulate their own conduct by the examples of happiness or misery which they see around them. These are precisely the habits and the views which are destined by nature to regulate the operation of the principle of increase; their developement, therefore, is materially aided by the acquisition of that character which general information is fitted to bestow.

" It is important, however, that the real effects of education upon the lower orders should be understood, and that visionary consequences should not be anticipated from the adoption of a system which is so ardently pursued by the humane and philanthropic in this country. Great as its effects are, they reach only a *limited number* of the working classes, and cannot be compared with the influence of artificial wants upon the great body of mankind. Few, comparatively speaking, of the poor can ever be brought to appreciate the enjoyments of knowledge ; but there are hardly any who do not feel the advantages of comfort if it is once placed within their reach : many will neglect the discoveries of Newton, but hardly any are insensible to the advantages of substantial clothing, or the enjoyment of a plentiful repast. It must always be recollected that the minds of the lower orders are originally the same as the higher : we must not expect a system to operate *universally* upon them which is only *partial* in its effects upon their superiors. How many of the higher orders are permanently influenced by the enjoyments of literature, or would be found willing to make any sacrifices in the vigour of life for its acquisition ? How many, even in the learned professions, where a certain degree of knowledge is indispensable, make study a habit, or prove by their conduct that it is one of their greatest sources of happiness ? If any man has found a fifth of his acquaintances, in any rank or condition of life, to whom these enjoyments were habitual, he may consider himself singularly fortunate."— Vol. I. pp. 87–96.

He then proceeds to enumerate and describe other elements in this moral restraint on population, as the artificial wants of civilized life, the passion to accumulate wealth, the desire to rise to higher *ranks* in society ; all which, in the advanced stages of the world, operate extensively to postpone the period of marriage, or to deter from it altogether. Of these, the 'extension of artificial wants amongst the people is by far the most important, and he thus dilates upon this antagonist to the principle of population :—

" The acquisition of one comfort, or the indulgence of one gratification, not only renders its enjoyment necessary, but excites the desire for another. No sooner is this additional comfort attained and become habitual, than a new object of desire

begins to be felt. To the succession of such objects there is no end. From the time that mankind first pass the boundary of actual necessity, and begin to feel the force of acquired wants, they have entered on a field to which imagination itself can affix no limits. The highest objects of luxury in one age become comforts to the one which succeeds it, and are considered as absolute necessaries in the lapse of a few generations. The houses that are now inhabited by the lowest of the populace, were the abodes of rank and opulence three centuries ago ; the floors strewed with rushes, which were the mark of dignity under the Plantagenet princes, would now be rejected even by the inmates of workhouses ; and the vegetables which were known only to the court of Queen Elizabeth, are now to be seen in the garden of every English labourer.[*]

" This great and important change which ensues in the progress of society, in the habits and desires of all its members, is the principal counterpoise which nature has provided to the principle of population. The indulgence of artificial wants is incompatible with a rapid increase of the human species. If the labourer finds himself burdened early in life with a wife and children, he must forego many enjoyments which would otherwise be within his reach. When habit has rendered these enjoyments essential to his comfort, the want of them is felt as an excessive deprivation. The actual pangs of indigence are not so severely felt in savage life, as the want of artificial enjoyments by those who have been accustomed to the luxuries of civilized society. To descend to the habits of the lower orders, after having been accustomed to those of a superior class, is considered the greatest misfortune which can befall an individual. It is the great object of life, in all ranks, to avoid this calamity : to rise to the enjoyments of a higher sphere, not sink to the difficulties of an inferior. The slightest observation of human affairs is sufficient to demonstrate, even to the most unthinking,

---

[*] Amongst the wants and habits of civilized life, there are some which bear a peculiar relation to the article of food, as their gratification usually absorbs a large portion of agricultural produce. The number of horses kept for pleasure or ostentation, the quantity of grain consumed in breweries and distilleries, seem at first to operate disadvantageously by diminishing the amount of human food. But that share of the produce which, in ordinary years, is appropriated to these purposes, forms a sort of reserved fund which, in seasons of scarcity, can be made available for the sustenance of man. The pressure is partially thrown from the human being to the animals he is accustomed to feed. And this reserved fund is one of no small magnitude. " The number of horses is now at least 1,500,000 ; which, taking the food of each horse at that of eight men, which is the usual computation, would make the food raised for these animals, annually in Great Britain, as much as would be required for twelve millions of men."—P. 45.

that an imprudent marriage is the most effectual method of incurring the evils, and preventing the acquisition of these advantages. Strong as the principle of population is, experience proves that prudential considerations, when suffered to develope themselves, are still stronger, and are perfectly sufficient to restrain the rate of human increase, according to the circumstances in which the human race is placed.

" To be convinced of the truth of this observation, it is only necessary to consider the situation of the higher classes of society, and the principles which determine the increase of their numbers. That they are placed above the level of actual want, and that no imprudence in contracting early marriages could reduce them to a situation where they might want the necessaries of life, is in general sufficiently evident. Yet population advances with exceedingly slow steps among these classes; and so far from sending forth multitudes to compete with the inferior orders in their departments, they are unable to maintain their own numbers, and require continual accessions from the middling classes of society. The common observation, that the nobility of every country are on the decline, and would speedily become extinct if not recruited by new creations from the sovereign, shows how universally the truth of this observation has been experienced. Marriages in that rank are contracted with extreme circumspection, and seldom before one of the parties at least has attained the middle of life. The universal complaint of the excessive difficulty of getting young women established in life in the higher ranks of society, proves how generally the preventive check prevails in those elevated spheres. In no class of society is the rate of increase so slow as in that which is furthest removed from actual want. Whatever may be the rapidity with which population is advancing in some parts of the British empire, in the class which composes the Houses of Peers and Commons, it is stationary, if not declining.

" The same principle influences the rate of increase in the middling ranks of society. The desire of rising in the world, and extending the sphere of their enjoyments, is equally felt in that station of life. So strongly, in consequence, does the principle of moral restraint operate, that their numbers, as well as those of their superiors, increase very slowly, or remain stationary; and it is from a continual influx of persons from an inferior class in society, that the growth of that important body is secured.

" It is a most important and luminous fact on the subject of population, that in every well-regulated society, the rate of increase is slowest in the most opulent classes; rarely perceptible in the middling ranks; and rapid only in those situations where comfort and the influence of artificial wants are unknown. By a singular anomaly, the rapidity of increase is in the inverse ratio of the means which are afforded of maintaining a family in comfort and independence ; it is greatest when these means are least, and least when they are greatest.

" It is impossible to give a whole people the habits of prudence and the artificial wants of the higher ranks ; but it is possible to make them descend so far as to influence the conduct of the majority of their members, and decidedly to regulate the progress of population. The slightest observation of mankind in different parts of the world, is sufficient to demonstrate this. Holland and Flanders have long been remarkable for the density of their population, which exceeds that of any other part of Europe ; yet nowhere does more comfort or opulence prevail amongst the people. The small cantons of Switzerland, and the Pays de Vaud, are more thickly peopled than any part of the known world ; yet nowhere is the condition of the peasantry so comfortable, or moral restraint so universally diffused through the lower orders."—Pp. 103—113.

Thus it is that the law of property may be said to counterbalance the law of population, and here, as elsewhere, the different principles with which humanity abounds are observed to produce, conflicting as they may seem, an harmonious result. Those who would throw one of these two great laws out of the world, pronouncing property to be usurpation, may find some difficulty in dealing with the other. Such world-architects will, as they proceed, make many difficulties of the same description, and they must meet them how they can. How Mr Owen would keep his parallelograms from overflowing, or any other gentleman would accommodate his Utopian population so that they should not crowd and jostle each other, or strive together for the vulgar necessity of aliment, is more than we can divine. It is their task, not ours. Contented with the old world we live in, we are happy to recognize in the principles here developed, another and very striking instance how all the energies of nature, mental and physical, co-operate, not indeed for the *best*—for optimism is a mere vain presumption—but "work together for good." We are happy in believing that the future prospects of mankind are not overclouded by many new or magnified disasters; but that the cloud that hangs over ourselves will probably disperse as the fulness of the day advances. We said that to measure out the tracts of unoccupied territory, or to estimate the unelicited capabilities of half-cultivated soils, was not an answer to Mr Malthus; but having found an answer to the anxious doubts he had raised, and being persuaded that the increase of population may be controlled and accompanied by the unceasing industry and ambition, and the growing skill and opulence of society, it becomes a calculation of some interest, how far and to what amount population has still room to extend itself. It is reckoned, that if the soil were thoroughly cultivated, Great Britain and Ireland, on the most moderate calculation, would be capable of maintaining in ease and affluence 120 millions of inhabitants, (p. 50.) France, it is calculated, might support no less than 360 millions. Such being the capabilities in reserve, even in the cultivated soils of most populous nations, we have only to carry this calculation with us as we glance over the map of the world, to feel convinced that man hitherto has hardly taken possession of his dwelling-place, and that the injunction " to increase, and multiply, and replenish the earth, and subdue it," still bears upon him, and is but half fulfilled.

When Mr Malthus took a single principle out of the many which constitute the great scheme of human society, and brought it not unnecessarily before the attention of mankind, he dwelt upon it with the eagerness and haste of novelty; and in doing so, exaggerated, perhaps in the minds of others even more than in his own, the power and operation of his principle. Succeeding speculators have redressed the balance, and the result has been, that the problem and its solution are now presented with beautiful distinctness to the mind. Nor perhaps has the Essay on Population been without some species of practical benefit. The chief application made of its doctrine, we have observed, and shall have again occasion to observe, was most unwise, and might have been most disastrous; but it

was well perhaps that men should be told, and told in a very striking manner, that there was a moral duty, as well as a prudential consideration, forbidding them to enter upon reckless improvident marriages. Whatever prospect may lie in wide expanse before the community, a man, when he marries, must not think of peopling the world, but must look near and around him for some probable provision for his offspring. It may be true, that though duty be the more solemn word, it is prudence which will be the more effective restraint; yet the auxiliary of a moral opinion is not to be slighted.

On this topic much light wit is often expended; and this is in the usual order of things. We are all grave and gay by turns, and all subjects, at least with one exception, that are worth a serious thought, are sources also of merriment and humour—and the gayety of one moment is no hinderance to the saddest reflexion in the next. The jest is nothing; it brings its laugh, and passes. But that this portion of the speculations of Malthus should have been regarded with a grave disapprobation, and as unfriendly to the cause of virtue, has indeed surprised us. His teaching may be inefficacious—it may be least likely to make impression where the impression is most wanted — prudence may be thought to do all that can, or will be done in this matter—the subject may be one on which no distinct rule whatever can be laid down; for what is reasonable hope to one man, is blank despondency to another; and, without doubt, the calculations of genuine hope are to be here esteemed as valid provision for the future family; for what would life be in all its stages, and especially in this, if expectation were not somewhat in advance of probability? All these reasons may lead us to see, that the subject can only partially and imperfectly be reduced under ethical discipline; but yet, most assuredly, if a man rushes, with his eyes open, into a palpably improvident marriage, bringing human beings into the world for whom he can provide no sufficient sustenance—to whom he can give no wealth, no measure of education—the act is something more than imprudence; it is a moral delinquency. This follows on no peculiar theory of population, nor does the man sin only against society at large: he offends against that circle of friends or relations on whom he will endeavour to throw his burden ; but he offends most grievously against that progeny towards whom he has placed himself in the relation of a father without the ability to nourish, protect, and educate them.

There seems to be in some minds an unaccountable repugnance to admit the operation of a moral principle in restraining from improvident marriages. They readily allow—they look upon it as a providential arrangement —that the desire of a comfortable, or even a luxurious mode of life should postpone the period of marriage, or altogether deter parties from entering into that union ; but they shrink from the proposition that man should do that from a moral motive, which, nevertheless, they applaud as the happy effect of vanity or prudence. Will the moral motive be so much more stringent than those social and selfish influences, that the " holy and comfortable estate of matrimony" will incur a risk of being deserted ? Or can it ever be an holy and comfortable estate when extreme poverty, and the vice which extreme poverty generates, are suffered to enter? Should we even suppose that some perverted minds might find in the perusal of Malthus an argument against marriage, but no confirmation of the practice of chastity, for this they themselves would be solely and entirely responsible. If one man teach abstinence from ardent spirits, and another abstain, but take to opium instead, this last evil habit is worse than the first, but the teacher is not responsible for its adoption.

As the application of his principles to the subject of the poor-laws was, in our apprehension, the gravest mistake of Mr Malthus, so do we esteem the application of these views of Mr Alison to the same subject, to be the most important portion of his work, the most felicitous, and the most convincing. It is no exaggeration to say, that in stepping forward, and demonstrating in so masterly a manner a momentous practical truth, he has laid his country under an obligation. We, in England, seemed at one time on the verge of surrendering our poor-law, of resigning our poverty-stricken multitudes to unrelieved, unprotected destitution. How lamentable—how fatal

a step we should have taken, may be gathered from the following exposition of Mr Alison :—

" The most important effect of the poor-laws, however, is to be found in their influence upon the *principle of population*, and their tendency, by relieving extreme distress, to prevent the growth of those habits from which a redundant population takes its rise. As this is the most important consequence of their establishment, so it is the one concerning which the greatest mistakes have been generally received. If it were true that by providing an asylum for the poor in sickness, distress, or old age, an uncalled for impulse is given to the principle of population, it would unquestionably follow, that such establishments are productive of more misery than they relieve. It deserves the most serious consideration, therefore, whether these consequences really flow from them; and whether it is the duty of the legislator to remain deaf to the calls of humanity, lest, from mistaken lenity, he defeats the object which he has in view.

" It will be found on examination, that these consequences are deduced from an erroneous view of the causes which restrain the increase of the lower orders; that they are not only incorrect, but diametrically the reverse of the truth; and that there are no measures so effectual in checking the growth of a redundant population, as those which relieve the present distress of the poor.

" Among the labouring classes generally, and the destitute portion of them in particular, inability to rear a family may check the growth of mankind, *but it never will alone prevent the contracting of marriage*. To all who are practically acquainted with the condition of the poor, this truth must be matter of observation ; to all who are familiar with the varied appearances of the species, it is matter of history. Nor is it difficult to assign the reason for this peculiarity. The passions of our nature are universal and inherent ; the controlling principles partial and acquired ; the former act most powerfully where the latter are unknown. The limitations to population acquire, in the progress of society, an entire ascendancy over the physical propensities ; but these limitations are slow of growth, and uniformly prevail most strongly in those classes whose condition is the farthest removed from real suffering. They are to be found in the highest degree among the aristocracy of England, to whom indigence is unknown; they will be looked for in vain among the peasantry of Ireland, who are continually in danger of wanting the necessaries of life.

"It results from these considerations, that nothing encourages a redundant and miserable population so powerfully, as the existence of *unrelieved suffering* : because it spreads those *habits* among the poor, from which a diseased action of the principle of population takes its rise.

" On the other hand, nothing tends to *check* an undue increase of mankind so effectually, as those institutions which, by relieving distress, dry up the sources from which an indigent population invariably springs. This is the great and important effect of such establishments Every individual who is withdrawn from a state of extreme indigence, is prevented from contributing his share to the diffusion of the habits from which a redundant increase of mankind arises. Suffering among the poor, like contagious fevers, never remains stationary : if it is not checked, it spreads its ravages; if the rich will not relieve its distresses, they will speedily be made to feel its bitterness.

" There is no such error as to imagine that by providing an asylum for the poor, we give an impulse to population which otherwise would not have existed. Such an opinion results from supposing, that the destitute portion of mankind are governed by the same views in contracting marriages as the opulent; a supposition contradicted by every thing we know of human nature. The supporters of this opinion forget, that animal passion precedes, both in the individual and the species, the desire of gain; that its influence is greatest where the other enjoyments of life are the least ; and that to leave the poor in unaided misery, is to consign them to circumstances where experience proves that no restraints upon the principle of increase are to be found. It is by relieving suffering wherever it exists ; by preventing the poor from sinking to that extreme depression where hope is extinguished ; by diminishing the frequency of perfect destitution, and thereby *augmenting the dread of incurring it ;* that the most effectual barrier against an undue increase of mankind is to be provided ; because it is in that. way that the habits are arrested which precipitate the poor into sensual indulgence, and level their multiplication to that of the lower animals. *

* * * * *

" Without leaving the British islands, the strongest proof of these principles may be discovered. For above two centuries and a-half, a system of legal relief has been established, and acted upon throughout the whole of England; and in the last half century it has gradually extended through all the great cities of Scotland. Are the poor of Great Britain in consequence redundant in numbers, reckless in habits, improvident in conduct ? So far from this being the case, the comfort and opulence of the middling and lower orders, at least in England, exceed that of any country in the world. The principle of population is more limited in proportion to the demand for labour, than in any other state where an equally complicated condition of society exists ; and fewer mendicants are to be seen than in any nation of Europe. The parliamentary committee, after the fullest investigation into the state of the poor, even during a period of extraordinary commercial distress, have reported, that the *native* poor of the island have no tendency to increase beyond the means of their comfortable subsistence.

" And whence is it that the crowds of unemployed poor have been generated, who now overwhelm the British empire ? Is it in the workhouses of England, or among the numbers whom her vast parochial assessments have called into being, when the state of society did not require their production ? It is, on the contrary, among the morasses of Ireland, among those whom want and misery have driven from their homes, and who now seek, from the wealth and the charity of Britain, that succour which is denied them by the institutions of their native land. It is amidst the indigence and misery of her *unrelieved poor*, that the principle of population has displayed its terrible powers ; and from the squalid habits of her reckless inhabitants that the multitudes have issued, who now fill every part of the empire with distress. A more extraordinary, a more memorable example of the consequence of neglecting the poor, never has been exhibited in the civilized world. The system of repressing the numbers of the poor by depriving them of relief, has there been tried to its *fullest extent ;* for centuries misery and want have stalked through the land; and the redundancy of the people, as well as the density of the population, are in consequence now greater than in any country of the world."—Vol. ii. p. 205-213.

A most important contribution to the advocacy of a legal provision for the poor may be found in an excellent pamphlet by Dr Alison, brother to the historian, " On the Management of the Poor in Scotland." Dr Alison makes the observation, refined as it is true, " that the existence of a legal provision for the poor—fixing at a proper standard the ideas of the higher orders as to what ought to be their condition and comforts—strengthens rather than weakens the feeling of benevolence and sympathy with which they are regarded by their superiors." It might be also added that it not only keeps up our charity to a certain pitch; but by imposing a contribution upon all, strengthens that public opinion which calls for industry, and censures sloth.

We hope soon to give a full account of Dr Alison's views; but meanwhile request attention to the following extract: it contains an anecdote not a little amusing, while it will be found to carry on the train of remark in which we are embarked.

" The simple fact of the habitual *cleanliness* of the English poor, as compared either with the Scotch or Irish, is sufficient evidence on this point, (namely, their superiority in diet and comfort.) That there are differences in nations as in individuals, in this last respect, independently of their difference in other comforts, is admitted; but that the lower ranks of a whole people should be habitually cleanly, and yet much impoverished, or should be habitually destitute, and preserve any habits of cleanliness, may be fairly asserted to be moral impossibilities. The Chief Secretary of Ireland, in describing to Parliament the great epidemic fever of Ireland in 1819, expressed a hope ' that the lower Irish would be better prepared in future to guard against such a calamity; that they would be more cleanly in their persons and domestic habits, fumigate their houses, and change their bedding and clothes.' This really recalls the remark of the French princess, who expressed her astonishment that any of her father's subjects should not have lived on bread and cheese, rather than have died of famine. A medical observer of the disease more practically acquainted with the poor Irish, observes, with perfect justice, ' It may be asked, How can those wretched beings, scarcely able to procure a meal's meat, be expected to be more cleanly in their domestic habits; or how can they, who have scarcely a rag to cover them, and who are obliged, for want of bed-clothes, to sleep under the raiment they wear by day, change their bedding and clothes?' Before we can be justified in using such language towards the poor of Ireland, we must remove the causes of their poverty, and then allow half a century to eradicate the bad habits of ages."— *On the Management of the Poor in Scotland*, p. 18.

In a note further on, Dr Alison says—

" It is well observed by Mr M'Culloch, that persons belonging to the higher ranks continually deceive themselves, if they attempt to conjecture, from their own feelings, how those in the lowest rank will conduct themselves in any particular circumstances; and therefore we can trust only to experience and observation in any speculations involving anticipations of that conduct. The simple illustration of this is in the regard paid to cleanliness among the lowest of the poor. As pure water costs nothing, we do not see why even extreme poverty should necessarily indispose mankind to the use of an article so essential to the comfort of the higher ranks; but experience shows that it *uniformly* does so. Again, in the higher ranks, on a sudden change of fortune, and near prospect of destitution, we know that suicide is not uncommon; but in the lowest ranks I believe, from that cause it is almost absolutely unknown. At least, although I have seen as much as most men of the distress and anguish of mind resulting from extreme destitution among the poor, I have met only with a single case in which this remedy for the evils of life was even talked of; and in that case, the proposal excited a strong expression of horror in those who heard it."

In the comparison that is drawn, both here and in Mr Alison's work, between the poor of Ireland and England, we beg to be understood as by no means assenting to the proposition (if, indeed, this is distinctly made by either of these writers) that *all* the difference between them results from the presence of a poor-law in the one country, and its absence in the other.

It is not only, however, by a legal provision for the destitute that we ought to attempt the amelioration of the condition of the poor. Something should be done, if only *possible*, for the reform of the Factory System, of which Mr Alison has added another painful description to the many that were already upon record. To facilitate to the poor the investment of their small capitals in the purchase of a portion of the soil, would be a wise and salutary measure. The law expenses on every transfer of land are enormous, and are felt the more in proportion to the smallness of the purchase. We know well that these expenses cannot be materially diminished, unless some reforms are first carried out in our systems of jurisprudence; but we are also thoroughly persuaded that such alterations as would simplify the laws of real property, would not only be received as a boon by the whole public, but would be energetically called for, on this and a thousand other reasons, if the study of jurisprudence was more generally cultivated. Mr Alison thus explains and illustrates the advantages resulting to the poor from the possession of some share of the soil :—

" There is, in fact, so great an aversion to labour in uncivilized man, and so great an affection for a listless, indolent habit of life, that nothing but some strong and predominant feeling is able to overcome it : something which can create new desires in the human breast, and give a permanent direction to that energy which is then only occasionally developed. The impressions of the present moment also are so strong, and the habit of attending to the future so utterly unknown to unenlightened man, that nothing but the formation of new habits, and the acquisition of a durable object in life, is adequate to correct the strong propensity, and enable him to sacrifice the gratification of existence at the instant from a view to his ultimate advantage.

" This change in the human character, by far the most important which occurs in the history of his species, the *division and appropriation of land* is mainly instrumental in producing. It is this, and this only, which can overcome the habitual indolence which characterises the savage and pastoral state ; which can induce men to submit to the fatigue and the restraint inseparable from agricultural labour ; which is able to check the wandering disposition which has been nursed amid the freedom of their steppes and forests ; and which can confine their views and their wishes to one spot, and the steady prosecution of one employment. It is this, in another view, which by accustoming them to continued labour, and a certain return for it, induces them to look into the future ; which shows them the effect which their exertions must of necessity have upon their happiness ; which induces habits of privation and self-control, from a view to ultimate enjoyment ; and developes the faculties of prudence, foresight, and frugality, which had hitherto lain dormant in the human breast. It is this, in short, which unfolds new desires and propensities in the mind of man, capable of overcoming those to which he is originally subjected ; which engenders those habits and views which lay the foundation of the progress of society ; and converts the indolent inhabitant of the forest or the desert into the laborious assistant of cultivated nature. Rousseau has said, that he who first enclosed a field, and called it his own, has to answer for all the misery which has ensued in society. He would have been nearer the truth, had he

said, that he had laid the foundation of the greatest improvement and happiness which man is capable of receiving.

" As the appropriation of land was destined to produce such important changes in the state of society, and in the habits and manners of mankind in general, a provision was made for it in some of the most powerful feelings of which our nature is susceptible. The desire of acquiring property in the soil, the attachment to a home, and the love of the place of their nativity, are among the strongest feelings of the human breast, and which, in the progress of society, are the first to be developed. In every part of the world, where agricultural labour has been commenced, these dispositions are found to exist. Mr Young tells us that in France the attachment to landed property is so strong among the lower orders, that the inheritance of their fathers is religiously preserved, and made the object of unceasing affection, though it sometimes consists only of a single tree. ' The universal object of ambition in the French peasantry,' says the Baron de Stael, ' is to become proprietor of a little piece of ground, or to add to that which they have received from their parents. This desire is of very ancient date, and the only effect of the Revolution was to confirm this tendency, by furnishing them with more extensive means of gratifying it. They generally purchase inconsiderately in this respect, that they give more than the land is worth ; counting their labour for nothing, as it forms the univeral condition of their existence. Land in Ceylon is so much subdivided, and tenaciously held, that an inheritance sometimes consists only of the 154th of a single tree. The same principle is mentioned by Mr Park, as influencing in the strongest manner the African negroes. ' This desire is felt,' says he, ' in its full force by the poor African. To him no water is sweet but that which is drawn from his own well ; and no shade refreshing but the tabbe tree of his native dwelling. When he is carried into captivity by a neighbouring tribe, he never ceases to languish during his exile, seizes the first moment to escape, rebuilds with haste his fallen walls, and exults to see the smoke ascend from his native village.' Nor are the Hindoos less strongly influenced by the same attachment. Considering, as they invariably do, their little possession as their own property, which it clearly is, according to the general custom of the east, they cannot, by any amount of misfortune, be torn away from the village of their nativity. ' Their villages are, indeed, frequently burned and destroyed by hostile forces, the little community dispersed, and its land returned to a state of nature ; but when better times return, and the means of peaceable occupation are again restored, the remnant reassemble with their children in the paternal inheritance. A generation may pass away, but the succeeding generation returns ; the sons take the place of their fathers ; the same trades and occupations are filled by the descendants of the same individuals ; the same division of land takes place ; the very houses are rebuilt on the site of those which had been destroyed ; and, emerging from the storm, the community revives, another and the same.' * * * *

"As the division of land is thus the great step in the progress of improvement, so its distribution among the lower orders, in civilized society, is essential to maintain that elevation of mind which the separation of employments has a tendency to depress. It is too frequently the melancholy effect of the division of labour, which takes place in the progress of opulence, to degrade the individual character among the poor ; to reduce men to mere machines ; and prevent the developement of their powers and faculties, which, in earlier times, are called forth by the difficulties and dangers with which men are then compelled to struggle. It is hence that the wise and the good have so often been led to deplore the degrading effect of national civilisation ; that the vast fabric of society has been regarded as concealing only the weakness and debasement of the great body by whom it has been erected ; and that the eye of the philanthropist turns from the view of national grandeur and private degradation, to scenes where a nobler spirit is nursed, amid the freedom of the desert, or the solitude of the forest. To correct this great evil, nature has provided various remedies, arising naturally from the situation of man in civilized society ; and one of the most important of these, is the distribution of landed property among the labouring poor. It is this which gives elevation to the individual character ; which gives a feeling of independence to the industrious labourer, and permits the growth of those steady views and permanent affections ; which both strengthens and improves the human mind." —Vol II. pp. 2—9.

"It is to be observed, however," our author continues, "that it is only where the possession of property takes place under a government which permits the developement of the limitations intended for the modification of the principle of population, that these beneficial effects result from its establishment. Under an oppo-

site system, the consequences which flow from it are very different. Where a subdivision of landed property exists among a people who are oppressed and degraded, who have no rank in society to support, and no prospect of bettering their condition to look forward to ; who are not suffered to enjoy the fruits of their toil, and acquire the artificial wants and habits of prudence which spring from their posses. sion, it may often lead to the production of a great and redundant population. By affording the means of subsistence, at the same time that the propensities destined for the limitation of the principle of increase are prevented from being unfolded, it affords greater facilities to the operation of that principle than any other state of society which can be imagined. These habits are transmitted from generation to generation, and multiply with the subdivision of the property, which thus comes to be only regarded as subservient to their indulgence : till at length the population becomes greater than the means of subsistence can adequately support, and poverty in its various shapes affords that check which the iniquity of government, or the wickedness of the people, prevented from being imposed at an earlier period, by the intelligence and prudence of the people themselves."—P. 20.

To this it should be added, and always borne in mind, that there is all the difference in the world between proprietorship of a portion of the soil and a mere tenancy. "Give a man," says Arthur Young, "the secure possession of a bleak rock, and he will turn it into a garden : give him a nine years' lease of a garden, and he will convert it into a desert."

As the leading view here taken of the subject of population consists in upholding the moral restraints as sufficient, whenever found in healthy action, to preserve society from the dreaded evil of over-population, it follows that every institution, custom, or opinion, which bears upon these restraints, becomes a part of the author's subject. Thus the topics of good government, equal laws, education, secular and religious, pass in review before him. The freedom requisite to give to proprietorship its full enjoyment, is indispensable to that legitimate conflict and co-operation of the laws of property and population on which so much has been shown to depend. An average share of education also, as well of what the schoolmaster as the clergyman supplies, is necessary before society can be said to be put upon its *fair trial.* Into these collateral though pertinent topics we cannot enter ; and, therefore, we feel it impossible to convey to the reader a just impression of the varied interest of Mr Alison's book. We cannot run over such a work as this, extracting here and there, without comment or connexion, passages which may have struck upon our fancy, or aroused our own reflection. Yet one such specimen we will venture to give; it shall be on a topic of equal interest to every subject of the British empire. Mr Alison is not disposed to exempt from the law of decay and mutability the great cities and great nations which are now flourishing on the earth ; he sees their fate written in the decline and fall of their predecessors ; nor does he promise to Great Britain any peculiar immunity from this common lot of nations. He provides for it, however, such a euthanasia as is almost covetable. The improvement which the agriculture of a country receives from its commercial wealth, is not always lost with the loss of commercial greatness. The population driven into the fields sustain these in their advanced state of culture, and even keep up their own numbers. Quoting from Chateauvieux, he says,—" Notwithstanding the great diminution of the population of the Italian *towns,* there is reason to believe, not only that the inhabitants of Italy, upon the *whole,* have gone on progressively increasing during all this period, but that they are at this moment more numerous than they were at any former period of its history, not excepting the most flourishing days of the Roman empire."—Vol. I. p. 176. Now, if a similar fate should attend England, and she should draw a large portion of her population out of her factories and her great towns, and spread them over her well cultivated fields, there would, perhaps, be little to regret, supposing always she retained her national independence. Mr Alison, in a very eloquent passage, prefigures such a destiny.

" It is impossible to expect, however, that this state of extraordinary prosperity, arising from colonial advancement, is to continue permanent ; or that England, by having planted her seed in so many distant parts of the world, is to avert the weak-

ness of age, and escape the common lot of mortality. The parent of so mighty a progeny will herself descend to the grave; her full-grown offspring will break off from the empire ; they may even themselves stab their progenitor to the heart. Already the British empire seems to stand on a dizzy pinnacle, and a false step in any direction might speedily precipitate it into ruin. Whether the present state of the empire be suited to withstand the shocks of adverse fortune, and whether the government which its vast and mercantile community has established, is endowed with the strength and foresight requisite to maintain inviolate so colossal a power in the midst of innumerable dangers, it is not the object of the present work to enquire. But this much may be considered as certain, that, sooner or later, by the violent strokes of fate, or by the insensible decay of time, the industry and population of the British islands will become stationary or decline. Whether her naval supremacy is at once to be destroyed, and her colonial empire severed from her grasp, by a single or a few dreadful shocks, as was the case with Athens at Aigospotamos, with Carthage at Zama, or with Pisa at La Meloria, or with Genoa at Malmocco ; or whether the gradual influence of the decay of time and retarding causes, in the later stages of society, is destined to weaken her resources, and she is to descend from her present pinnacle of greatness by as slow a decline as the Byzantine empire in ancient, or the Italian republics and Flemish commercial cities in modern times, at present lies buried in the womb of fate. But in either case, the loss of our colonial empire and maritime superiority must undoubtedly ensue in process of time ; the kind of decay and period of dissolution are alone doubtful. It is neither possible nor desirable for the interests of humanity, even in this country, that such a perpetual tenure of greatness should be assigned to any single state. And it is therefore a matter of the very highest importance to every friend of mankind and of his country, to consider what would be the probable fate of the people of the British islands, in the event of such a catastrophe either gradually or suddenly occurring.

" Involved in uncertainty, as all such speculations in regard to the future necessarily must be, there is yet reason to hope, from the experience of former ages, that this transition would not be attended either with the convulsions or sufferings which are generally anticipated. Other commercial states have undergone similar vicissitudes, and it is in them that we may see the mirror, if national sins have not called for some extraordinary national punishment, of the stationary condition, or declining years of the British Empire. The wealth of the world has fled from the Italian cities; but the cultivation of the plain of Lombardy at this moment never was surpassed: all the pendants of Europe are no longer to be seen on the banks of the Scheldt—but the fields of Flanders still flourish in un-diminished fertility: the merchants of Florence no longer number all the kings of Europe among their debtors—but cultivation has spread to an unparalleled extent through the terraces of the Arno, and rural contentment exists in its most enchanting forms on the vine-clad hills of Tuscany. It is in these examples that we may see and hope for the prototypes of the euthanasia of British greatness. It is in the transference of mercantile wealth to agricultural industry, and the rapid absorption even of the greatest manufacturing population in the labour of the fields, that the real security, in an advanced stage of civilization, against the destruction of commercial prosperity, is to be found. Vast and overgrown as is the present manufacturing population of Great Britain, the experience of former states which have undergone similar vicissitudes, warrants the hope that it could be absorbed in a very short time, and permanently and comfortably maintained in the labour of the fields. The single alteration of substituting the kitchen-garden husbandry of Flanders in our plains, and the terraced culture of Tuscany in our hills, for the present system of agricultural management, would at once double the produce of the British islands, and procure ample subsistence for twice the number of its present inhabitants. And humanity has no cause to dread a change which, reducing to a third of their present numbers the inmates of the British factories, or the operations in the British towns, should double the number of its country labourers, and overspread the land with rural felicity."—Vol. I. p. 215.